RESET

BEYOND
FUKUSHIMA

福島の彼方に

Kazuma Obara
小原 一真

RESET

BEYOND FUKUSHIMA
福島の彼方に

Will the
Nuclear Catastrophe Bring
Humanity to Its Senses?

原発の巨大事故は私たちを
目覚めさせるだろうか？

Edited by Adriano A. Biondo
and Lars Müller
編集　アドリアーノ・A・ビオンド
& ラース・ミュラー

Lars Müller Publishers

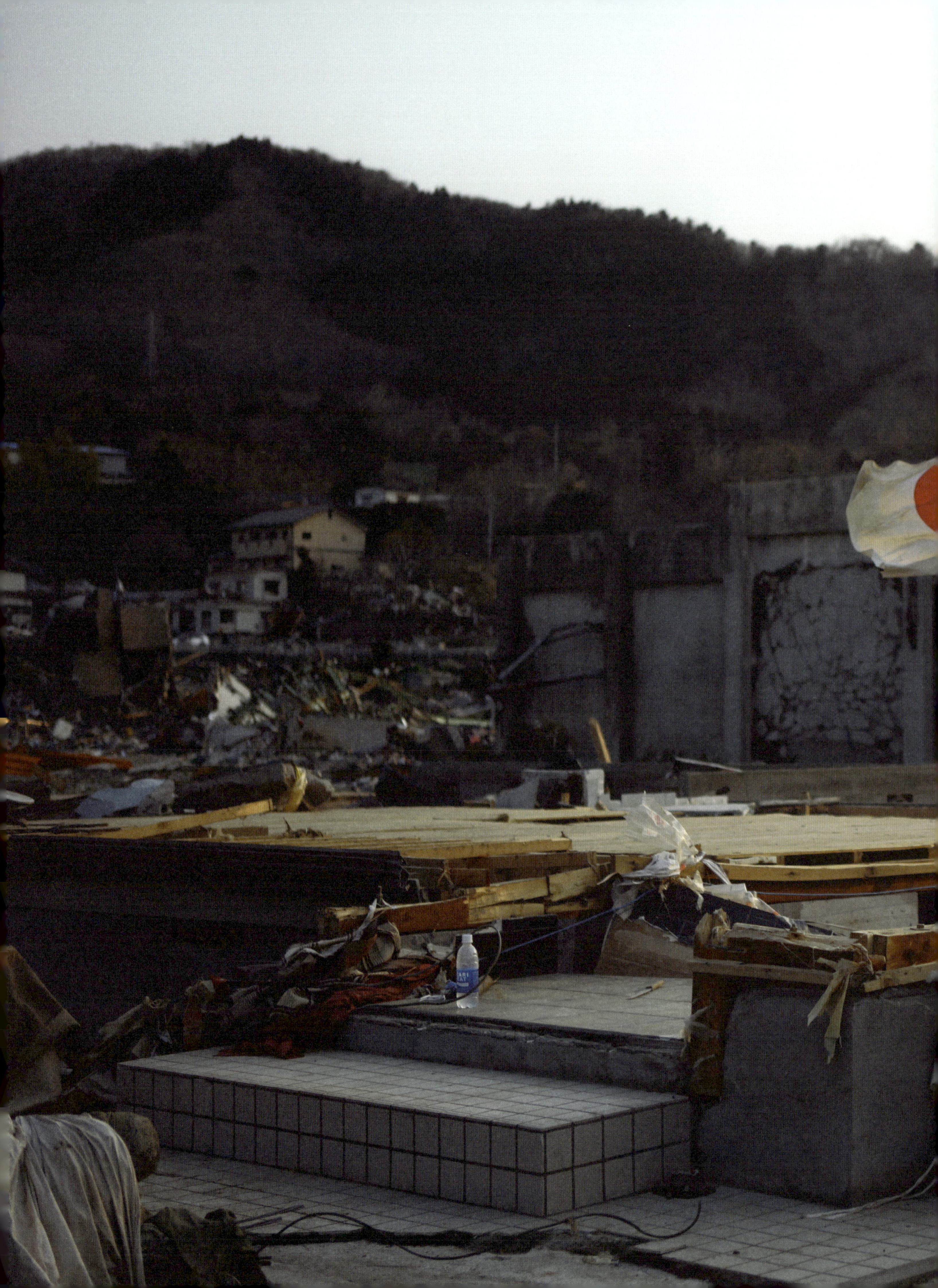

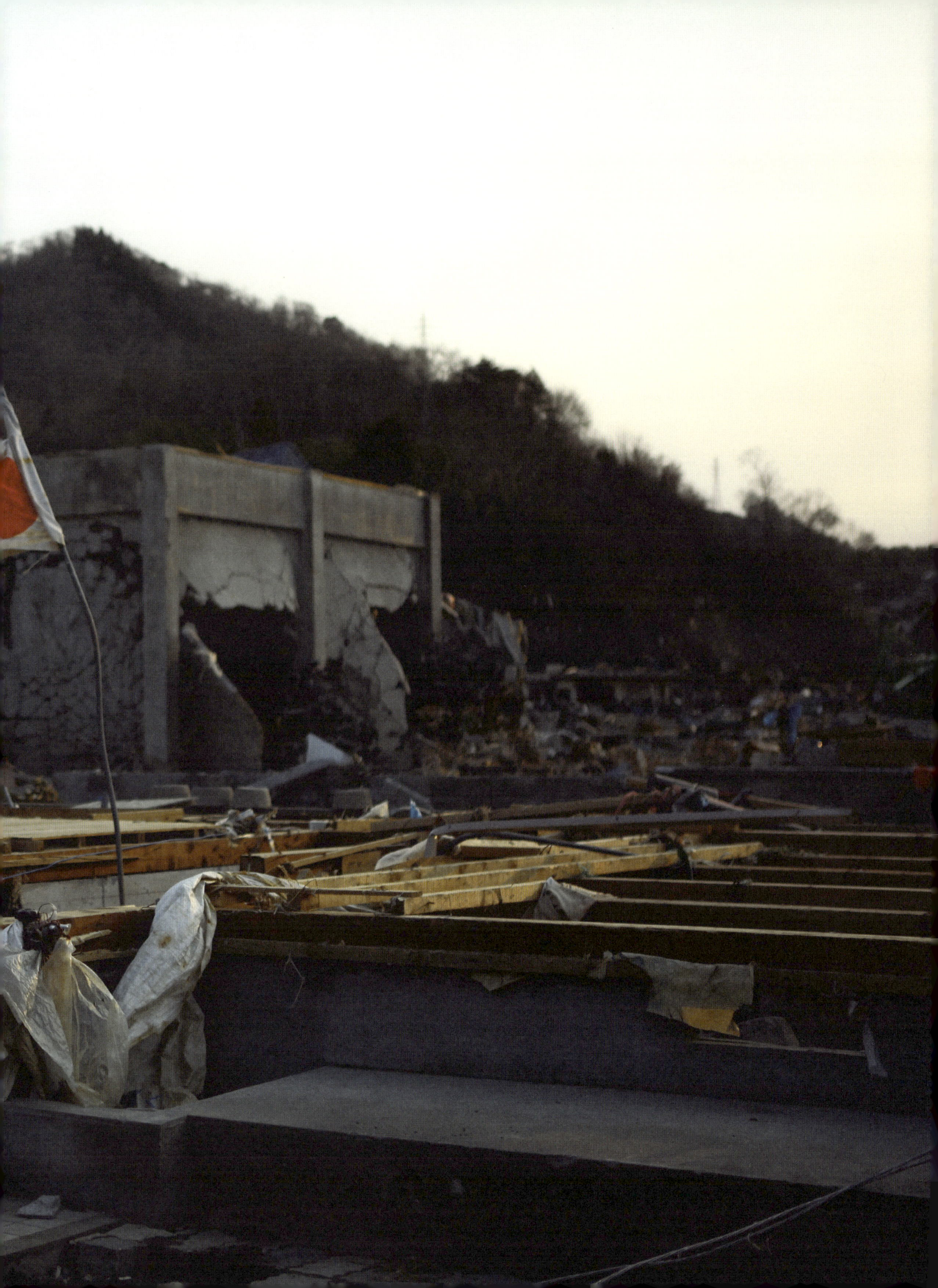

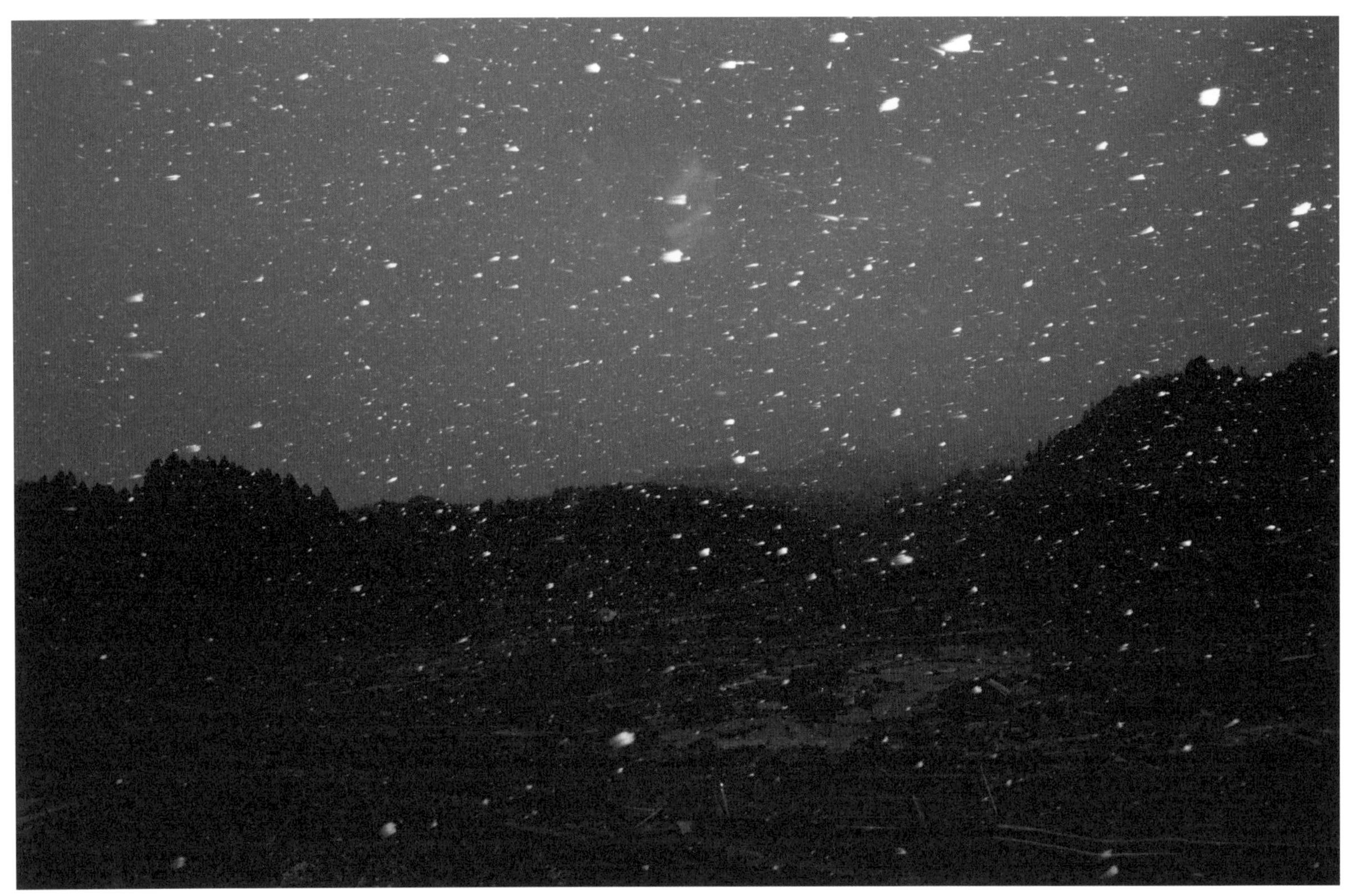

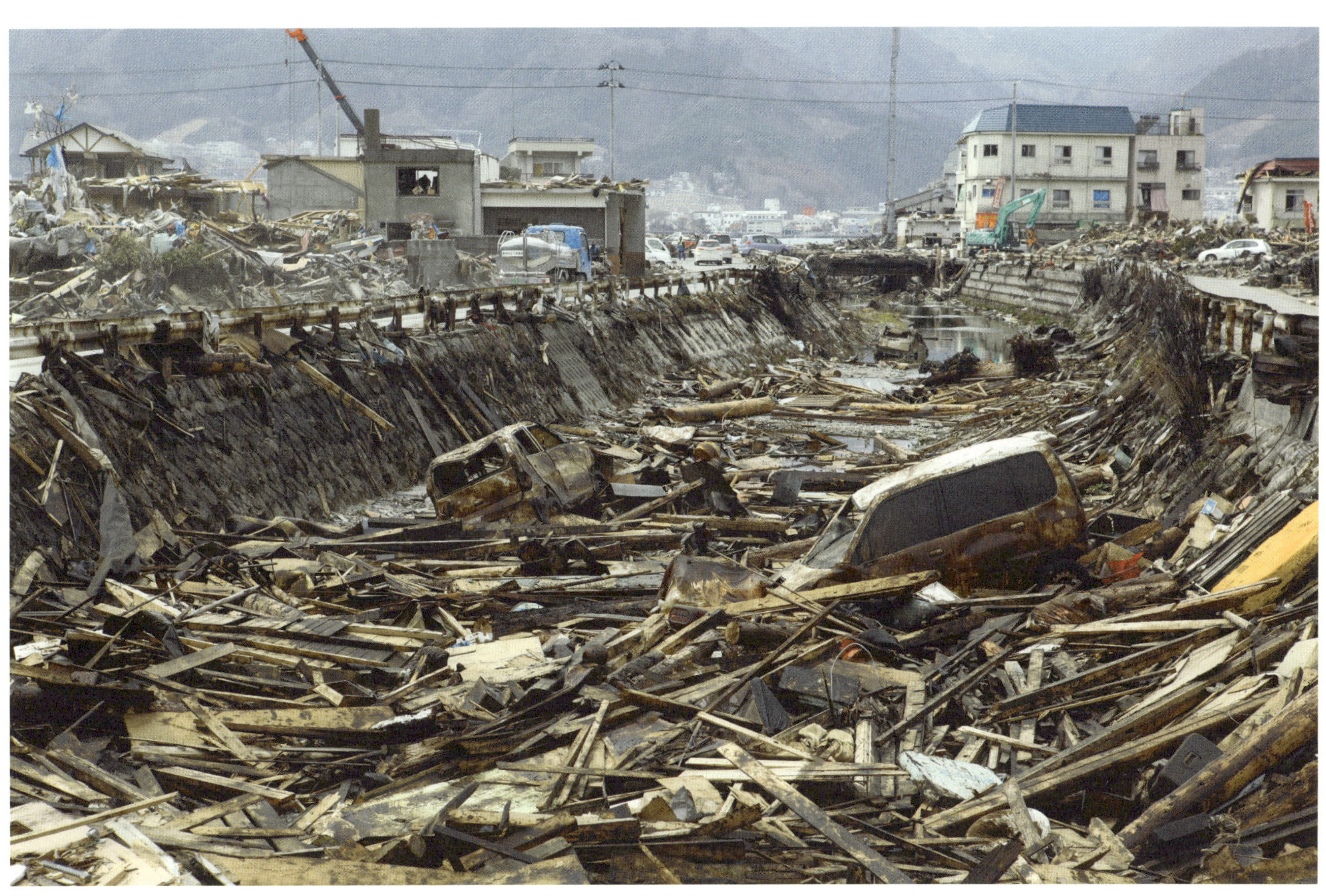

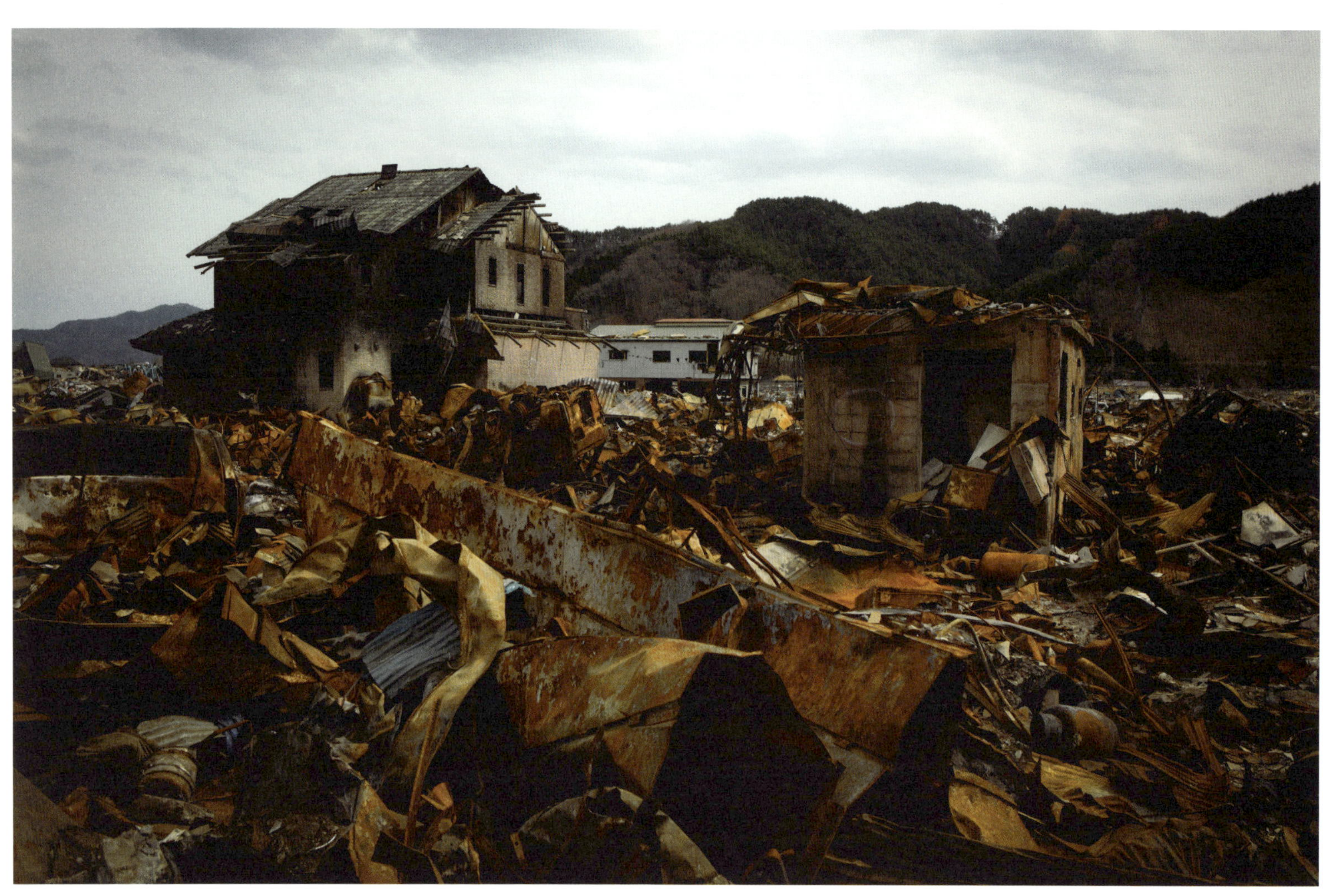

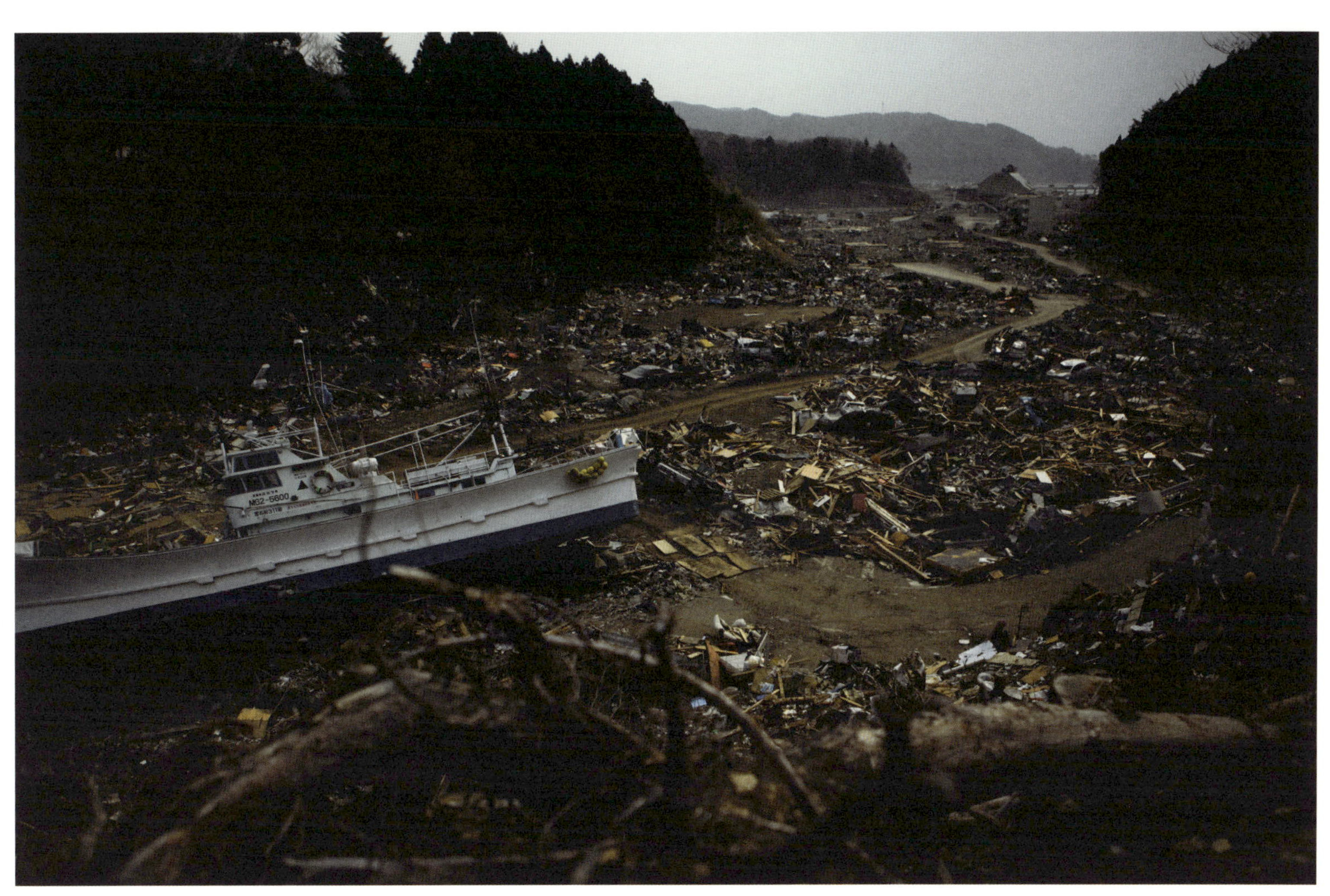

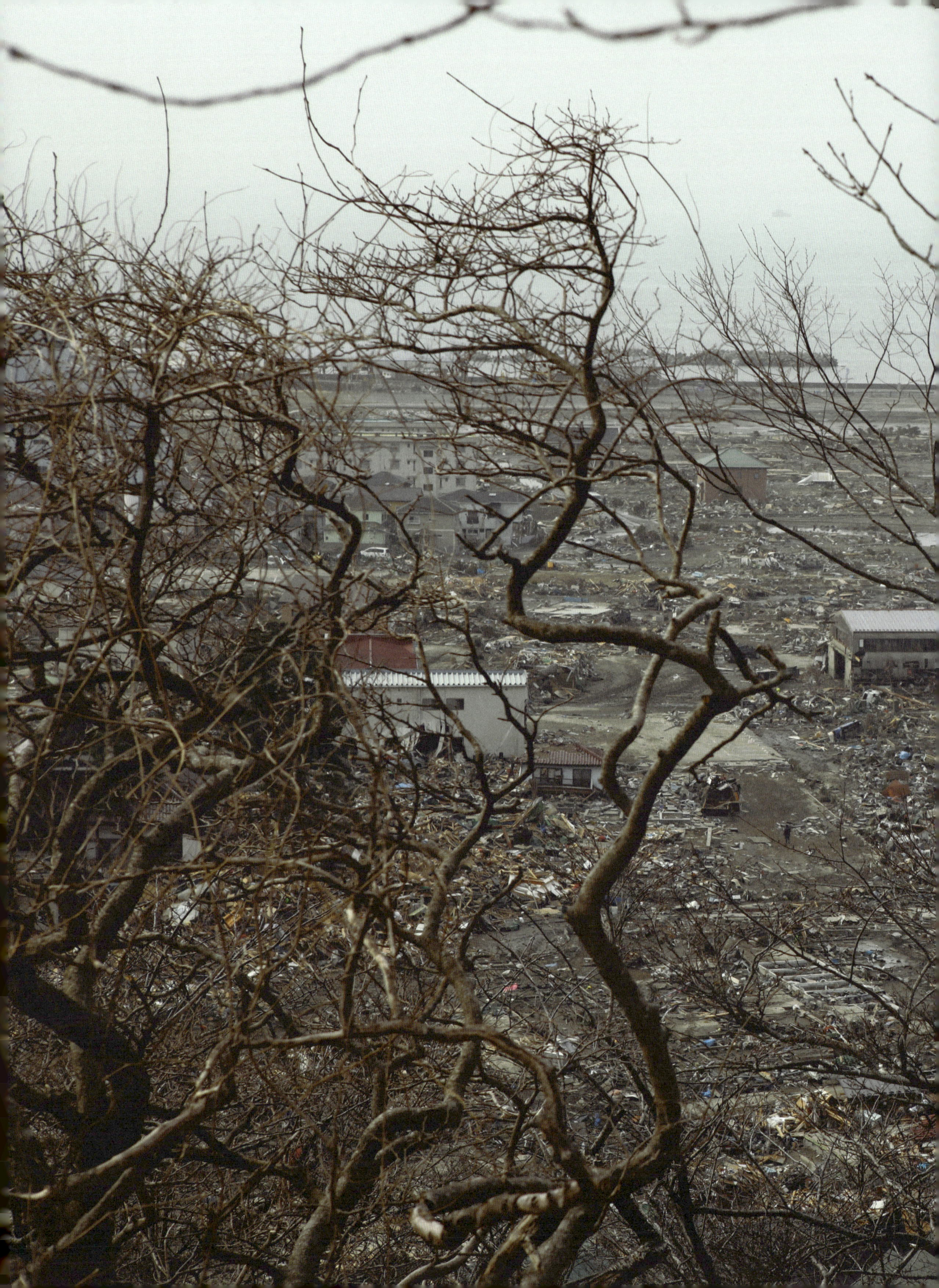

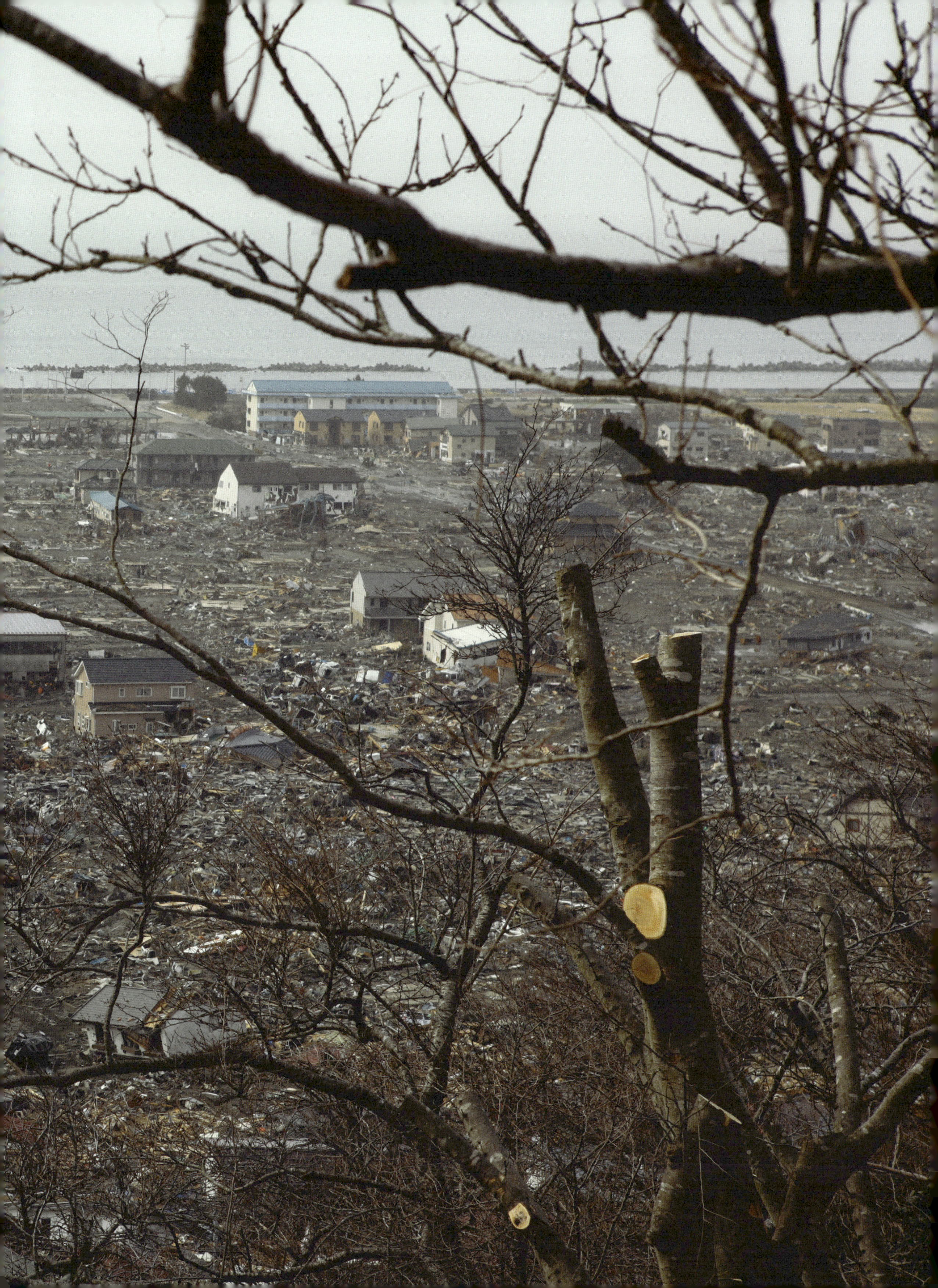

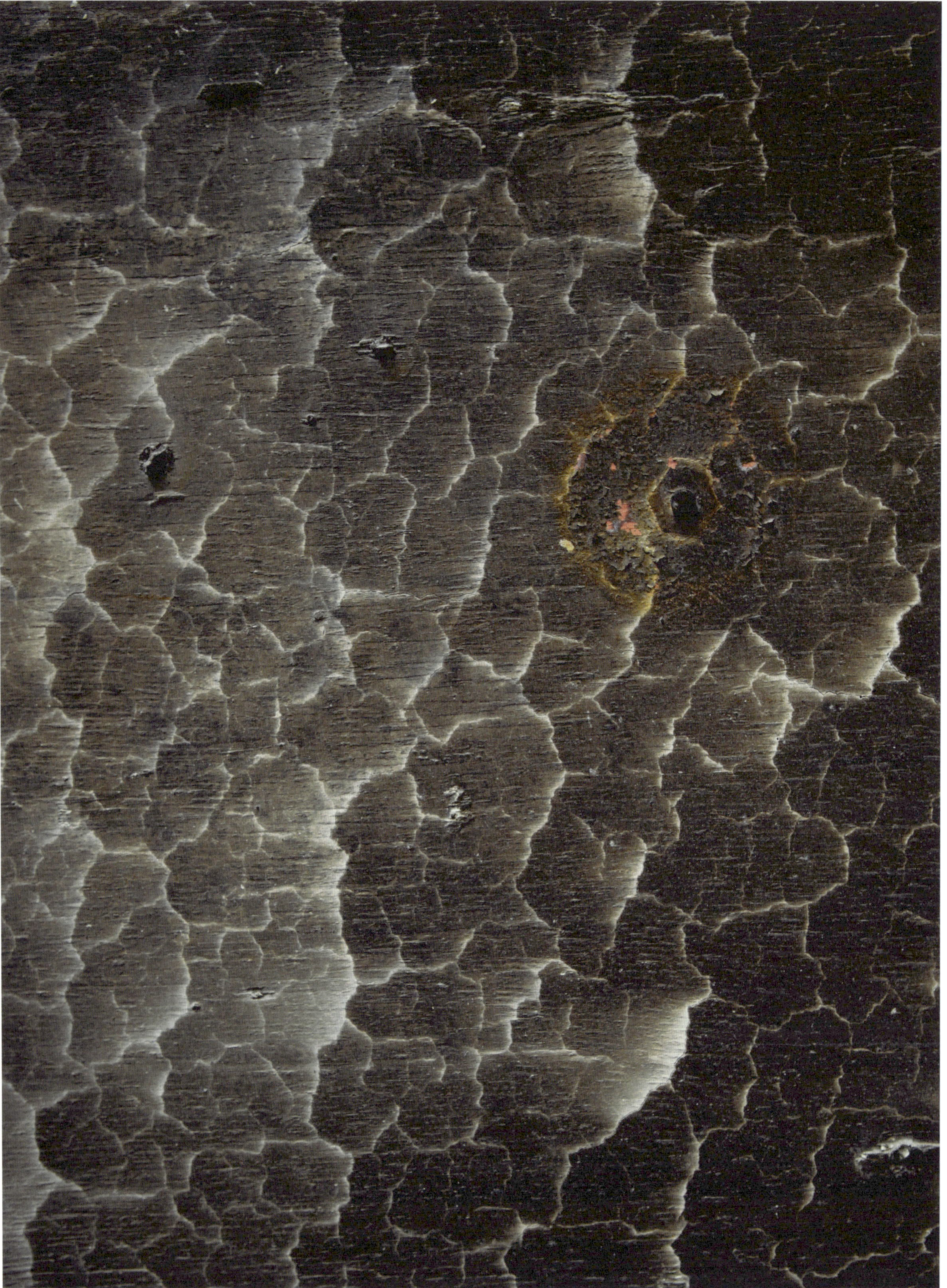

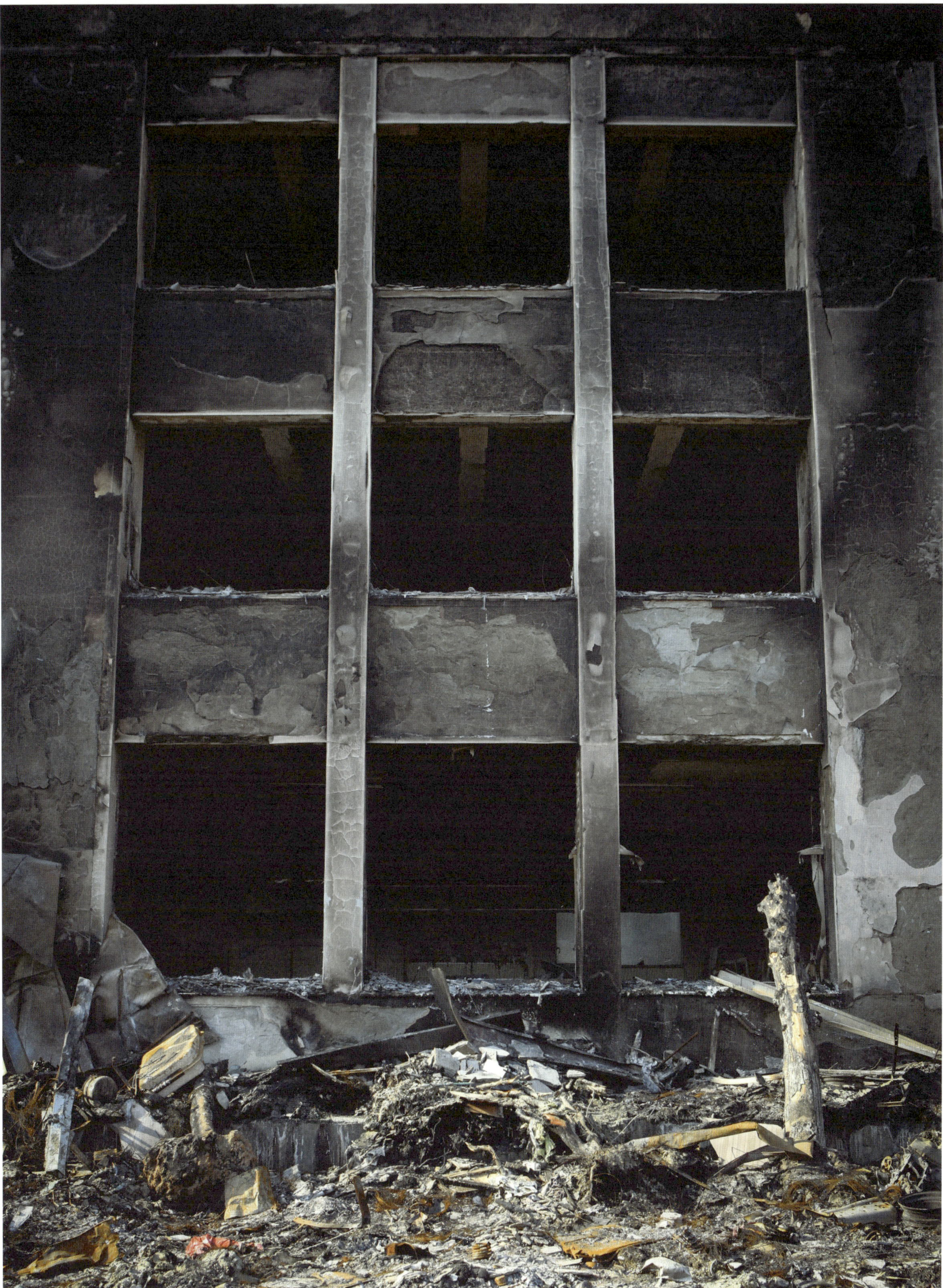

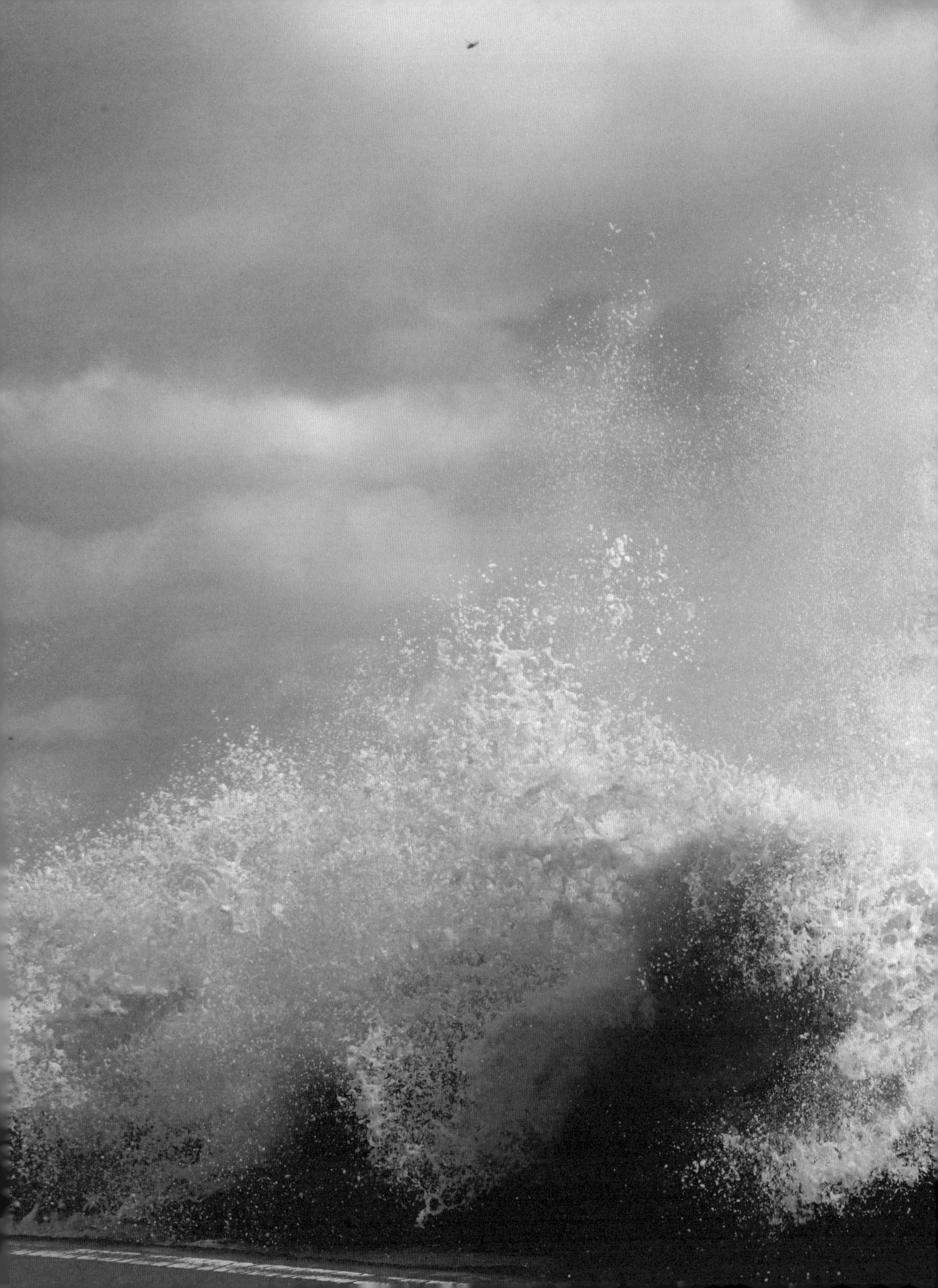

Prologue

On March 11, 2011, an earthquake measuring 9.0 on the Richter scale
and a subsequent tsunami wreaked havoc along 800 kilometers of
coastline from Aomori to Chiba, leaving a very deep scar. 16,000 people
lost their lives and more than 3,000 remain unaccounted for. A third
of the 330,000 evacuees have been deprived of their homes due to
contamination by the accident at the Fukushima Daiichi Nuclear Plant.
The immeasurable damage caused has left us all speechless. A year later,
we continue to grieve and face a paralyzing reality, unable to reset and
look ahead.

It is the close relationship that I established to the people I met in the
affected areas that keeps bringing me back to Tohoku. When I first met
them, when their lives became a part of mine, my perception of rubble
and radiation changed: it became more than just a hazard. As more
issues rise to the surface, my values are overthrown and society is urged
to rethink.

I take it as my duty to convey what I have experienced to distant places,
to create an opportunity for the world to meet the people through
my photography and have us all think about the plight of the victims.
This is the wish of one single photographer who is determined to
continue documenting the areas struck by this disaster.

Kazuma Obara, photojournalist

プロローグ

2011年3月11日、マグニチュード9.0の大地震は青森県から千葉県の800キロ
以上にわたり、津波の巨大な爪痕を残した。
1万6000人もの命が奪われ、未だ3000人以上の命の確認がとれていない。
その後に追い討ちをかけるように起きた福島第一原発の事故によって、総避難者数
33万人の約3分の1が汚染により、安心して戻れる場所も奪われた。
私たちは途方もない被害のあらゆる数字に打ちのめされ、言葉を失った。

あの日から1年。
リセットなどできない悲しみと、先の見えない現状に被災地は対峙し続けている。
僕を強固に東北の地に引き付けているのは、被災地で出会った人たちと
築いてきた繋がりである。
彼らと向き合い、彼らの抱える問題が僕の一部となった時、瓦礫の見え方が変わり、
放射能が危険物質という以上の重みを持ちだした。
浮上してきた様々な問題に、これまでの価値観が覆され、私たちの社会は見直し
を突きつけられた。

僕がやるべきことは、当事者に出会った自分の経験を遥か遠くの人にも届け、
写真を通して被写体と出会い、被災地に思いを馳せてもらうことである。
それが、被災地で写真を撮り続けている一人のカメラマンの願いである。

小原 一真 (フォトジャーナリスト)

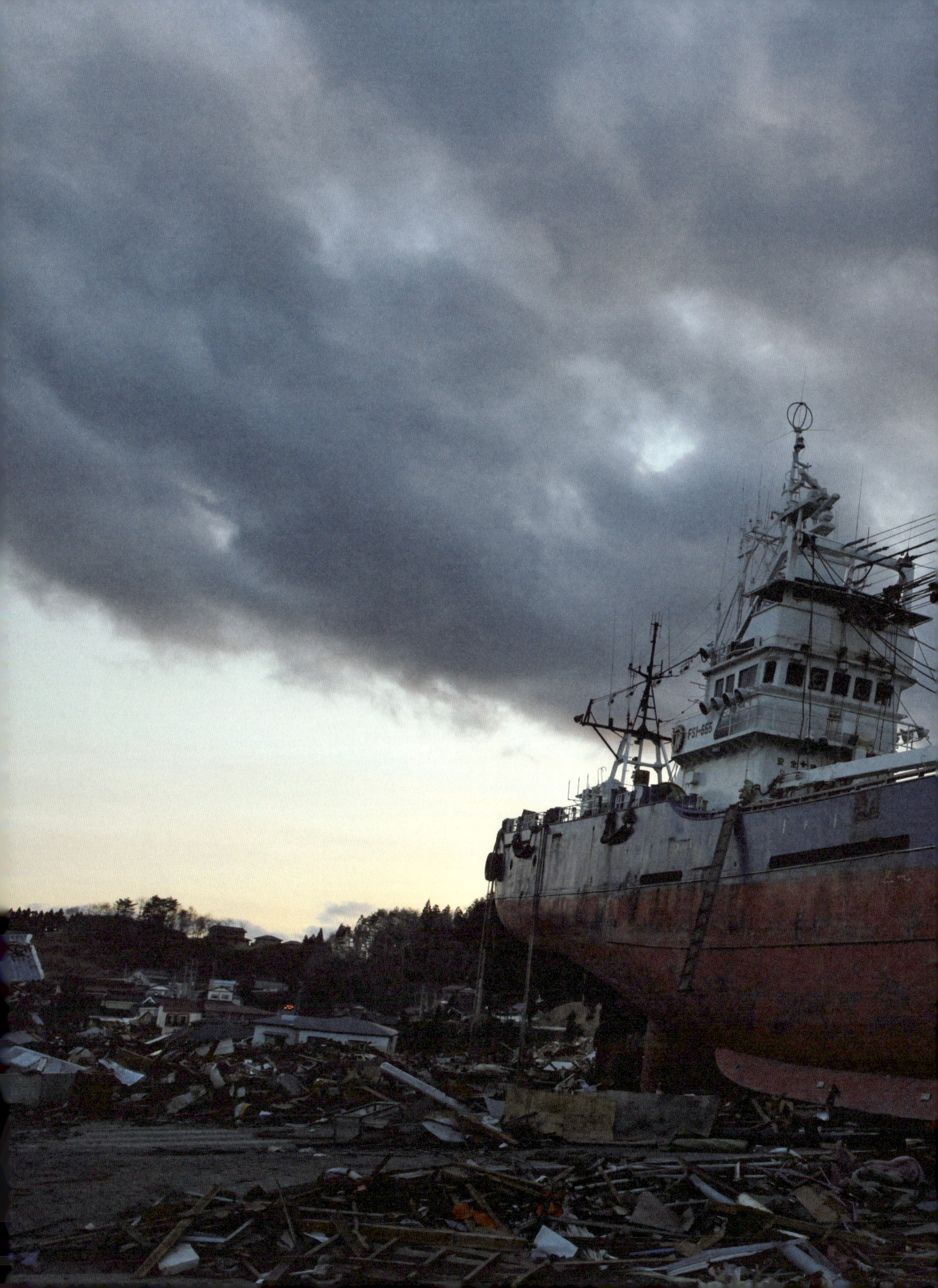

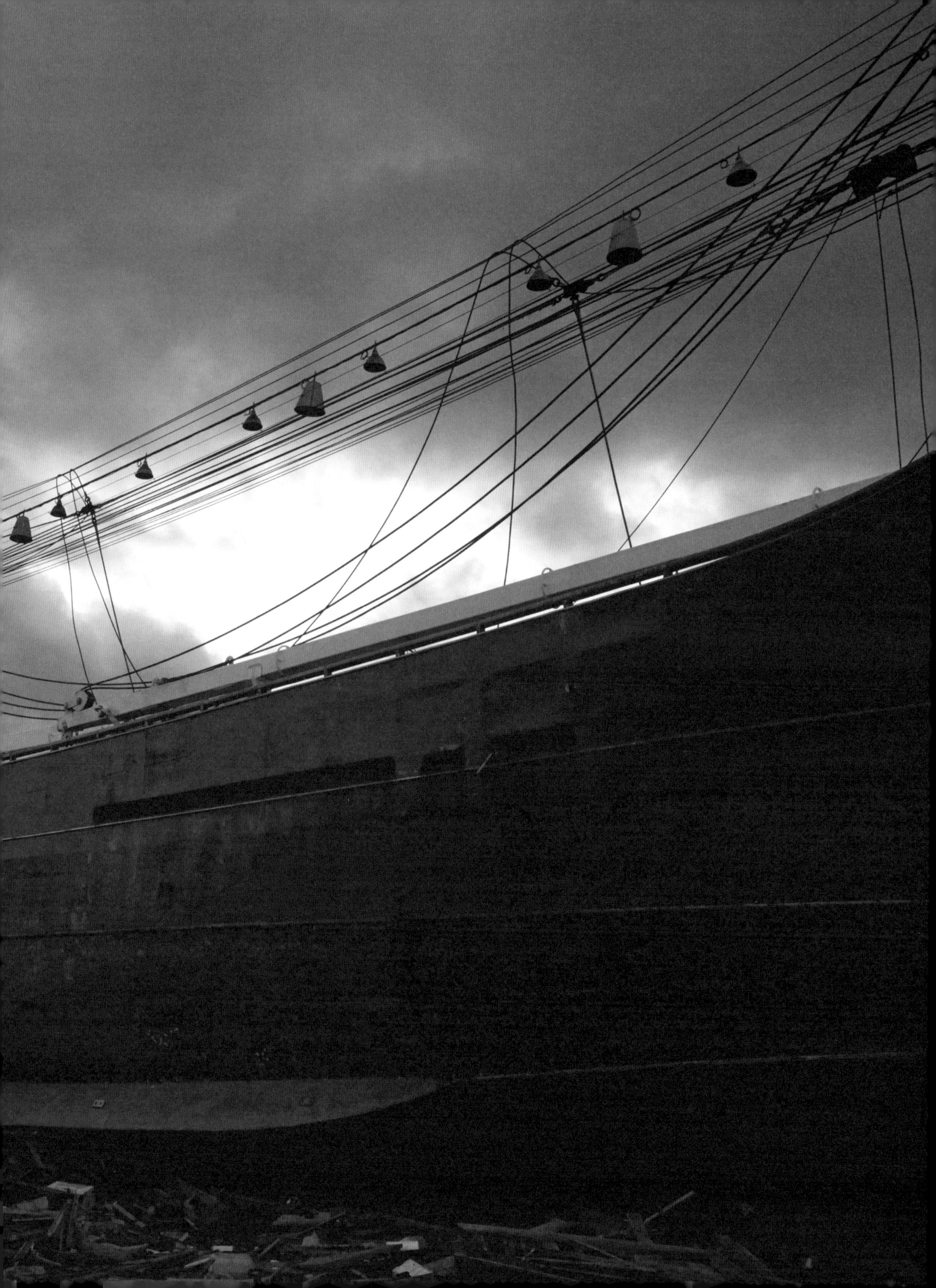

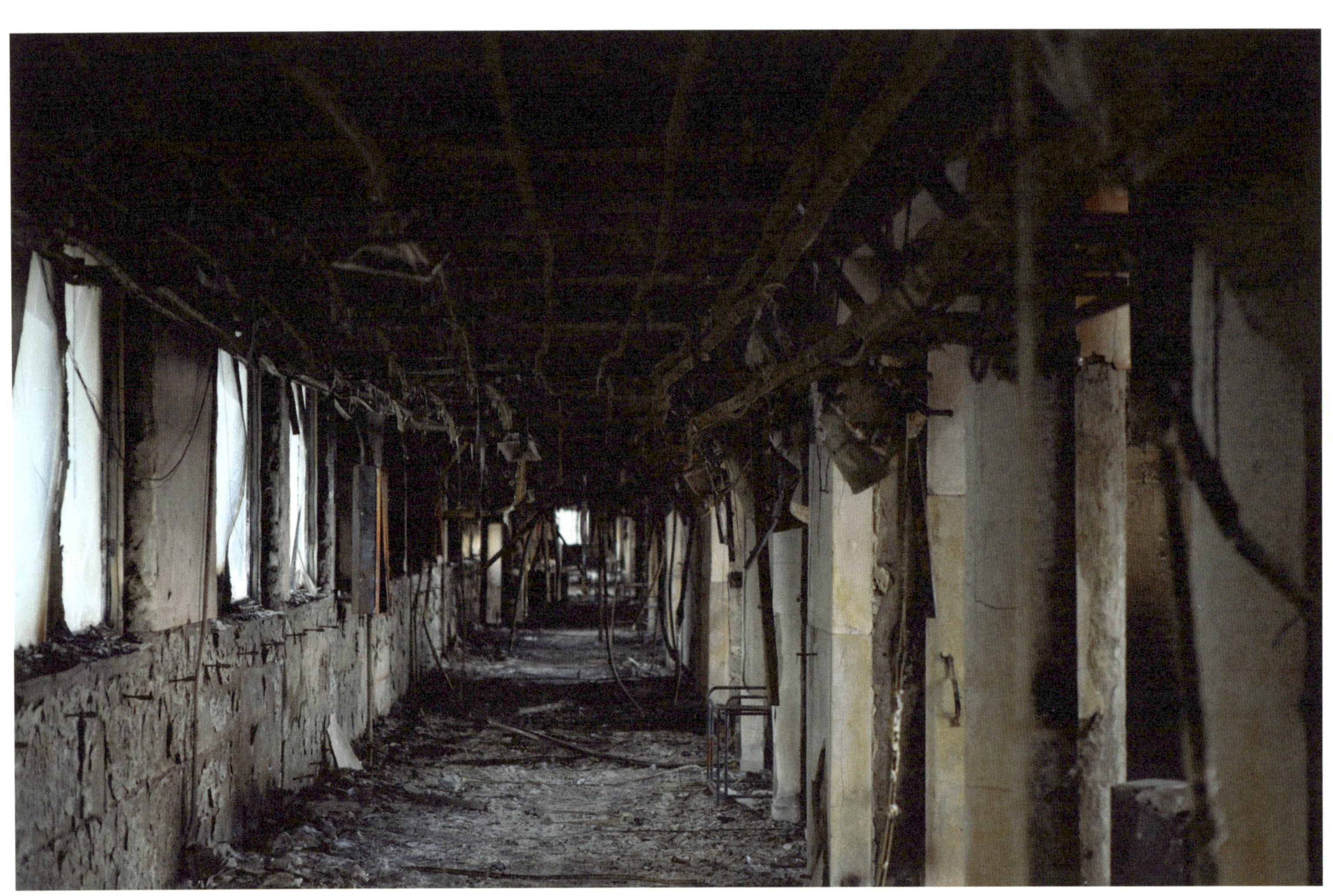

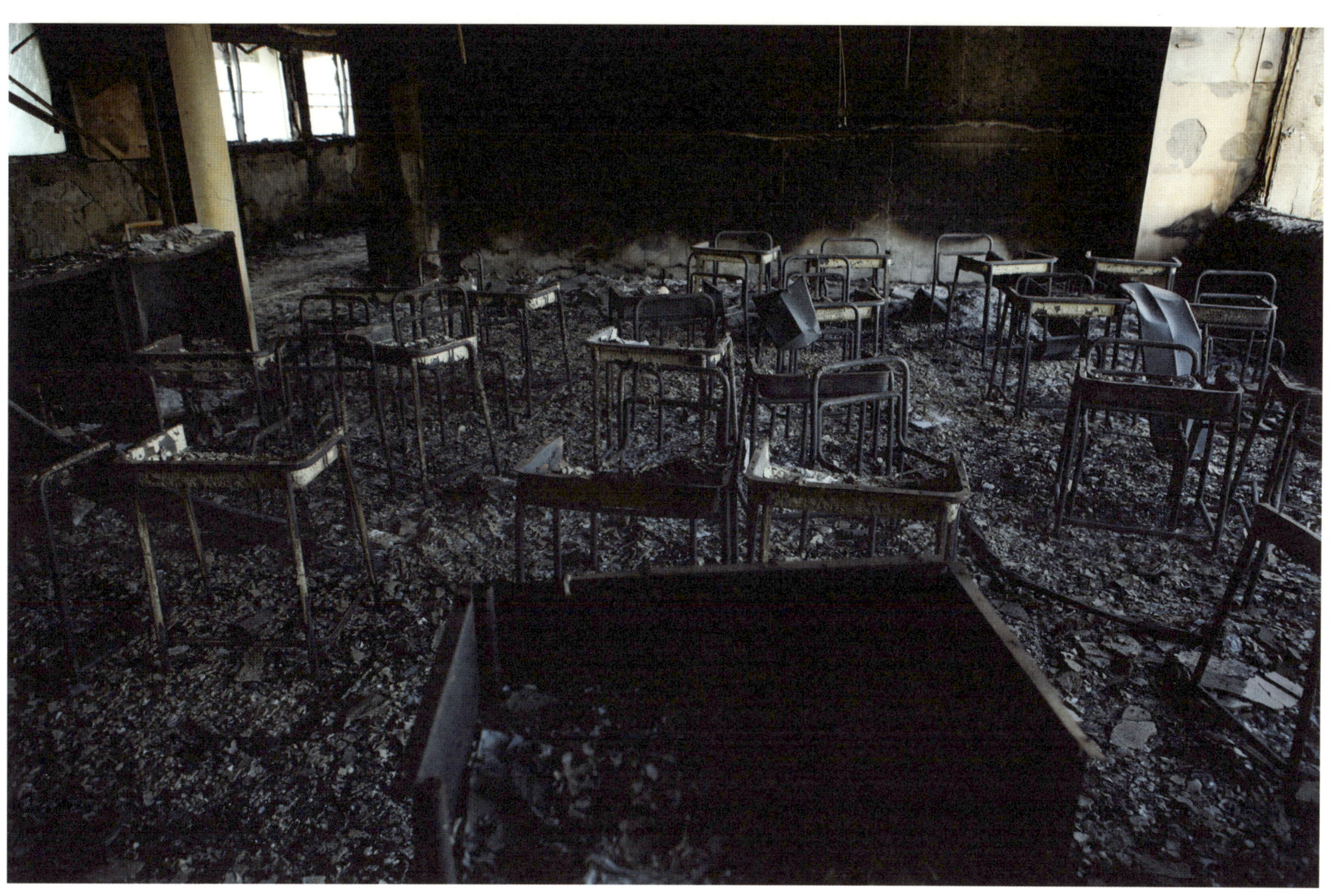

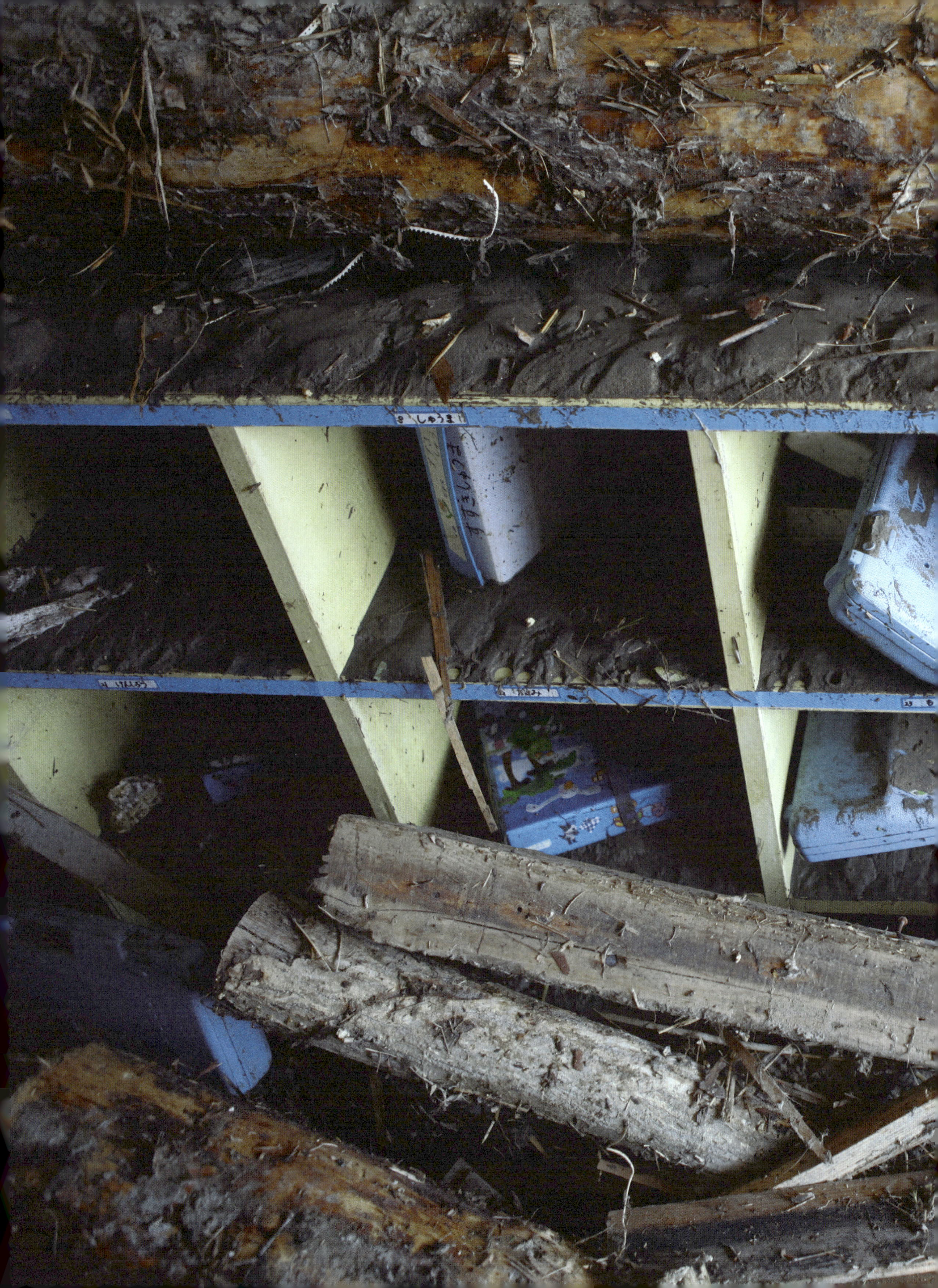

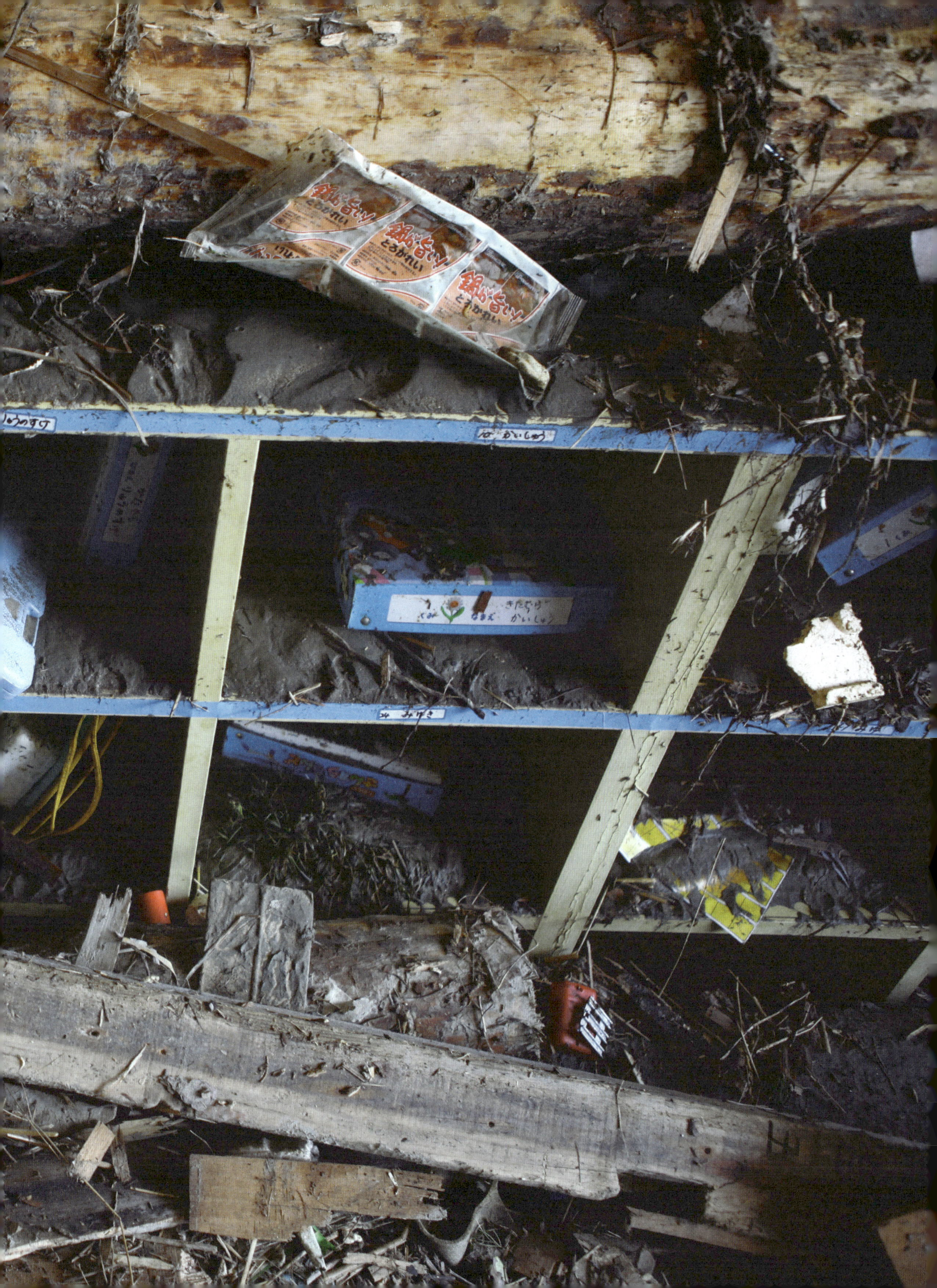
銀が言い！
とろかれい
いわのすけ
かいしゅう
とみ　なまえ　きたむら　かいしゅう
みぎき

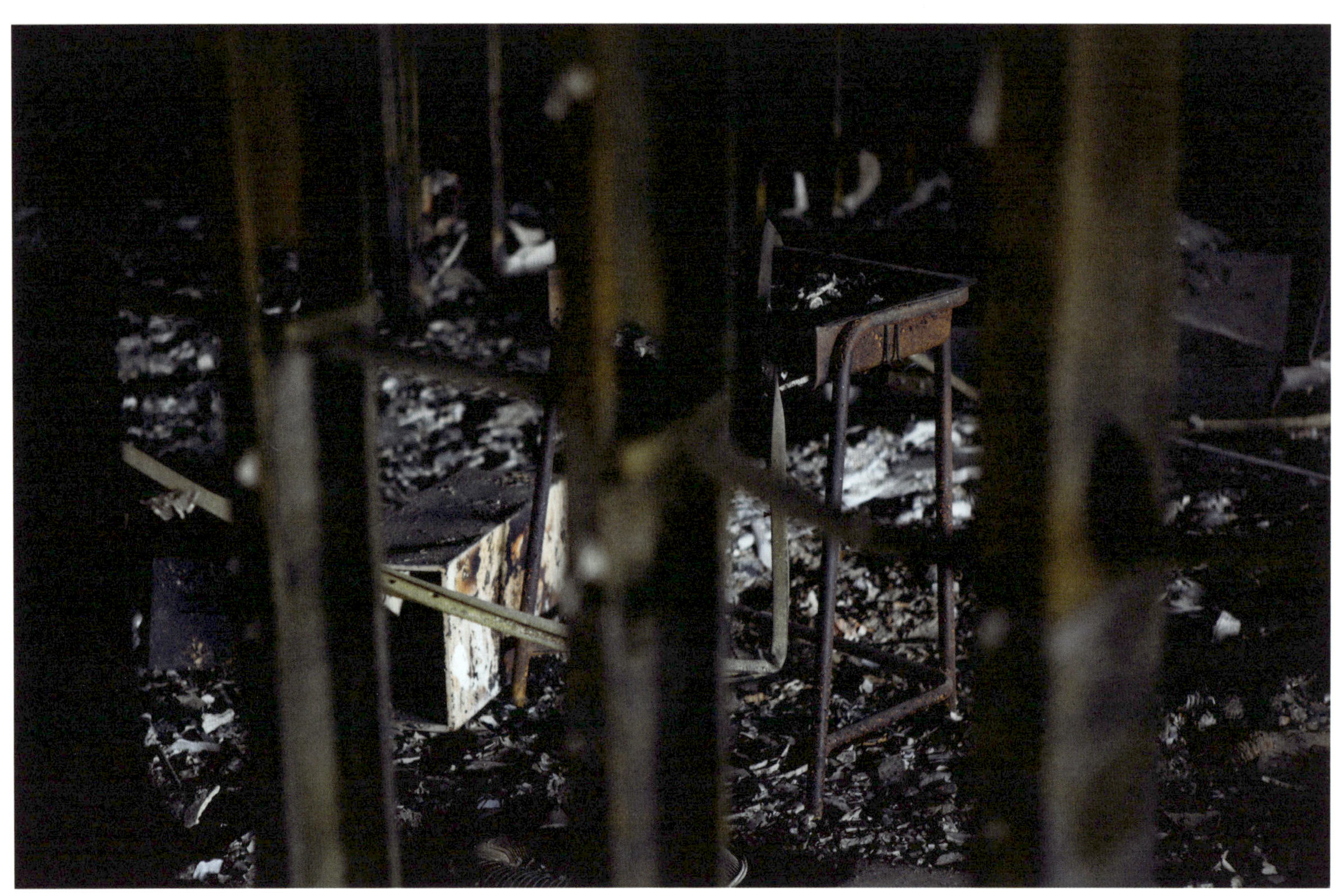

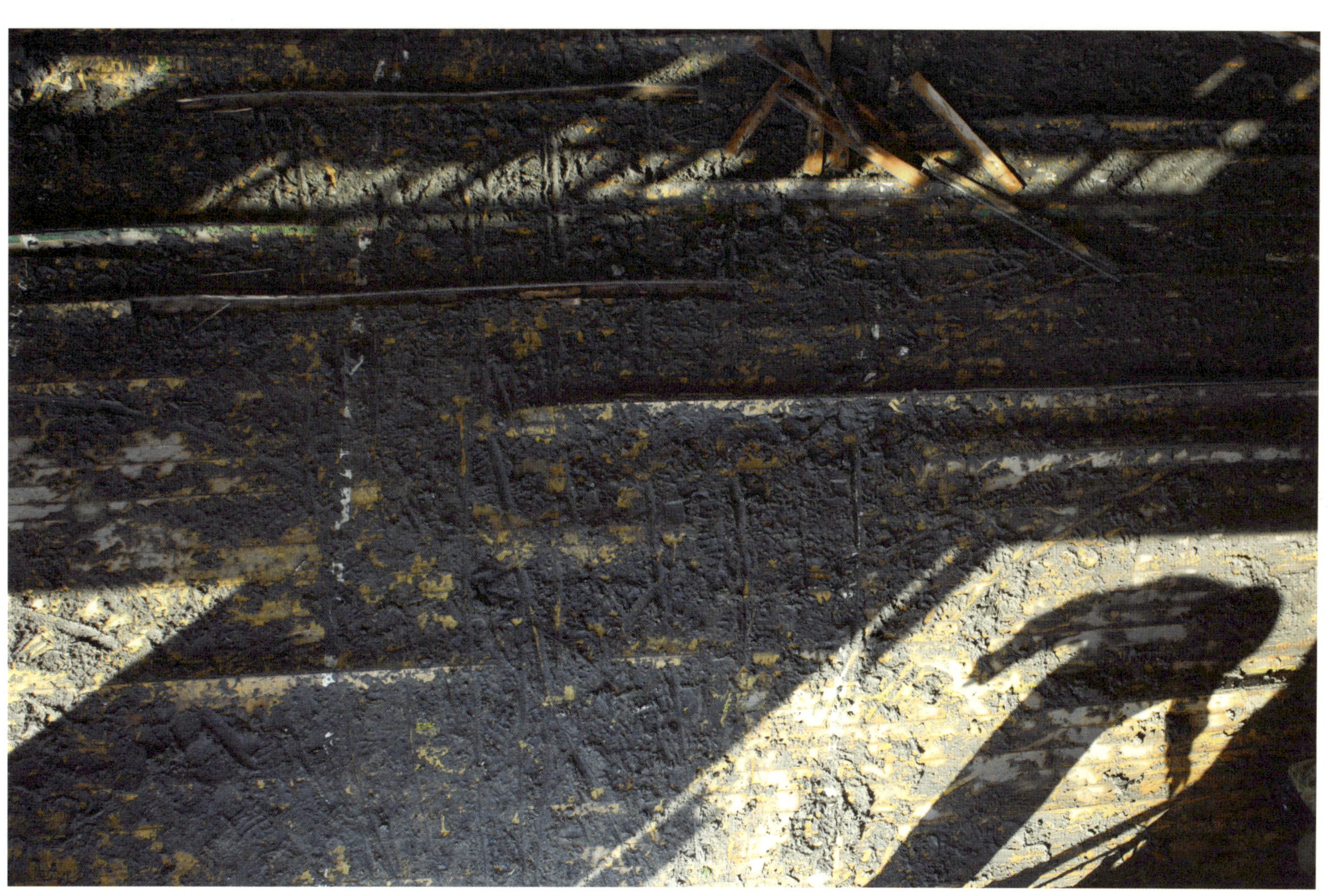

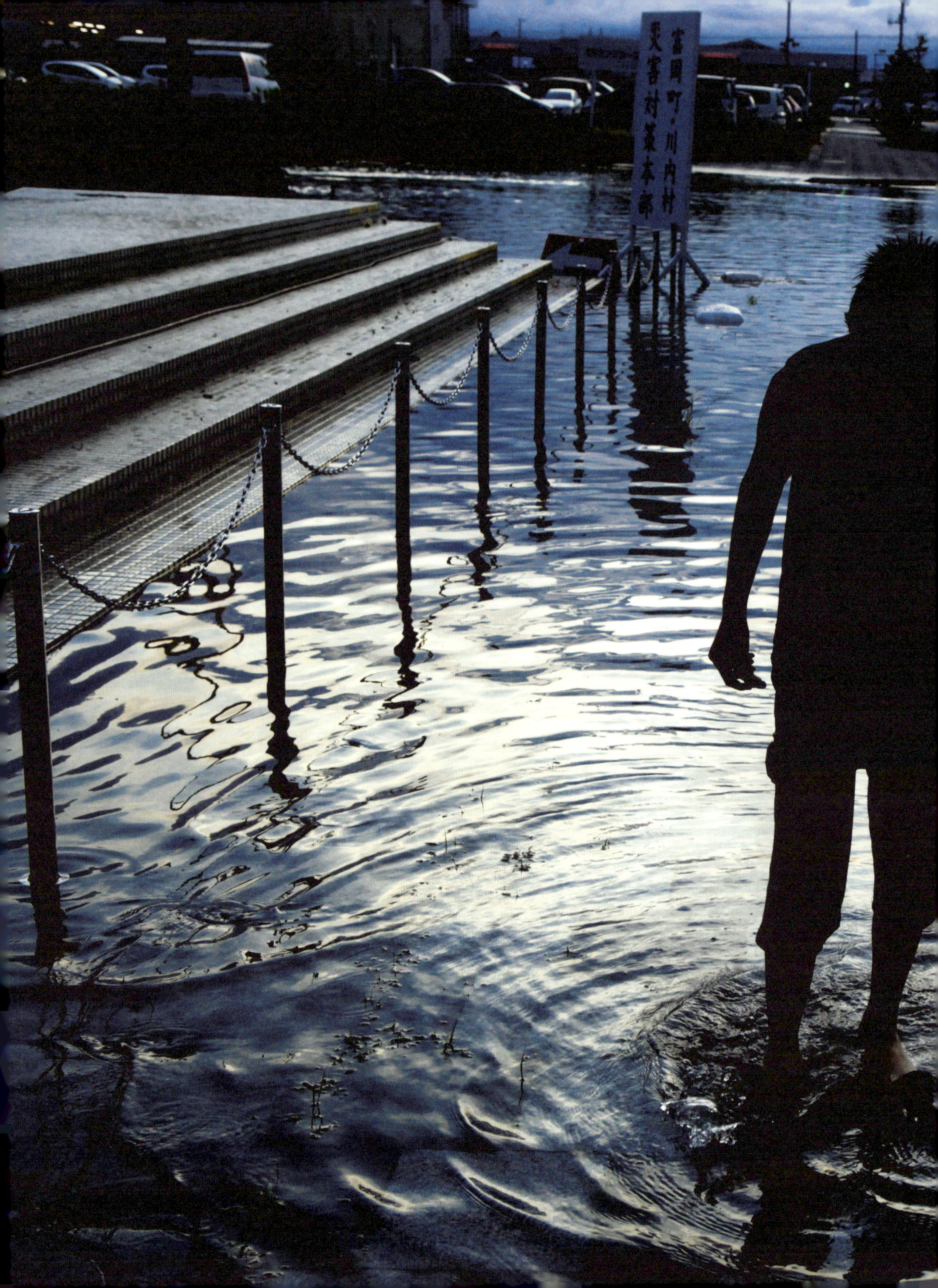

富岡町・川内村
災害対策本部

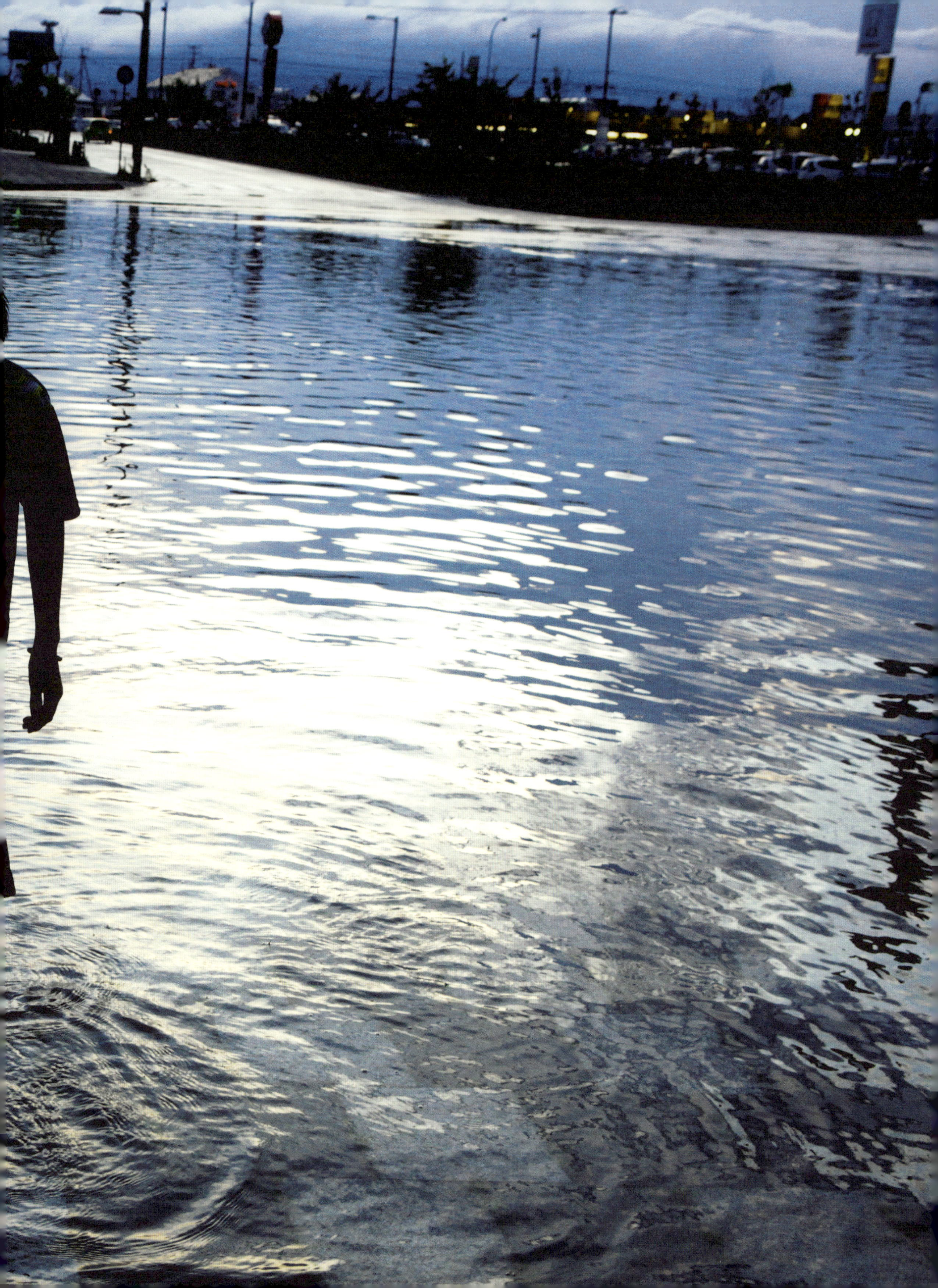

"…Experts Fear Japanese Chernobyl"

Le Monde, March 13, 2011

Shortly after the earthquake and the tsunami of March 11,
events around the Fukushima Daiichi Nuclear Power Plant cause
serious worldwide concern about a nuclear catastrophe
happening in Japan and the dangers of nuclear energy in general.

専門家、日本での
チェルノブイリを恐れる

2011年3月13日　ル・モンド紙

3月11日の大震災発生直後に福島第一原発で起きた大事故は
核の大惨事と原子力の危険性について世界中で深刻な懸念を引き起こした。

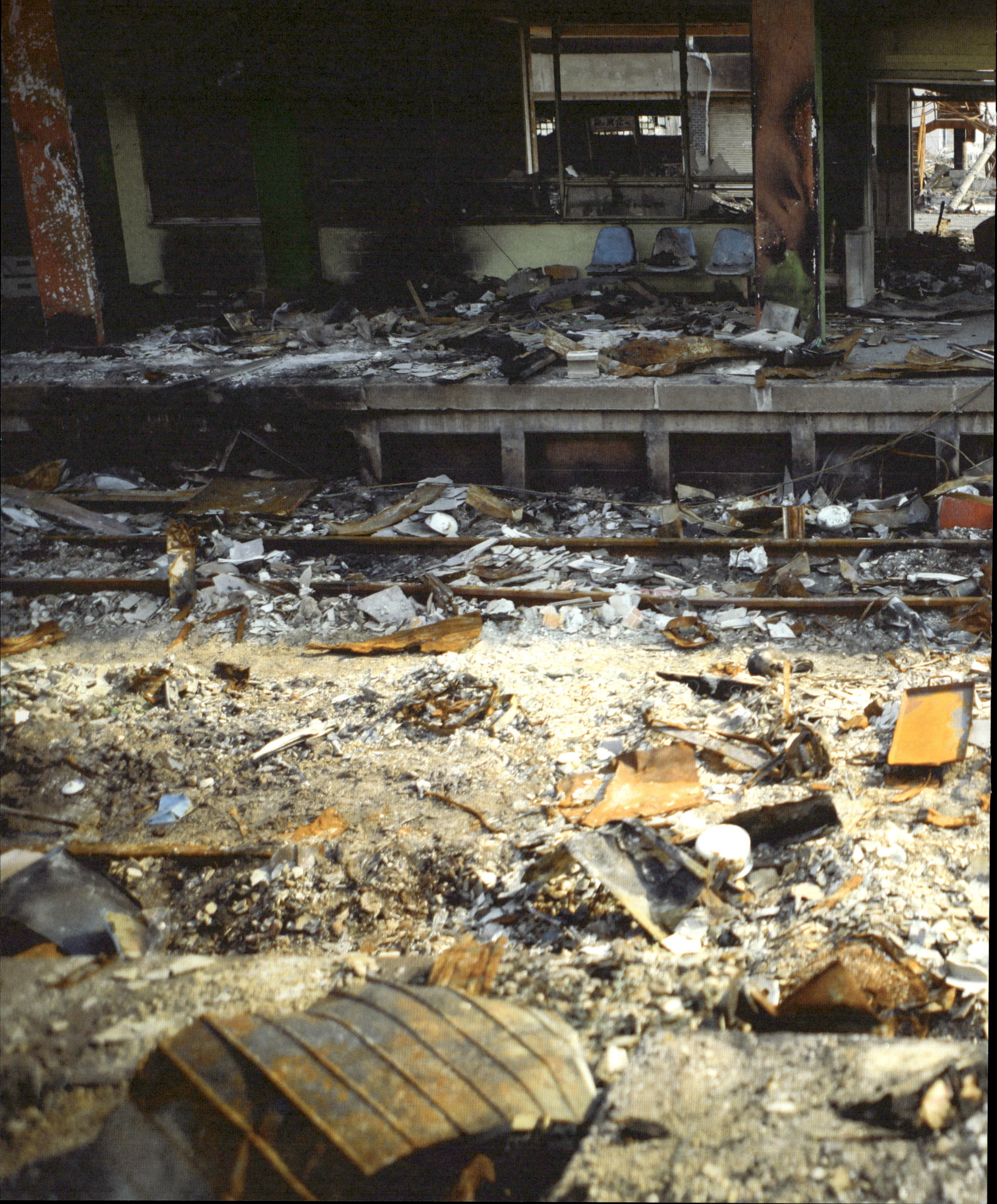

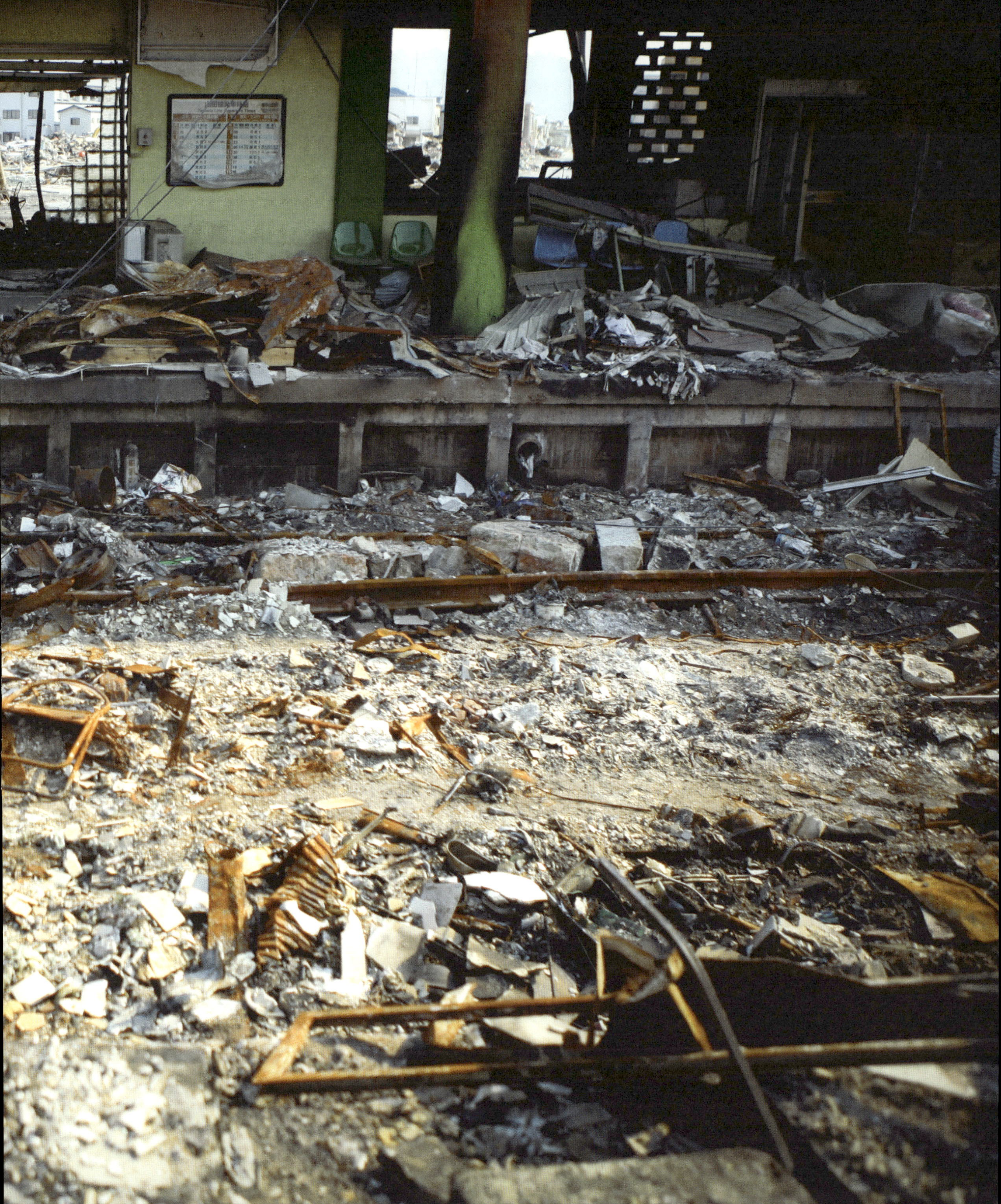
Tōhoku Line Departure Times

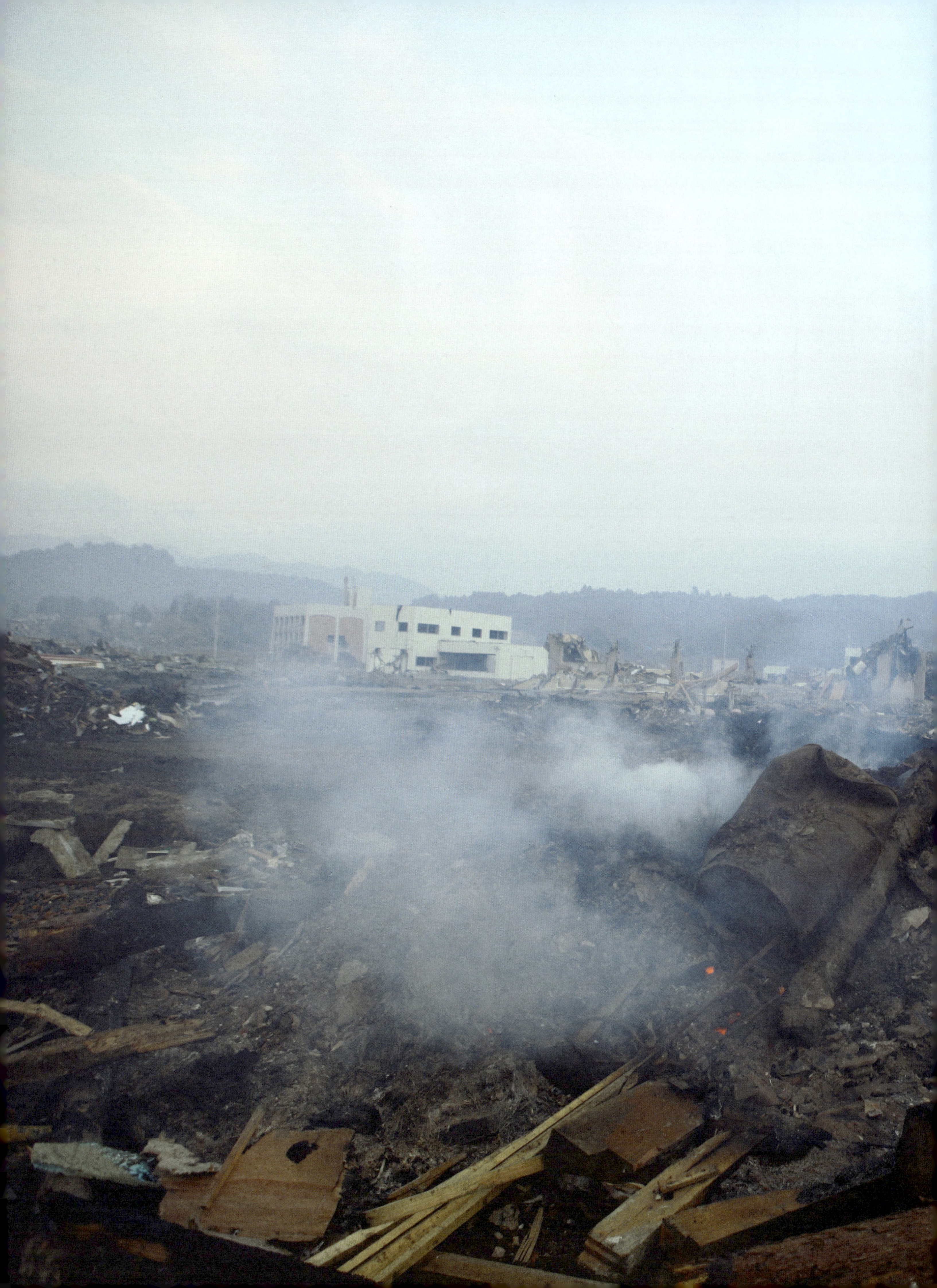

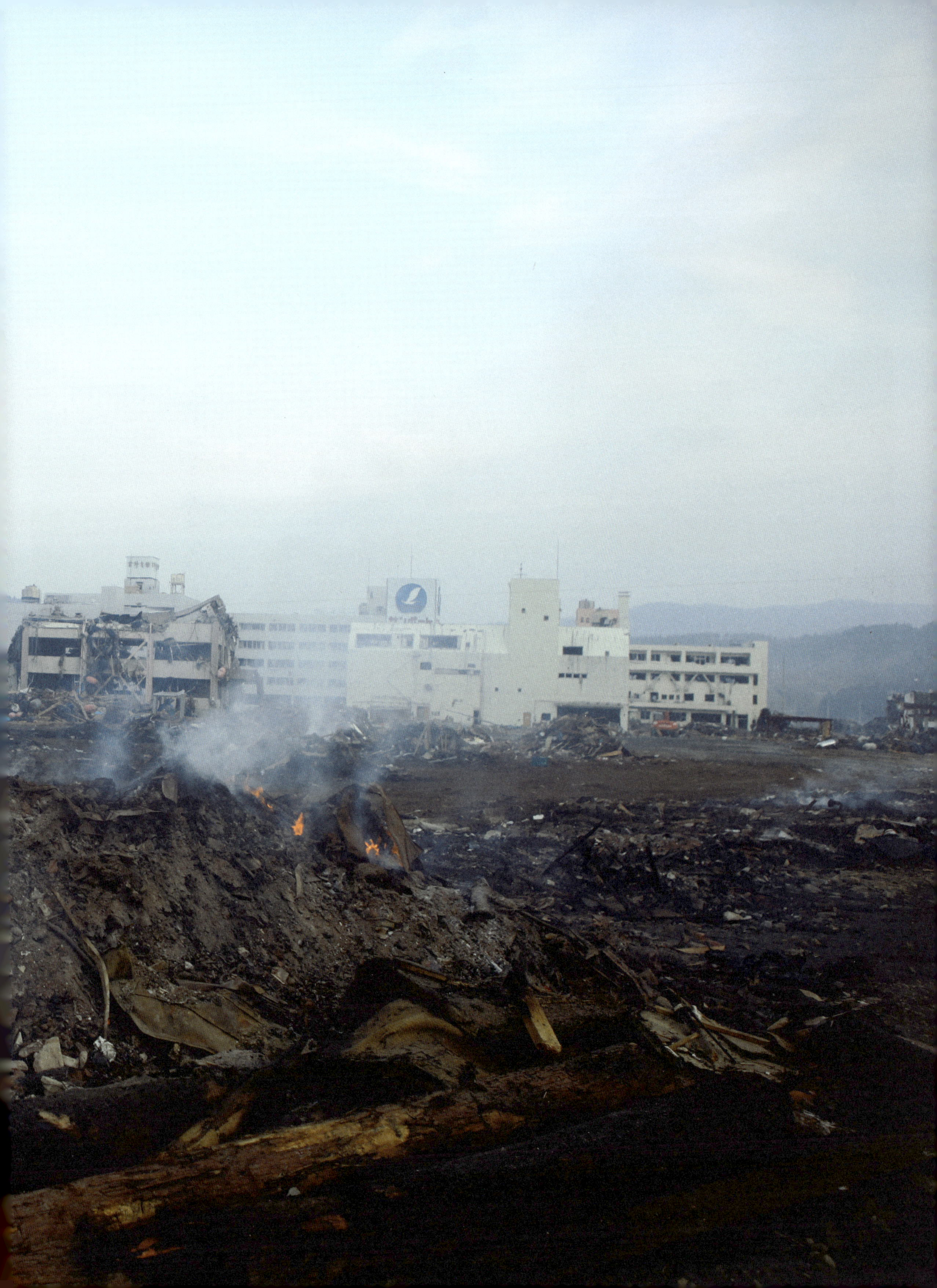

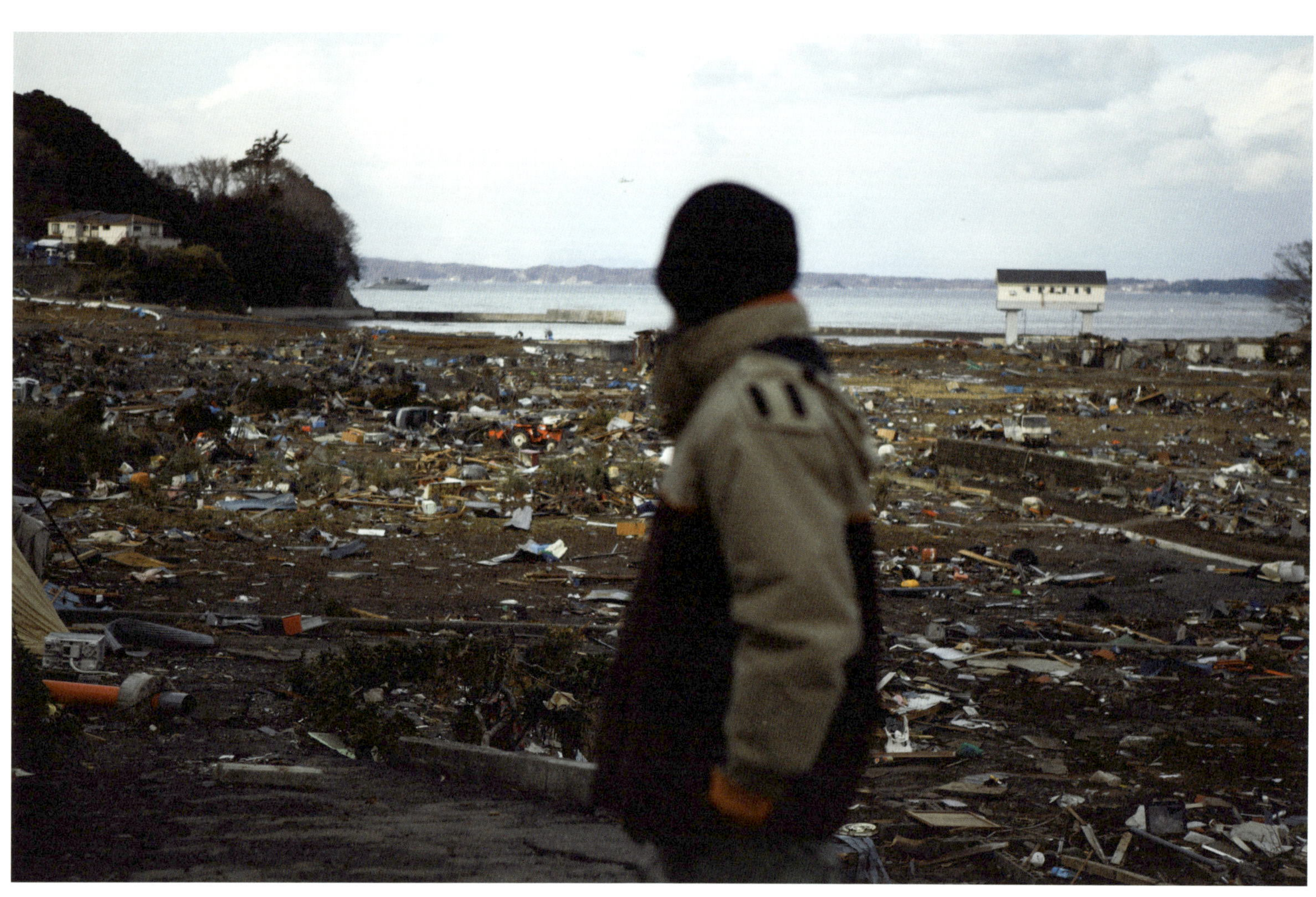

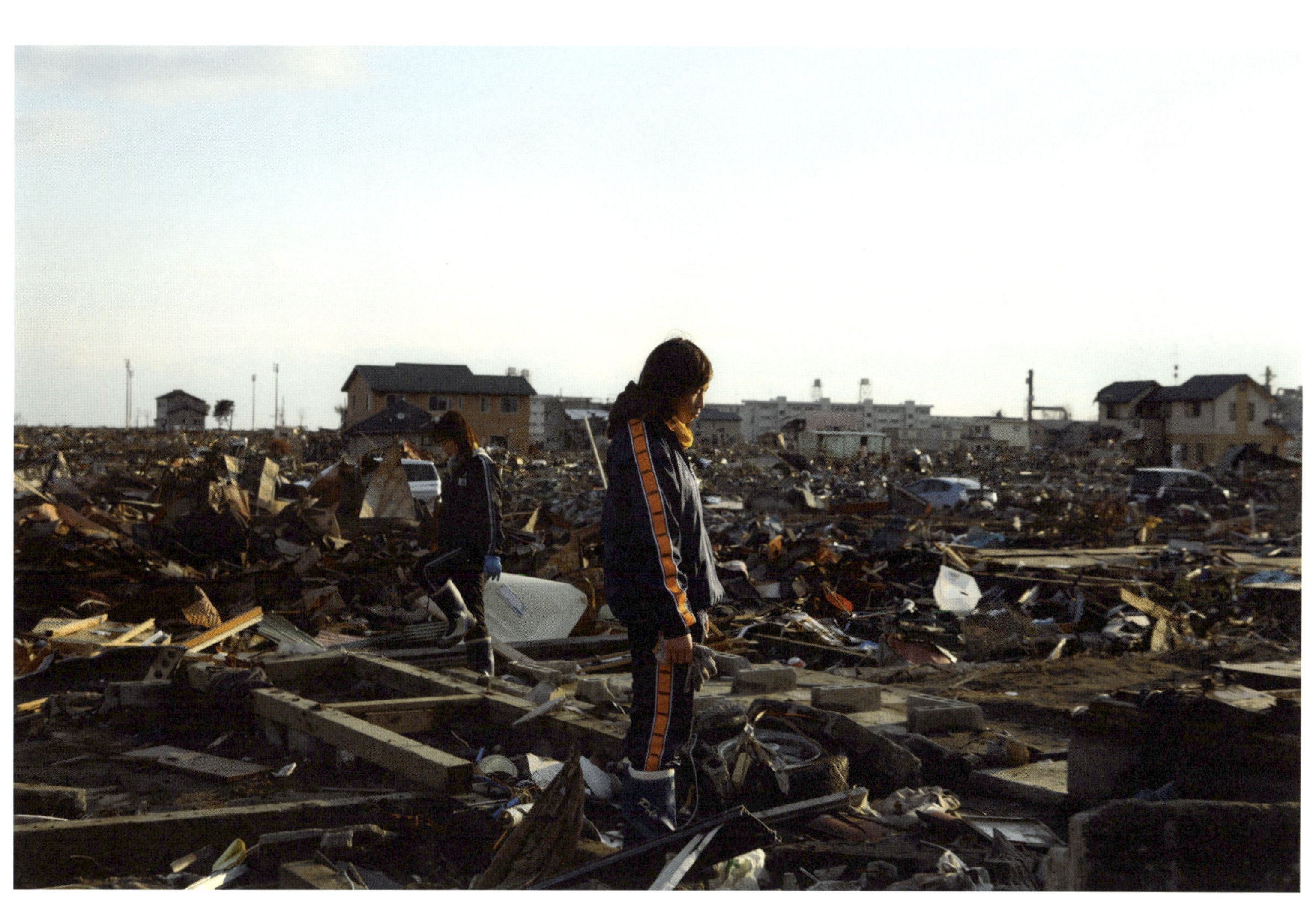

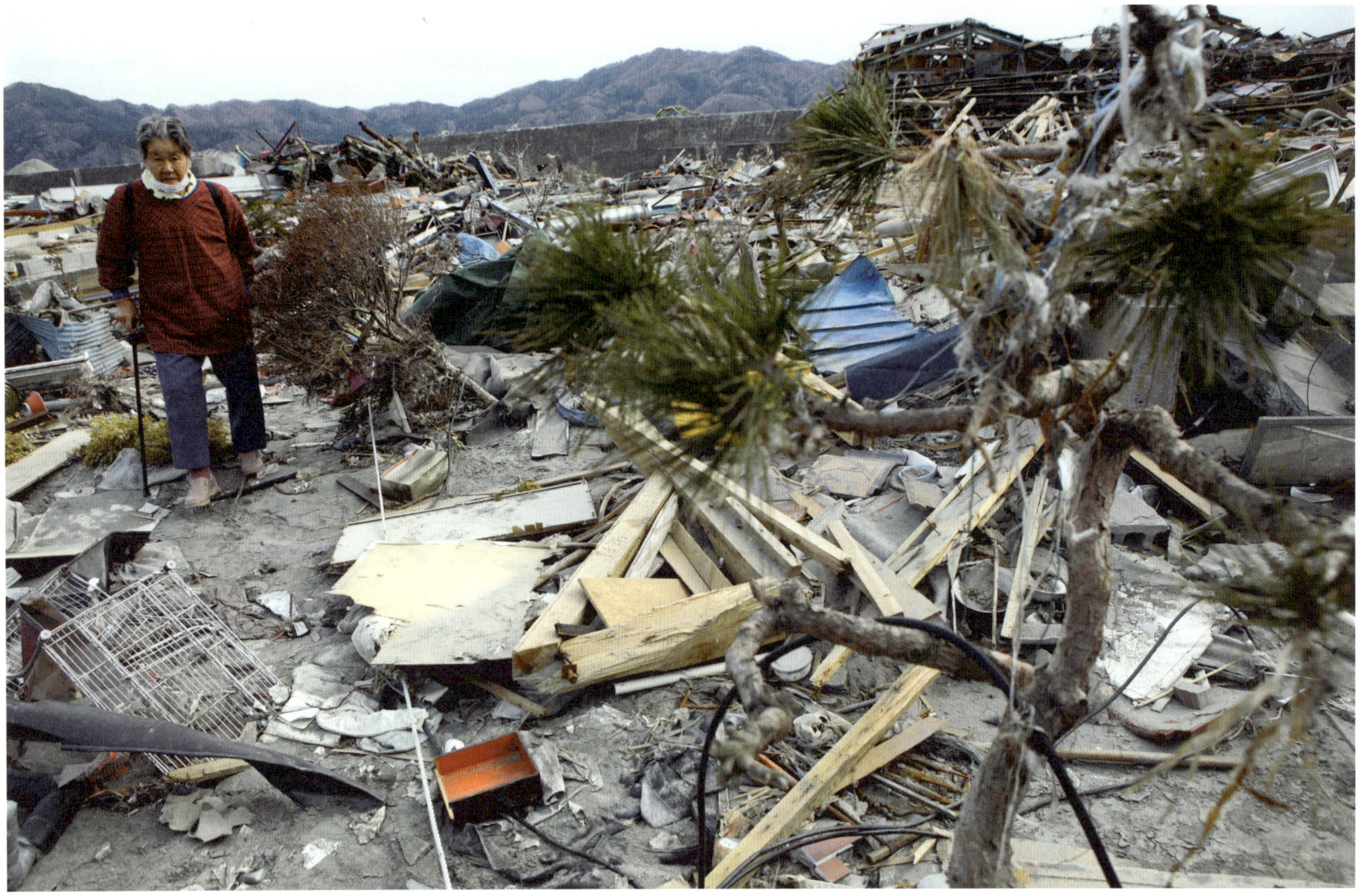

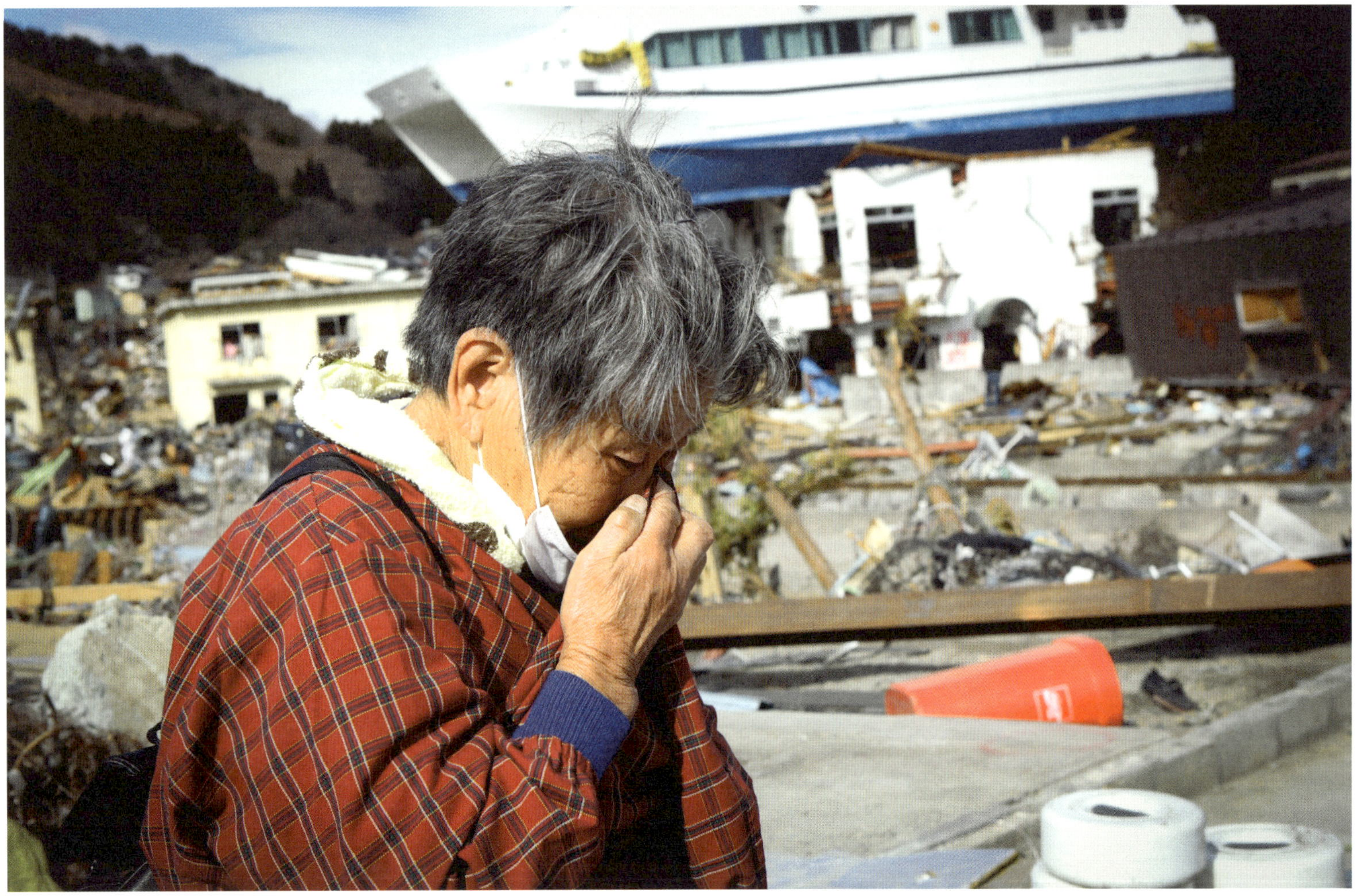

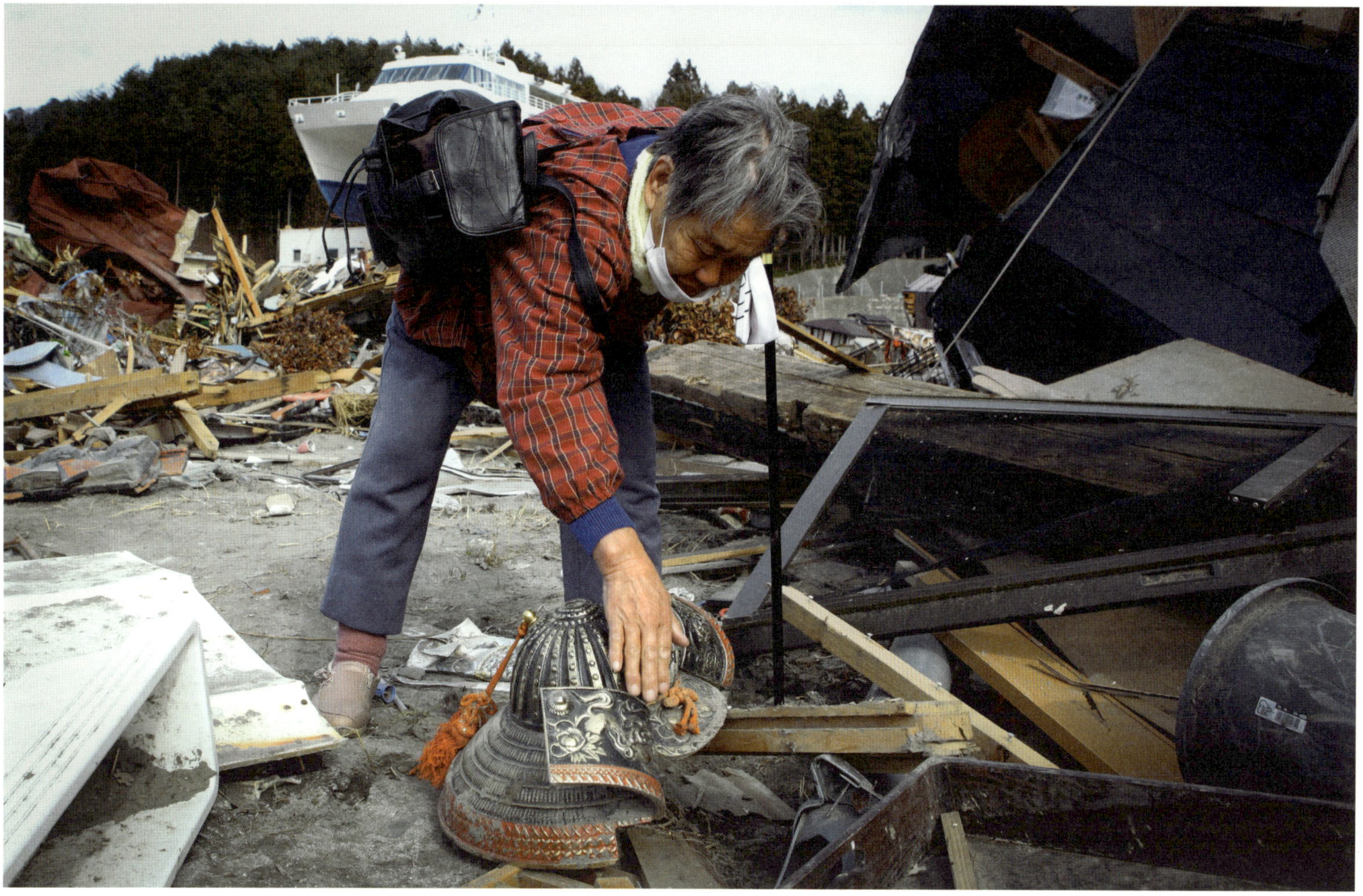

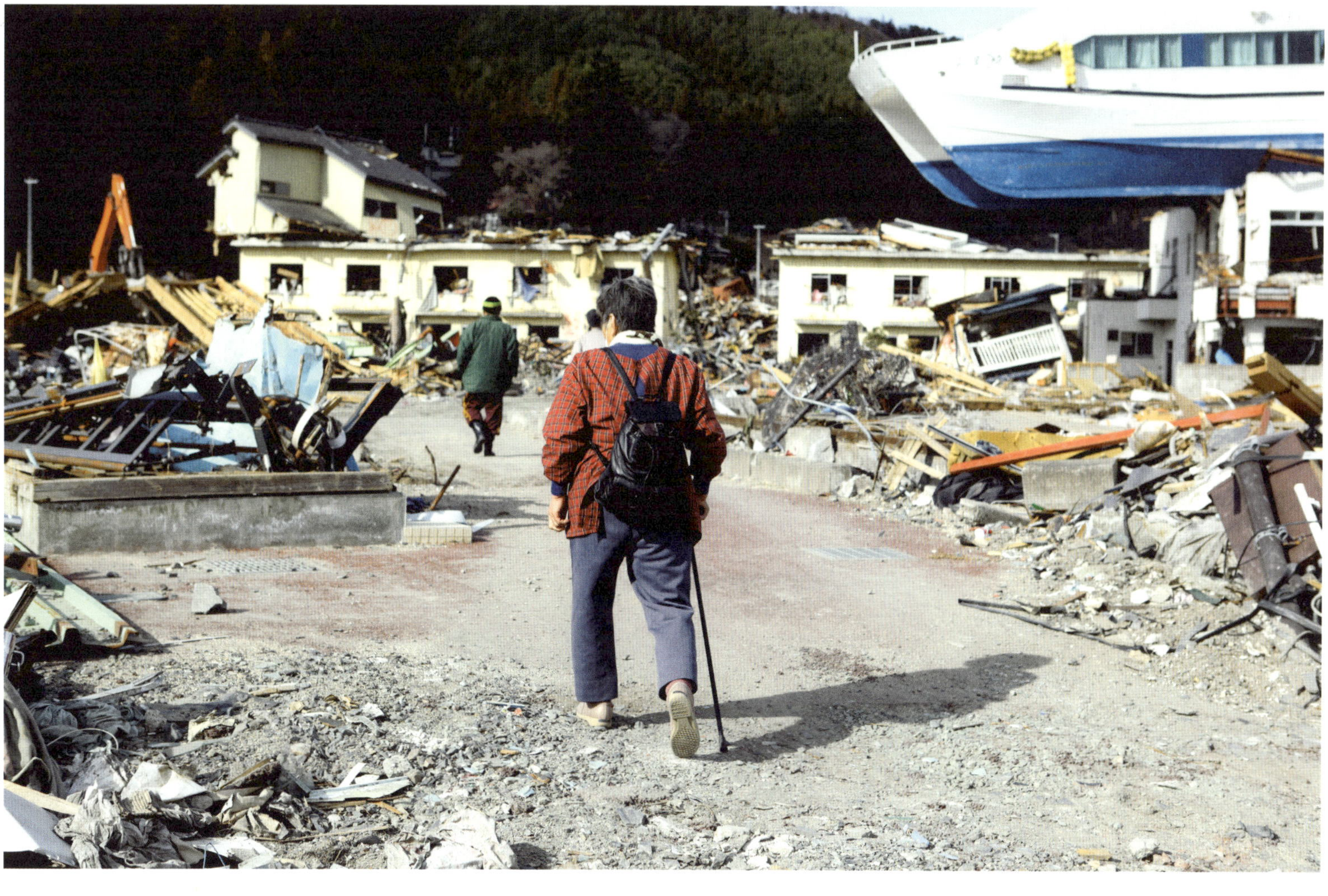

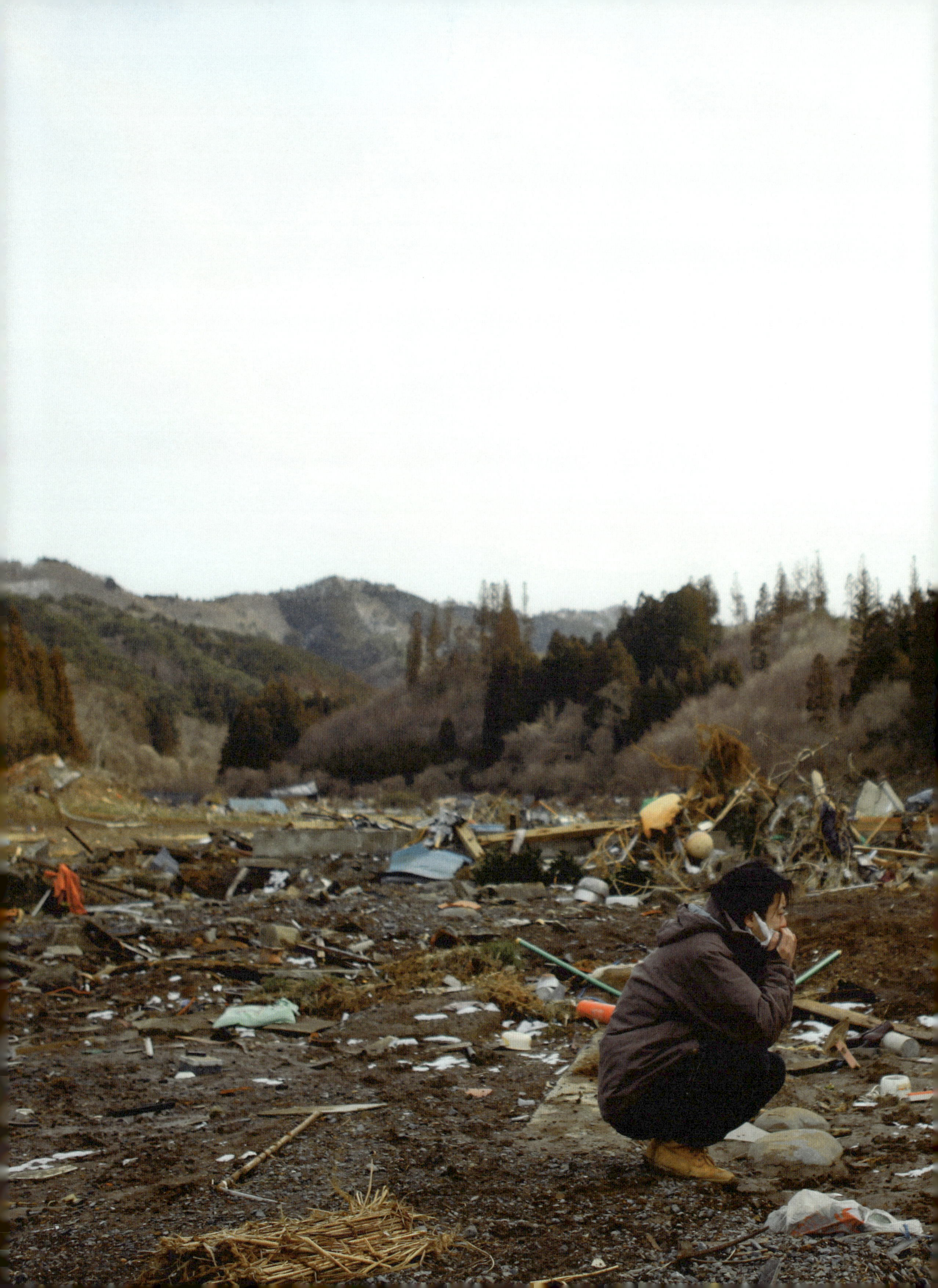

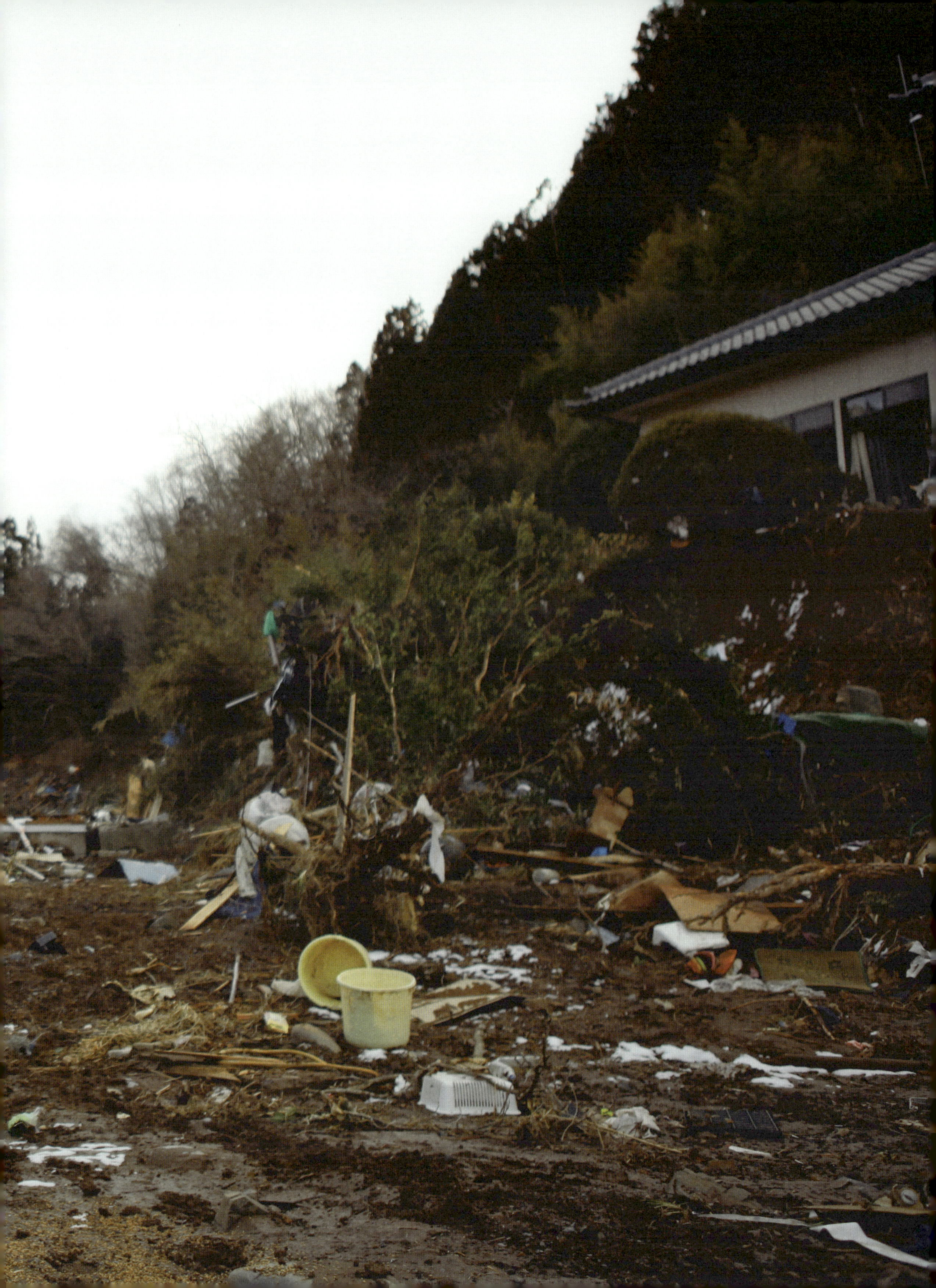

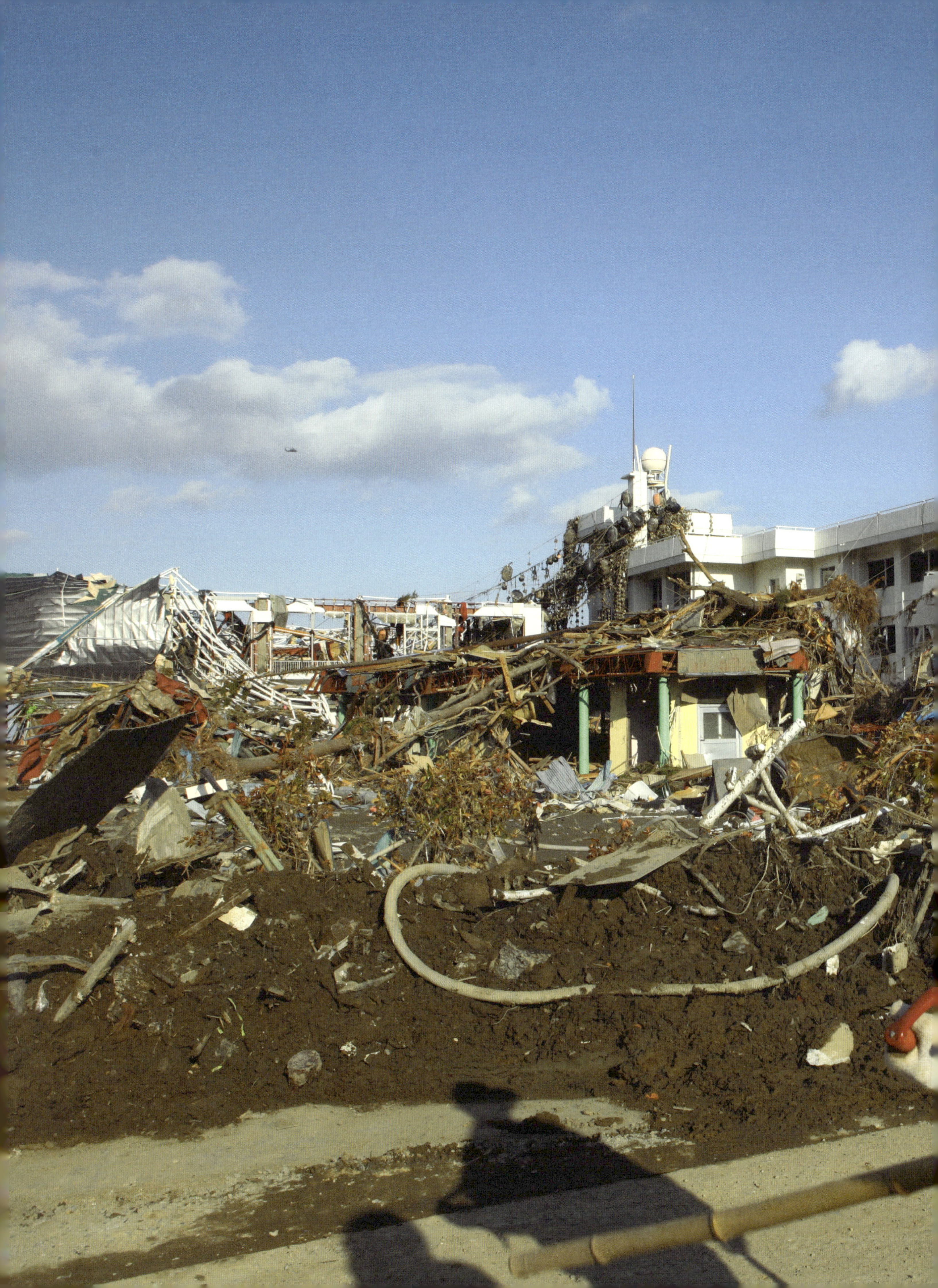

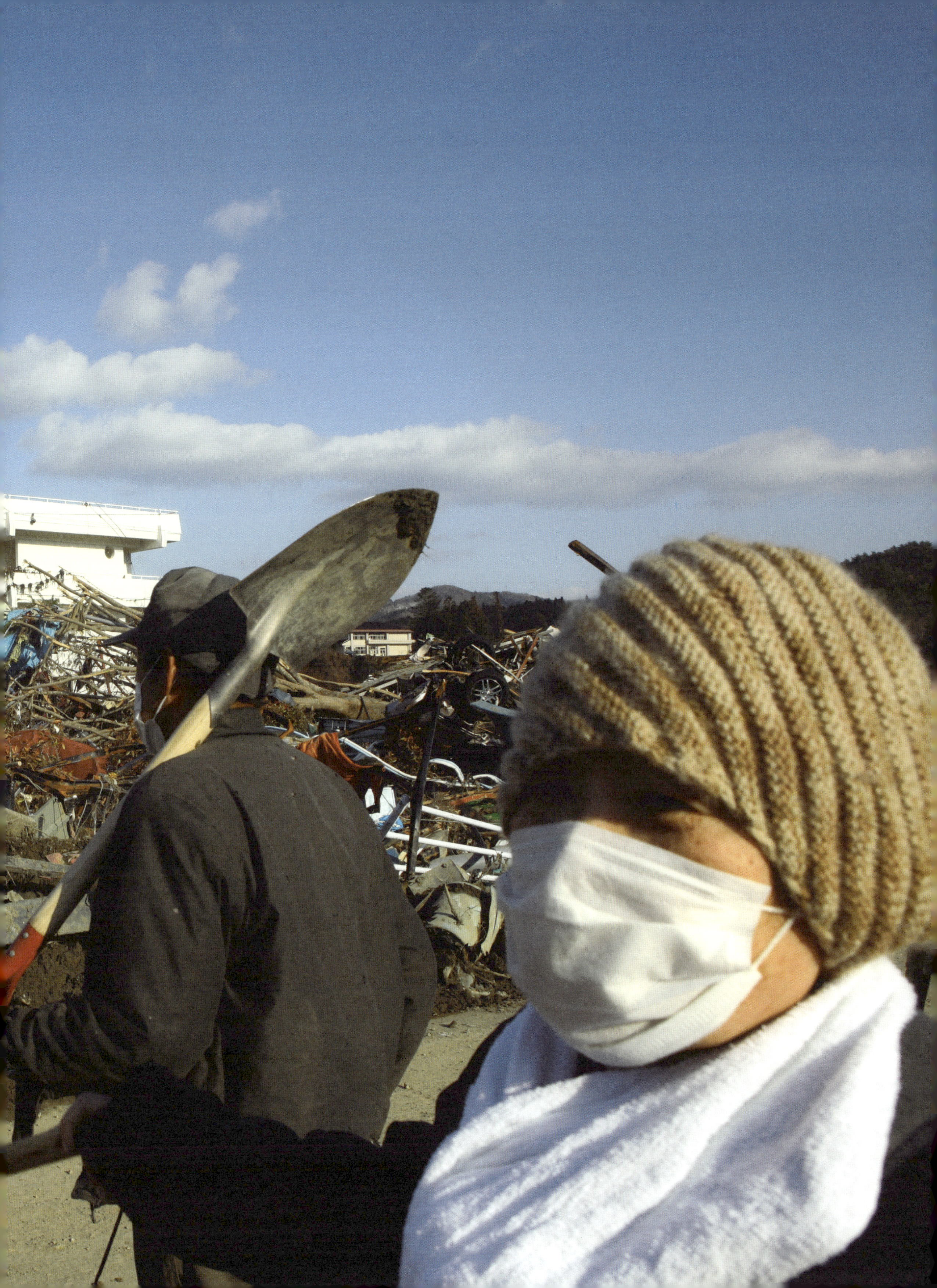

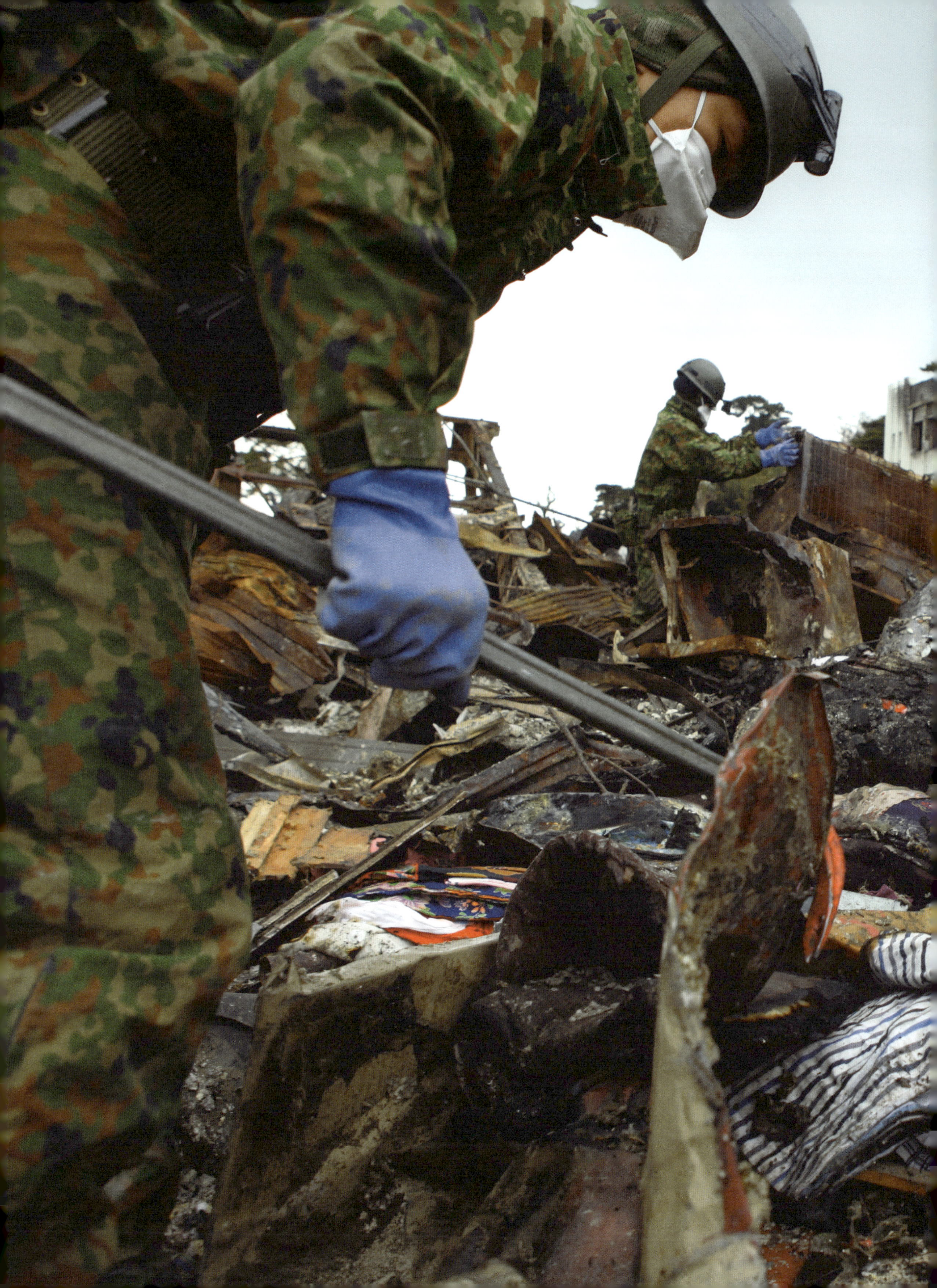

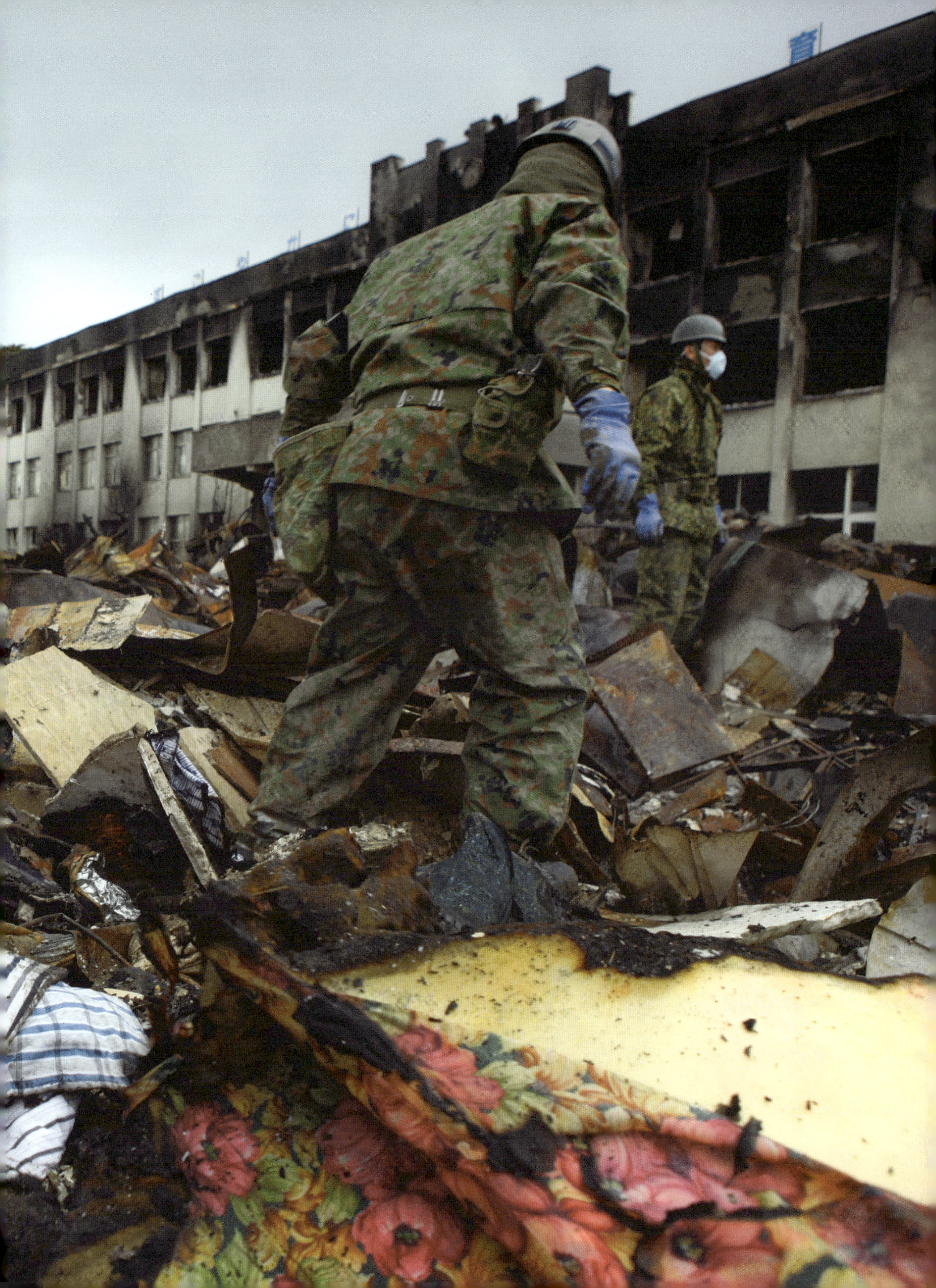

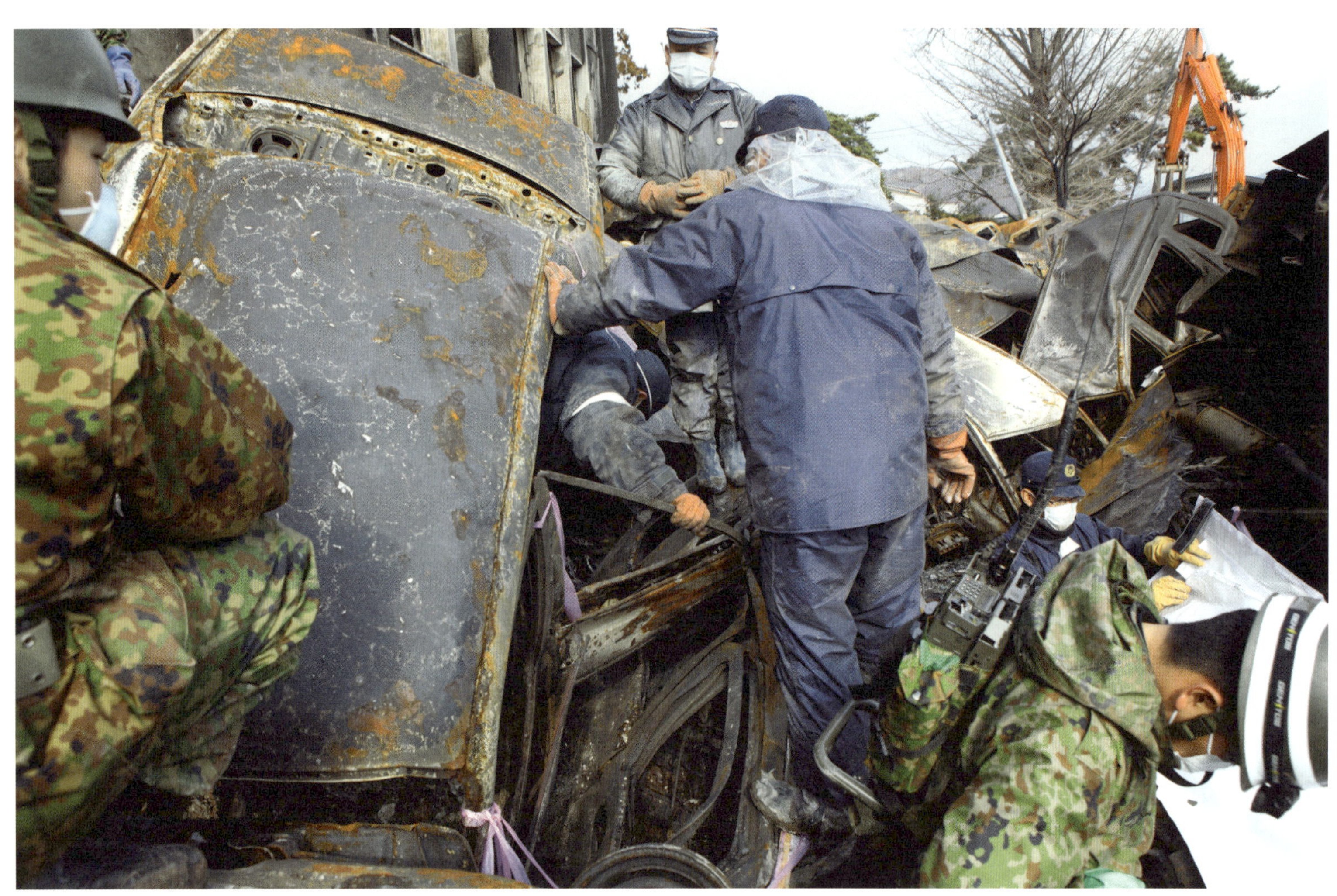

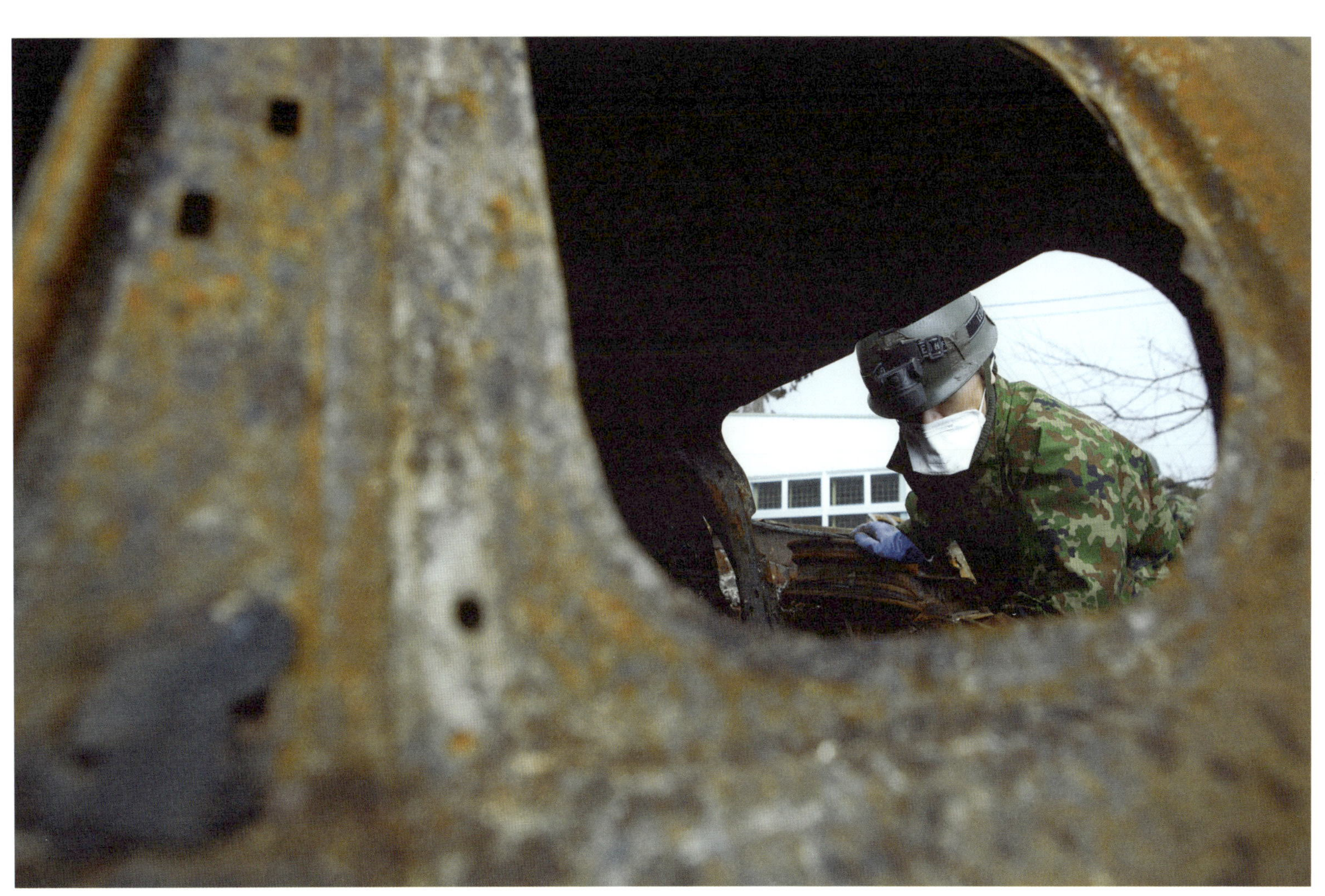

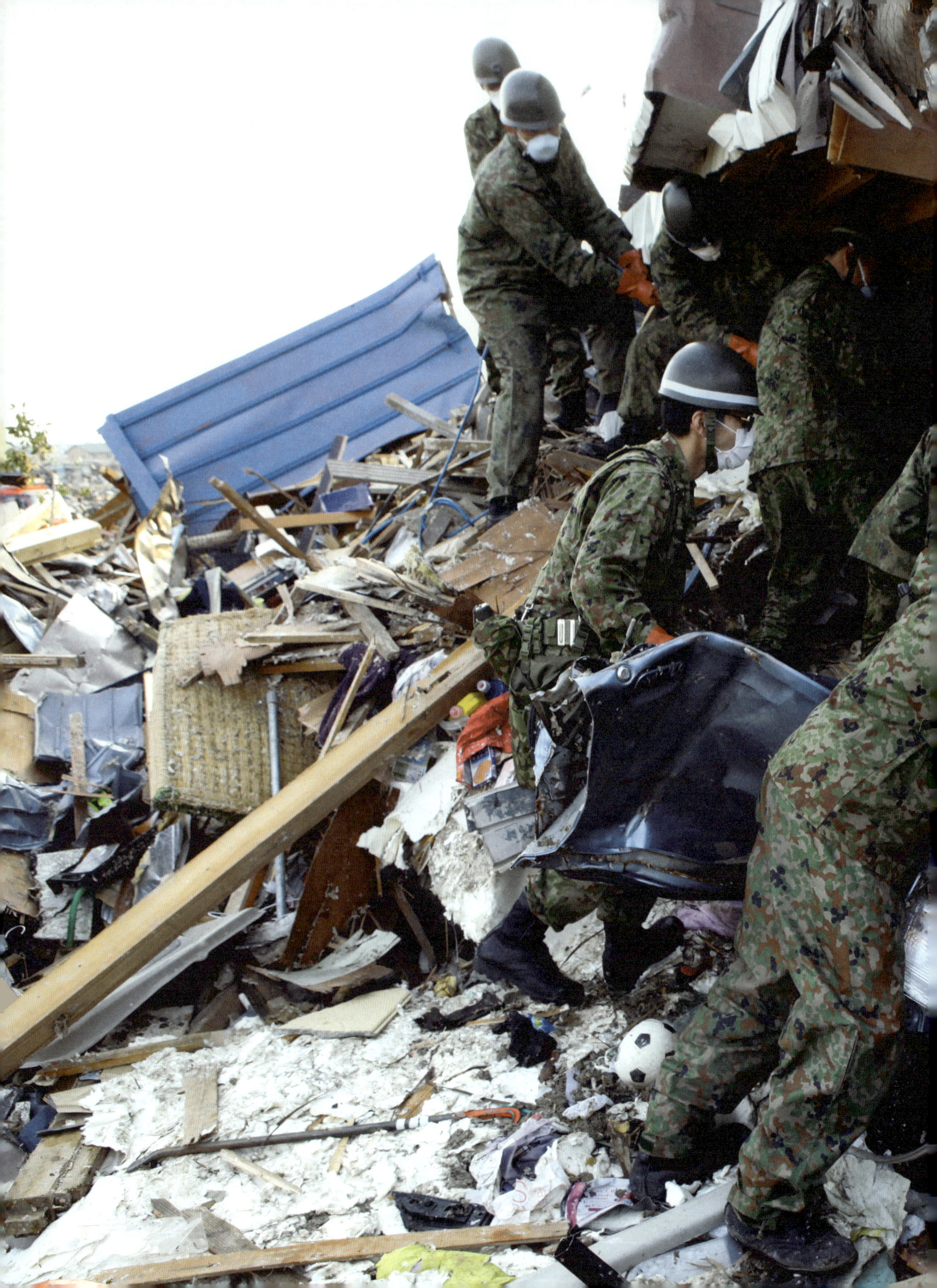

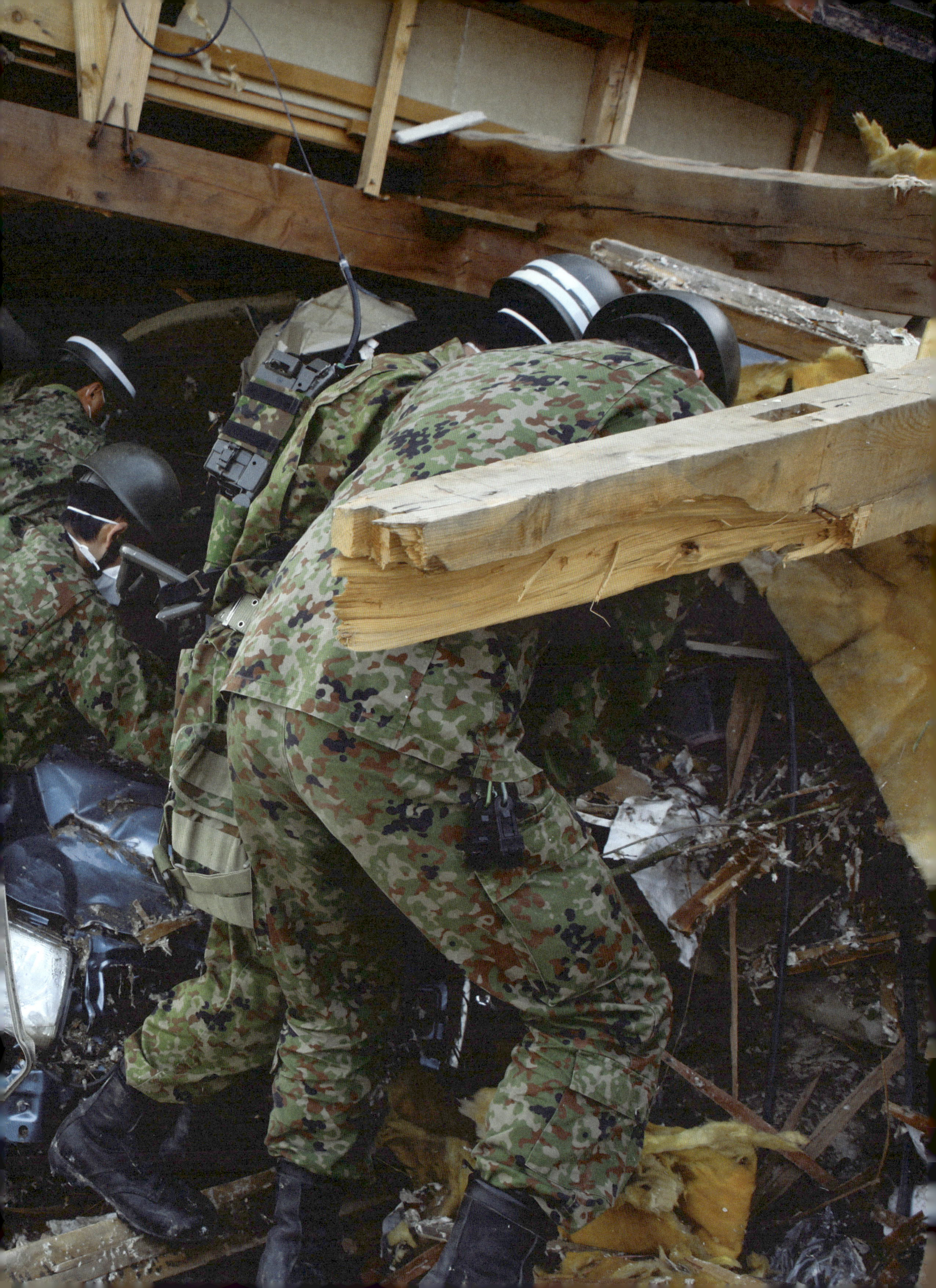

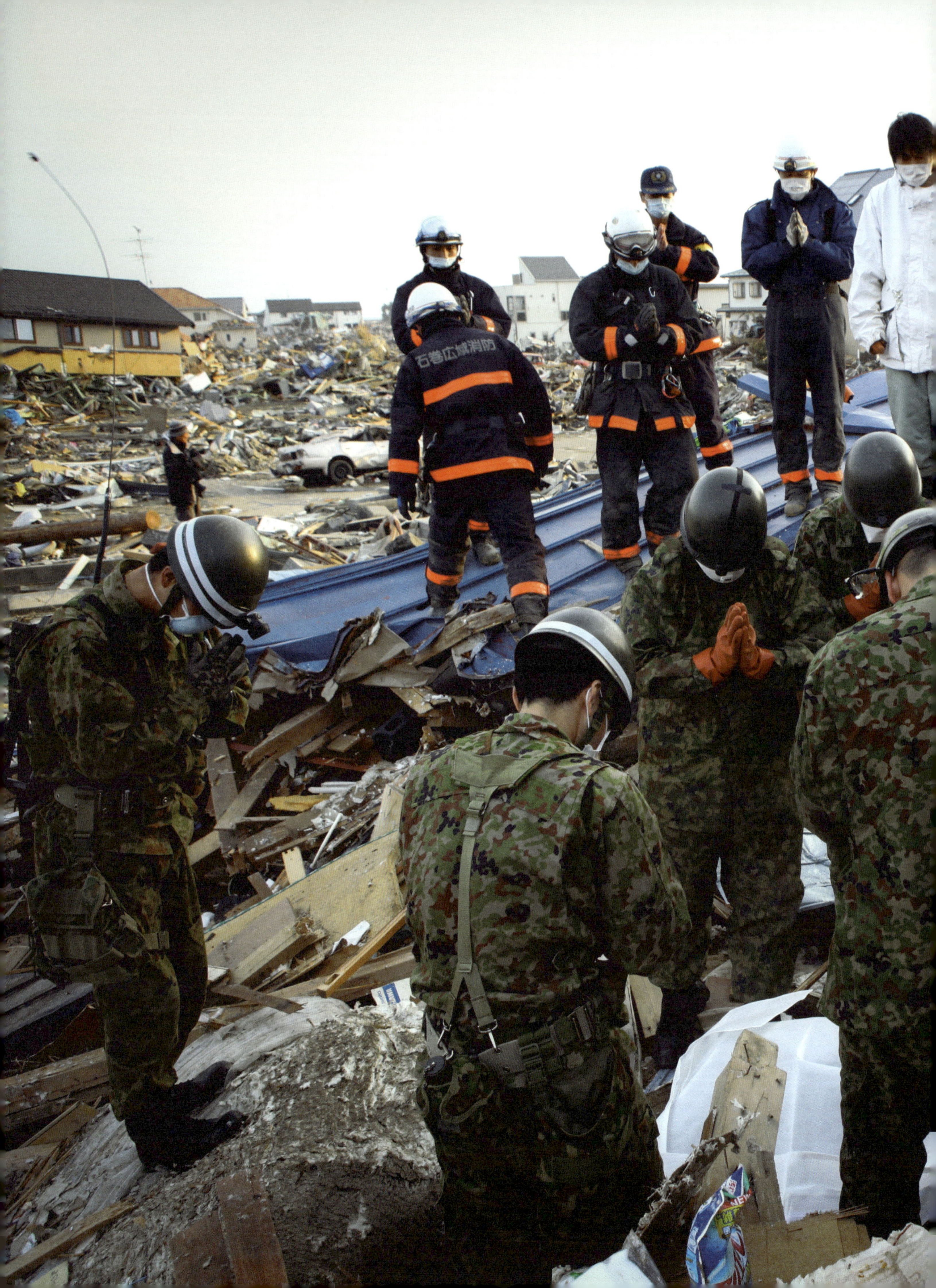

石巻広域消防

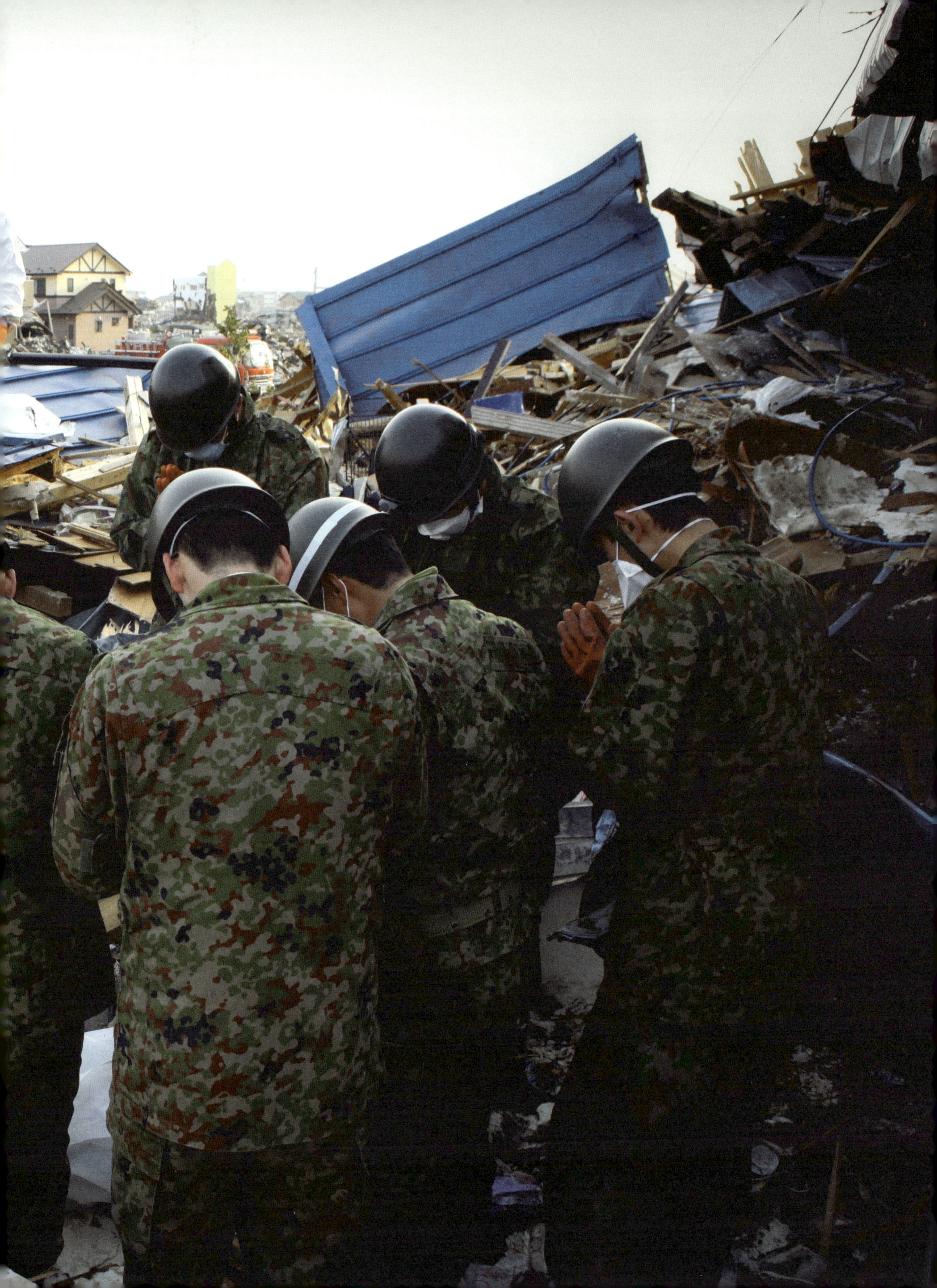

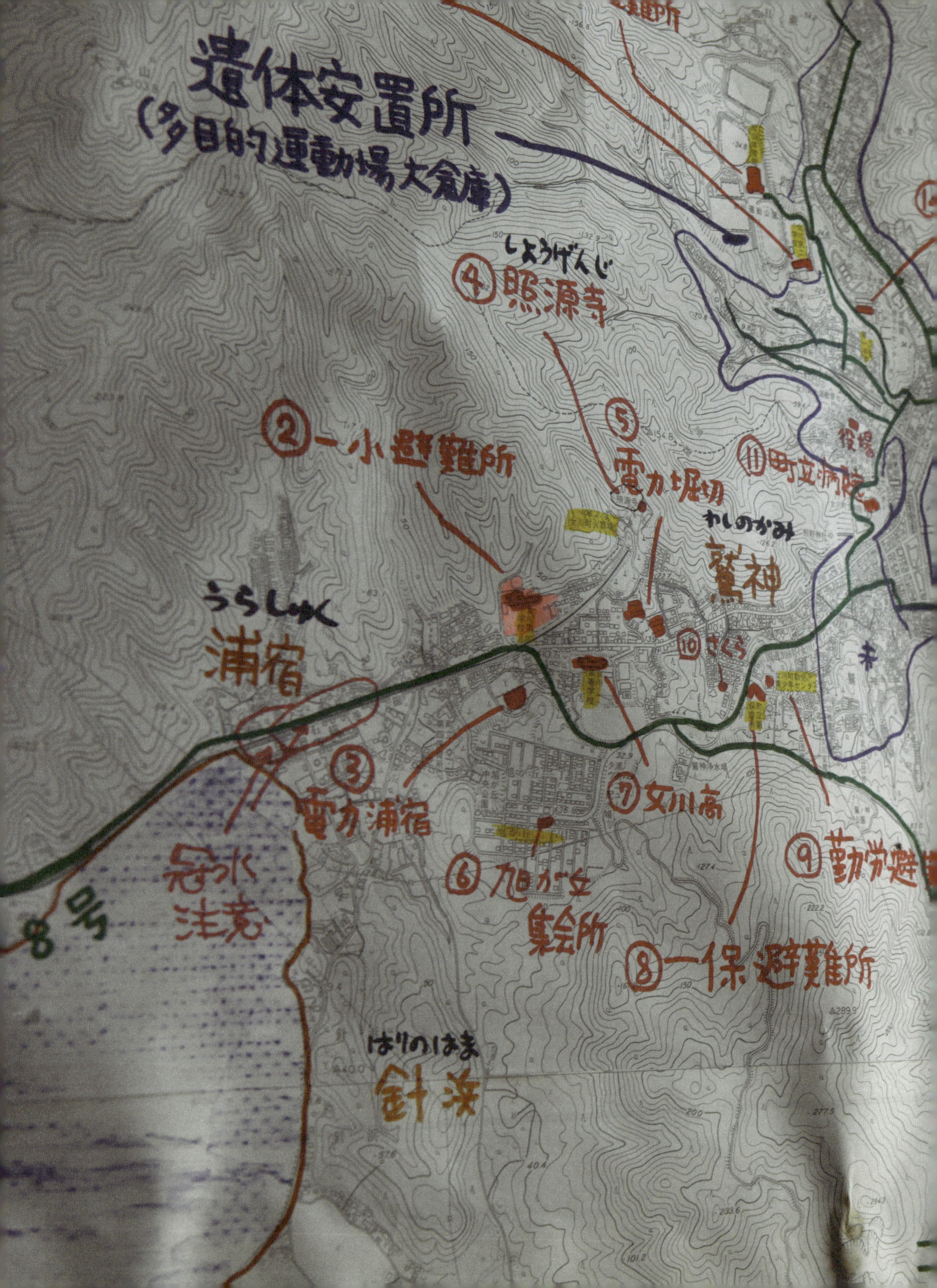

遺体安置所
（多目的運動場 大倉庫）
④ しょうげんじ 照源寺
② 一小避難所
⑤ 電力堀切
⑪ 町立病院
役場
わしのかみ 鷲神
うらしゅく 浦宿
⑩ さくら
③ 電力浦宿
⑦ 女川高
⑨ 勤労避難
⑥ 旭が丘 集会所
⑧ 一保避難所
8号
洗水洗浄
はりのはま 針浜

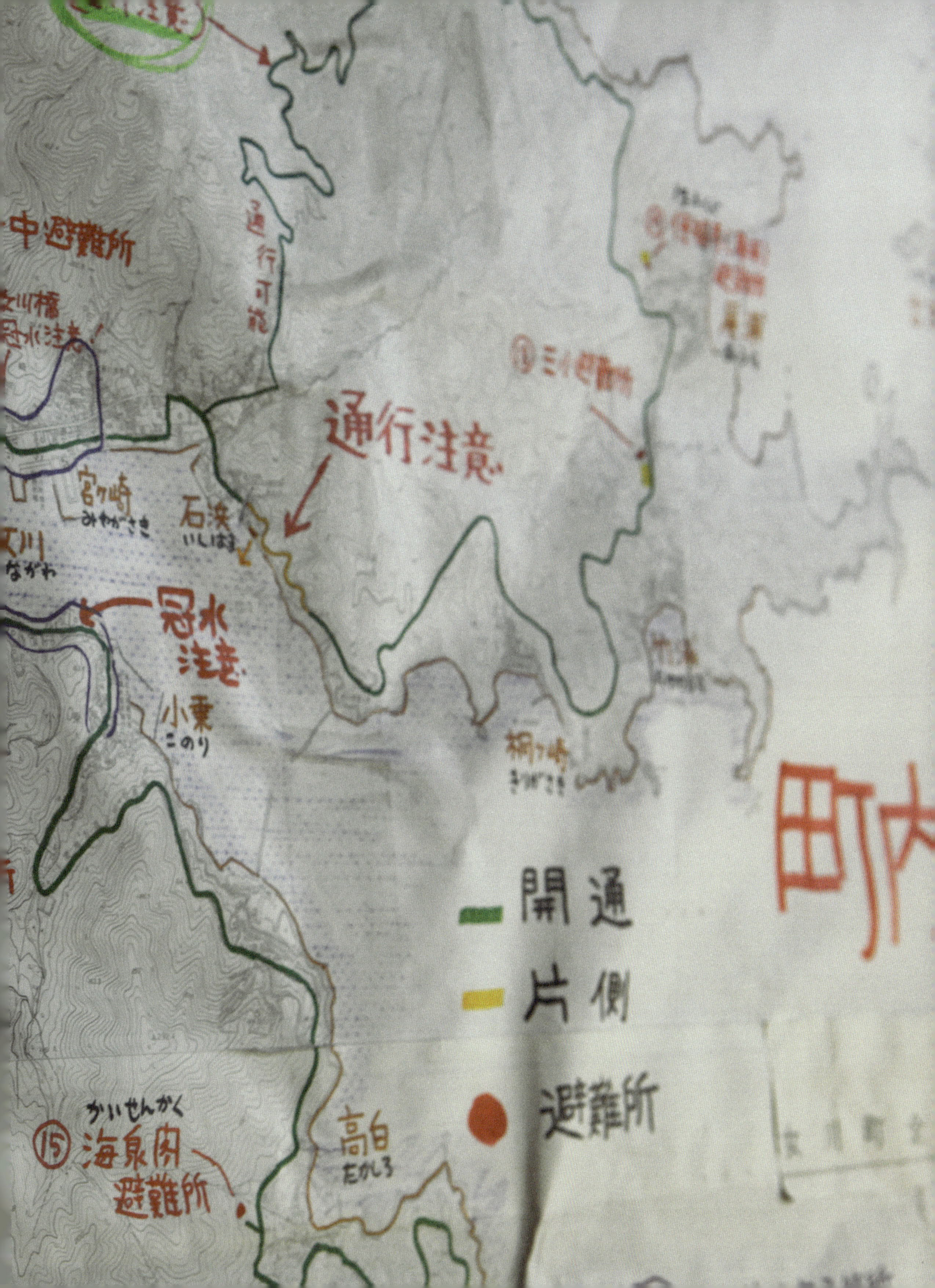
中避難所
溪川橋
冠水注意！
通行可能
通行注意
宮ヶ崎
みやがさき
石浜
いしはま
又川
ながわ
冠水注意
小栗
こぐり
桐ヶ崎
①ミハ避難所
かいせんかく
⑮海泉閣
避難所
高白
たかしろ
開通
片側
避難所
町内

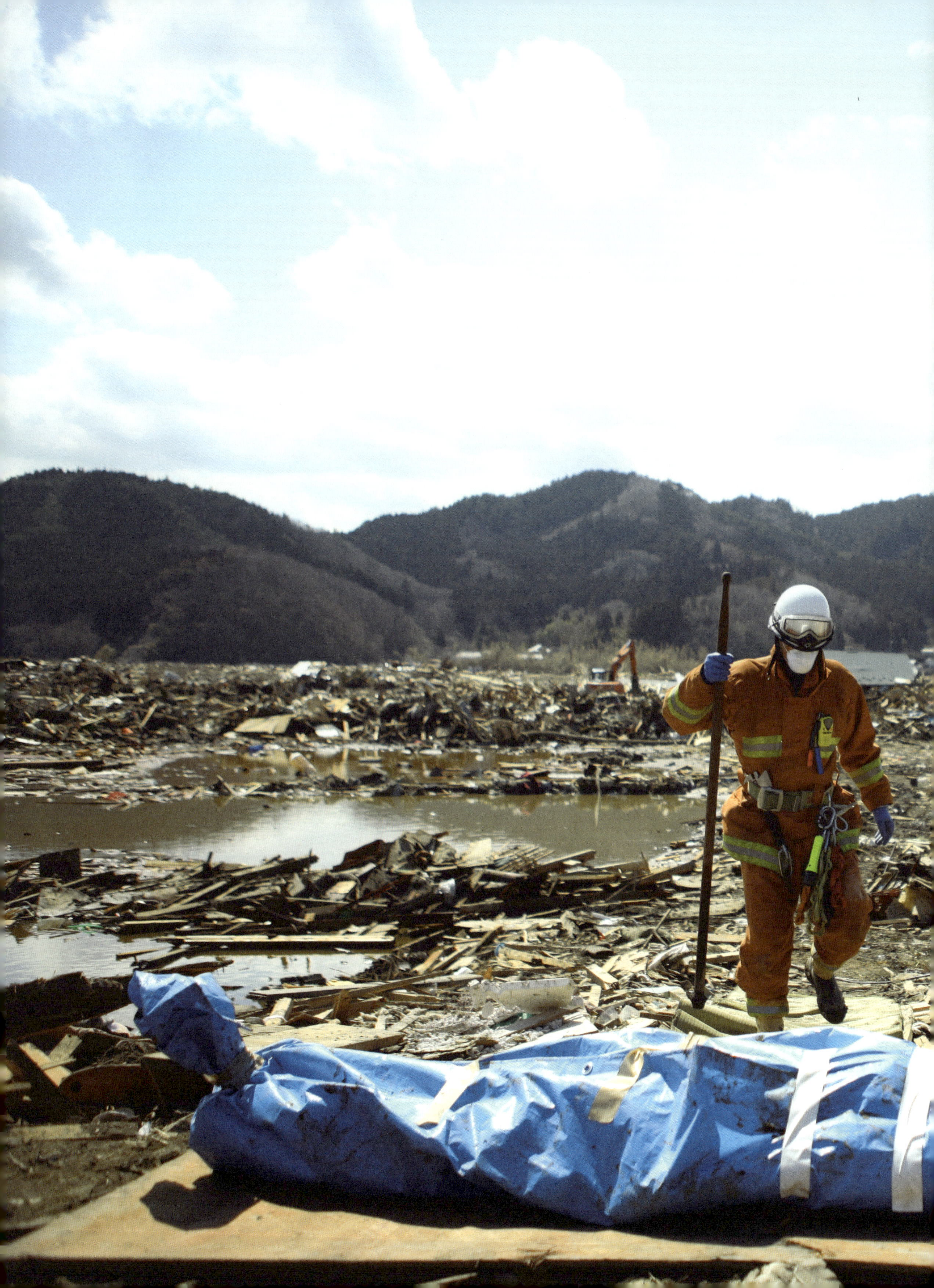

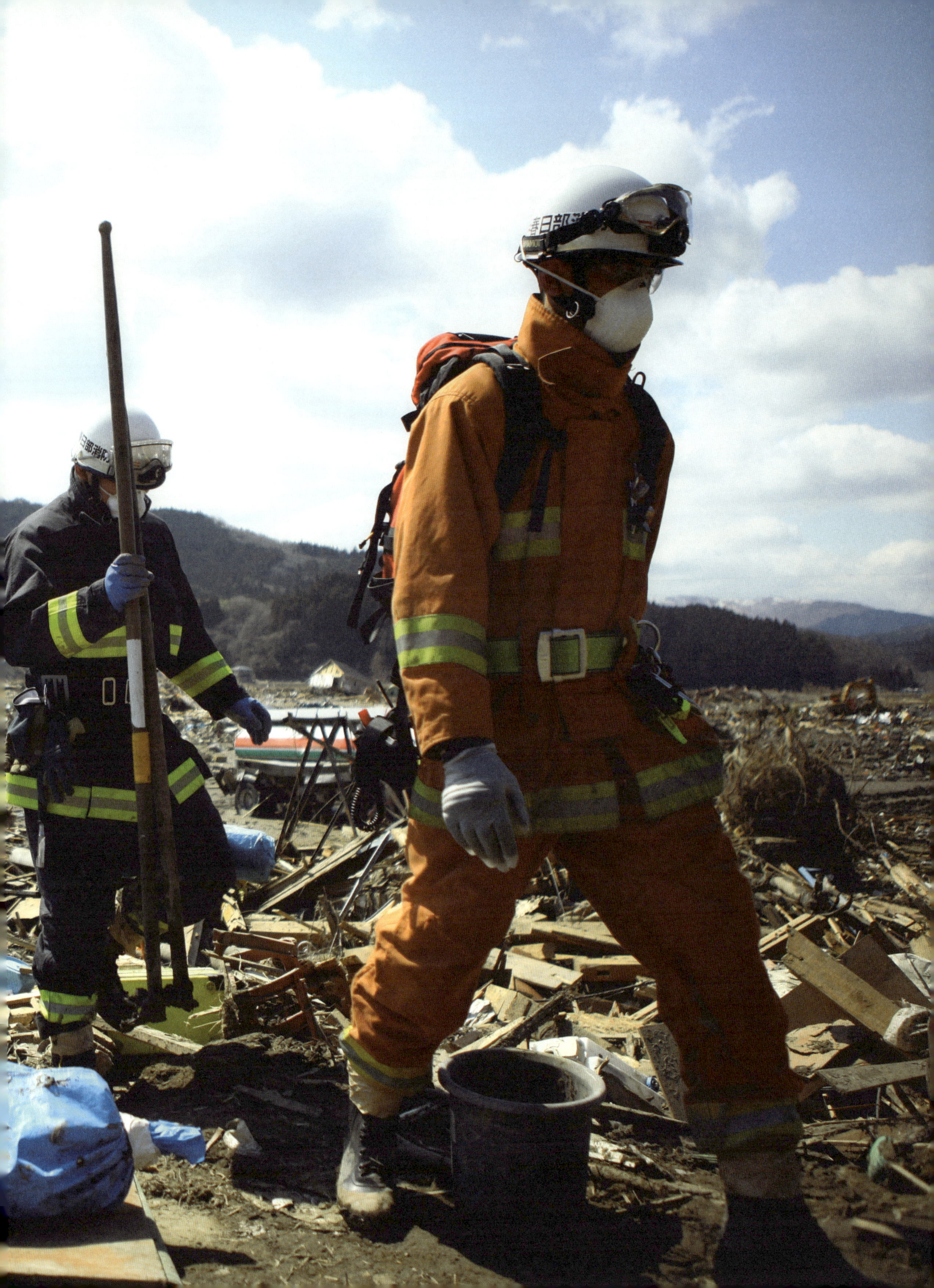

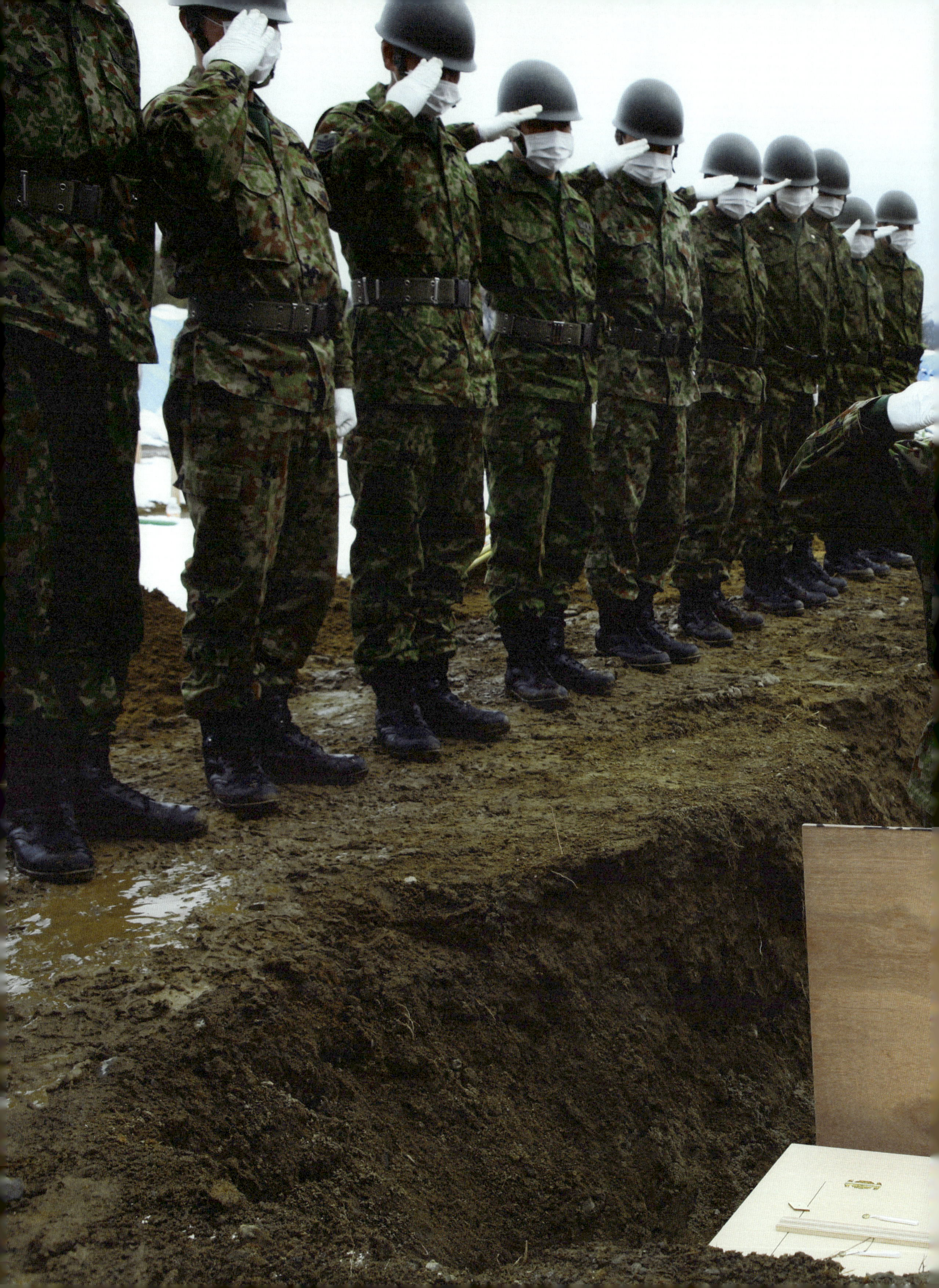

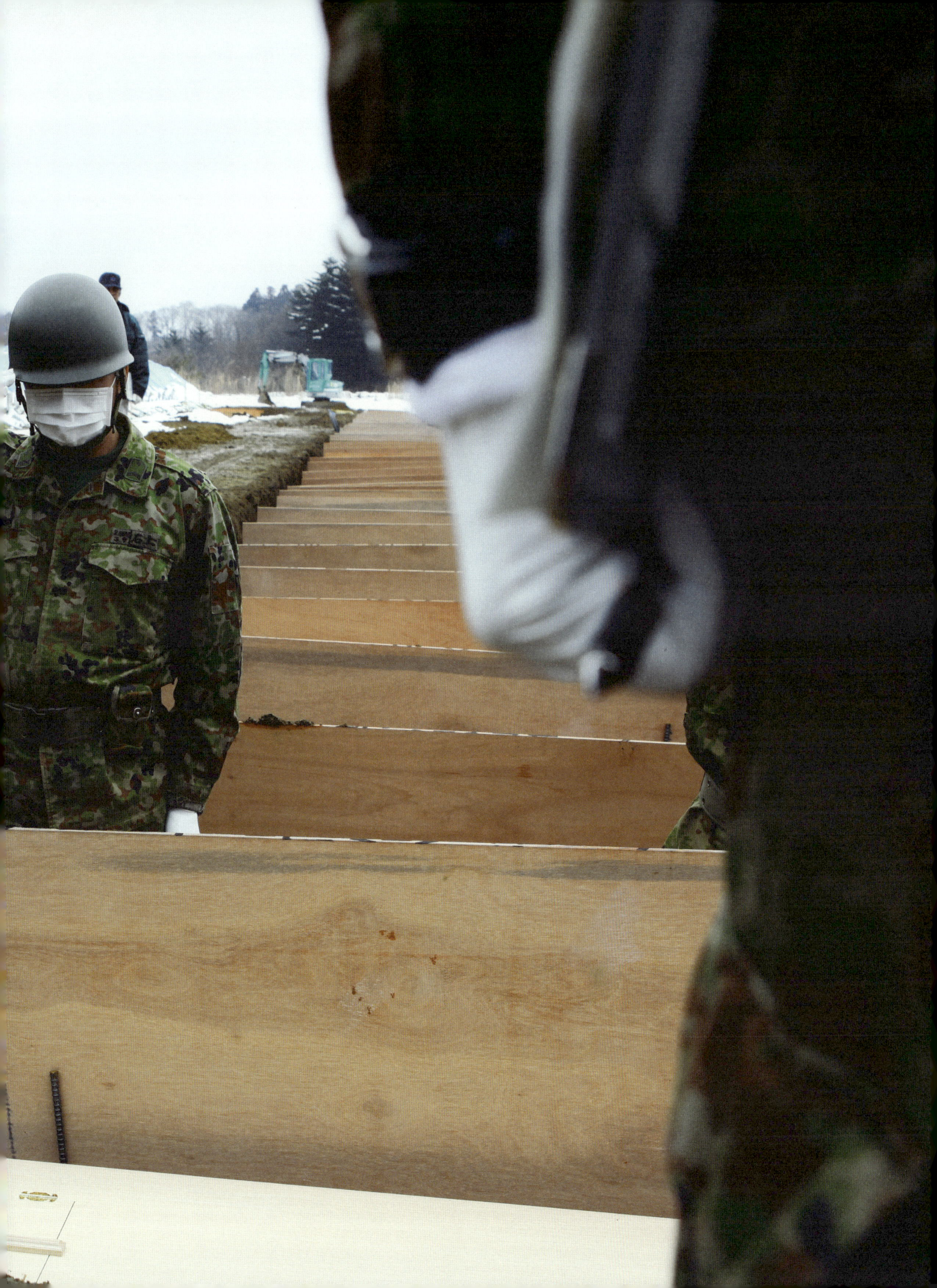

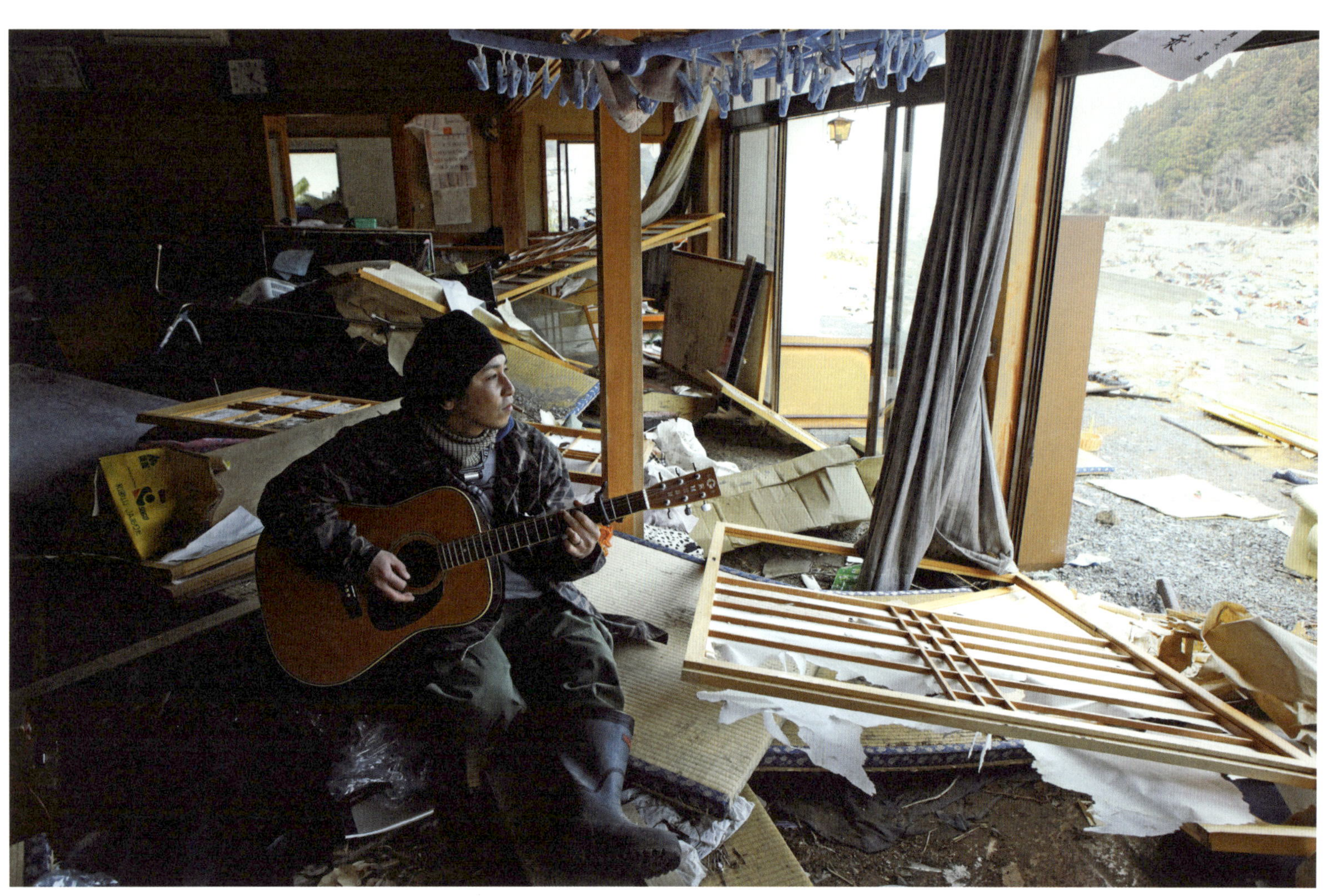

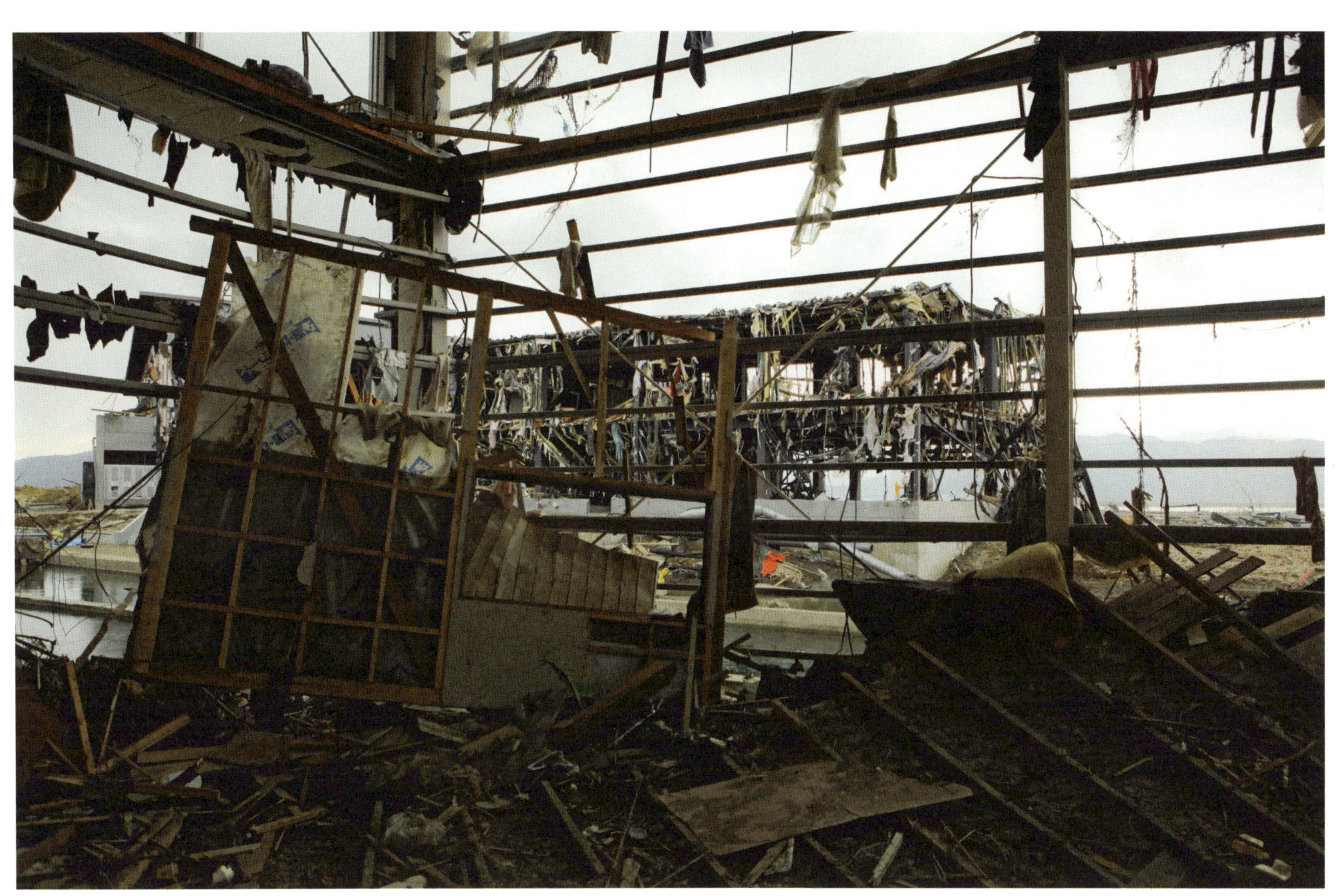

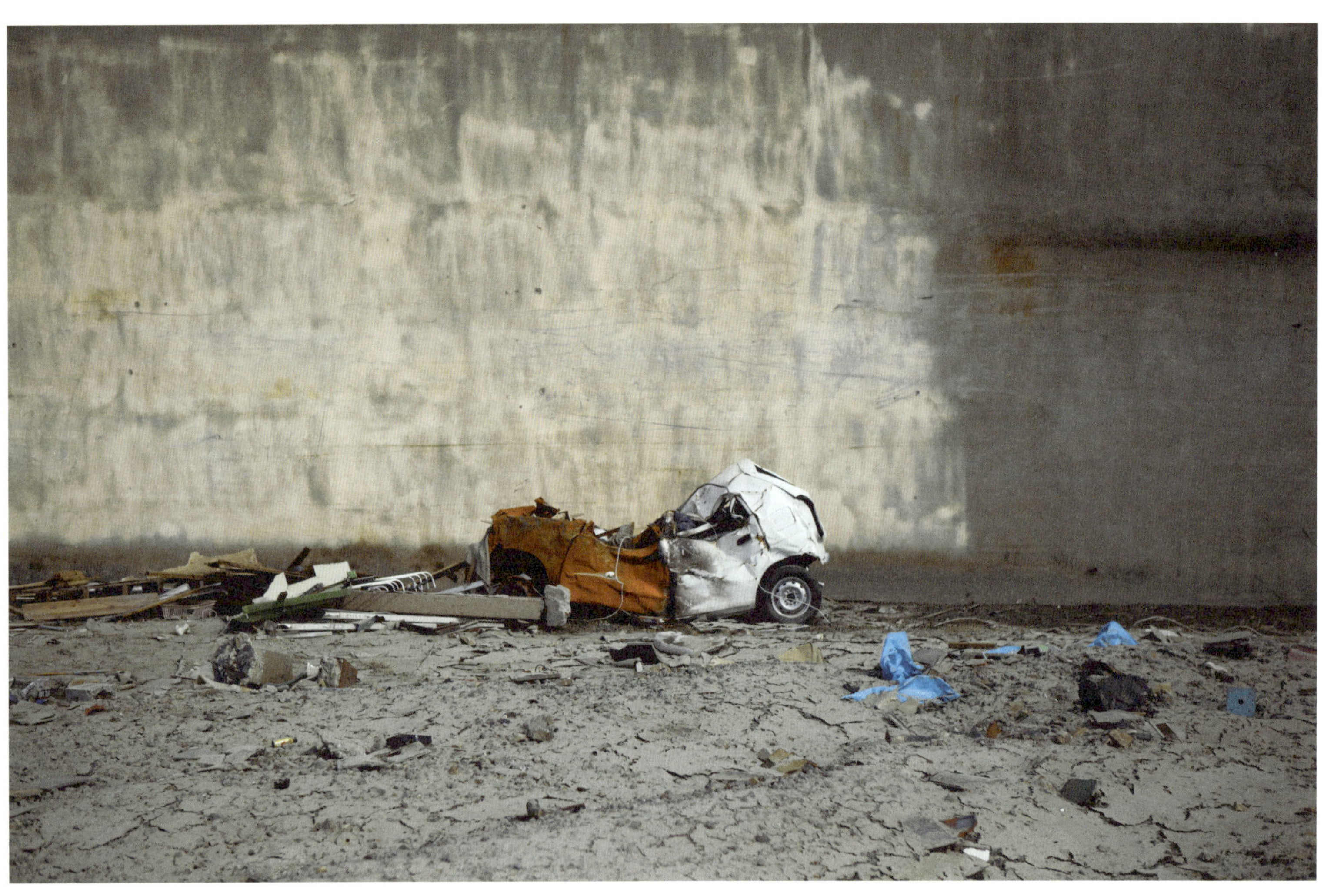

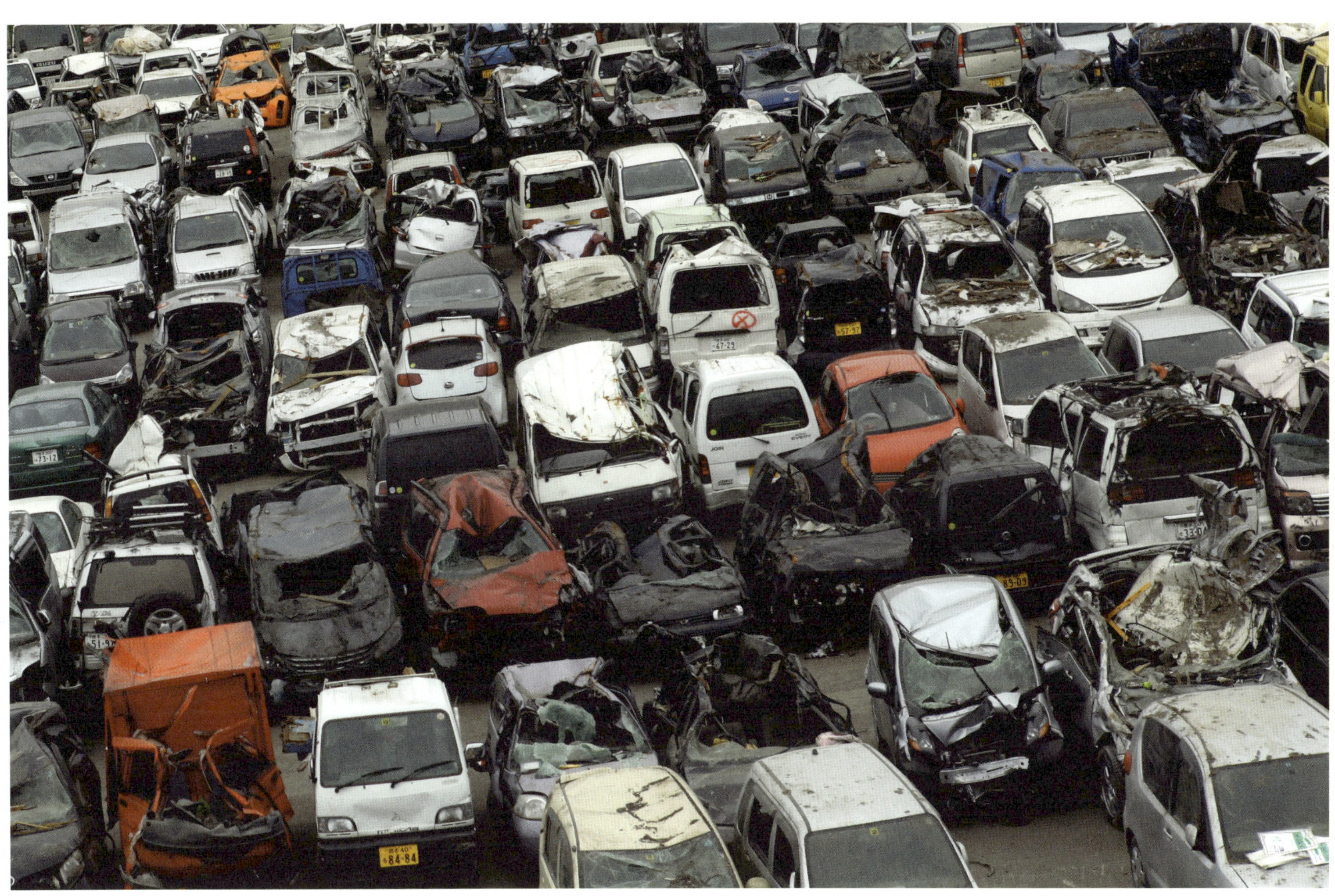

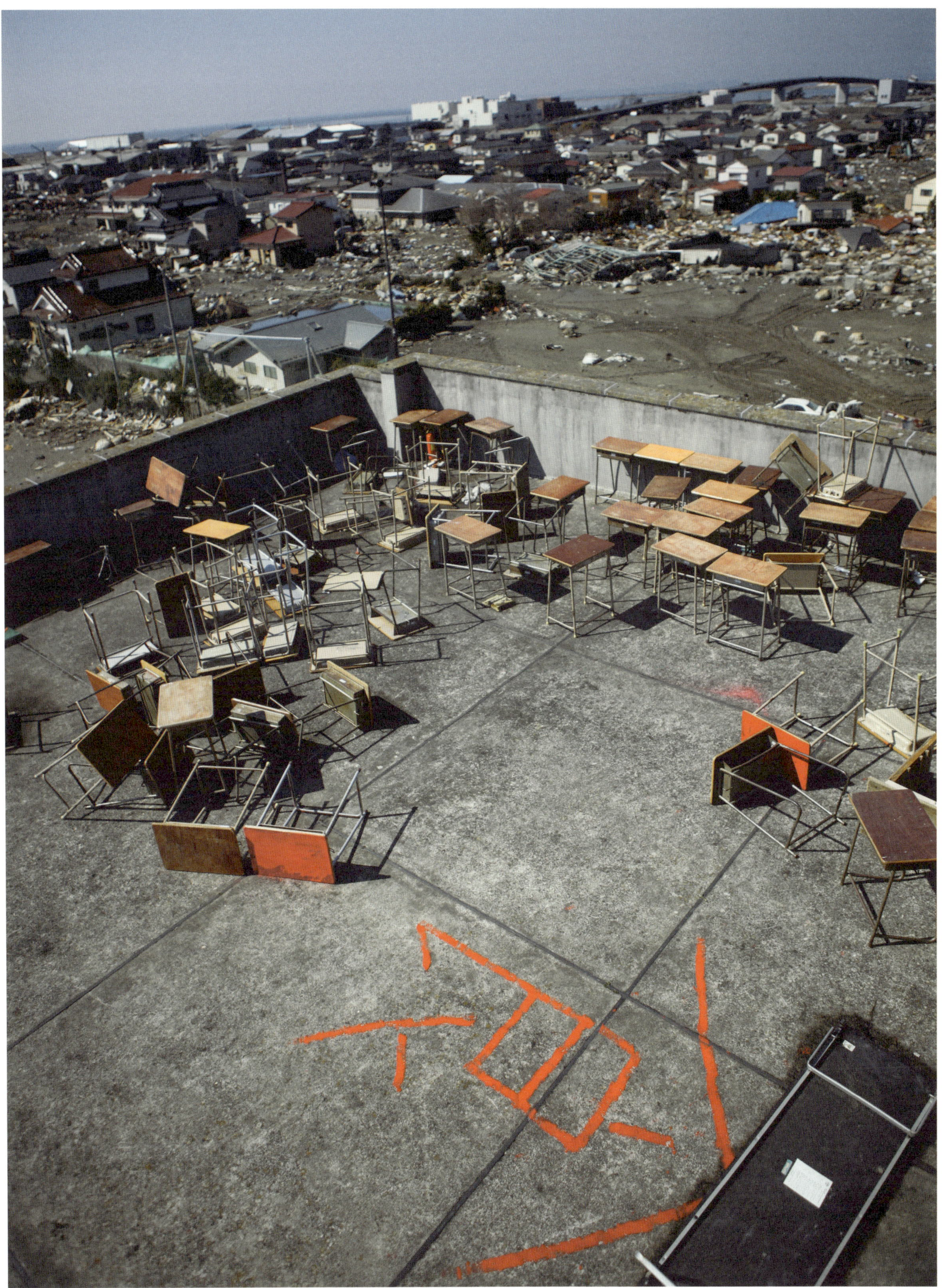

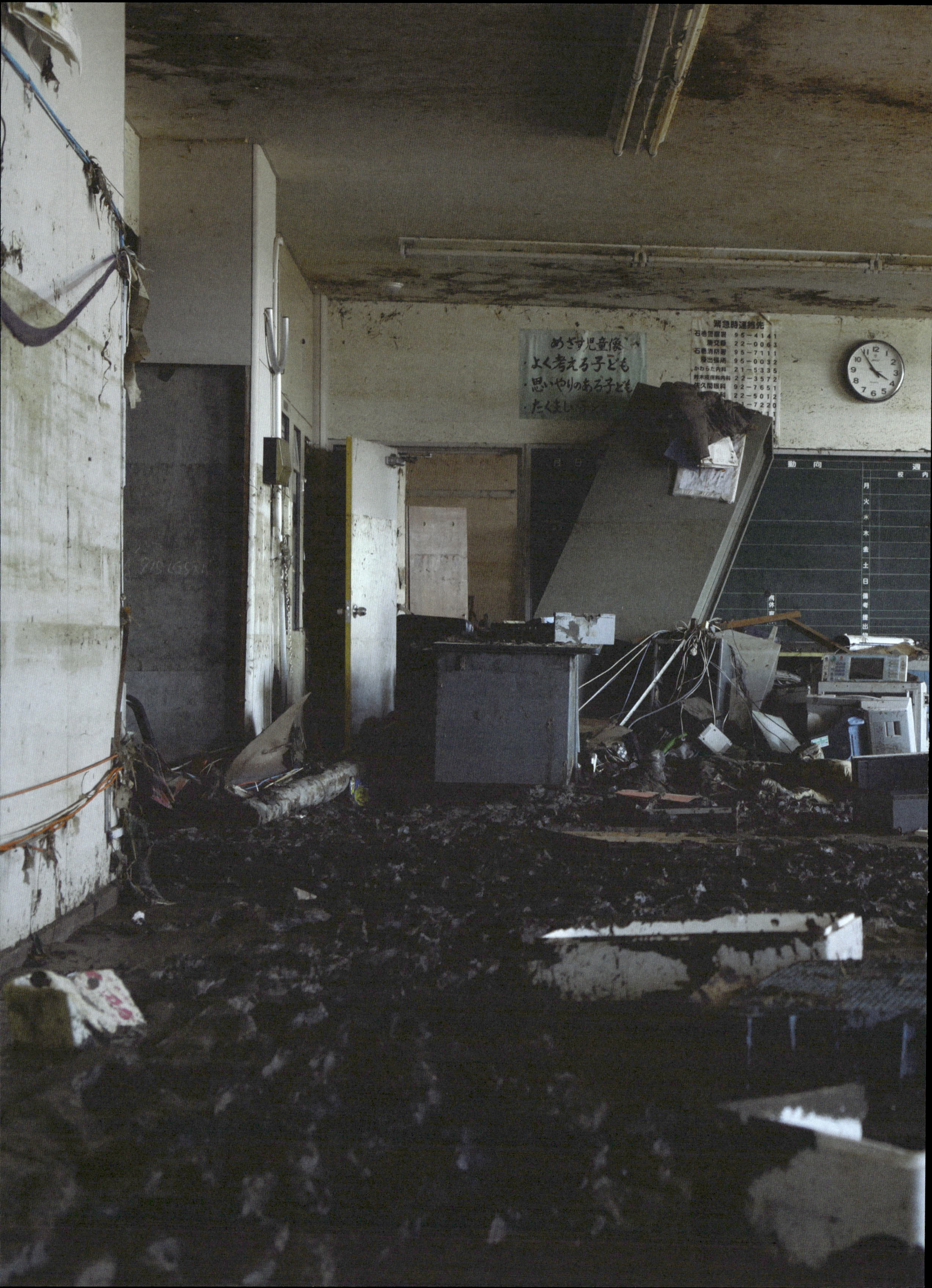
めざす児童像
・よく考える子ども
・思いやりのある子ども
・たくましい子ども
緊急時連絡先

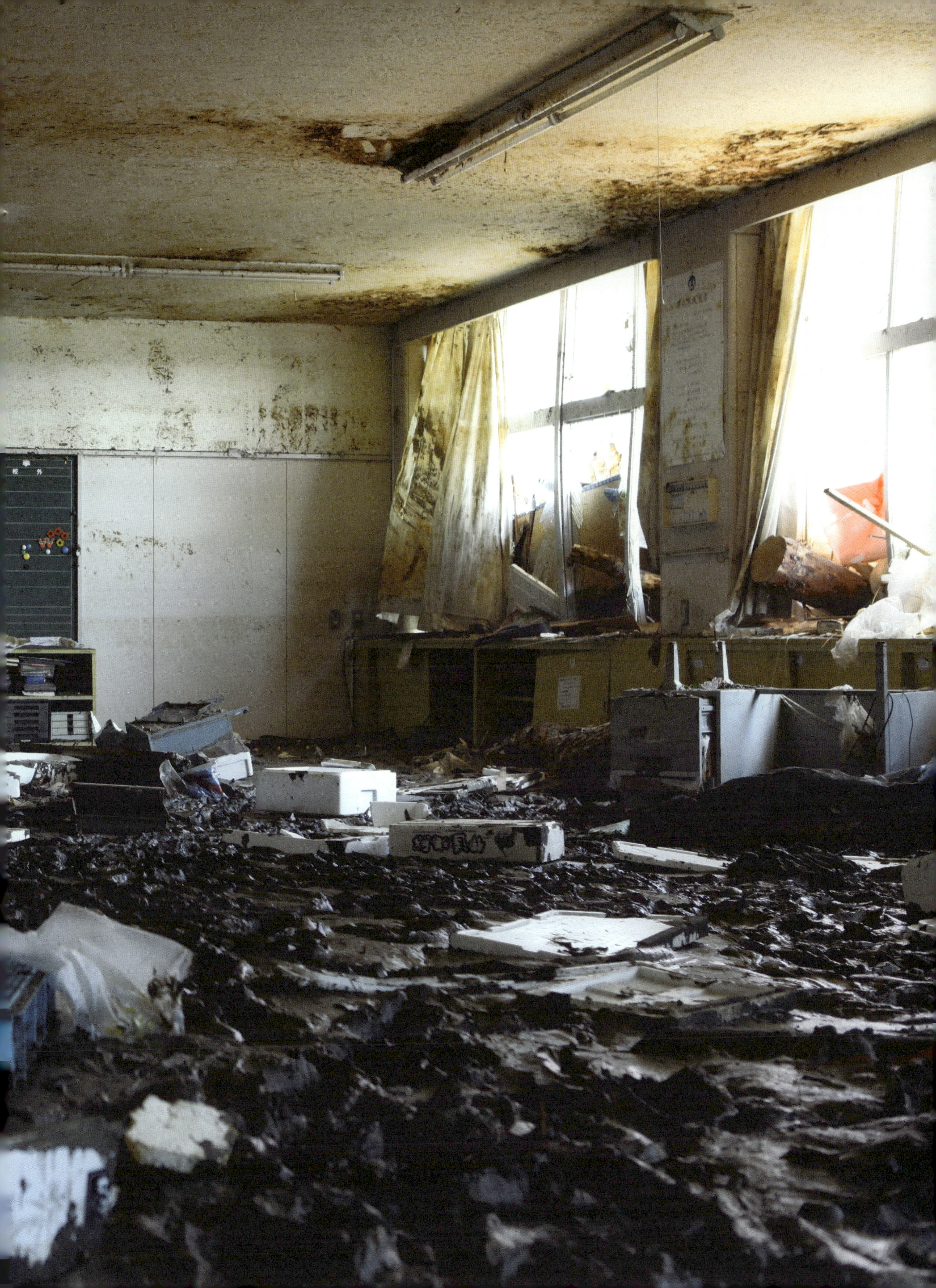

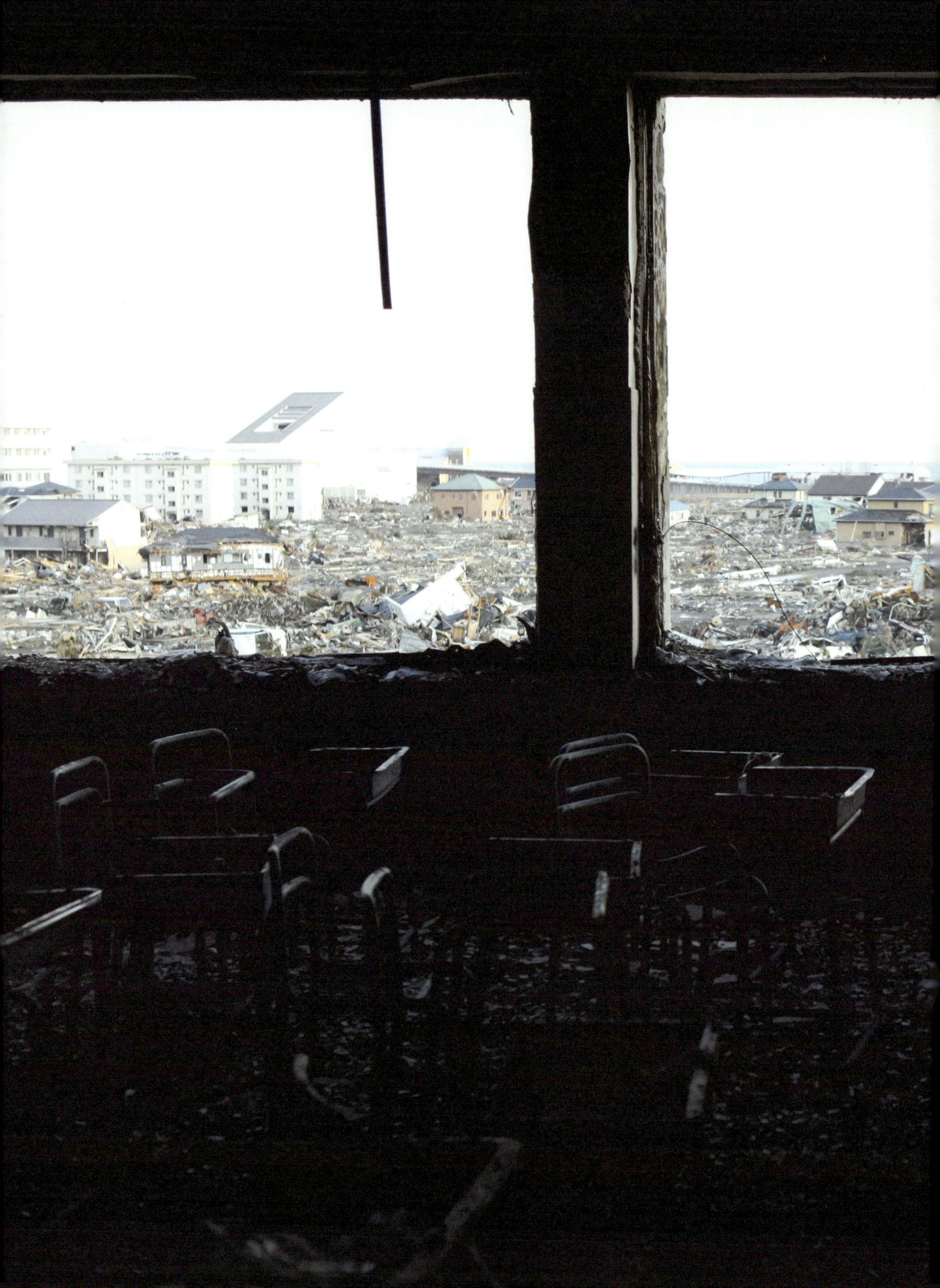

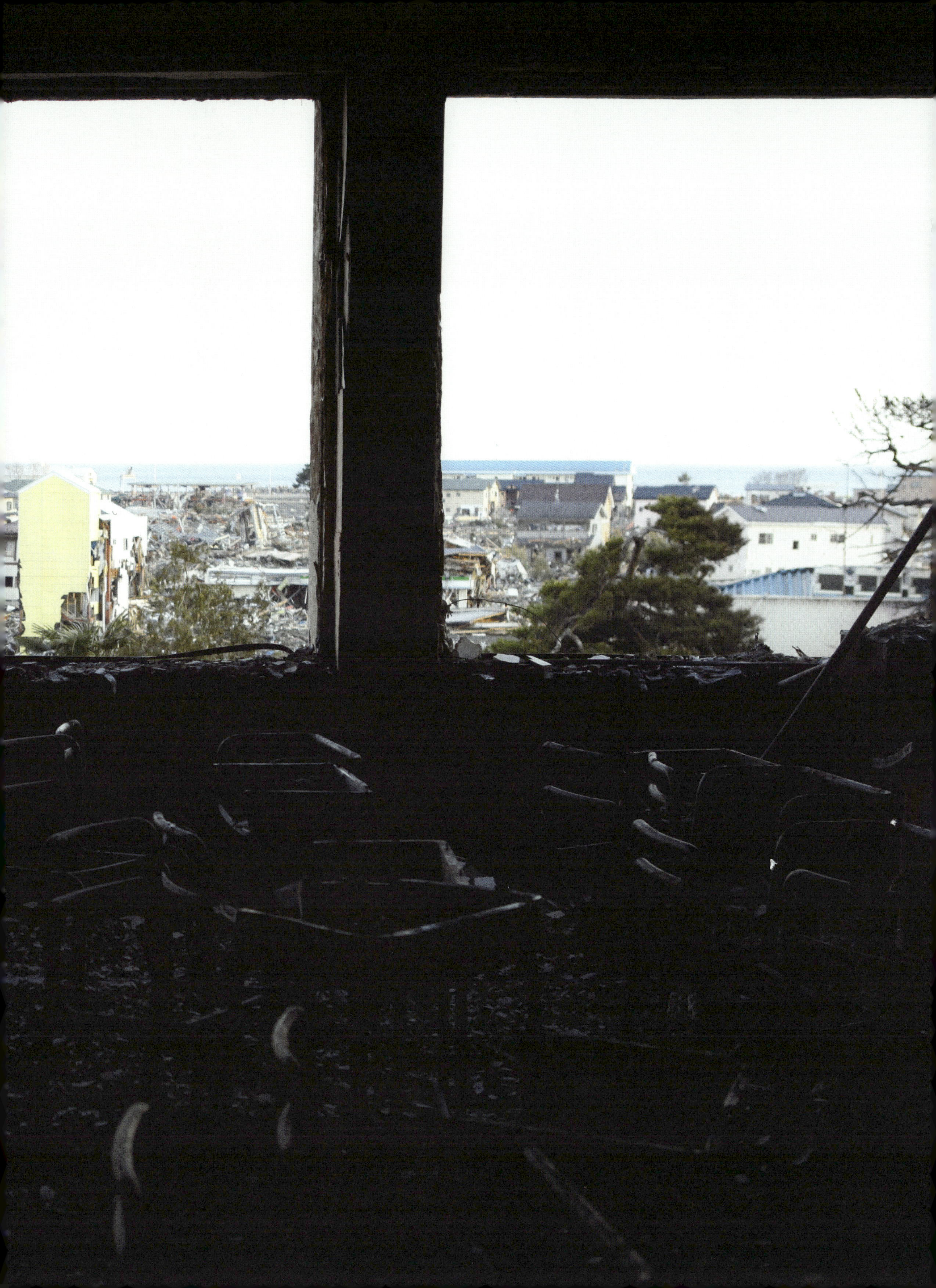

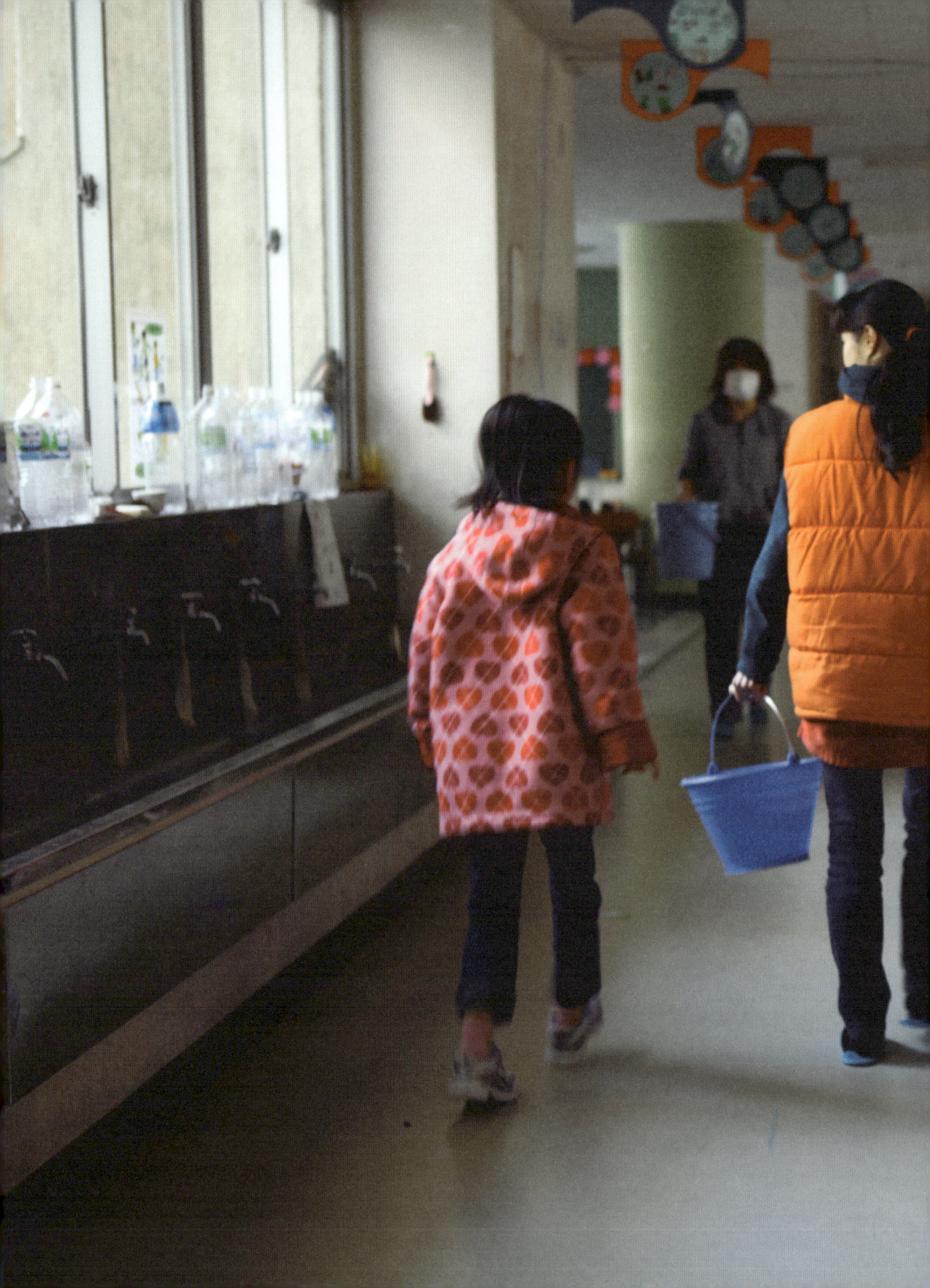

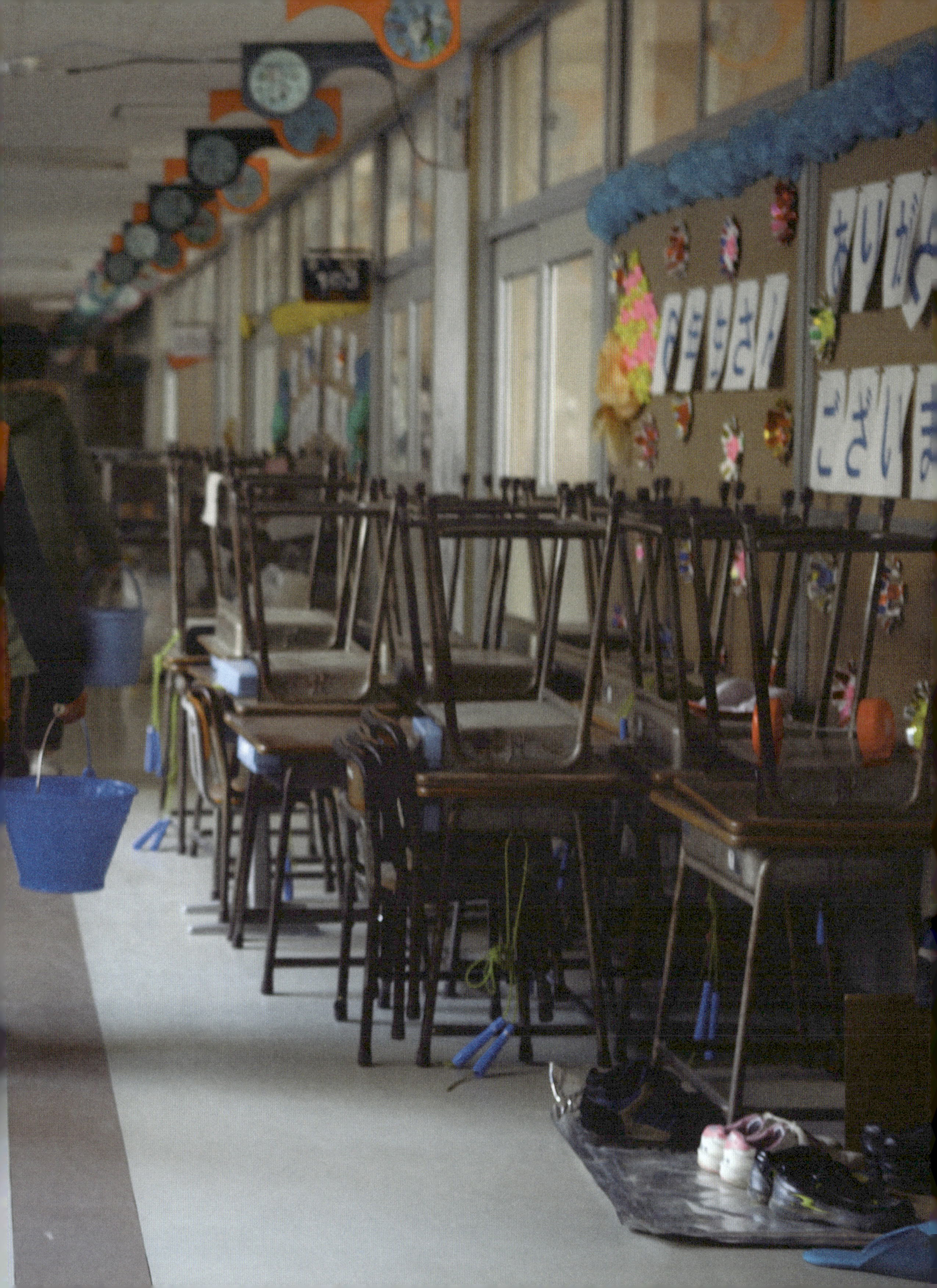

あいだ
ごさい

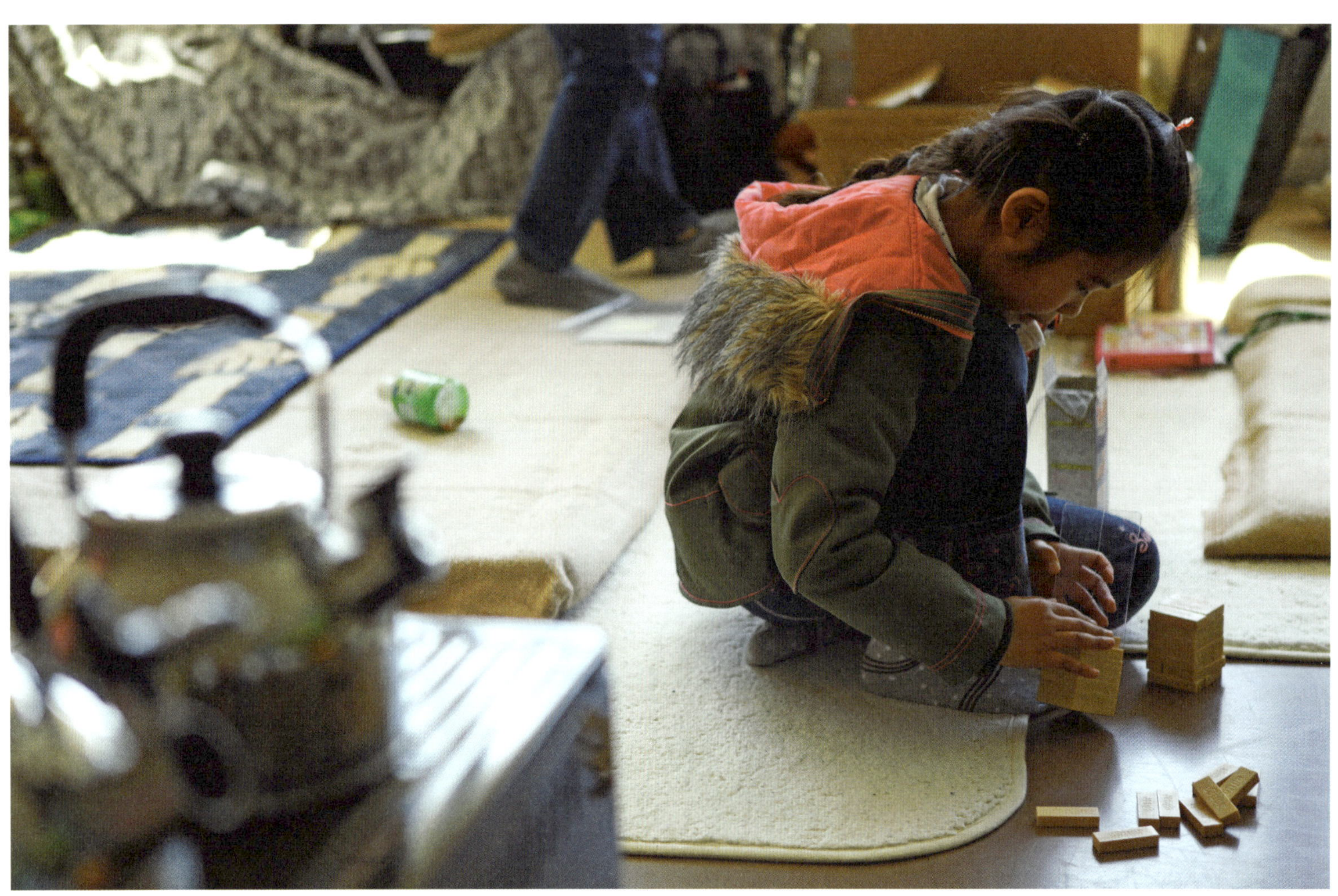

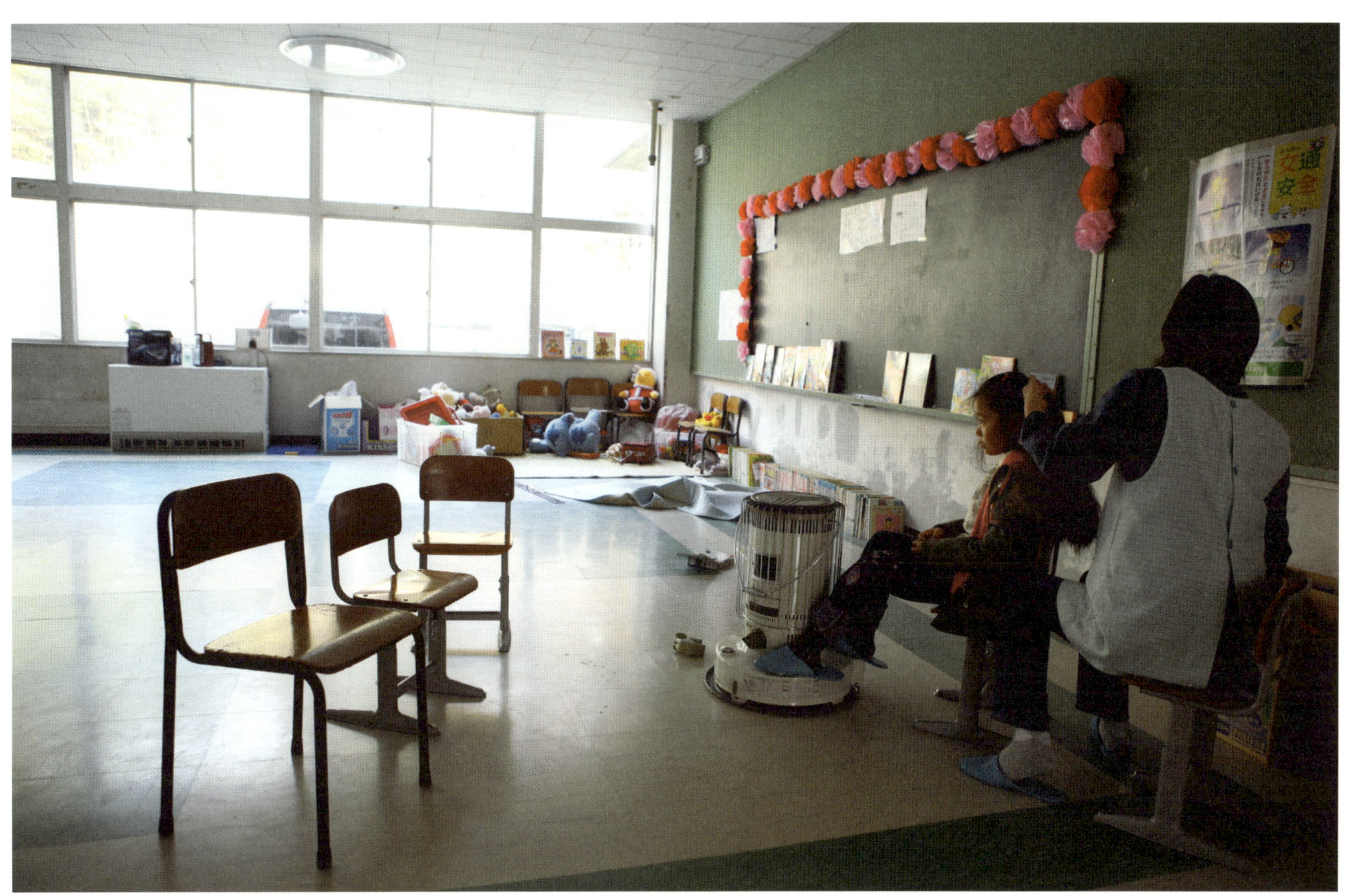

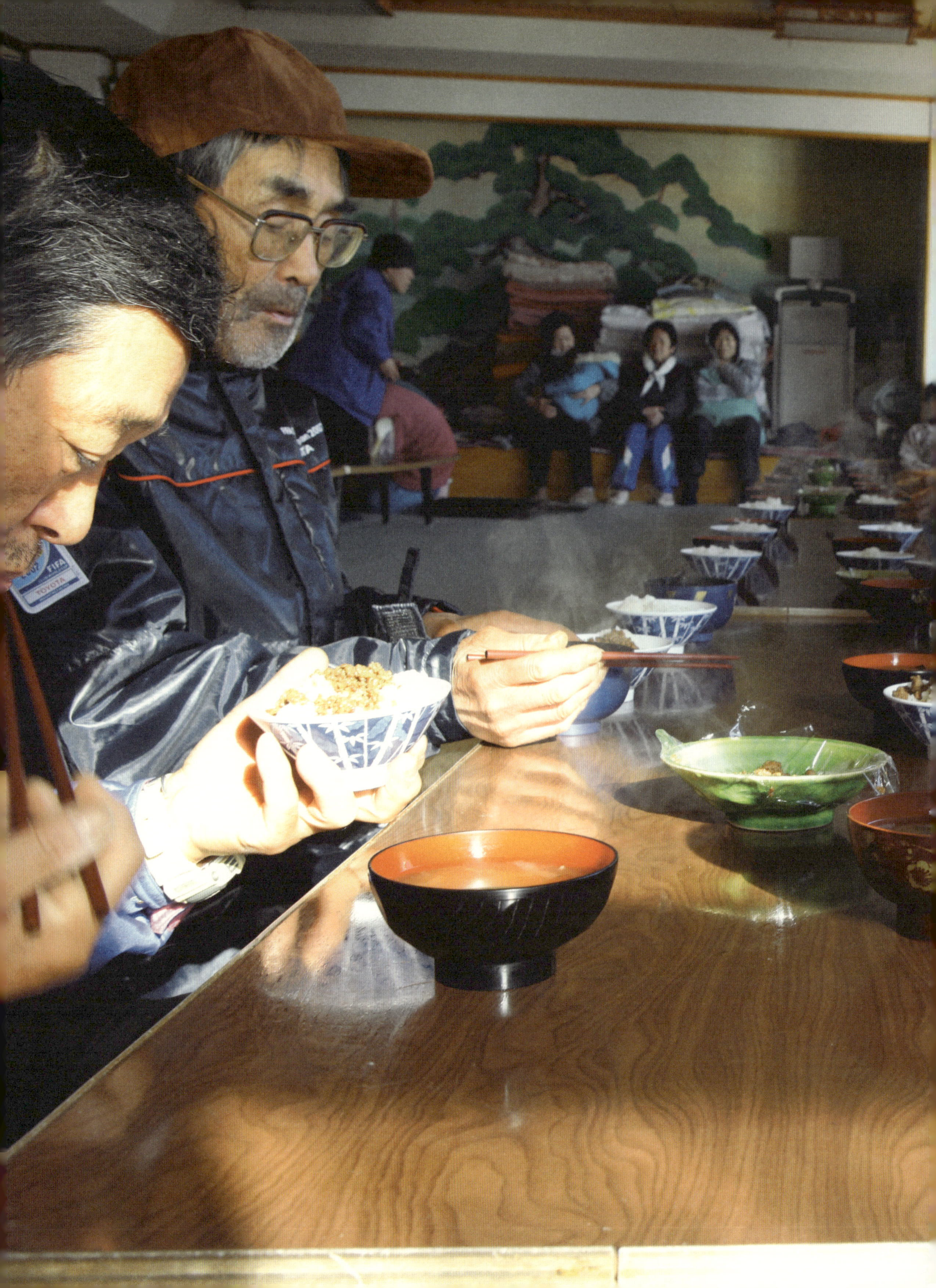

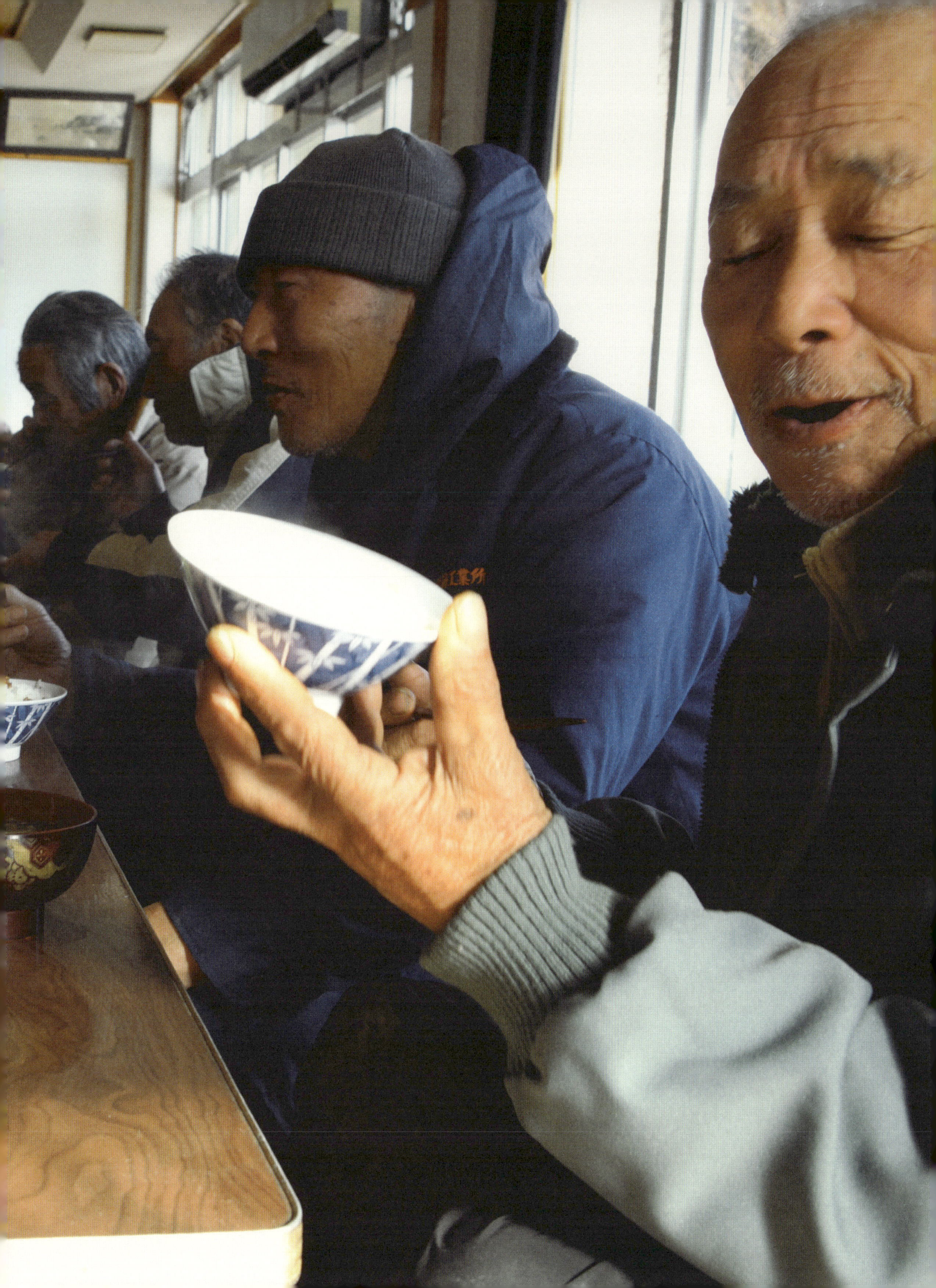

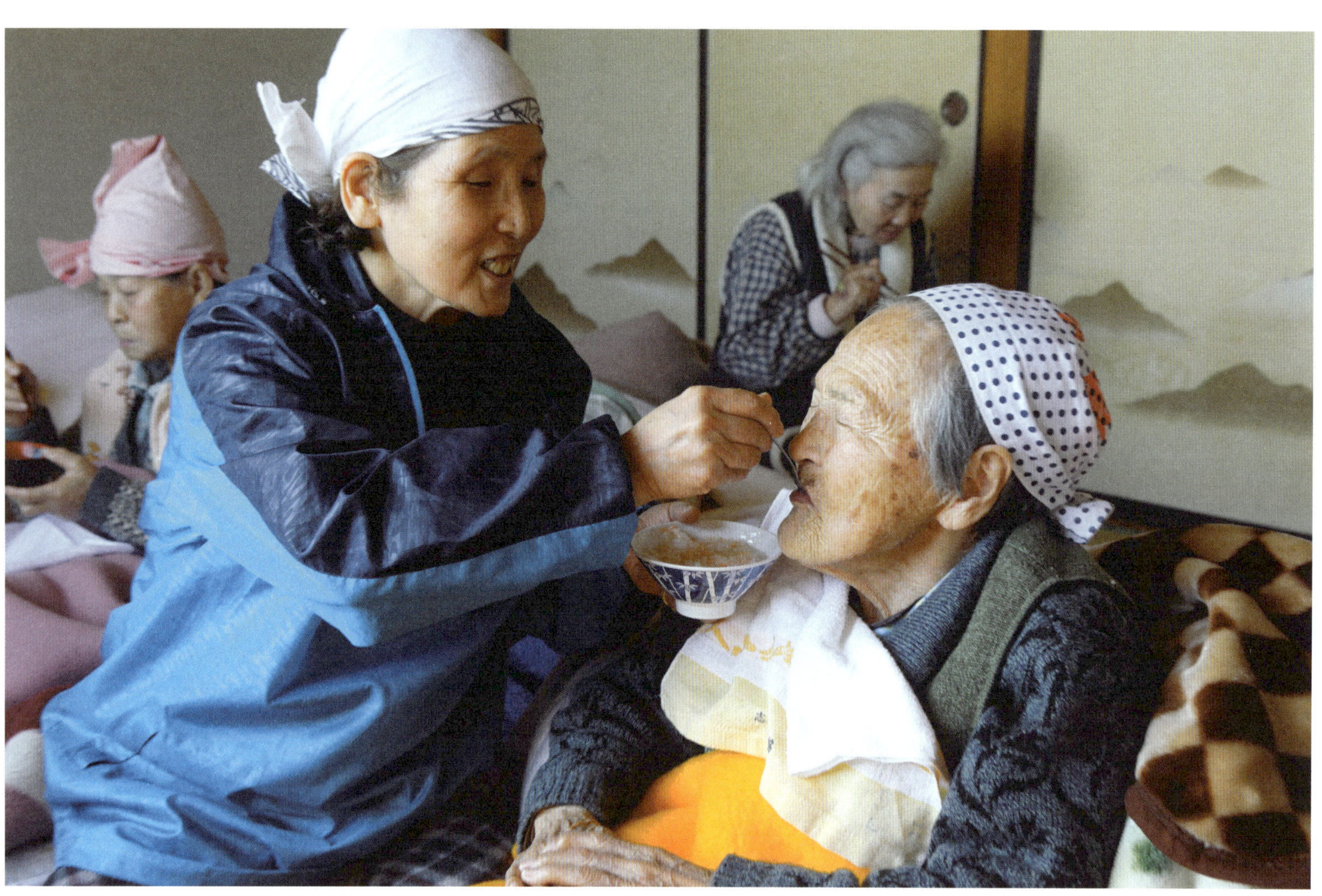

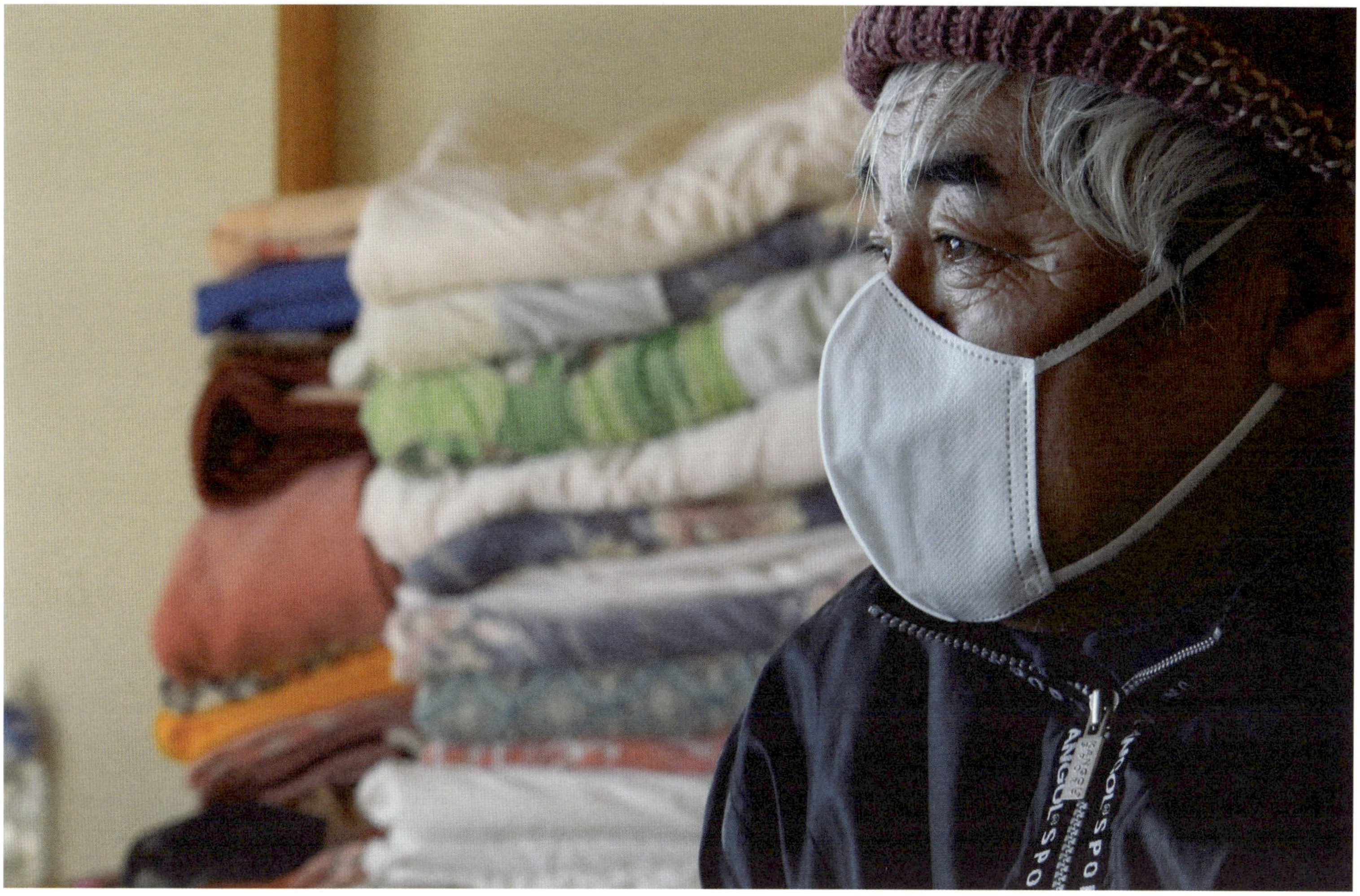

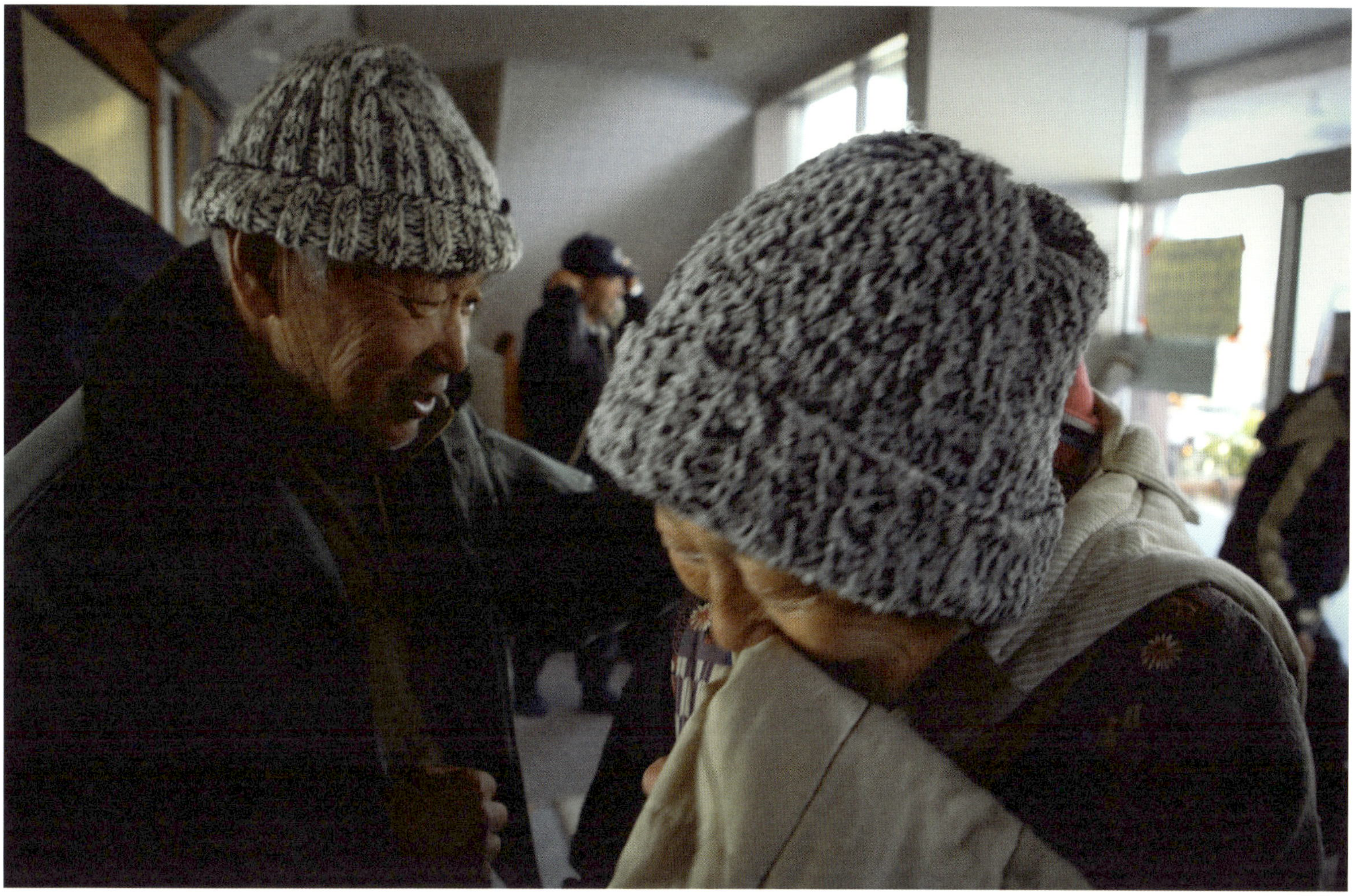

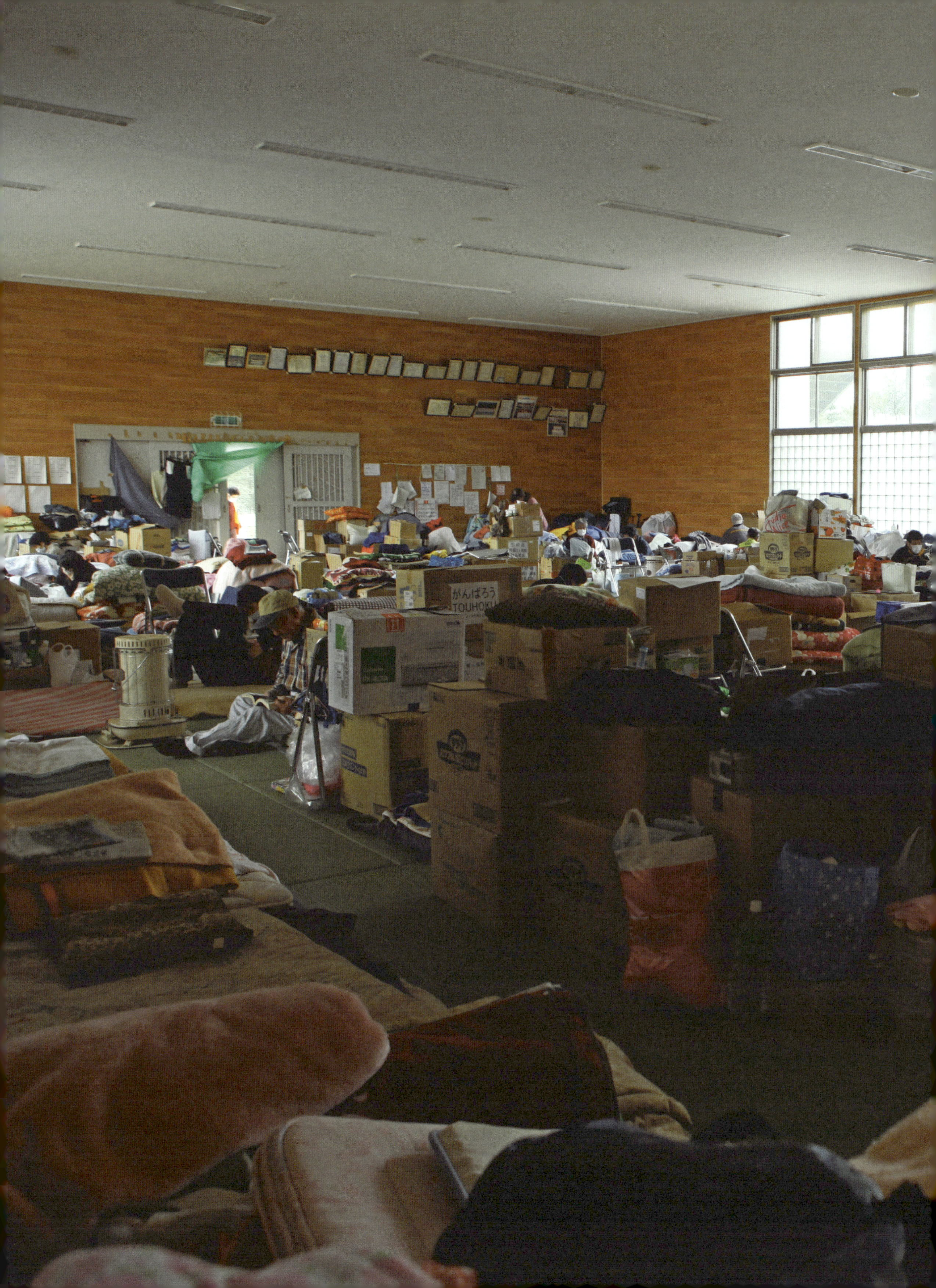

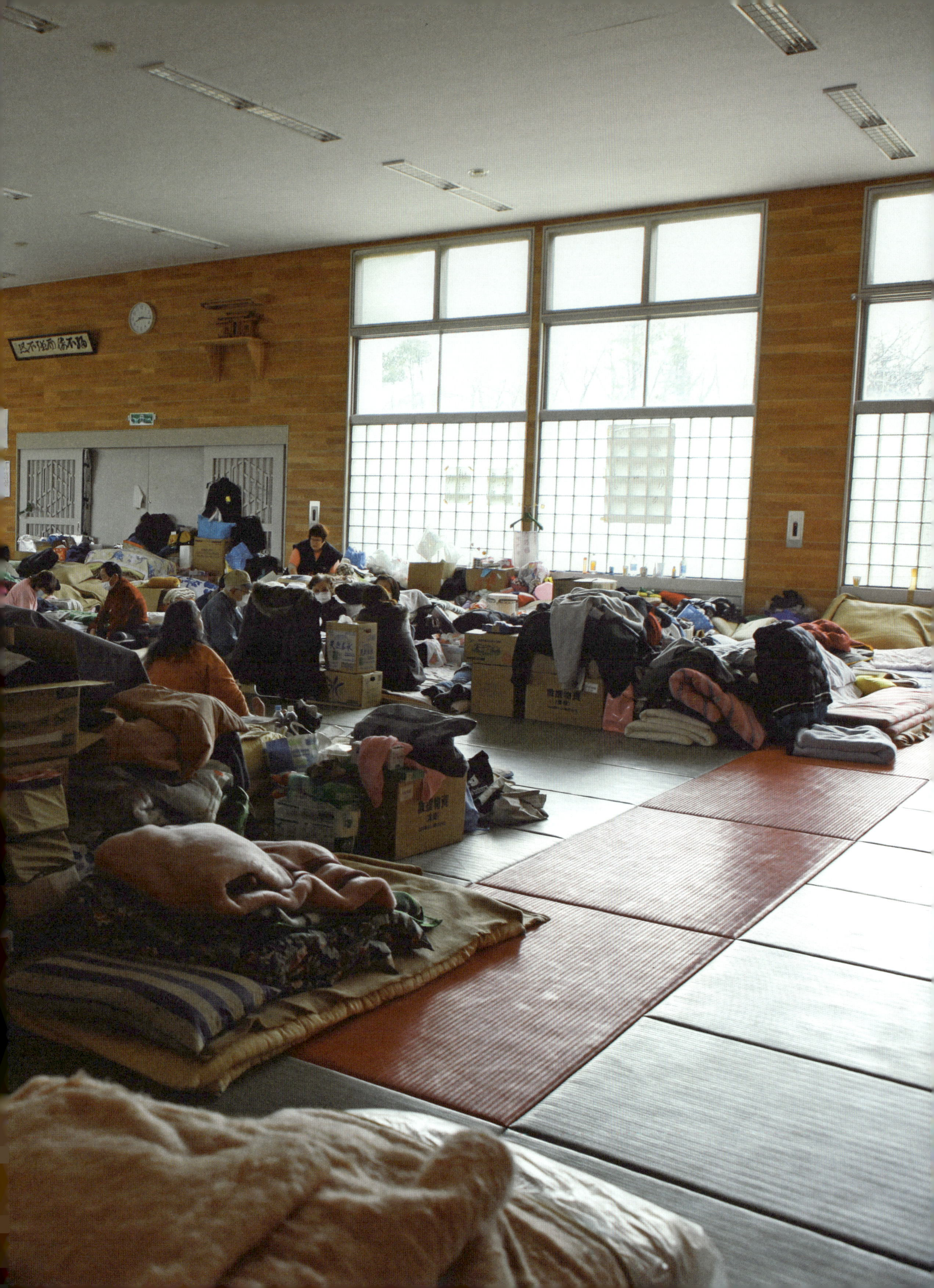

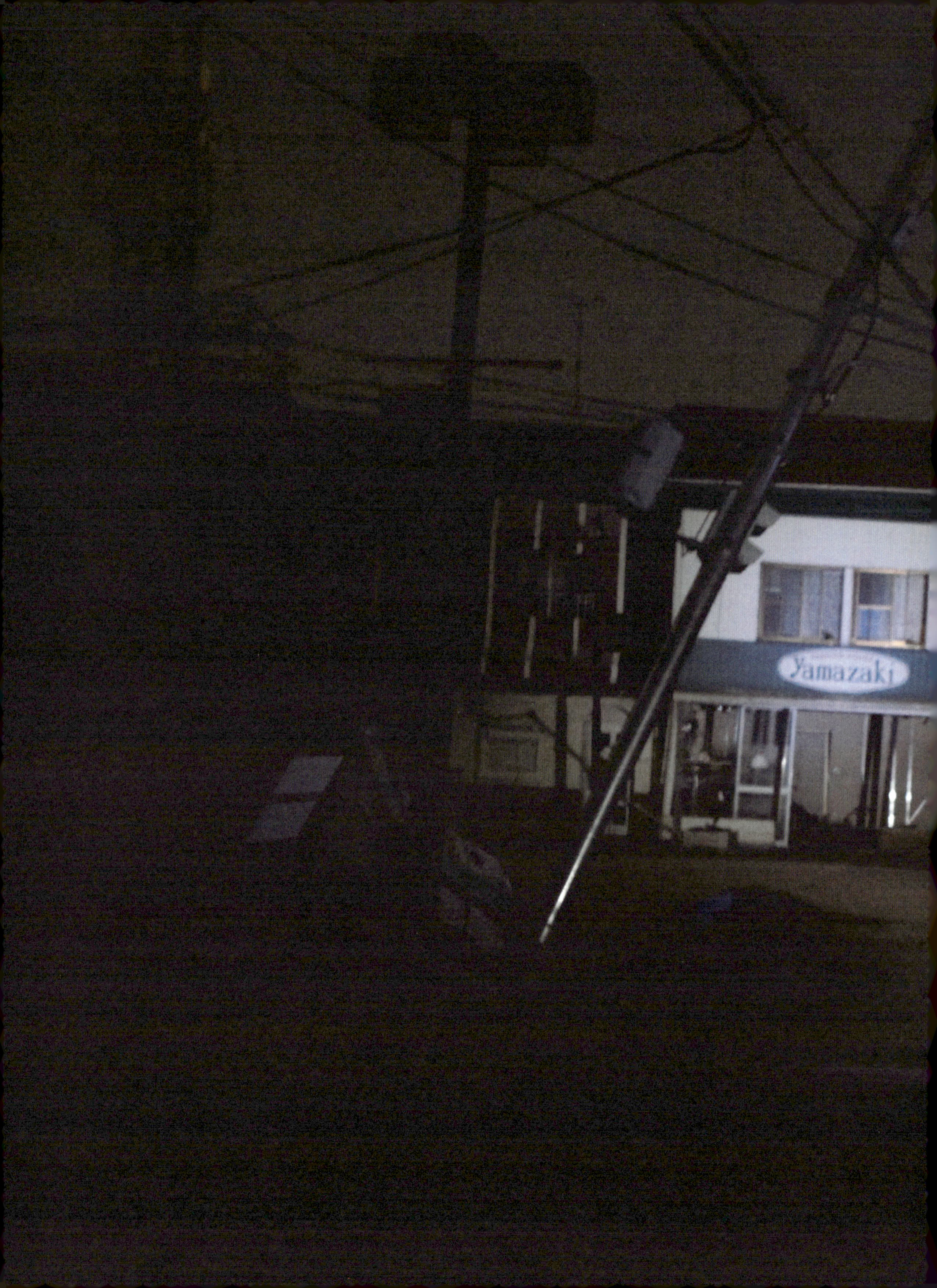

Yamazaki

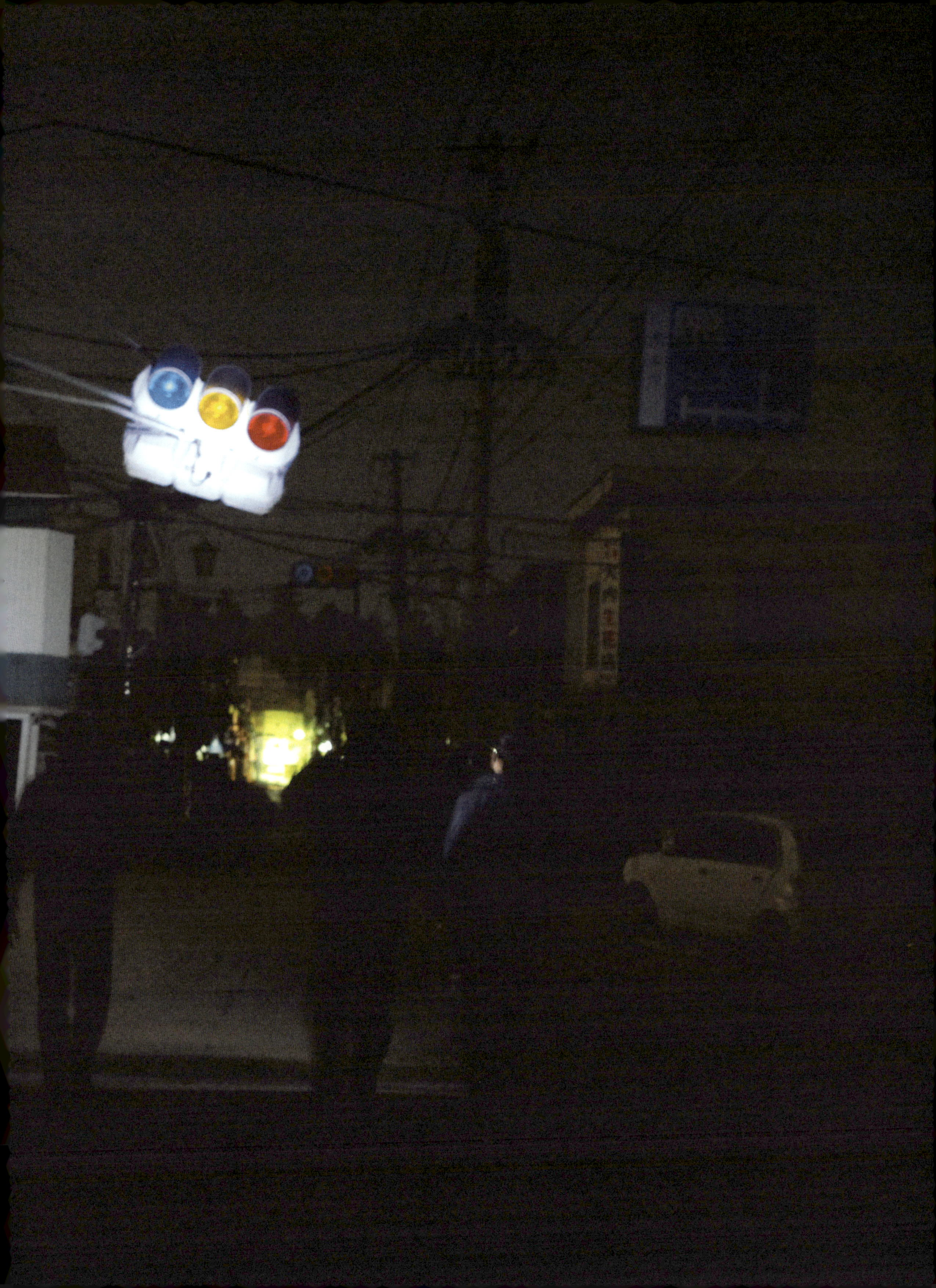

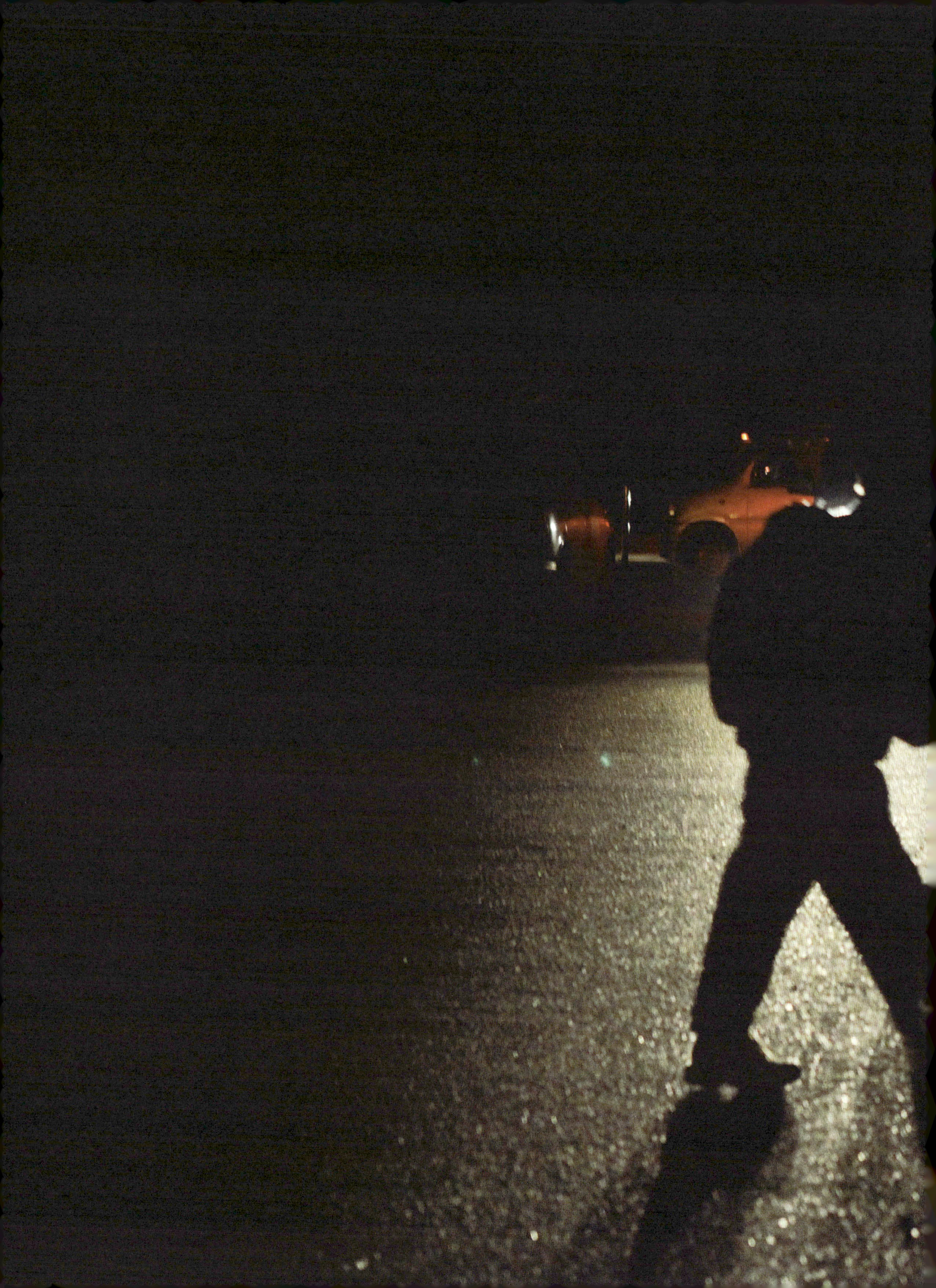

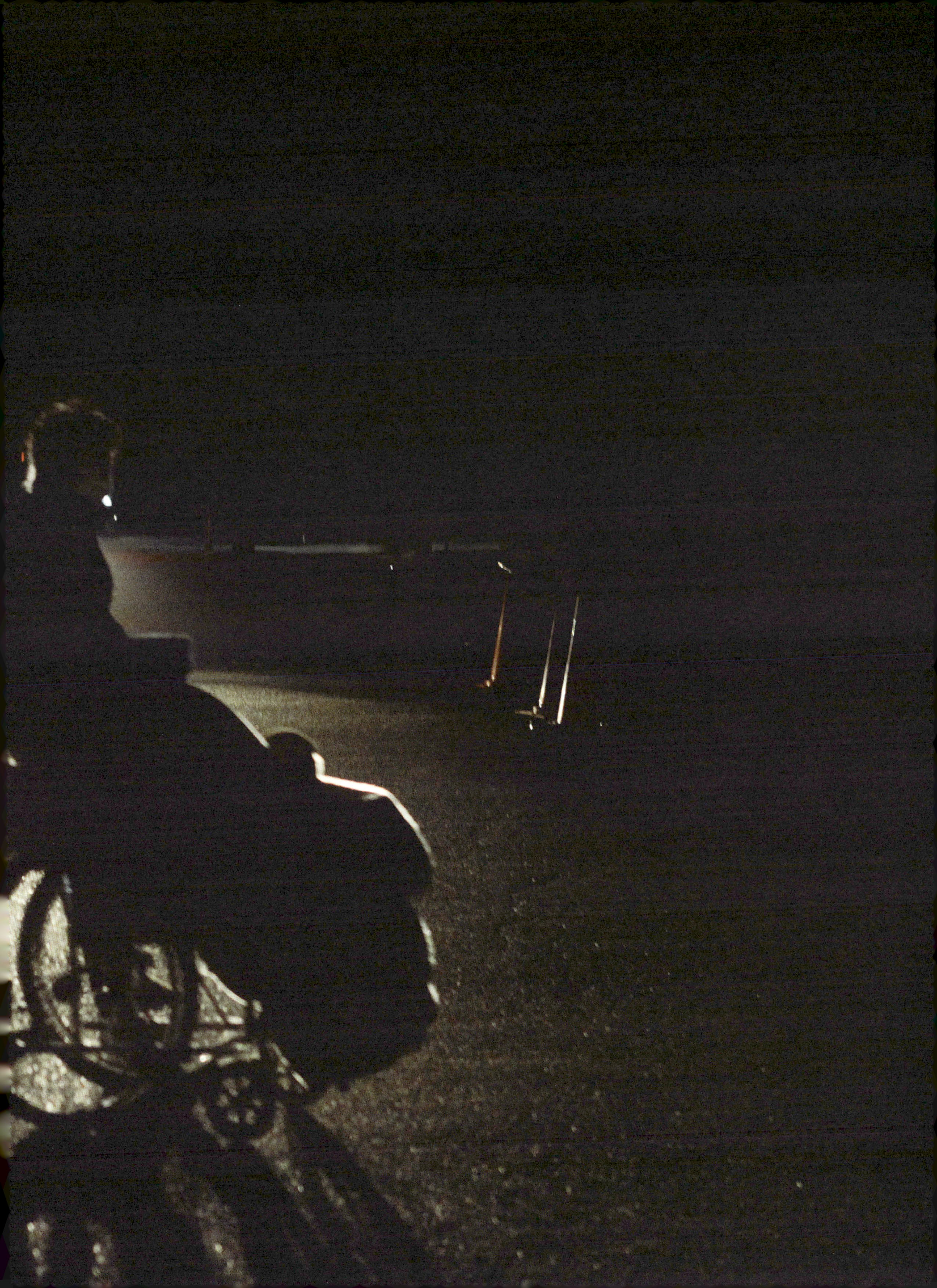

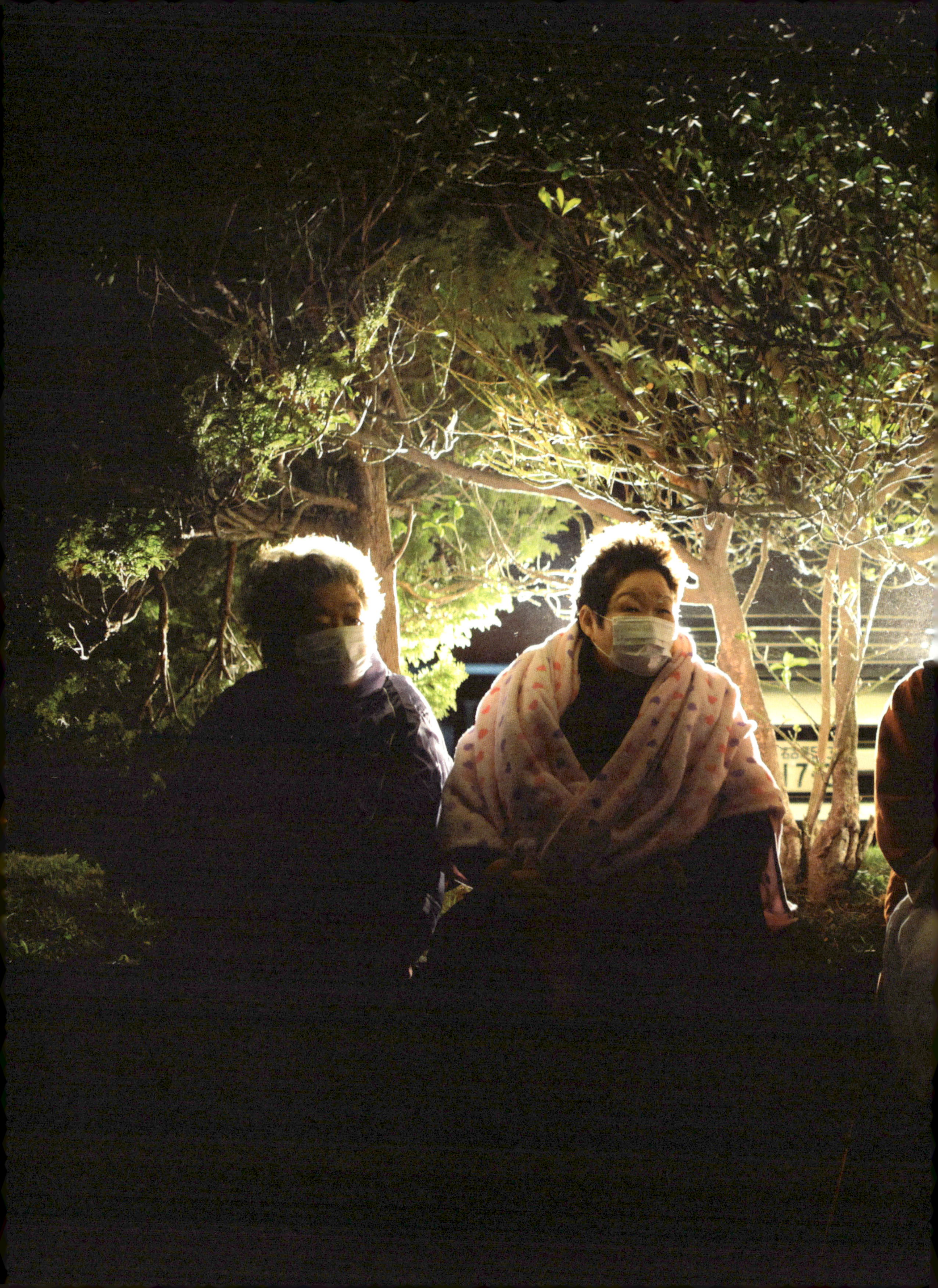

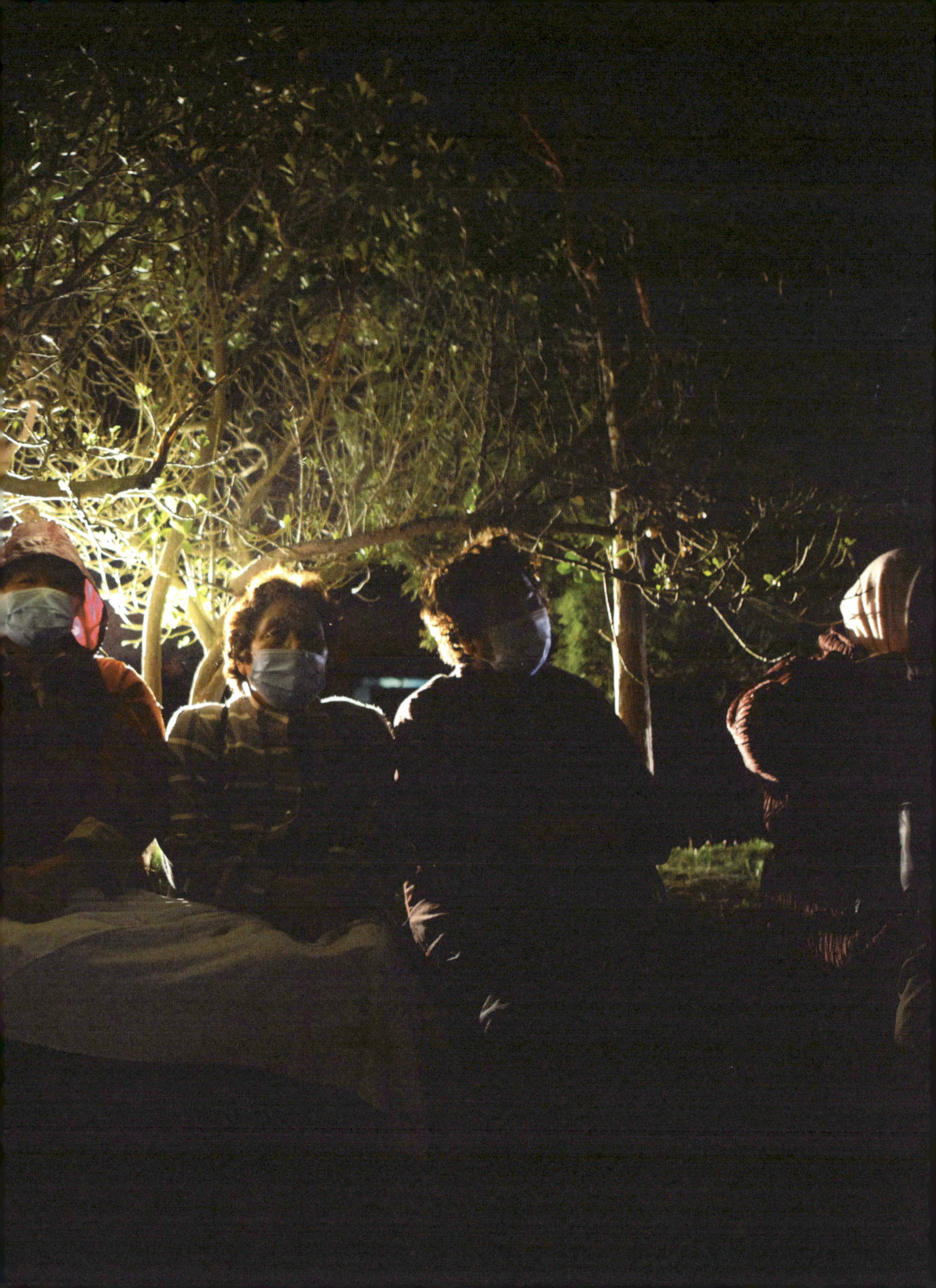

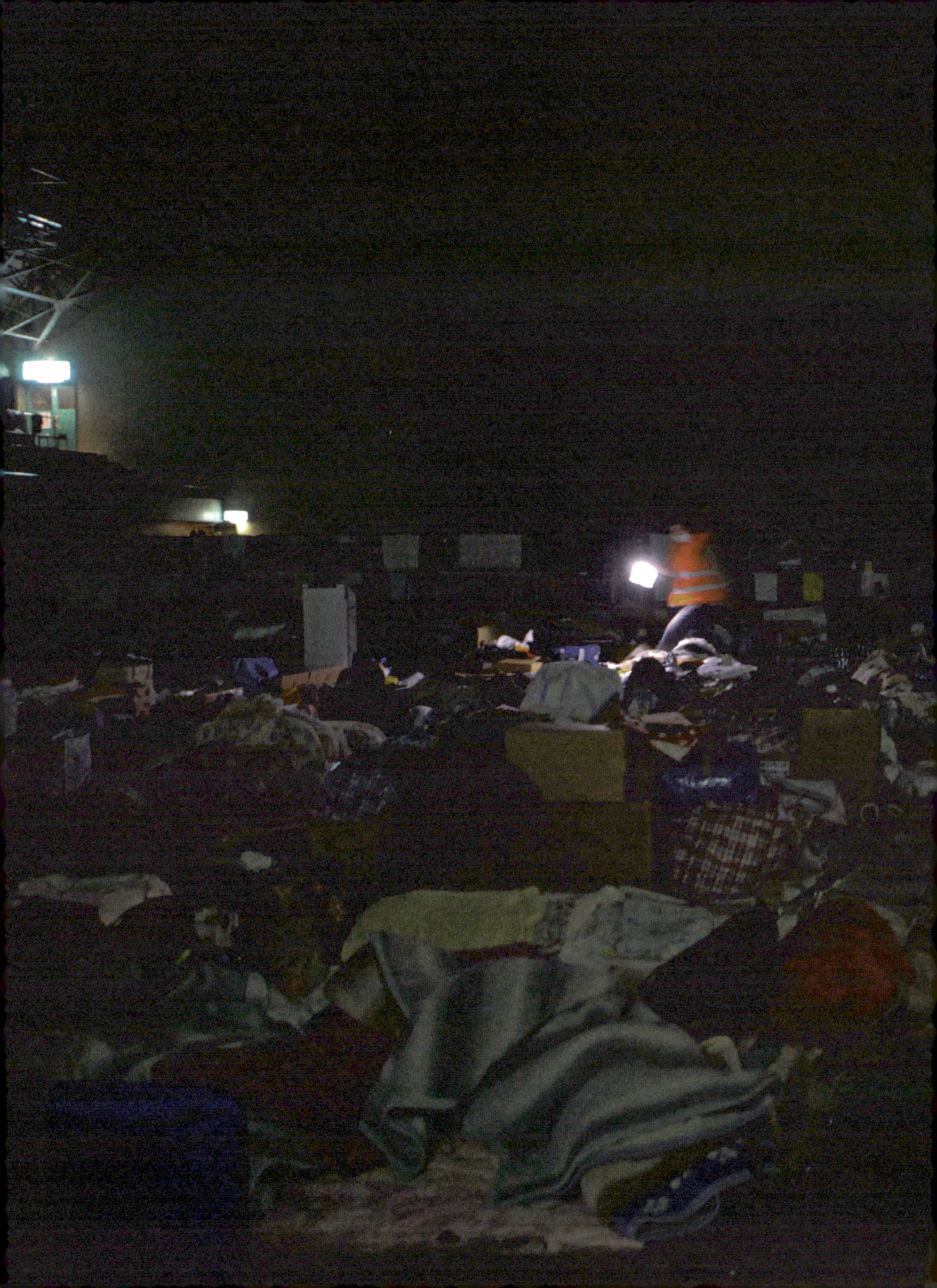

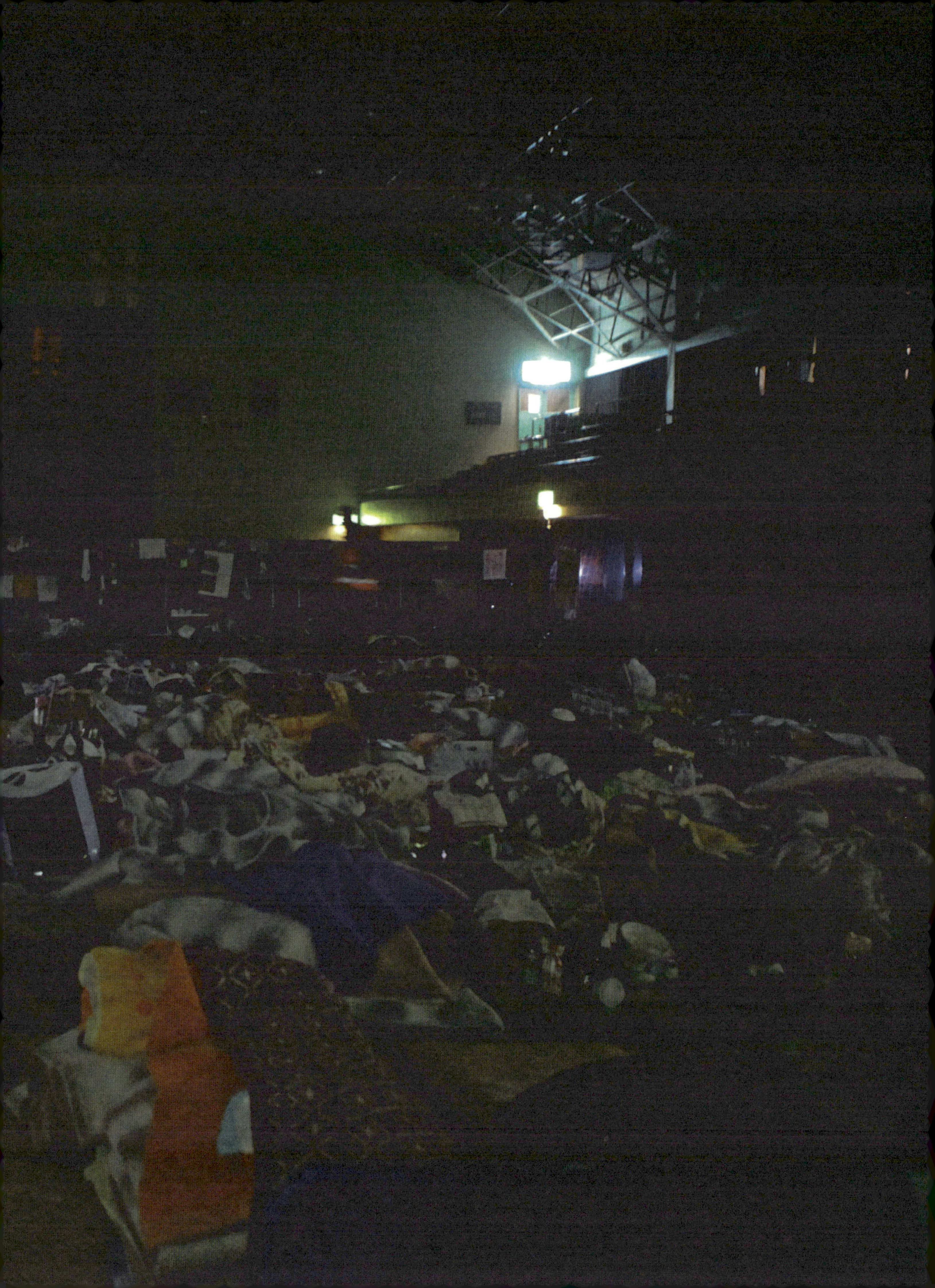

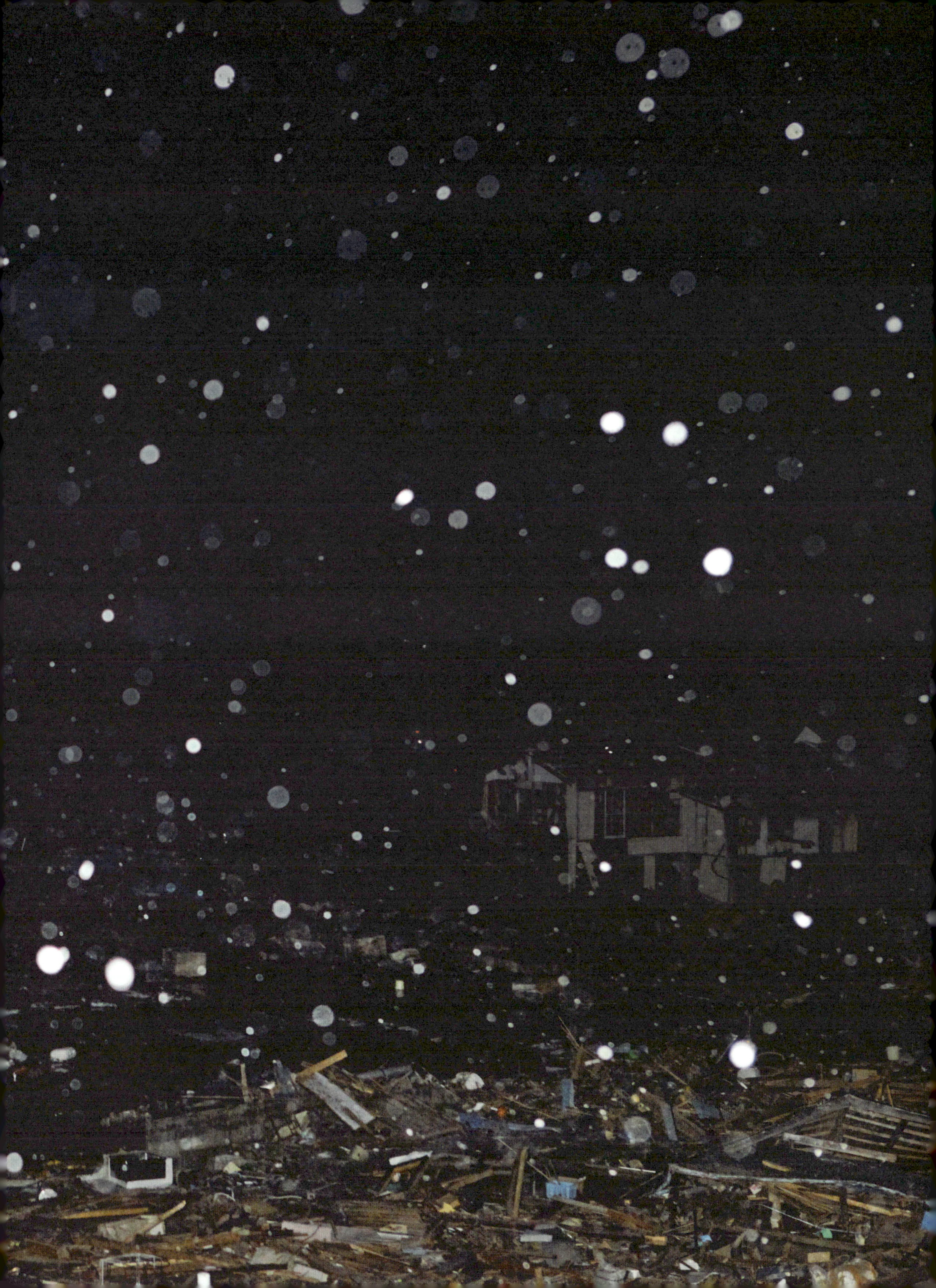

"Atomic Chancellor Announces Nuclear Phaseout"

Süddeutsche Zeitung, June 9, 2011

As a reaction to the events in Fukushima,
formerly pro-nuclear German chancellor Angela Merkel decides
to have nuclear power phased out in Germany by 2022.

ドイツ "原発首相" が 原発廃止を表明

2011年6月9日　南ドイツ新聞

福島の大惨事を受け、原発推進派だったアンゲラ・メルケル独首相は、2022年までに
ドイツの原子力発電を段階的に廃止することを決定した。

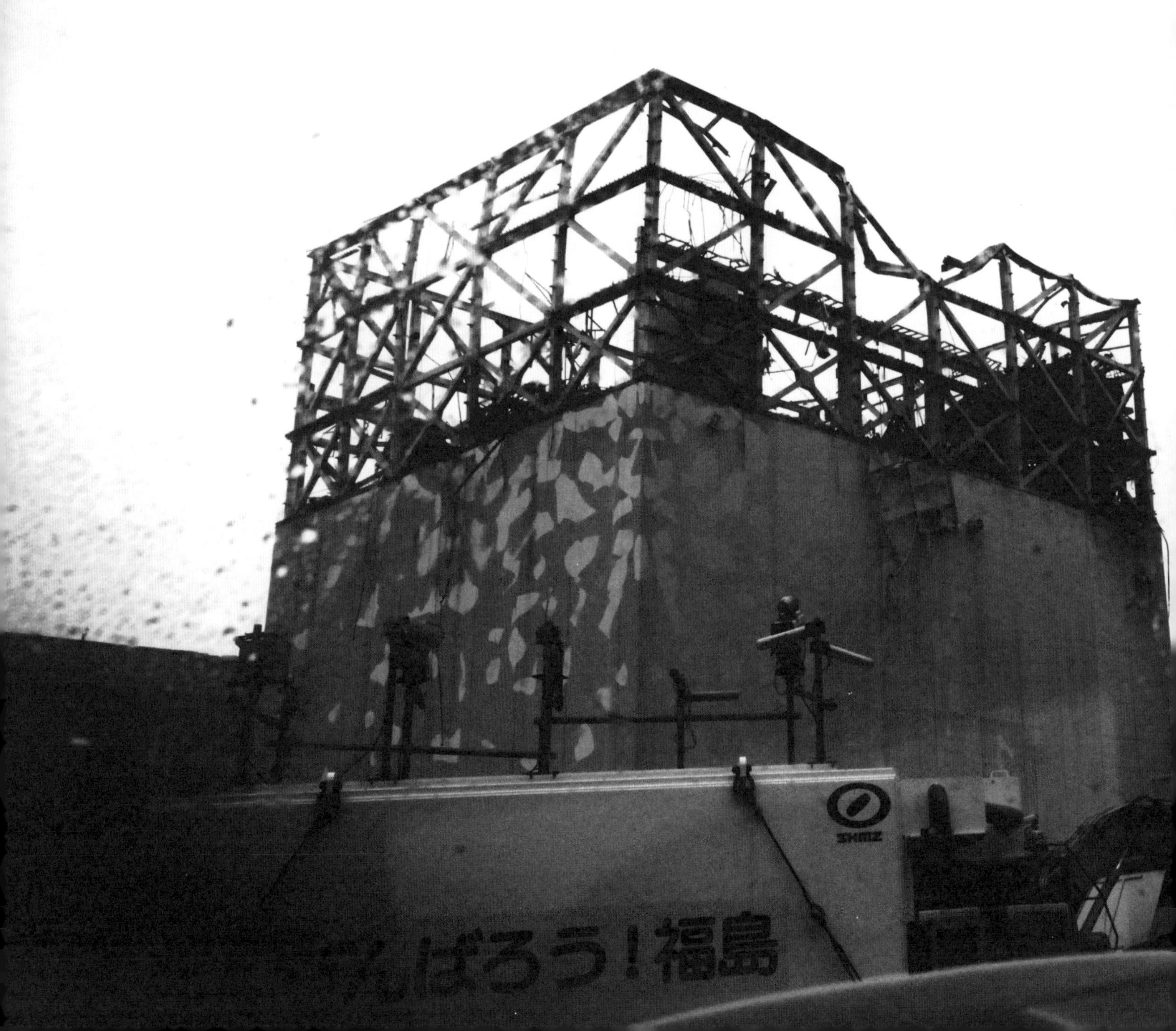
ばろう！福島

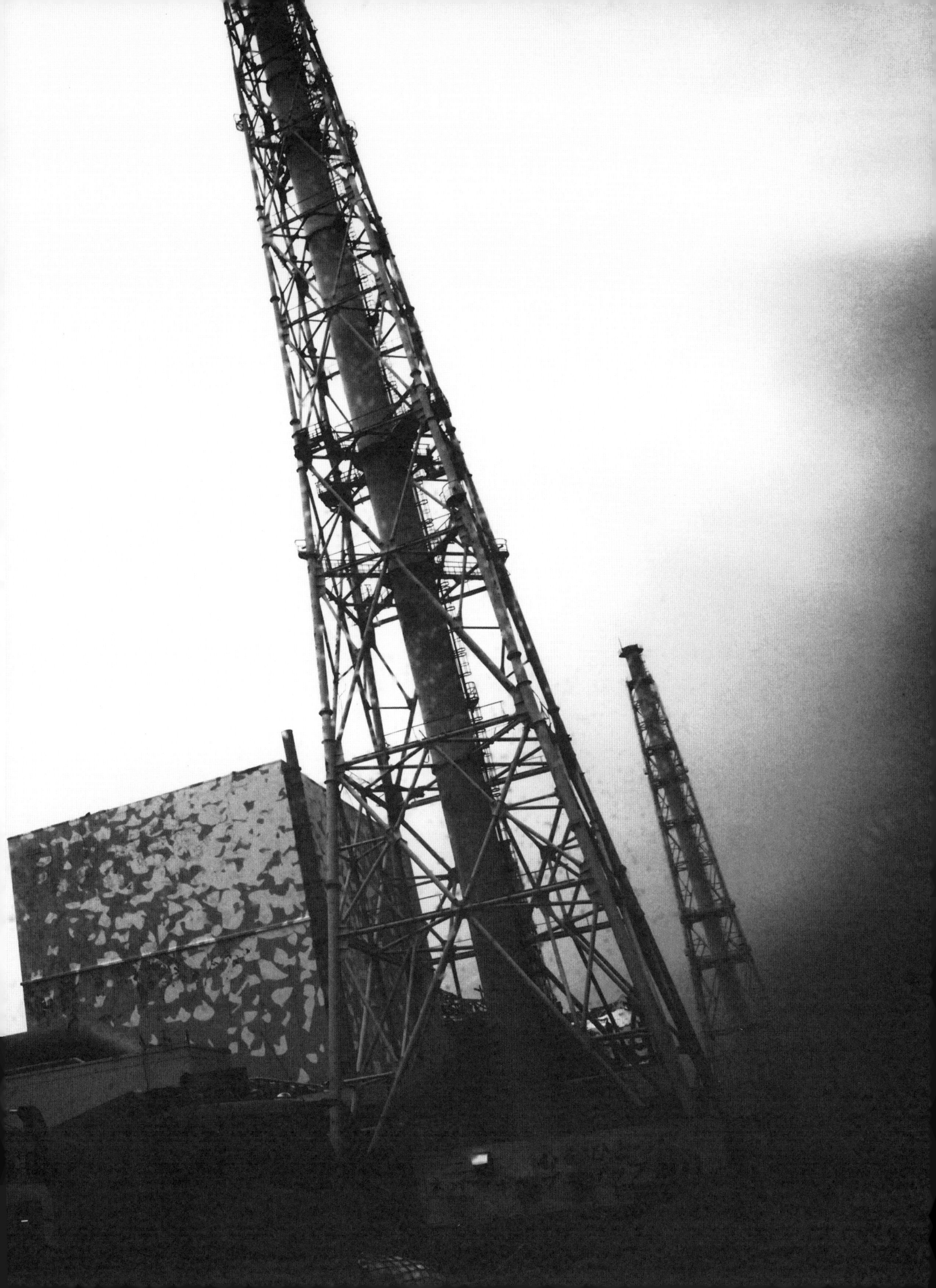

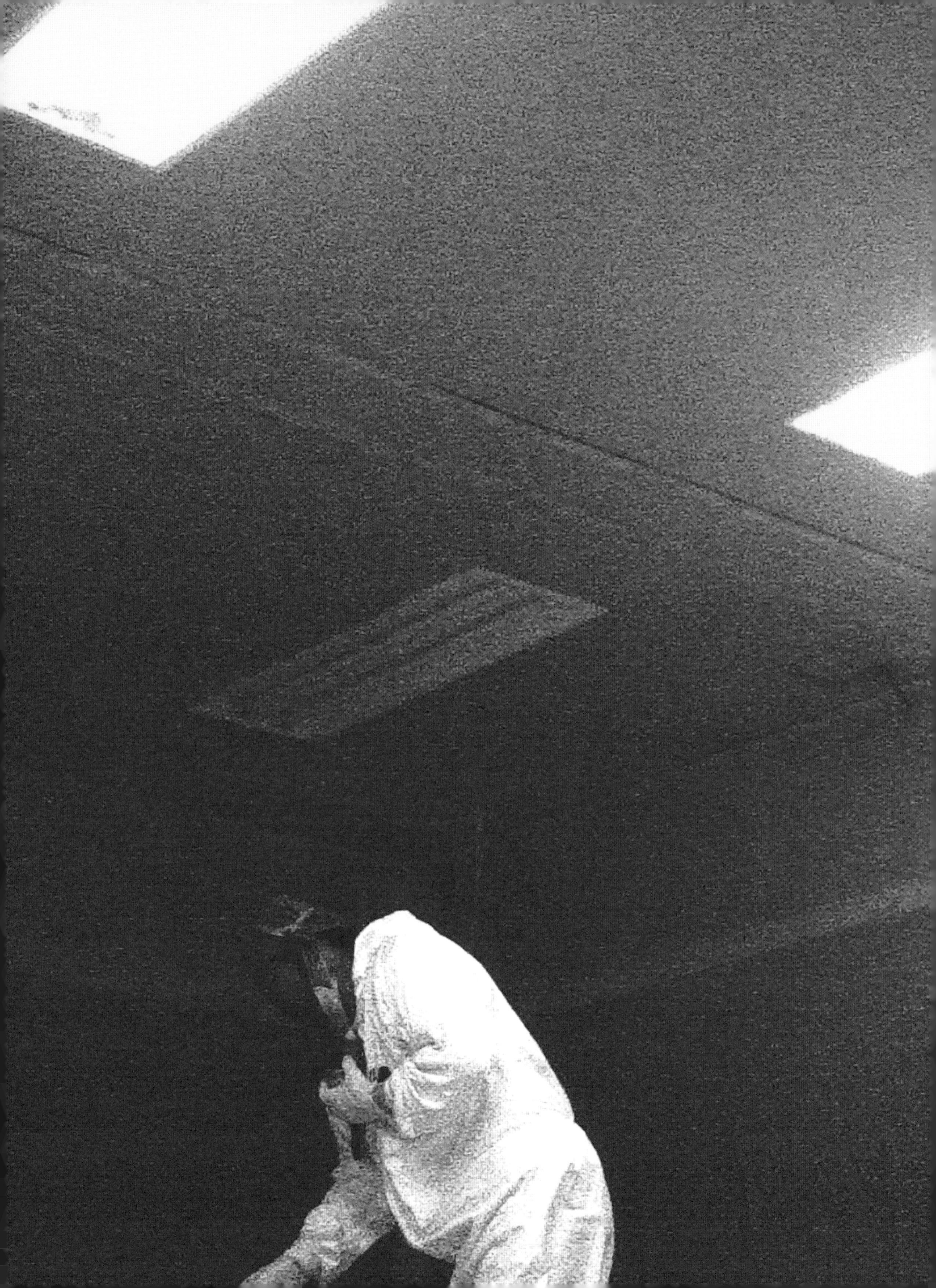

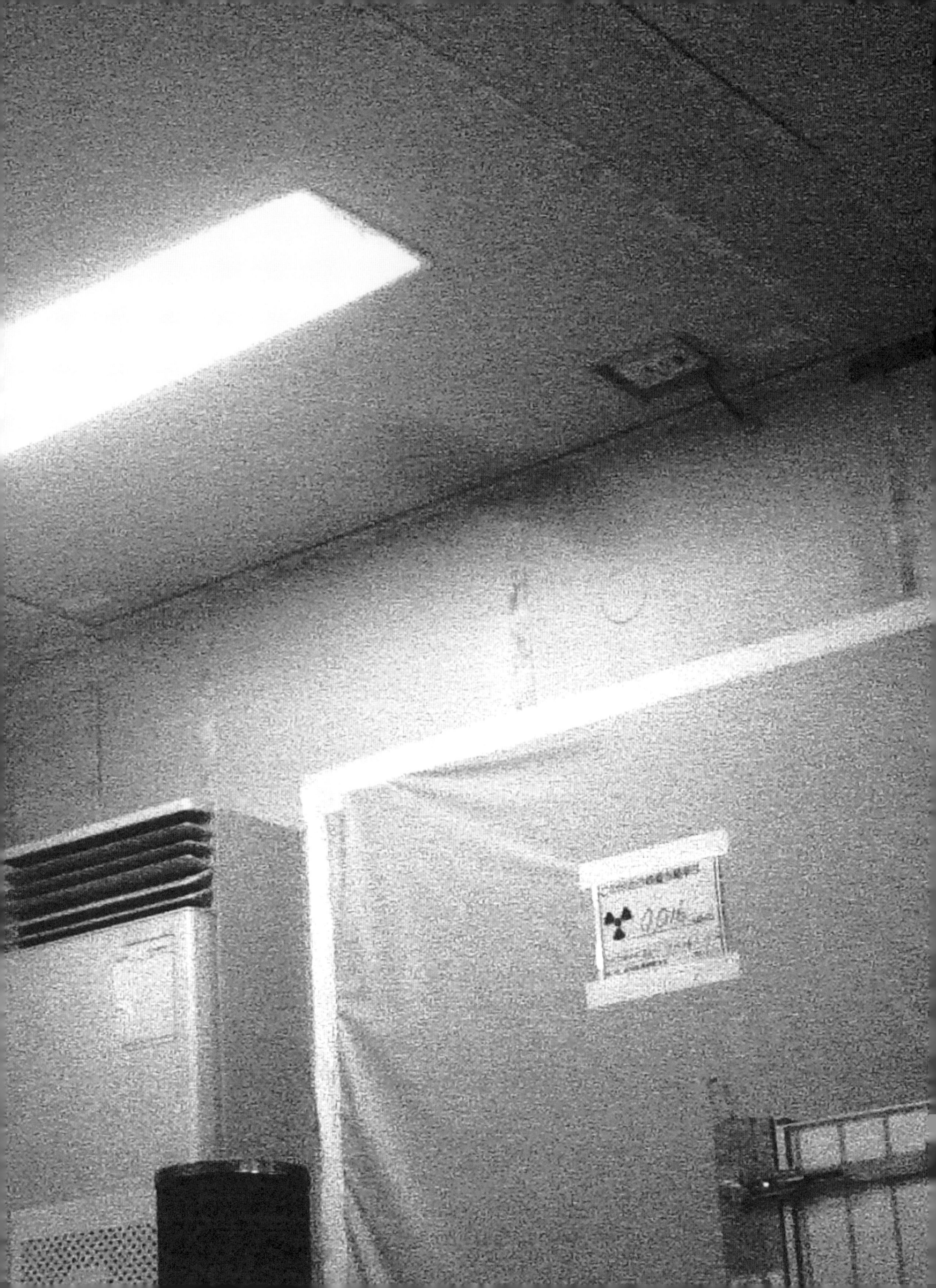

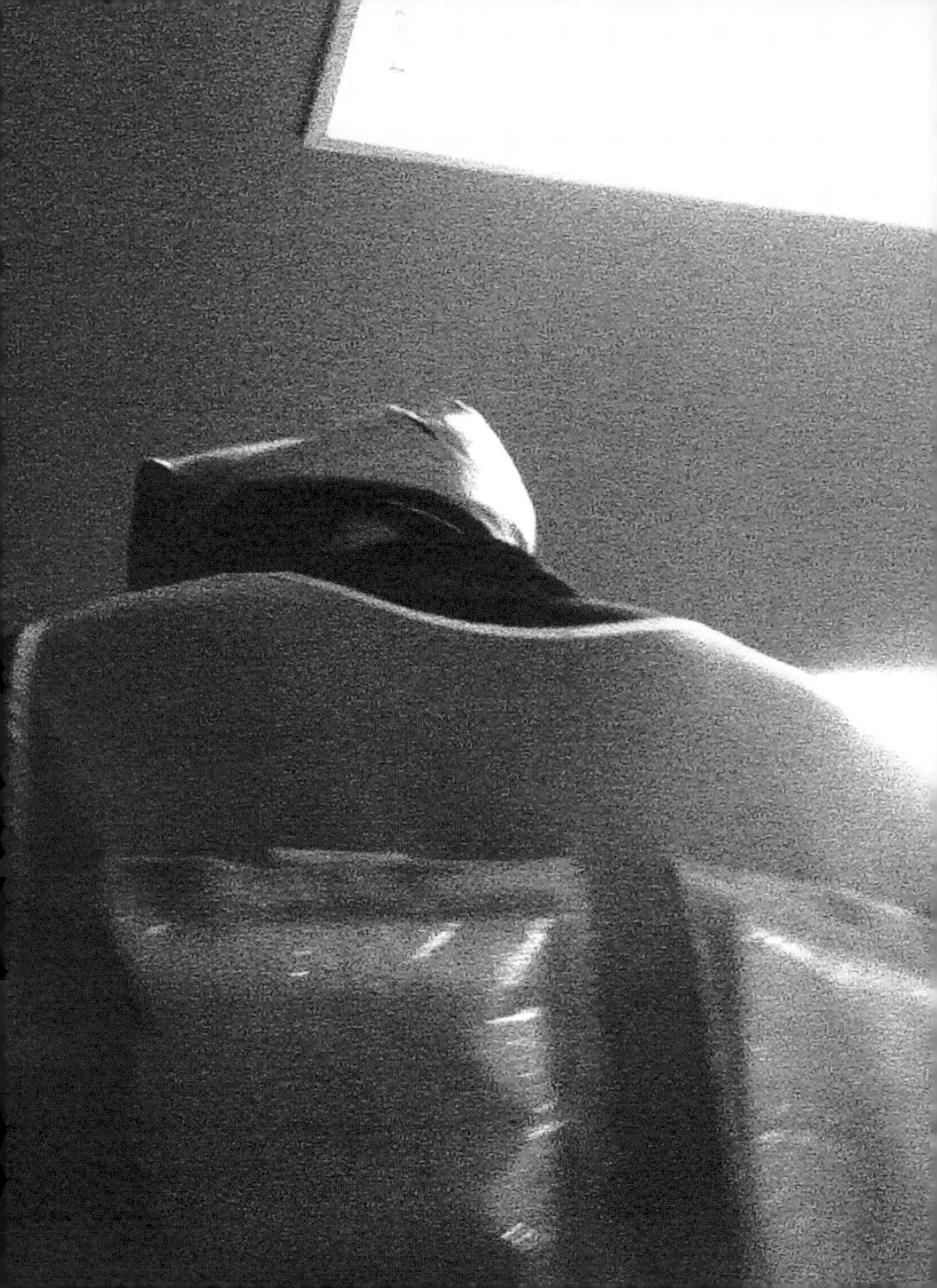

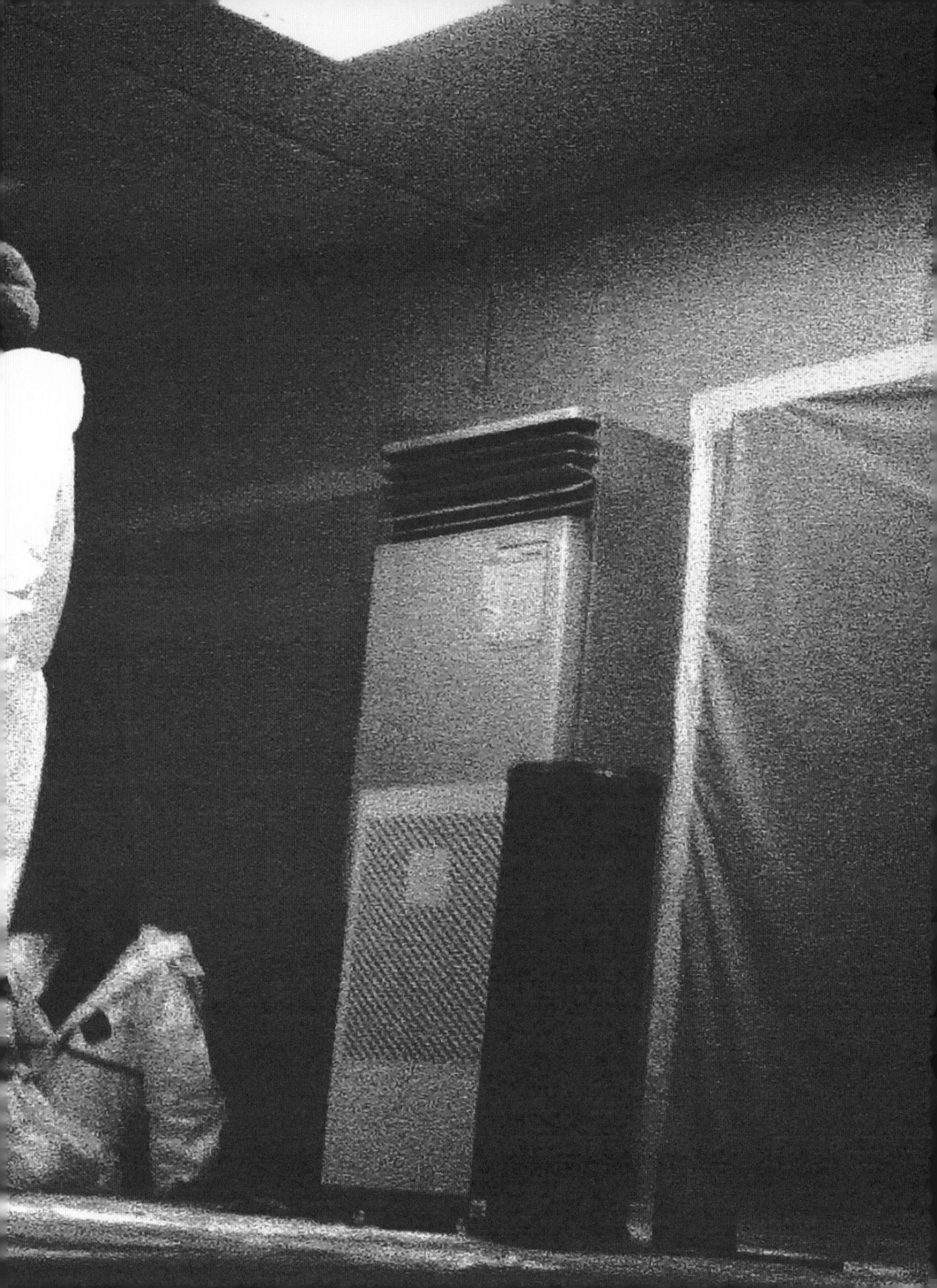

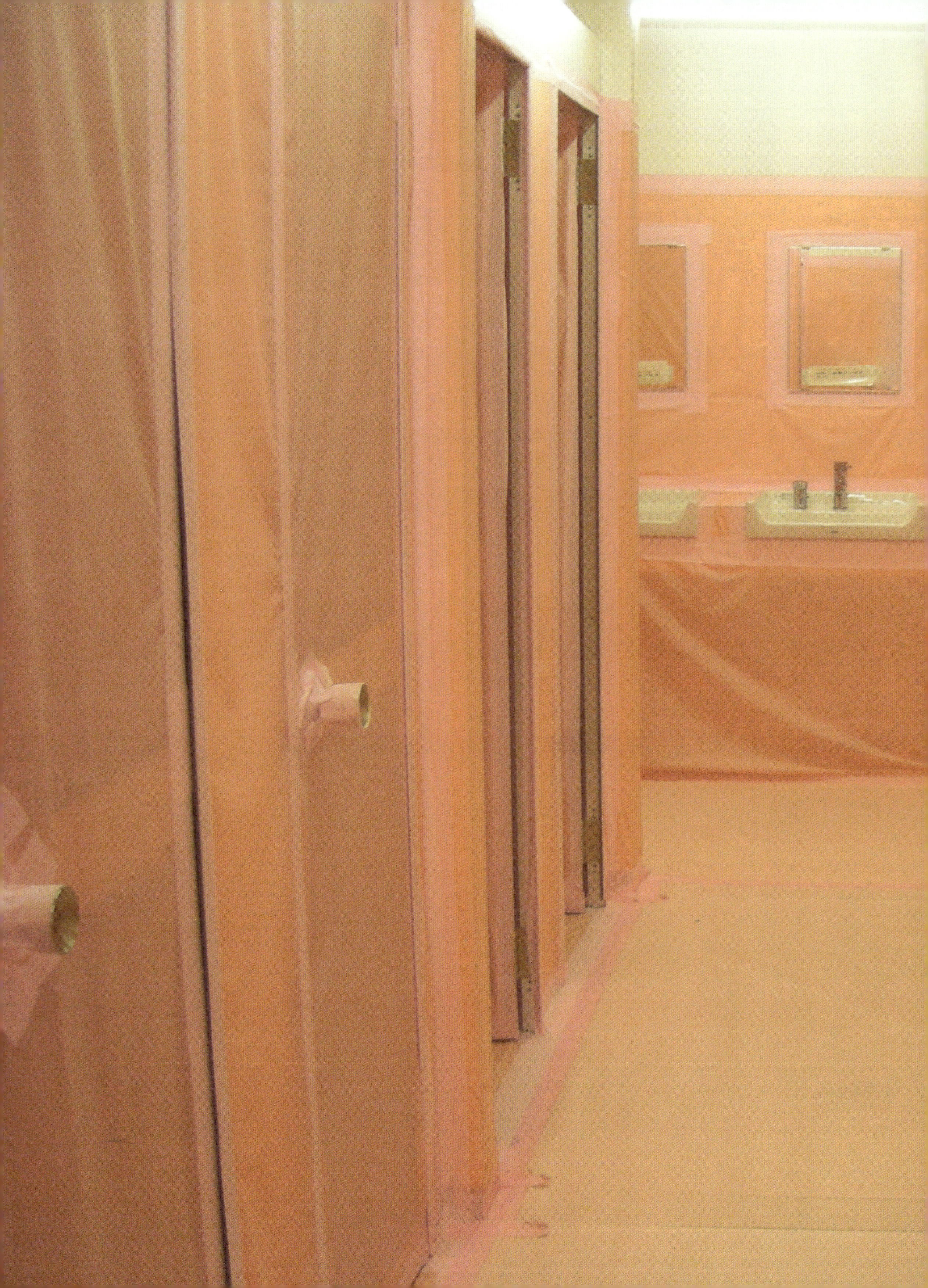

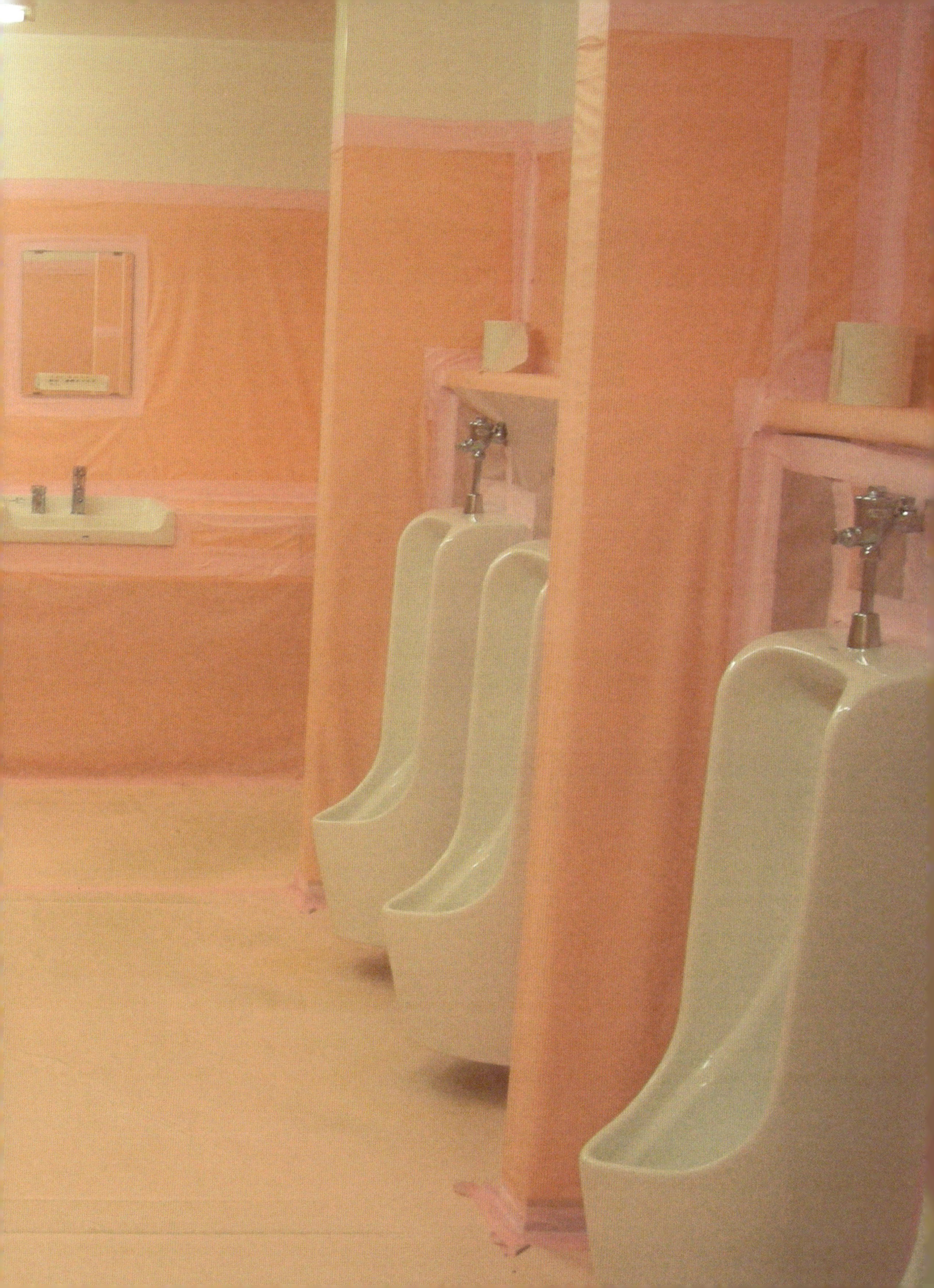

The Frontline

It is yet unknown when the Japanese nuclear accident at the Fukushima Daiichi Nuclear Plant will be resolved. A year has passed since the accident happened, but the government and Tokyo Electric Power Company (TEPCO) continue to conceal information. After the accident, the mass media were only allowed to report officially for one day, on March 12.

The fact that they conceal the situation of the workers, who are protecting our lives, is something we need to take very seriously. The following recounts what I experienced when I entered the reactor in early August 2011.

At 7 a.m., the workers' identities were verified at the gate of Daiichi and they headed toward a seismically isolated building (Menshinto). The building is located 200 meters away from the number one reactor of the plant that exploded. After the explosion, they had set up their "Emergency Control Department" in this building, where the workers come to rest.

When I entered the building with its walls and floors covered in pink plastic, a man walked by and I heard his Geiger counter's high-pitched beeps. Many workers took off their full-face masks and protective suits to rest. In each of the rooms, I find radiation measurements. Most show a rather high measurement of above 15 microsieverts per hour, though they are not very recent. Some have not been updated since April.

My dosimeter showed 10 microsieverts per hour. Note that the annual allowance for ordinary citizens in Japan is 1000 microsieverts per year (0.11 microsieverts per hour). Meaning that the place where the workers eat and rest is 100 times more contaminated than the legal limit. The workers told me that this was unbelievable and had never happened before.

At 9:30 a.m., I joined them outside wearing the same protective gear as they did; the gap between mask and suit sealed with the plastic tapes, wearing two pairs of cotton gloves and another pair of plastic ones over them and two pairs of socks.

Walking down the hill towards the shore along which the nuclear reactors were standing, I caught sight of Daiichi. Although TEPCO announced that radiation as high as 10,000 millisieverts per hour had been detected near the ventilation system between reactors 1 and 2, the workers were not informed of the finding: not on that day, nor afterwards. They only learned of the danger from the broadcast news.

After wearing the mask for 20 minutes, I felt a piercing pain at the back of my nose. Breathing became difficult. Within 30 minutes, the left side of my head hurt. I wasn't sure if this was because I had put on the mask too tightly for fear of any air penetrating. After an hour, the pain was so unbearable that I considered taking the mask off. Because most of the workers finish their shifts at the same time, they need to wait in long lines to be screened to measure their radiation exposure. One of the workers told me that, "Though we only have one hour of break including transfer times, it's very common to be stuck in line for more than 30 minutes here. So sometimes I wink at the guy responsible for the screening to go through the tests quickly."

The workers returned from their shift. Exhausted, they all lay down on small mats. Where space is scarce, they squat along the corridors to sleep. Some of them look awfully young. The laughing and talking from the early morning could no longer be heard. They seemed focused on trying to recover from the exhaustion. At 1 p.m., they went back to their houses.

The process of restoration will last decades. This was only a single day.

Kazuma Obara

フロントライン

未だ収束の目処が立たない福島第一原発。事故から1年が経過しようと
する今でも、政府、東電は取材を規制し情報統制を行っている。事故後、公式に
報道陣が取材を行えたのは11月12日の1日限りだ。

私たちは今ある生活を守ってくれている人たちの、隠された状況を、
もっと重く受け止めなければいけない。以下は私が8月上旬に作業員として
入構したルポルタージュである。

午前7時、1F（イチエフ：作業員が呼ぶ福島第一原発の通称）のゲートで
入構手続きを済ますと、作業員は免震重要棟と呼ばれる建物に準備のため向かった。
爆発した1号機から200メートルほどしか離れていない建物は、事故後、
緊急対策室が設置され、作業員の休憩所としても利用されている。ピンク色のシート
に壁面や床が覆われた棟内に入ると、すれ違った男性の胸ポケットから
線量計の警報音が突然鳴りだした。多くの作業員が全面マスクと防護服を脱い
でいる場所だった。棟内の各部屋を回ってみると、空間線量が書き付けられた
紙が掲示されていた。そのほとんどが毎時15マイクロシーベルト以上の結果
を示しているが、測定時期が4月と書かれたものも更新されずにあった。私の線量
計は毎時10マイクロシーベルトを示していた。国内に置ける一般市民の被曝
限度基準は、年1000マイクロシーベルト（毎時0.11マイクロシーベルト）であり、その
100倍近く汚染された場所で作業員は飲食を行い、仮眠をとっている。
事故前であれば、そのようなことなどあり得なかったという。

午前9時半過ぎ、作業員とともに現場に向かった。全面マスクと防護服の隙間を
テープで埋め、綿の手袋を2枚、その上にビニールの手袋を重ねた。靴下は二重に
はいて、免震棟の外に出た。原子炉が並ぶ海岸線に続く坂道を下っていくと、
1号機建屋が見えてくる。8月1日、東電はその1号機と2号機の間の排気筒付近
で毎時1万ミリシーベルトが検出されたと発表。しかし、その日もそれ以降も
作業員は、その事実を東電から知らされてはいない。彼らはテレビを通して、
その事実を知った。

免震棟を出て20分ほど経った頃だった。鼻の奥にツンとした痛みを感じ、
呼吸が非常に苦しくなった。30分ほど経つと、マスクの装着部が痛み始めた。
少しの空気でも侵入させまいと、マスクをきつく閉め過ぎたからだろうか。
1時間が経つ頃には頭痛が限界に達し、マスクを外したい衝動に駆られた。夏の
暑さも厳しさを増し、連日熱射病で倒れる作業員が続出していた頃でもあった。

労働を終えた作業員たちは同じ時間帯に戻ってくるため、渋滞が起きて
しまう。「現場との移動時間を含めて休憩時間が1時間しかないのに、30分以上
ここで並ぶこともざらにあるので、スクリーニングを担当する作業員と目配せをして、
簡単に済ませてしまうこともある」と、ある作業員は愚痴をこぼした。

休憩場所に戻ると、疲れきった作業員たちが、床の上に敷かれた銀マットの上に
所狭しと横たわっている。そこからあぶれた何人かの若者たちは、廊下に体育座り
で仮眠をとっている。頬が赤く、あどけなさの残る青年もいる。朝のうちは談笑し
余裕が見られた作業員たちだが、この時間帯は会話も少なめになり、ただ体力の回復
に努めていた。

午後1時、仕事を終えた作業員たちが家路につく。
これから数十年続いていく収束作業。その1日が今日も終わった。

小原 一真

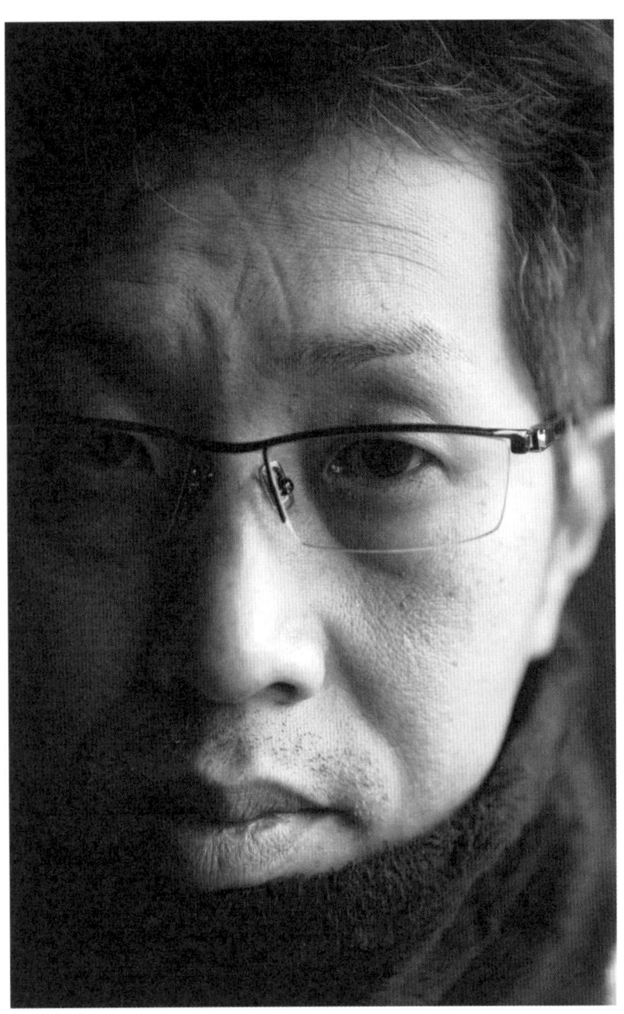

Atsushi Ogawa
小川 篤
43

"Subcontracted workers are treated as inferior by TEPCO's staff. I greet them on purpose, only to find that they won't even react."

「お疲れ様です」ってでっかい声で言っても、
まず「お疲れ様です」って返すことはない。
お前ら事故起こした会社の人間だろ、俺は
わざと言ってんだけど、まず反応がない。

What has the situation been like since the accident?
After evacuating, I volunteered while living as an evacuee. Then, I returned to Fukushima in November to do restoration work. It was so mortifying when I had to enter my own house in raincoat and boots back in March. Why do I need to be dressed this way to enter my own house? I'm not playing this game! I took everything off. It's beyond paralysis; it's mortifying. Of course, I'm afraid of the invisible, but panicking won't help either. I just told myself that'll be okay, I won't have any immediate health damages. My mother is already 77 years old. She probably won't live to see the day they tell us we can return to stay in our house after decontamination. But I can't take her to see the house because she'll think she is able to return. But let's face it, that's pretty unrealistic.

What was it like entering the Daiichi reactor?
I wonder what difference I would have made if I had come right after the accident. I ask myself why I didn't. That feeling of regret is stronger.

How do you feel about young people working at the reactor?
I don't want them to be here. They still have their lives ahead of them. That's why I always try to take on the assignments in the more contaminated places, but maybe that's only a drop in the bucket. It's not a place for them to be in.

Your thoughts on the Japanese government and TEPCO: how do you feel after having entered Daiichi?
Despite the fact that TEPCO caused a major global accident, nothing has changed about the hierarchy. It's the same at J-Village as well. Subcontracted workers are treated as inferior by TEPCO's staff. I greet them on purpose, only to find that they won't even react, let alone respond. It's almost shocking. Just because we are the ones working in the reactor, they treat us like strangers. We're the dirty workers. Only the employees of TEPCO and the subcontractor work in rotation and make sure there are no health damages. If we're unlucky, they order us to work on Saturdays as well, to exclude any personal sentiments and to only think about work, they tell us as if it was the most normal thing to do. I still come back every day and obey, telling myself that I'm not doing this for TEPCO.

Are there people who think differently about TEPCO?
You might think of them as good if you have personal contact to TEPCO's employees or other representatives but that's a wholly different position.

How do you feel about the government backing TEPCO?
Politics and money, TEPCO and the Ministry of Economy. I knew that already before the disaster, but after the accident the Nuclear and Industrial Safety Agency's (NISA) irresponsibility has been disclosed. If they're allocating a trillion for decontamination, I want them to think about compensation as well. I don't think decontamination is really going to do a thing. Building temporary storage infrastructure for the rubble in Futaba is the equivalent to saying, "Forget about Futaba. It's hopeless." Only those sitting at a table, the talkers, will dare send people back here. All the ministers should put on full-face masks and Tyvek suits and stay on the grounds for four, five hours. The only way to fathom this is by experiencing it physically.

Considering how much is hidden from the public, what would you like everyone know the most?
The statement about accident resolution shouldn't read "suspension of operations," but, "We're pumping water into the basin where

the fuel rods are," but they're melting anyway, aren't they? Without knowing where the rods are, nor in what condition they're in, they declare the cooling process completed. That's how negligent this "accident resolution" is. I can only take this as a please-calm-down-act for the international community and the Japanese people. I want everyone to know that we're far from resolving anything here. It looks a lot better organized and clean now and much of the rubble has been removed but it's only a cover that's been put over Daiichi Unit 1, and we probably won't be even able to cover up Units 3 and 4. If there's another magnitude 6 quake or a tsunami, I don't think it could withstand it.

What are your thoughts about the future?

I think the amount of construction work needed for the nuclear decommissioning is going to decrease. After that it's going to be the infrastructure maintenance for the circulation of the cooling water that will gain importance. Time will tell if I continue with the decontamination work or if I quit to work in a safer environment. Employment in the area is going to be one of the problems. I backed off the nuclear industry soon enough because I feared I wouldn't be able to work anything else. But the people who have become dependent on the industry for the good money, for them to lose their jobs, that's devastating.

November 2011

震災後の状況は？
警戒区域から避難し、避難所生活を続けながらボランティアをして、その後11月から福島に戻って収束作業をしてます。3月に自分の家に、カッパを着て、長靴履いて入ったんだけど、悔しくて。なんで自分の家でこんな格好しなくちゃなんねえんだ、ふざけんな、と思って脱いじゃって。もう、麻痺とかいうよりも悔しさだよね。目に見えない怖さがあるんだけど、じたばたしたってしょうがねえし。自分で「直ちに健康被害はないからいいんだ」って言っちゃったよ。おふくろも７７歳。多分、除染して、はい、住めますよってなるまでは生きていないと思う。だから、余計今見せに連れてっていいものか。やっぱり年寄りは帰れると思ってるからね。でも、現実的に無理だよね。

１Ｆに入ってどうでしたか？
これが震災直後だったら、俺どんなことできたんだろうなって。何で俺すぐ来なかったのかっていう後悔が強いです。

若い人たちが原発で働くことについてはどう思いますか？
来て欲しくない。若い人ってこれからでしょ。だから、ちょっとでも線量の高い現場で、代われる所があればやってるし。でもどうなんだろ、焼け石に水なのかもしれない。若い人の姿は見たくないです。

国や東電に対する思い、１Ｆに入った後に感じていることは何ですか？
東電は世界的な大事故を起こしたにもかかわらず、実際体制は何も変わっていない。Jビレッジでもそうだけど、東電の人間に「お疲れ様です」ってでっかい声で言っても、まず「お疲れ様です」って返すことはない。お前ら事故起こした会社の人間だろ、俺はわざと言ってんだけど、まず反応がない。びっくりするぐらい。俺らが現場で働いてる人間だからって他人事のように思ってる。ちゃんと輪番組んで、作業環境が悪化しないように、健康被害がないようにやっているのは、東電と元請けの人間だけであって、末端の作業員は、へたすりゃ土日も仕事出ろとか、「個人的な感情一切抜きにして、仕事のこと考えて下さい」なんてことを平気で言われる。東電のためにやってるわけじゃない、って言い聞かせながら毎日行ってますね。

東電に対して、違う思いを持っている人もいるようですが？
東電の中でも担当者やメーカーの付き合ってる人間がいいとか、いい交渉ができるとかがあれば、良くも思うんだろうけど。立ち位置が全然違うからね。

東電を国が守っている状況をどう思いますか？
政治と金、東電と経産省、それは震災前にも分かっていたことだけど、震災が起きてから原子力保安院のいいかげんさも露呈してしまっているでしょ。除染に1兆円つぎ込むんだったら、保障の方に充てろって。除染しても何にもならないと思うし。双葉郡に中間貯蔵施設を作るってことは、実際双葉郡は諦めなさい、みたいなもんだしね。その近隣にまた戻って下さいなんて、全く他人事なんだよね。あくまでも国会議員なんてのは、机上論でしかないし。本当、大臣首を揃えて全面マスクにタイベックスーツで、現場に４、５時間いて、体感しないとわかんないよ。

国民に見えてない部分がたくさんある中で、特に知ってもらいたいことは？
事故収束宣言って、あれは冷温停止じゃなくて、冷温停止状態なんだよね。だって燃料棒が入っている窯に水をぶち込んでるけど、実際溶けて落ちてるわけでしょ。燃料棒がどこにあって、どういう状態にあるのか分かんないのに、窯を冷やしてある程度冷えたから冷温停止「状態」だって言って、事故収束って言ってるいいかげんさ。海外とか国民に対しての「ちょっと安心して下さい」みたいなパフォーマンスにしかとれなくて。だから絶対収束なんてしてないって本当に分かってほしい。確かに見た目は大分きれいになって、瓦礫も大分撤去されたけど、1号機はただカバーかけただけで、3、4号機はまだカバーもかけられないだろうし。もしまた6強の地震とか津波とか来たら持ち堪えないと思う。

今後の生活についてどう考えますか？
廃炉に向けて、その周りの関連の土木仕事って徐々に減っていくと思う。後は本当に冷却水の循環をしてる施設の管理とかのウエイトが大きくなると思う。除染の仕事に携わるか、お役御免になって安全な場所で仕事をするのか、どっちかかな。ただ、原発立地区域の雇用、それをどうするかっていうのが問題の一つ。若い頃はこんな仕事で潰しきかねぇだろうと思って、原発すぐ足洗ったけど。楽な仕事で原発に依存して、いいお金もらっていた人たちが職を失うと大変なんだな。

Atsushi Endo
遠藤 篤志
25

"I had a strong feeling that we were
by no means following any emergency
evacuation manual—something
that still doesn't exist to this day."

緊急避難マニュアルみたいなのも
未だに出されていないし、
守られてないなって。

What were you doing at the time of the accident?
I was working at a textile factory cutting material. The earthquake
was so monstrous I thought the earth had fallen apart. It just
wouldn't stop. At that point, I didn't spare a single thought about
the nuclear power plant.

How do you feel about your work at the reactor?
I must say it was tough going at the beginning, so tough. With people
passing out one after the other at the plant, I thought it couldn't
just be the radiation's influence. Thought I'd die of overwork or
mental stress. Your head gets heavy and I would feel unbearable
pain after only one and a half or two hours of work. I told myself
I would die anyway, whether I continued working or not. That really
was awful. I was afraid I wouldn't be able to go on. On top of
that I had a strong feeling that we were by no means following any
emergency evacuation manual—something that still doesn't exist
to this day. Still, I'm not as pessimistic as the TV reports. They just
pick up those people, not that they were entirely wrong either.
But it wouldn't hurt if they showed more people who hang in there
like us, those who persist and remain optimistic. Everyone must be
thinking that the people of Fukushima are worn-out and exhausted,
the city discouraged. They keep on encouraging us to hang in
there, but we already are.

November 2011

震災時は何をしていましたか？
服飾工場で生地を裁断してました。地震は地球が割れたかと思うぐらいすごかったです。
全然収まらないんですもん。そん時は原発のことなんて頭になかったですね。

現場での作業はどうですか？
最初はきつかったですね、本当に。原発でばたばた人が倒れるっていうのは、放射能
の影響じゃないなって思いましたもん。あっ、こんなことやってたら死ぬわって。
俺でも過労死しちゃうと思いましたね。全面マスクは、これで本当に仕事できんのって
思いました。すごい苦しいのもあるし、頭も重くなっちゃうんですよね。最初は
１時間半とか２時間の作業でも、堪え難い苦痛でした。死んじゃうぞ、このまま仕事
してなくても、って。あれはきつかったな。本当にこれで作業できるか不安
でしたもん。それに緊急避難マニュアルみたいなのも未だに出されていないし、
守られてないなって。でも、テレビで見るほど、俺らって全然悲観的じゃないですよ。
ああいう人（暴力団によって仕事を斡旋されている人など）だけを取り上げて、
まあ、それも間違いじゃないと思うけど。でも、もうちょっと俺らみたいに頑張ってる
よって人を取り上げてもいいと思うんですよね。多分よその県の人から見たら、
福島って、皆どんよりとして、げっそりとした町に思われてるんじゃねえかなって思う
ところもあるし。福島頑張ろう、とか言われても頑張ってるしねえ。

2011年11月

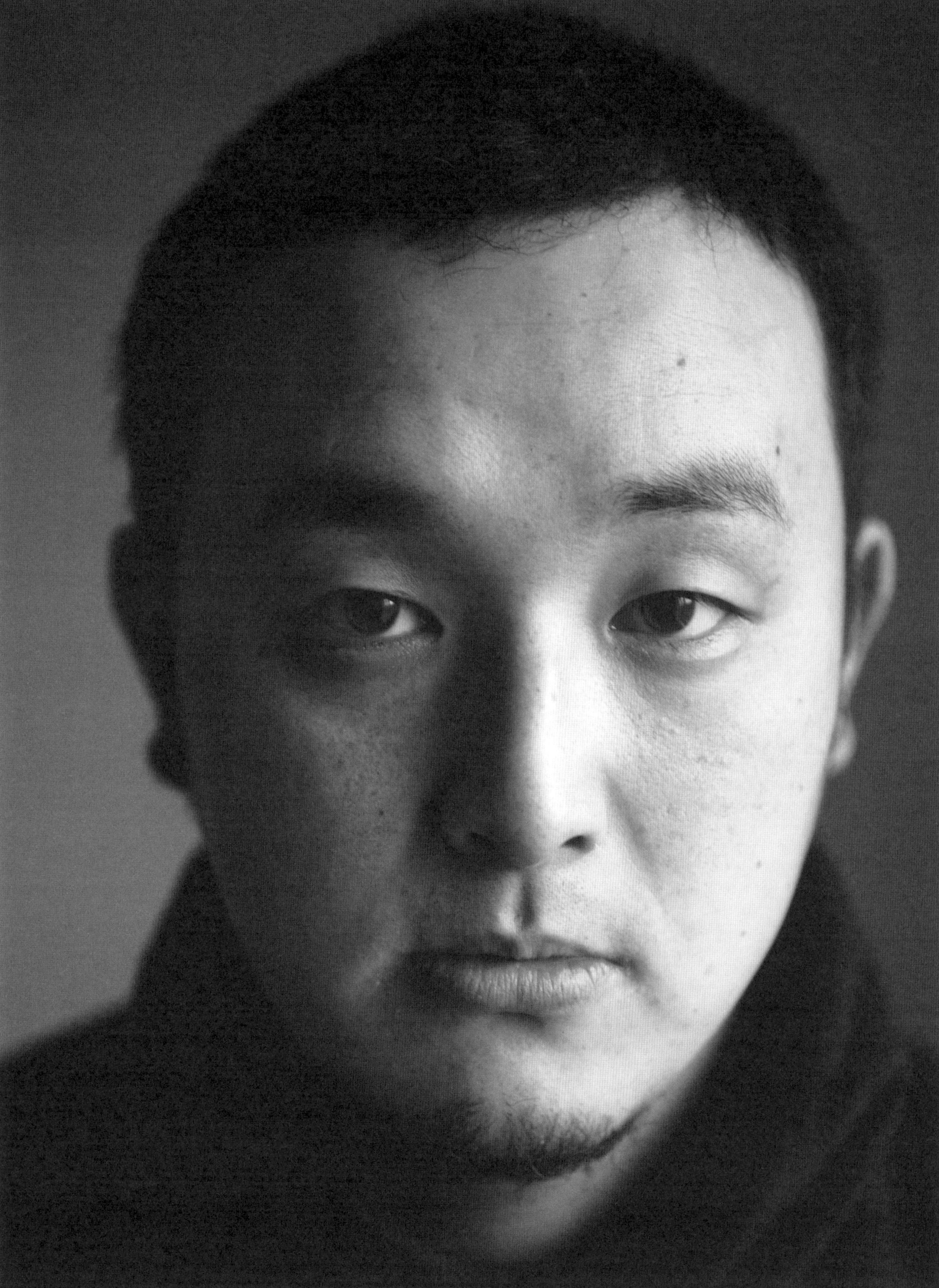

Jin Watanabe
渡辺 仁
39

"There are issues about the work
and the pay and you can't trust anyone
when it comes to safety."

作業とか賃金の問題、安全性も信用
できないですよ。

Why did you not evacuate?
My daughter's grave is here. I had the rest of my family evacuate
but I decided to stay. In fact, it's not as if my business makes huge
profits. In addition to that, there are many risks: high risk, low return.
If my workers wanted to quit, I think that would only be legitimate.
But everyone believes in making the best of the situation and
continues on.

What is your opinion regarding TEPCO and the government?
TEPCO has been a dishonest corporation from the very beginning
and the government has been in cahoots with them. Their version
is the only one out there at the moment and people have been buying
it. TEPCO reports to the government and they leave undisclosed
whatever doesn't sound quite right. I don't understand why the towns'
administration believes them at all.

TEPCO is where the money comes from and I'm working here,
but I want to be clear about what is wrong. How can it be that the
truth about the worker's working circumstances hasn't come to
light after ten months? And even if it did become public, the story
would be forgotten very soon. There are issues about the work
and the pay and you can't trust anyone when it comes to safety.
And on top of that, isn't it absurd that you need the perpetrator's
permission to enter the 20-kilometer exclusion zone? How can that
be? It's because of them that we can't return home anymore.
Even the police contribute to it. If you still go in without permission,
you'll get a 100,000 yen fine. It's absurd.

なぜ地元に残っているんですか？
娘のお墓がここにあるんですよ。家族はみんな避難させたけど、俺だけでも残
ろうって。実際のところ、会社として考えたら、利益の出る仕事じゃありません。
それに伴って危険性も高い。だから、ハイリスク低リターン。もし、従業員から辞め
ましょうよっていう話が出れば、すぐにでも辞めてもいいと思ってます。
でも、皆、地元を何とかしたいっていう思いがあって仕事を続けていますから。

東電と国に対しては、どう思われていますか？
東電は最初から嘘をついてる企業であり、国もそれに乗っかって嘘をついていた
わけじゃないですか。それを信用して、その人たちの情報しか今はないわけですよね。
東電から国に情報がいって、危ないような話は包み隠しながら言うじゃない
ですか。だから、各市町村が、なぜそこまで信用してやっているのかが分からない。
お金の出所は東電で、そこで仕事をさせてもらってますけど、やっぱり間違って
いることは間違ってるって言いたいですよ。なんで作業員の実態を明確に話さ
ないのか、10ヵ月も経っているのに、作業員が陽のあたる所に出てないっていうのは
本当におかしいことだなと。結局それが問題になっても、すぐに終わっちゃうじゃ
ないですか。作業とか賃金の問題、安全性も信用できないですよ。それに、悪い
事をやった会社の許可を持って20キロ圏内に入るっていうのがそもそも
おかしい。なんであの人たちの許可を得て20キロ圏内に入らなくちゃいけないん
ですか。あの人たちのせいで帰れないんでしょ。警察も協力して、入ったら罰金10万円。
そんなの、おかしいじゃないですか。

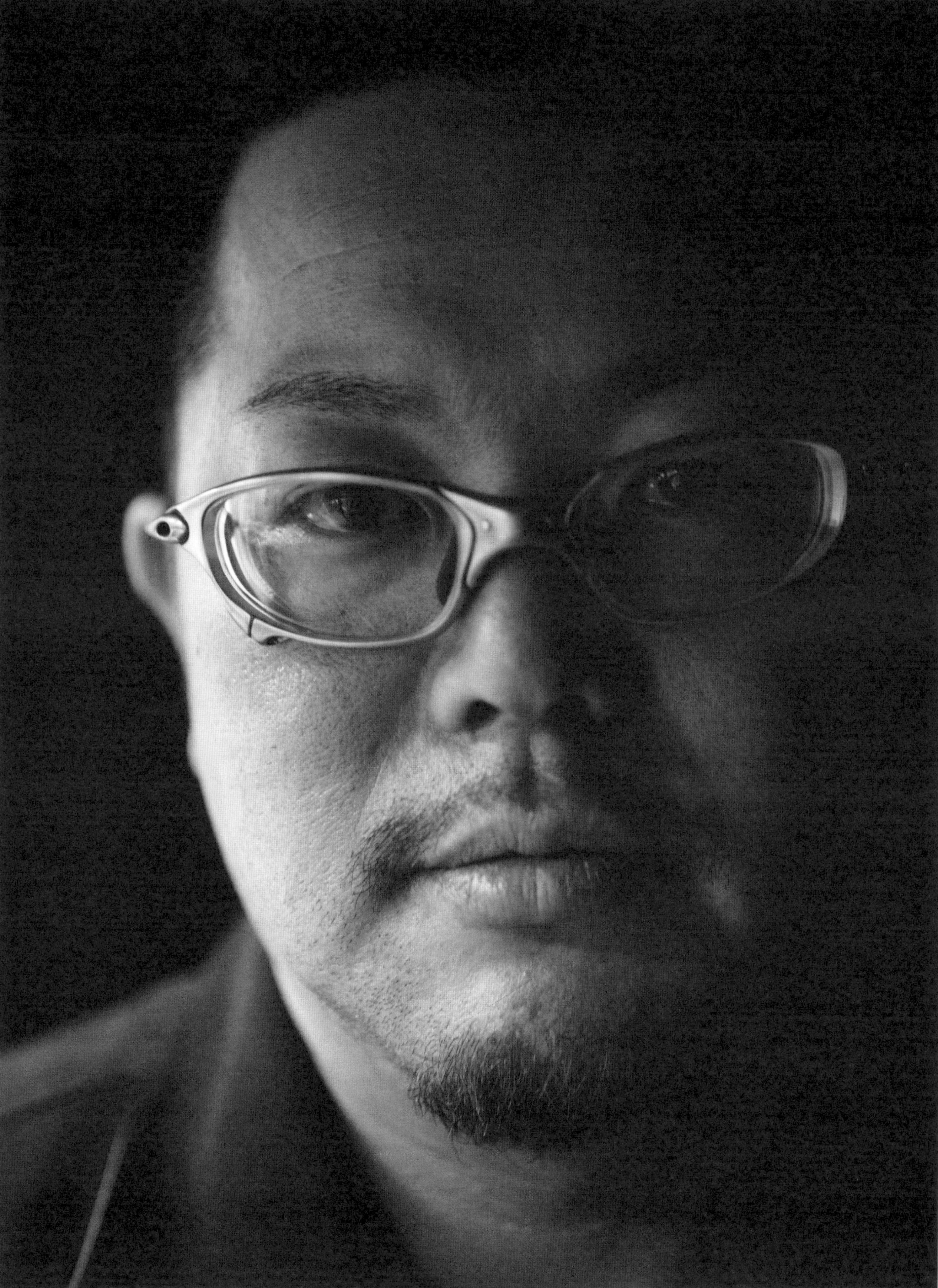

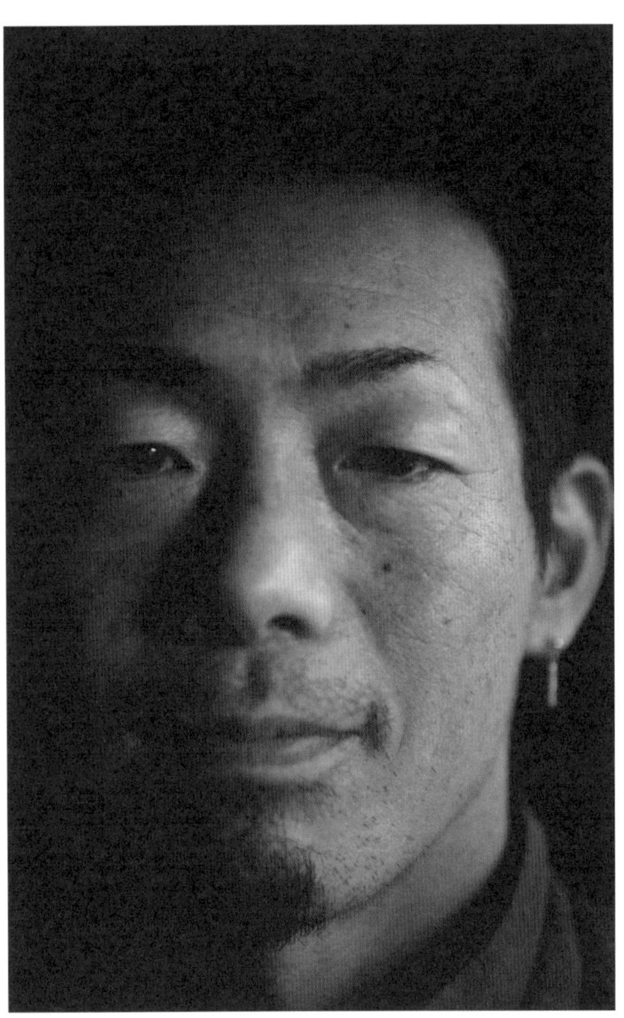

Takeshi Igari
猪狩 猛
39

"What the government and TEPCO
are saying on the news and what they're
actually doing are worlds apart."

国と東電がニュースで言ってることとやってる
ことが全然違うじゃないですか。

What has the situation been like since the accident?
Before the earthquake disaster I worked as a bus driver on
the grounds of the Daiichi plant. My house was located within the
20-kilometer exclusion zone so after the explosion I was forced
to evacuate. I would love to return to my own house and live
life as always but I have no idea what the future will bring. What
the government and TEPCO are saying on the news and what they're
actually doing are worlds apart. I need them to take honest action
and to be clear about how much compensation we will be granted.

January 2012

震災後の状況は？
震災前は1F構内のバスの運転手をしていましたが、20キロ圏内に家があって、
爆発した後に強制避難になりました。自分の家に帰って、今まで通りに生活したい
けど、これから先、全くどうなるか分からない。国と東電がニュースで言ってる
こととやってることが全然違うじゃないですか。本当にやってくれるんだか分からない。
嘘のない行動をして、補償金もどのくらいまで出るのかはっきりしてほい。

2012年1月

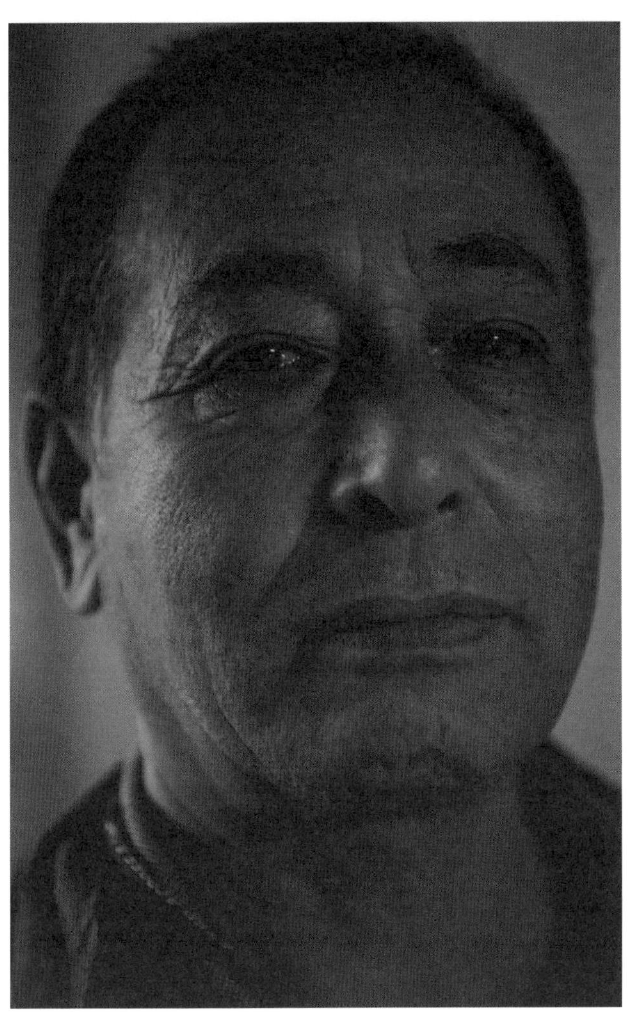

Terumitsu Shiraiwa
白岩 照光
55

"I knew radiation levels were high, but I'm already 55 and my kids are grown, so I thought it was my turn."

放射能が高いってのは分かってましたからね。
でも自分は55歳と年も取ってるしねえ。
子供もある程度大きくなってるから、そろそろ
いいかと思って。

What has the situation been like since the accident?
My workplace was within the 20-kilometer exclusion zone so I lost my job due to the earthquake disaster. I started working in rubble removal at the end of March and came to Daiichi in July.

Were you afraid of entering the Daiichi reactor?
I knew radiation levels were high, but I'm already 55 and my kids are grown, so I thought it was my turn. There's no getting around it, so I decided to be courageous. In the beginning I felt uneasy, but I had experience in construction work and reassured myself that I'd be fine.

How do you feel about the work?
What I was really surprised about was that young people were here as well. On the other hand, nothing would advance if nobody were here. For now, we need to do our best at this and then decontaminate the surroundings and make it a habitable place again. That's my wish. I think that being exposed to radiation at my age is not too bad but those young folks–I think it's intense. They still need to live their lives, get married, have kids. Men my age should be working in there.

January 2012

震災後の状況は？
震災時、職場が20キロ地点にあって仕事を失いました。3月下旬から瓦礫撤去の仕事して、7月から第一原発で仕事を始めました。

1Fに入ることへの恐怖心は？
放射能が高いってのは分かってましたからね。でも自分が55歳と年も取ってるしねえ。子供もある程度大きくなってるから、そろそろいいかと思って。だからこれはしょうがない、やるしかないと思って度胸決めてね。最初はやっぱり不安はありましたよ。でも経験のある土工の仕事だったから、これだったら大丈夫だなあと思って。

働いている中での思いは？
行った時にびっくりしたのは若い人が入ってるってことですね。だからと言って、人が結局いなかったら、いつになっても良くなんないんですよ。まずは現場に行って、今働いてる人たちが一生懸命やって。あとは周りを除染して、とにかく住める地域は住めるような形にしたいです。でも、放射能は私らの年齢だったら少しぐらい浴びてもいいかって思うんですけど、若い人はね。うわあ、すごいなって思いますね。若い人はこれから結婚して子供を作るんだから。やっぱり私らの年齢の人が頑張んないと駄目ですよ。

2012年1月

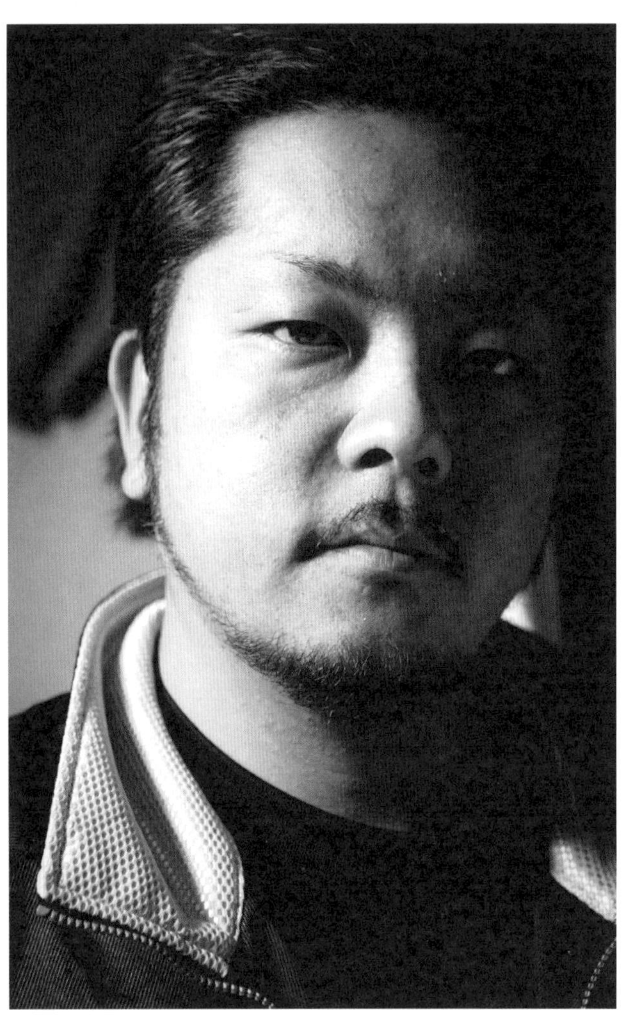

Yoshinori Suzuki
鈴木 良法
33

"Within the 20-kilometer exclusion zone
it feels like a deserted slum,
a no-man's land."

20キロ圏内なんて人のいないスラム街
みたいな感じやん。

What was it like entering the 20-kilometer exclusion zone?
The truth is that I came thinking it's worth putting one's own health
at risk for an income to sustain the family. But seeing the locals
refusing to evacuate, exposed to the radiation, because they want
to stay where they've grown old, the reality of the people who've
remained to live with their animals: that's shocking and intense.
Especially within the 20-kilometer exclusion zone it feels like
a deserted slum, a no-man's land where only buses packed with
workers and other authorized people come and go. That's when
I feel so sorry for the animals that were left behind there, animals that
can't escape even if they wanted to. It must have been so hard for
the people who kept the animals as part of their families to abandon
them, so that at least they had some freedom, instead of locking
them up in a stable.

What are your thoughts after the accident?
Some thought speaking out against nuclear power would get
them unemployed, but I think now everyone's eyes were opened.
If there really was a guarantee that nuclear power is absolutely
safe, they would be continuing the work at the new reactor that
is under construction. But there was a hydrogen explosion. So that
means the government hadn't thought that far and wanted to
build a new one.

November 2011

20キロ圏内に入ってどうでしたか？
実際、自分の体を張ってでも収入があれば家族を養っていけるっていう思い
で来てるけど、避難していない地元の人の姿、線量を浴びるけれども、生まれ育った
場所にいたいっていう現状を見たら受ける衝撃が大きい。特に20キロ圏内
なんて人のいないスラム街みたいな感じやん。人っ子一人いない、作業員が乗った
バスやそこに関係する人間が行き来するためだけの地域。そこに取り残された、
逃げるにも逃げれやん生き物を見ると、可哀想だなってすごい思う。牛舎入れとく
よりも自由があるって放した人の気持ちを考えると、家族と変わらないところがある
んで、もっとつらいんじゃないかなって。

事故後どのように思われていますか？
いつも働いている人間が原発を批判して食いっぱぐれになるやないかという
意見もあったけど、今回でみんなよく分かったと思う。原子力は絶対大丈夫っていう
保証が本当にあったら、今建設中の新たな原発も継続して工事を行っとる。
でも、震災が起きて、水素爆発を起こしたと。国はそこまで考えずに新しい建物を
作ろうと思ってたんかってことですよ。

2011年11月

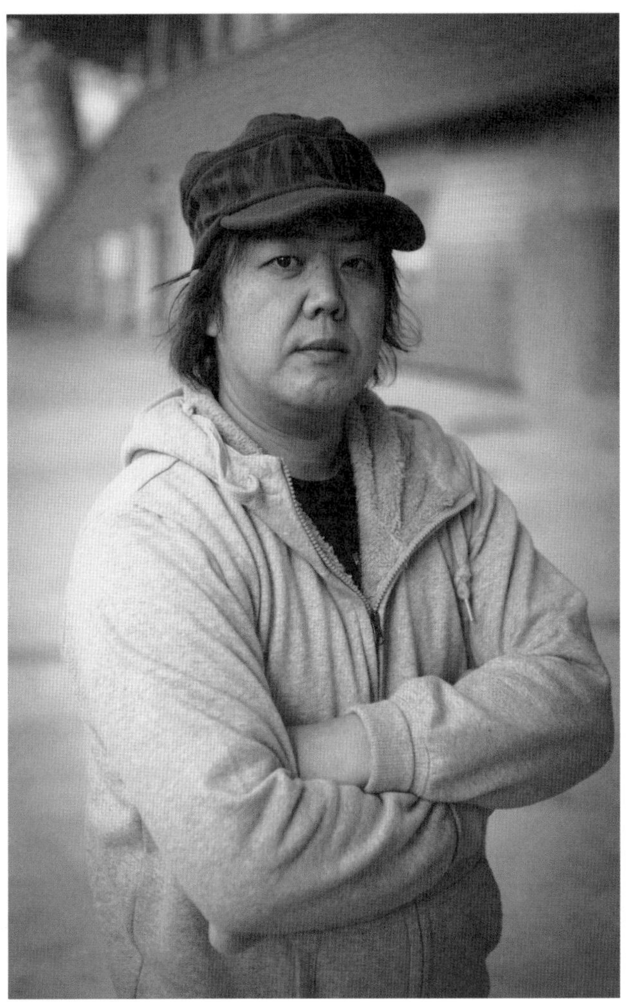

Makoto Takano
高野 信
42

"There is something about being able to tell to future generations that I was there, that I did my best back then."

他の代に変わった時に、あーその頃頑張った
よって後々残せるわけじゃないですか。

When did you first arrive in Fukushima?
This coming August it will have been ten years since the last time I was assigned to Fukushima. Before that I'd been working at reactors in Onagawa, Aomori, or Kashiwazaki, moving from one plant to the other. I had left after having worked at Daiichi and Daini for a long time because I wanted to see other places for myself and I ended up doing land rotations for about a decade.

How did you feel when they first allocated you to Daiichi?
Everyone was very reluctant about going, but for me, Daiichi was where I started working and where I learned the ropes. Also, I was kind of curious about what the inside looked like, and so I thought if no one else wants to go, I will. My company asked me if I had considered working at Daiichi. I replied immediately that I did. So when they asked me to begin that very day, I did. At the end of the day, it's not for Fukushima, not for Japan that I'm working here. At the end of the day, it's for myself. I've always lived here, and there is something about being able to tell to future generations that I was there, that I did my best back then. Daiichi really isn't a place people should be working in. But because there are people who think that something needs to be done the situation has changed quite a bit since the accident.

December 2011

福島にはいつ頃から？
8月に10年ぶりに福島に戻されたんです。それまでは女川、青森、柏崎の方を半年周期で転々と動いてたんです。最初は1Fとか2Fでずっと働いてたんですけど、自分、自らよそも見たくて、ずっと地方周りしてたんです。

一番最初に1Fにって言われた時どんな思いでした？
皆行きたくないって言ってたんですけど、逆に1Fって自分が最初から仕事してて、仕事覚えた場じゃないですか。実際その場所を見てみたいなっていう思いもありましたし、誰も行かないんだったら進んで行こうかなっていう思いはありましたよ。会社の方からも1Fに行く意思はあるかっていう確認はあったんです。もう即答で、ありますよって。地元への思いもありますよ。震災当時でも、行けと言われたら行きました。でもやっぱ福島とか日本のためじゃなくて、自分のためなんですよね。要は、ずっと今までそこで生活してきたわけだから、自分の代じゃなくても他の代に変わった時に、あーその頃頑張ったよって後々残せるわけじゃないですか。なかにはいましたよ。1Fなんか働く場所じゃないって。でも実際何とかしなくちゃいけないっていう人がいるから、震災当時と比べたら大分変わりましたよ。

2011年12月

Katsuhiro Akimoto
秋元 活廣
39

"It was an awkward feeling to enter
the reactor. Cherry blossoms blooming
and birds flying high while you're
hiding behind a mask."

最初に入った時は異様な感じでしたよね。
マスクしながら、マスクの外では桜のつぼみも
膨らんでるし、鳥も飛んでいる。

What was it like entering the reactor after the accident?
I wasn't that afraid. The TV reported x-thousand microsieverts but
working at the reactor I knew the difference between microsieverts
and millisieverts and wasn't too worried. I did make sure not
to inhale anything and wearing a mask is a given for me anyways.
The walls of the shock-absorbing structure had crumbled or
had holes in them but the building itself was fine. Also, there was
a no-entry-zone; so the only place you could take a break were parts
of the pathways on the first and second floor. At first people were
lying down and crammed into a pathway that was two meters wide
to rest. Some were barefoot, others had shoes on. Those were awful
conditions, indeed. Every company got an area marked-off with duct
tape. That situation went on for a while, until July or so.

**Has there been a change in your mental state since
the earthquake disaster?**
Not really, I take work as work. I'm not saving Japan or anything.
I don't think anyone is. Still, it was certainly an awkward feeling
to enter the reactor for the first time in April. Cherry trees blooming
and birds flying high while you're hiding behind a mask. What should
I say, as if there were a different world beyond the mask, maybe
like in an aquarium, separated by a glass wall. I was only wearing
a mask but the difference between the two sides was intriguing.
I've gotten used to it by now, though, a feeling that's hard to grasp.

November 2011

事故後、一番最初に入った時はどうでしたか？
怖さはあまりなかったですね。最初にテレビで報道されてたのは、何千マイクロ
シーベルトとか言うんですけど。結局、原発で働いているとマイクロシーベルト
とミリシーベルトの違いは分かるんで、そんなに大したことないなって。吸い込ま
ないようにマスクするのも当たり前の話なんで。ただ、免震棟も最初は壁が
崩れたり壁に穴が空いてたんですよ。建物自体は大丈夫でしたけど。立ち入り
禁止の部分もあったんです。だから休憩する場所は1階と2階の一部の通路だけ。
最初は2メーターぐらいの幅の通路に、人が横たわったりして休んでました。
そこを裸足で歩いている人もいるし、靴で歩いている人もいて、あれはかなり劣悪で
したね。通路にガムテープ貼って、会社の名前を区画して、大分続いてましたよね。
7月ぐらいまではそうでしたよ。

震災前と震災後で働く心境の変化はありましたか？
特にないですね。仕事だという意識で働いてますから。別に俺が日本を救うん
だなんてのは。実際、そんな人いないんじゃないかと思います。でも、4月に一番最初
に入った時は異様な感じでしたよね。マスクしながら、マスクの外では桜の
つぼみも膨らんでるし、鳥も飛んでいる。何となく、何て言うんですかね。マスク越し
の別の世界みたいな感じでした。水族館的な感じというか。ガラスの向こう
とガラスのこっち。実際はマスクしかしてないですけど。マスクのあっちとこっちは
違うっていう、異様な感じでしたね。まあ、だんだん慣れてきましたけど。
何とも言えぬ異様な感じでした。

2011年11月

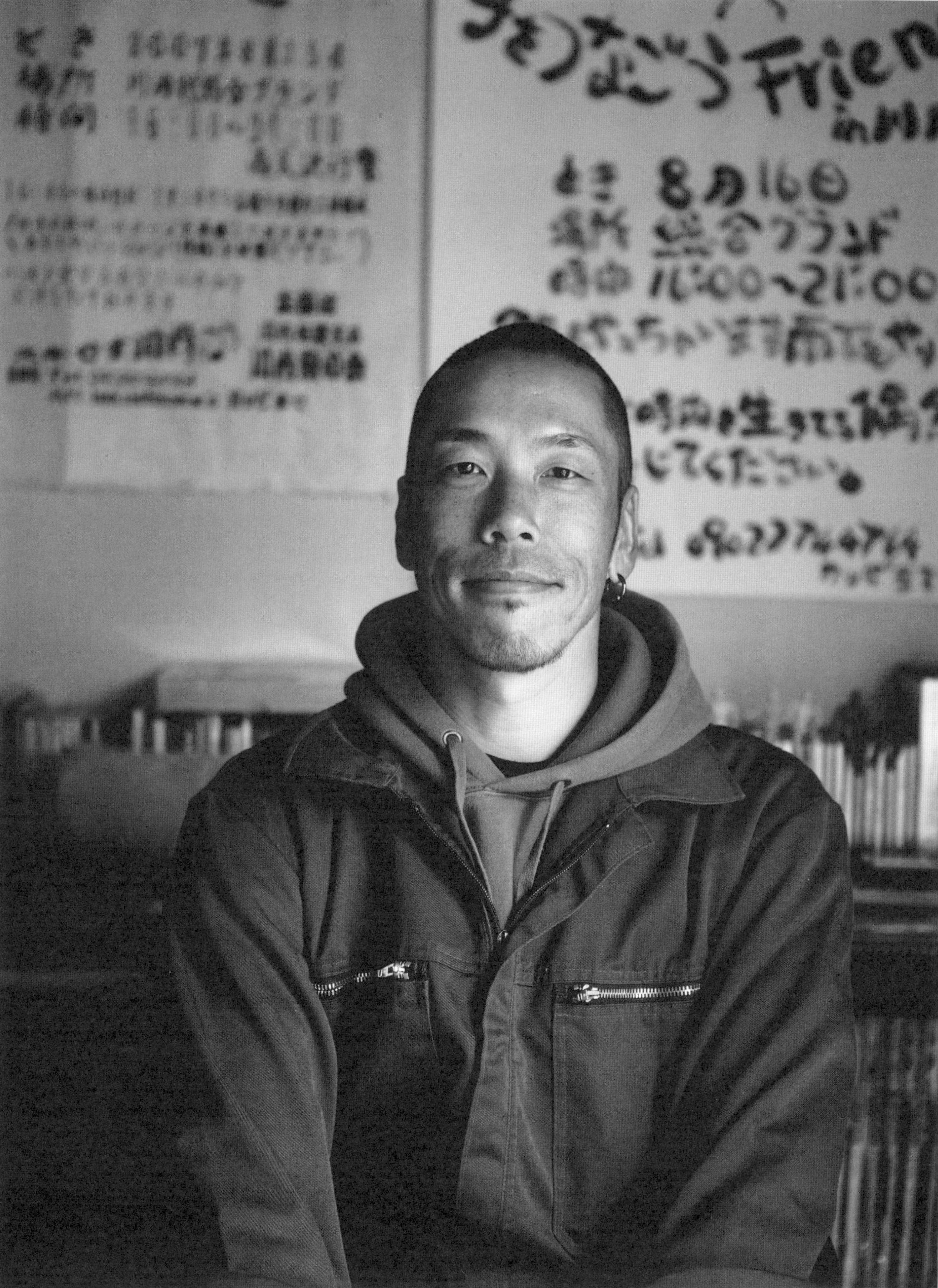

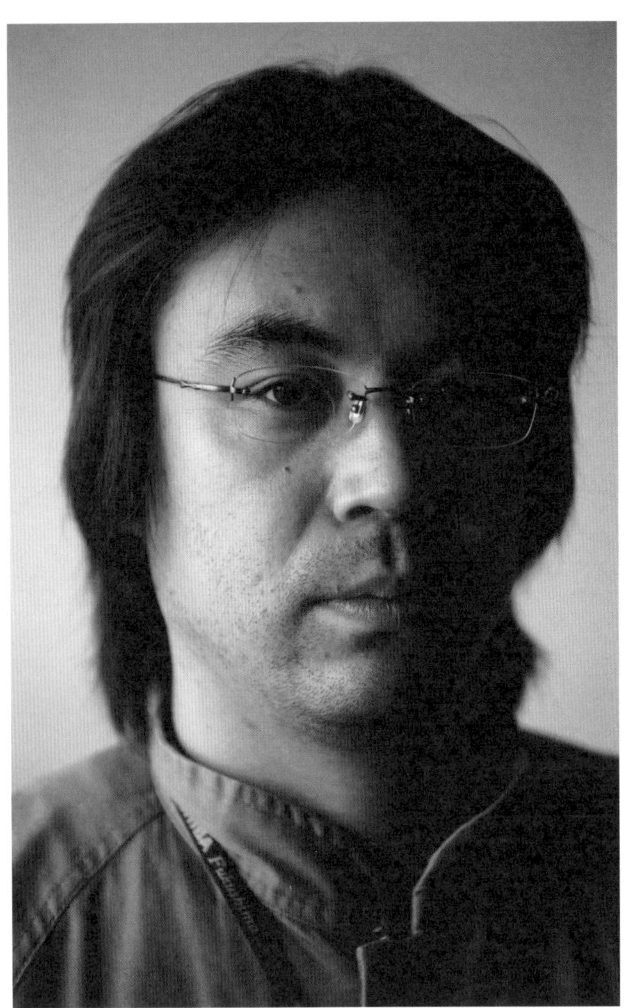

Kazuhiro Arasawa
荒沢 和宏
31

"Somebody has to do it, so why shouldn't that 'somebody' be myself, I thought."

誰かがやんなくちゃいけないし。
だったら、その誰かになればいいんじゃ
ないのって。

What has changed since the accident?
I don't think I had a real sense of responsibility for my job before the earthquake. Running regular checkups and tests, just to have it done. That's the way I was thinking, but then the earthquake hit, the explosion took place, and naturally restoration work begins. That's when that same reactor demands new work depending on the site, methods change. The experts are really needed to handle the situation. I didn't leave. I stayed in Iwaki all the time, always on call. I had been at the Daiichi reactor for a decade already, inspecting it and running tests. Yes, I was afraid because you can't see the radiation but if everyone is just afraid–somebody has to do it, so why shouldn't that "somebody" be myself, I thought.

Will you continue working at the Fukushima Daiichi reactor?
Well, I do have the knowledge, the skills, and the experience on the worksite. I know where everything is. Of course, there are always people who can work but when it comes to the crucial points, it's only us, the old-timers at Daiichi who can sort it out.

December 2011

震災後に何が変わりましたか？
震災前って、そんなに責任感とかなかったと思うんですよ。定検行ったり、作業タンタンとこなして、やることやっとけばいいやっていう気持ち。実際そうだったんです。でも、震災があって爆発したりして、当然復旧が始まるじゃないですか。となると、同じ発電所でもサイトによって仕組みが違ってたりとかして、やり方も変わるんで、やっぱり知ってる人間がやらなければ駄目だろって。それで私は逃げなかったんですよ。ずっといわき市にいて、呼ばれると思って。1Fの方も10年近くやってて、ずっと試験とかやってまして。目に見えるもんじゃないから怖いっていうのはありましたけど、皆が皆怖い怖いって言ってても、誰かがやんなくちゃいけないし。だったら、その誰かになればいいんじゃないのって。

今後も福島第一原発で働かれますか？
知識と技術を持ってますからね。サイトでの経験もそうだし。仕事できる人は当然いるんですけど。じゃあ、どこに何があるって、場所までとなると、第一原発で長年働いている、うちらにしか分からないこともあるし。

2011年12月

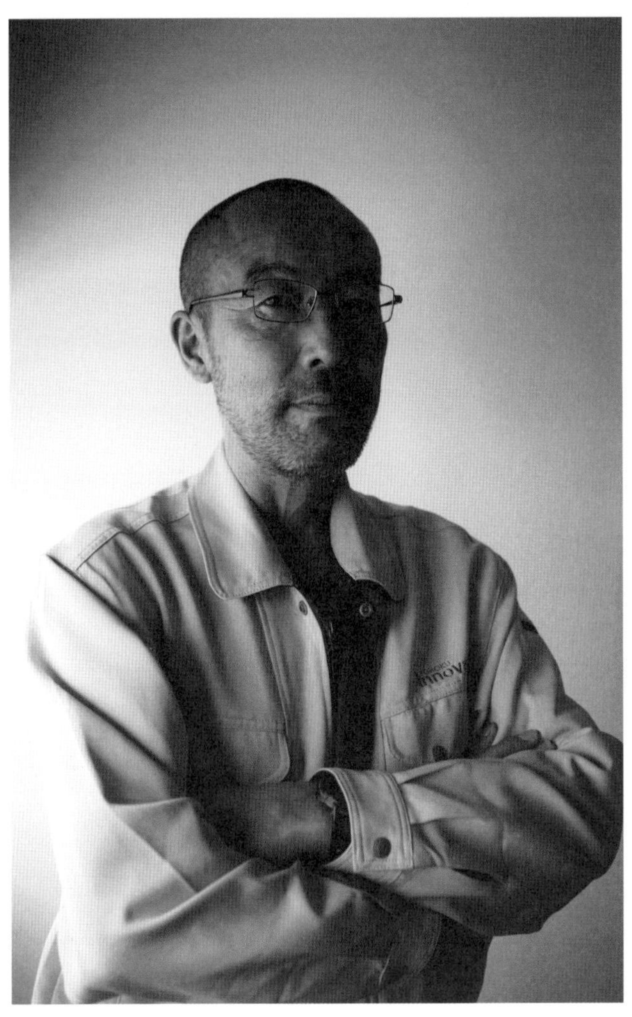

Yoshihiro Kimura
木村 好宏
46

"My perception's gotten so distorted. I used to think, 'You had better get out of here! Radiation levels are high.'"

感覚が麻痺してくるんですよね。そのあたり線量高いから走れーみたいな。

What are the working conditions at the Daiichi reactor like?
I entered the reactor for the first time only after the disaster. Can't tell you what it used to be like. But I can tell it's not business as usual when I see all the rubble, the wrecked buildings. So I can't do anything but obey my superior calling on me to do this and that. My perception's gotten so distorted. I used to think, "You had better get out of here! Radiation levels are high." But having been exposed to one or two millisieverts at once makes everything appear low now. "Micro"? No big deal.

Will you continue working at the Daiichi reactor?
Well, for the moment, the restorations are advancing well without setbacks.

December 2011

第一原発の仕事の状況は？
実際第一原発に入ったのは震災後が初めてなんですよ。元はどうだったかは分からないけど、普通じゃねえっていうのは、瓦礫だのぶっ壊れた建物見ちゃうと。先輩のあれやれこれやれって言うのに従うしかないじゃない。線量食らってるとだんだん感覚が麻痺してくるんですよね。そのあたり線量高いから走れーみたいな。1回に1ミリ2ミリ食らっちゃうと、今なんか低く感じちゃうんですよね。だから、マイクロとか聞いちゃうと感覚がね。別にいいんじゃね。みたいな。

これからも第一原発で働かれますか？
後退はしてない。着実に前進してるからね。

2011年12月

Minoru Tsuchida
土田 実
31

"As an evacuee you get money without doing anything, but I don't like not being independent."

避難してると、何もしてなくてもお金が
入ってくる。それを当てにして自立しないのが
嫌だった。

What was the situation at the time of the disaster?
I was at the Daiichi reactor. The tsunami came to a halt 200 meters before my house, which left it relatively undamaged but it's only 3.8 kilometers to the power plant, so my family, all four of us, moved from one evacuation center to the next for four months until moving to Iwaki in August.

How come did you return to your former work?
As an evacuee you get money without doing anything, through donations and temporary payments, but I don't like not being independent. I gladly received some aid in the beginning but how would that have gone on? Living as a charity case? I wanted work and looked for a job when luckily my former boss asked me to return to the company. And so I did in September.

What are your plans for the future?
The kids suffer most from these circumstances so I wanted them to be able to settle down and for me to return to my old position. We probably won't be able to return to Futaba in the near future but I want to build us a house as soon as possible without the kids having to change schools and get their grandparents to live with us. That's my new vision.

December 2011

震災当時の状況は？
当時は1Fにいました。うちは津波が200メーター手前で止まって、そんなに被害があったわけではなかったけど、原発から直線で3.8キロだったので、それから4ヵ月、家族4人で避難所を渡り歩いて、8月にいわき市に来ました。

なぜ元の職場に戻られたのですか？
避難してると義援金とか仮払金とか、何もしてなくてもお金が入ってくるんですよね。今もそうなんでしょうけど。それを当てにして自立しないのが嫌だった。だから多少は手助けしてもらいましたけど、それで、義援金とか当てにして生活してたらどうしようもないなと。やっぱり、仕事したいなって探したんですけれどもね。元いた会社の親方が連絡してくれて、戻って来いっていうことで出戻りさせてもらったのが9月に入ってからです。

今後はどうされますか？
子供がこんな状況で振り回されるのが、一番可哀想で。いわきで落ち着いて前の仕事に戻りたいって、もうそれだけでしたね。だからこの先も双葉町には帰れないだろうけど、今住んでいる近くで、学校変わらなくてもいい場所に早く家を建てて、親父とお袋と一緒にひとつ屋根の下でっていうのが、これからの理想ですね。

2011年12月

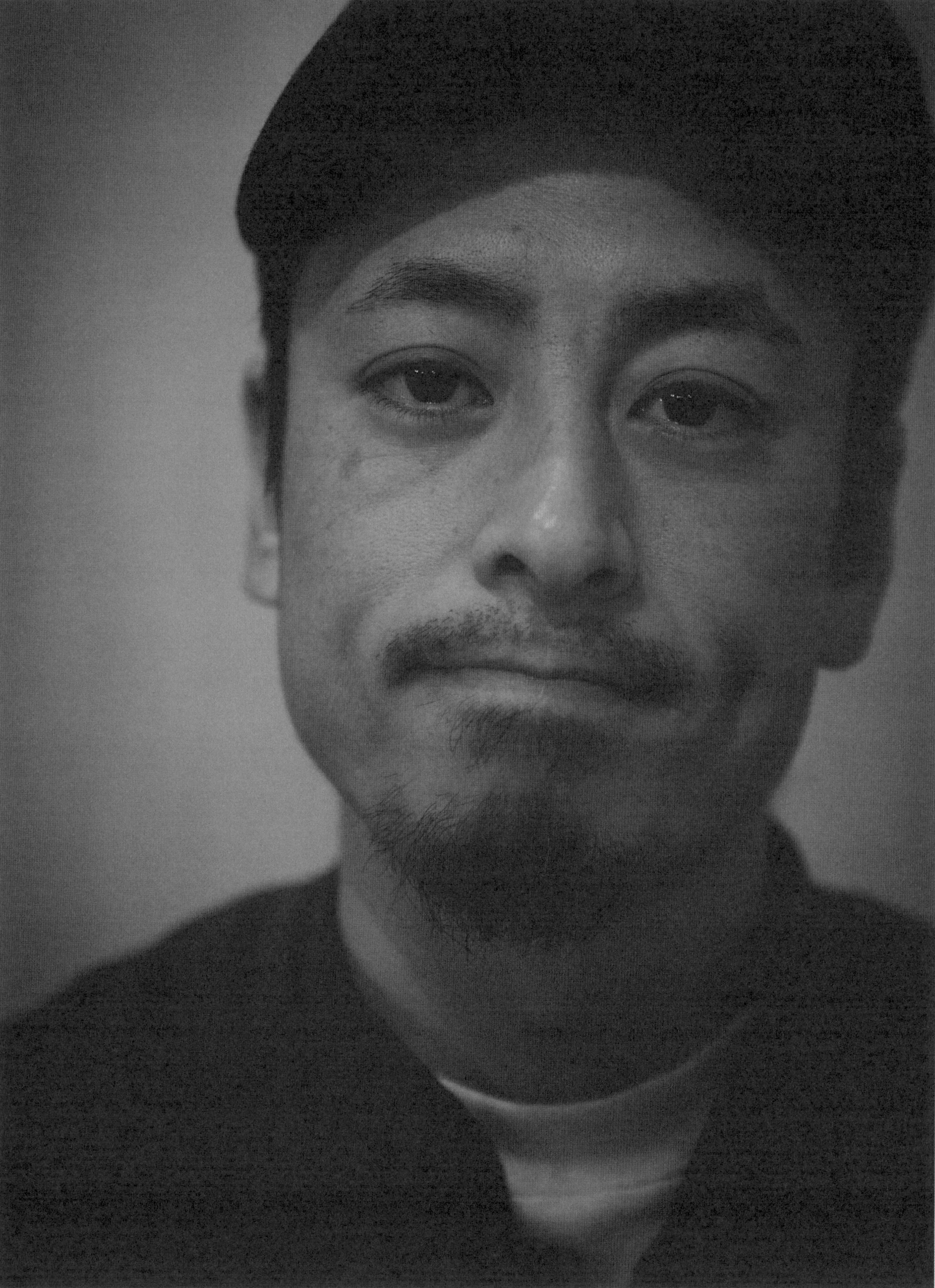

Hiroaki Niizuma
新妻 浩昭
51

"If my being here means that all
the work can get done, exposing myself
to radiation would be worth it."

俺が行って、全部が終了するんだったら
なんぼ線量食ったっていいって。

Why did you start working at the nuclear reactor?
It's an odd story but there weren't any employment opportunities
within Futaba District before we got the power plant. The same
is true of Onagawacho in Miyagi Prefecture. That's why there were
even school field trips to Daiichi's Service Hall when the plant
was newly built. When I was in high school, I took an employment
test at an electric company and the worksite at that time just
happened to be the nuclear power plant. So I've been working in
this industry for about thirty years now. Of course, I've worked
at thermal power stations as well, but I've spent two entire decades
at the Fukushima plant.

What is Daiichi like after the earthquake disaster?
If I compare current radiation levels with the ones before the disaster,
they differ by two or three orders of magnitude. I used to enter
the containment building for inspections, an area with slightly higher
radiation levels, and be alarmed about 0.01 millisievert. That's the
highest radiation level I had been exposed to in 20 years of work. But
now we're talking about 10 millisieverts! Even if it were 1 millisievert
per day, you can't work for more than one month. You use up
your annual allowance in a month's time. There no way you can
make a living that way. Given that neither TEPCO nor the other
companies will take care of you, we don't want to enter those highly
contaminated places either. If there were other jobs waiting in line,
I wouldn't mind, but on the other hand, if my being here means that
all the work can get done, exposing myself to radiation would be
worth it. But that's not the way this game works.

原発での仕事を始めた理由は？
変な話、双葉郡って原子力が来るまでは地元に仕事なんてなかったのよ。
女川町（宮城県）もそうなんですけど。俺らの小学校の頃に第一原発が出来たん
だけど、その頃の遠足っていうのが、第一原発のサービスホールだったの。
俺は高校の時に就職試験受けた先が電気工事だったんだけど、そこの現場がたま
たま原発っていうだけの話で、30年ぐらいやってる。もちろん、火力も経験
しているんだけど、まるまる20年は福島原発の仕事をしてるよ。

震災後の状況はどうですか？
以前入っていた時の線量と比べたら、桁が100倍、1000倍違う。だって検査の時、
ちょっと線量の高い格納容器にも入ったけれど、俺らなんて、0.01ミリシーベルト
でさえ、何だこれって大騒ぎだった。そんな所で作業したことぐらいしかない。
20年もやっていて、ほぼゼロだもん。なのに今は10ミリとかさ、毎日1ミリ
食ったって1ヵ月しか働けないし、1ヵ月で1年の仕事が終わっちゃう。それじゃ
生活できないじゃん。メーカー、電力さんが生活を見てくれるわけじゃないしさ。
そしたら自分たちも線量の高い所に行きたくない。そこ終わって、次の仕事、次の仕事
ってあるんだったら構わないけど。もちろん俺が行って、全部が終了するん
だったら、なんぼ線量食ったっていいって、そういう気持ちもあるけど、ただそういう
場合じゃないでしょ。

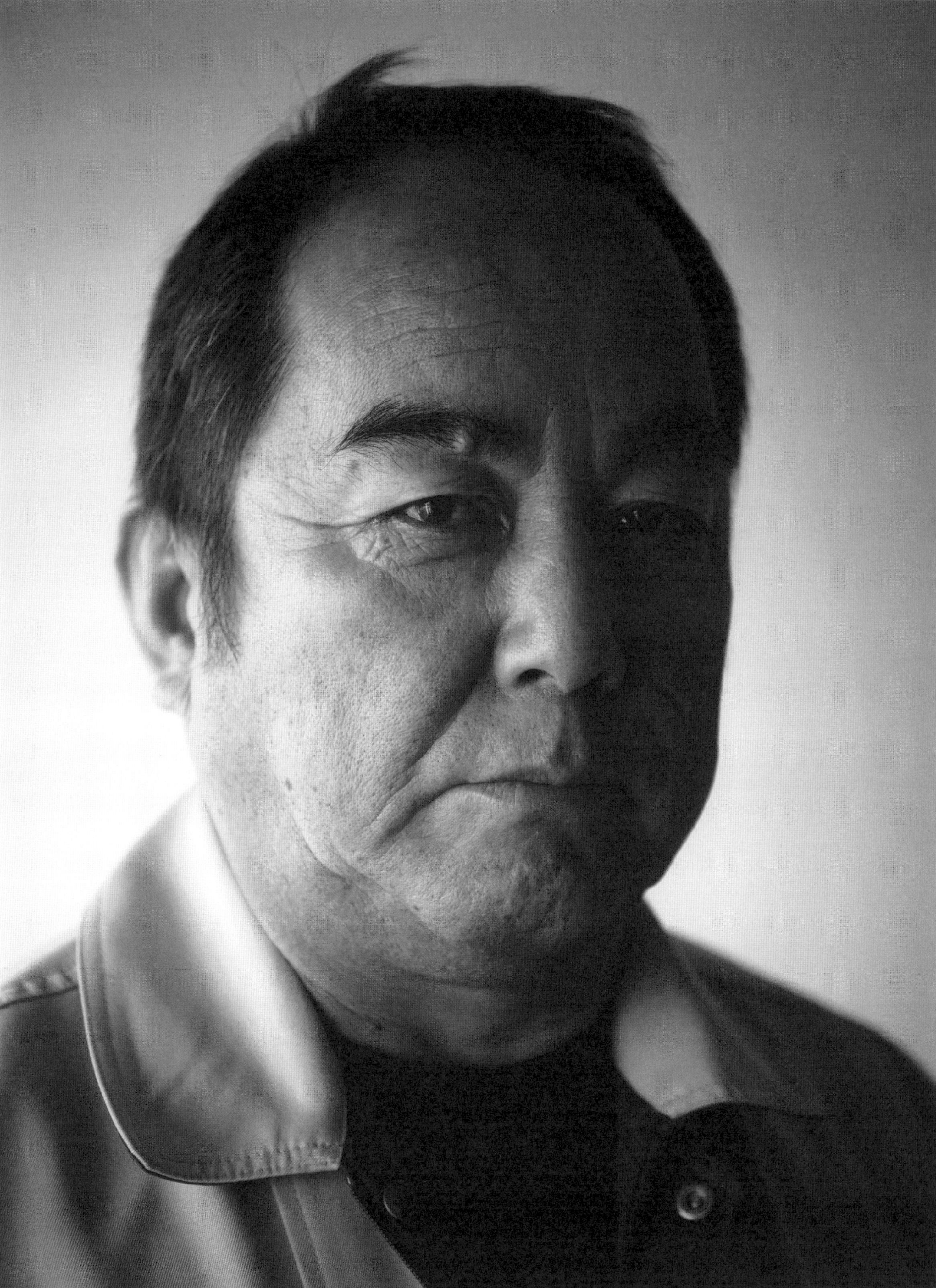

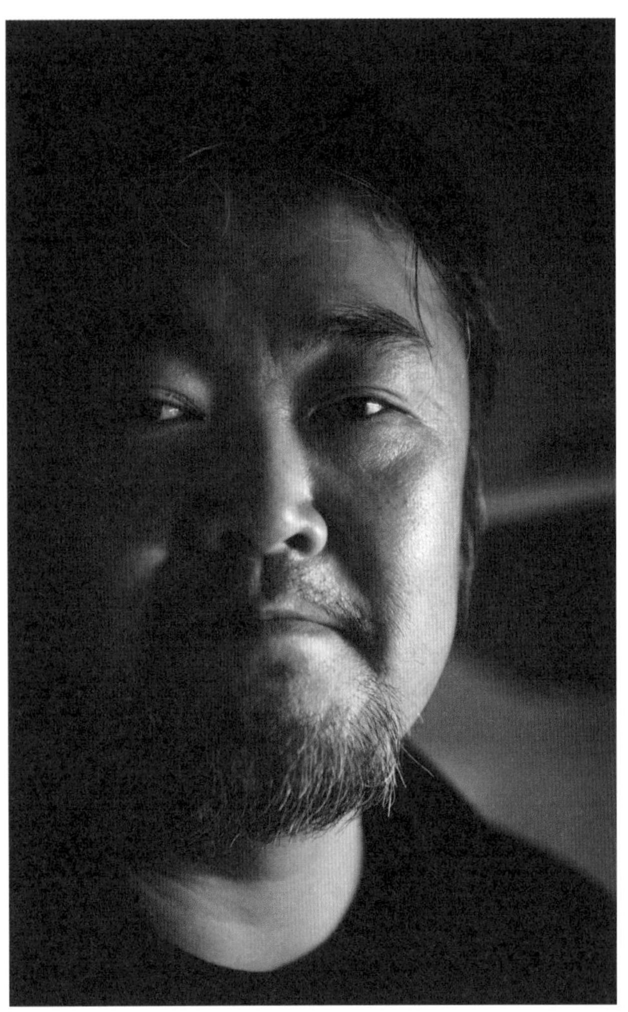

Seiji Nakamura
中村 誠治
40

"I'm not afraid about shortening my life expectancy due to being exposed to radioactivity, but I have concerns regarding the future."

一概に、放射線被曝したから、寿命が縮まるんじゃないかという怖さはない。ただし、将来的にどうなのかって思うけど。

Why are you at the Fukushima Daiichi plant?
I was at a nuclear reactor in Aomori and about a week before finishing up the inspection, my boss asked me to recruit members from the staff and to go to Fukushima. He didn't know the details about the work but that people were urgently needed for support. Personally, I had worked at Daiichi some years before and I was blown away by the sight of the reactor. That was my first impression.

Were you afraid?
I'm not afraid about shortening my life expectancy due to being exposed to radioactivity, but I have concerns regarding the future. We're doing repair work on our own initiative here, so we can't waste our time being fearful. We just have to do this, we just have to. If we don't, it's just going to get put off and become the product of government policies, going backwards with one thing after the other not working out. That's why I've come here, hoping to be of actual use. Nothing will change if you just try to escape from work. Also, some of the workers I've brought are already older, but four of them are in their twenties and thirties. I have a responsibility to get them back safely. I tell them over and over about the dangers but other than that we sit together casually when we get back to our rooms and drink.

December 2011

なぜ福島第一に？
青森県にある原発で、定検の作業が終わる1週間ぐらい前に、社長が今自分が連れて来ている作業員からメンバー募って、福島行ってくれって。作業の内容は分からない、とにかく人がいるから応援に行ってくれって言われたんです。私自身、何年も前に1Fで作業したことがあるんで、見た時はこんなにひどいのかって、自分でも唖然としましたね。それが第一印象でした。

怖さはありましたか？
一概に、放射線被曝したから、寿命が縮まるんじゃないかという怖さはない。ただし、将来的にどうなのかって思うけど。自分らで収束作業やってるので、怖いって言ってたら仕事になんないし。だから皆そうだと思いますよ。ひどいけれどやらなきゃ。まずはやらなきゃ。やらなかったら、どんどんどんどん先延ばしになってくことなんで。そうなると、まるっきり国の政策じゃないけど、後ずさりして、あれ駄目、これ駄目ってやってたら、なるものもならないし。俺はそう思うから自分でも来たし、どうにかできないかなって。仕事から逃げてたら何もならないしね。それとまあ、今連れて来てるメンバーには年配の方もいますが、その他4人は20代、30代なんですよ。そいつらを無事に返してやること、それが俺の仕事だと思ってます。危険だっていうことに関しては口うるさく言うけれども、それ以外のことに関しては何も言わないし、部屋に帰ってくれば皆無礼講で、お互いねえ、杯傾むけながら飲んでます。

2011年12月

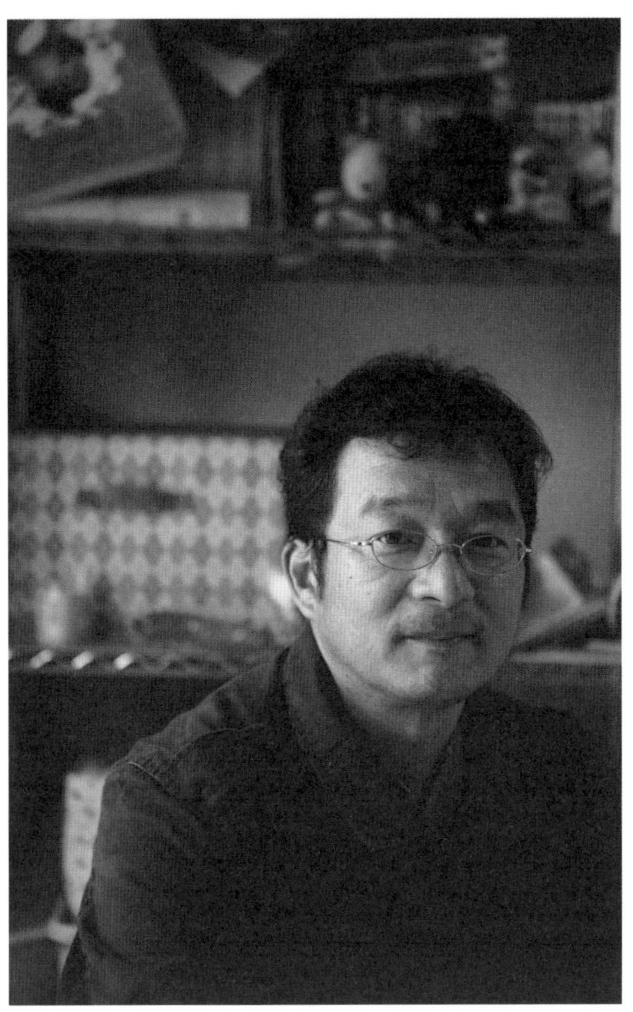

Takayuki Takeuchi

武内 孝之
48

"I was told that it was going to get
seriously dangerous if the power wasn't
reconnected. That if we go in now,
the city could possibly be saved."

今電気つながないとやばいらしいよって
話になって。今行けば町救われる
かもしんないって。

Why are you working at the nuclear power plant?
I was offered the job by my neighbor's company about six months
before the disaster, with the assurance that I could work there
until I'm 65. It was just about when I got used to working in the reactor
when the quake hit. A couple of days later I was told that it was
going to get seriously dangerous if the power wasn't reconnected
very soon. That if we go in now, the city could possibly be saved.
I had been working as a firefighter to help assist in evacuations
so I had no clue about the circumstances at the reactor. But I went.
Back then, that was the spirit. I had to do something.

How do you feel at the evacuation center now?
It's no good getting used to life at the evacuation center where you
are given everything. So I wonder if it would be possible to compile
the thoughts and feelings of evacuated? Free from any governmental
bias, just to trigger a grassroots movement.

December 2011

なぜ原発で働いていたんですか？
震災の半年ぐらい前に、近所の人がやってる会社から「65歳まで働けるよ」
と勧められて。ちょうど仕事に慣れてきた頃に地震があったんです。何日後かに、
今電気つながないとやばいらしいよって話になって。今行けば町救われる
かもしんないって。消防団活動で避難の手伝いとかしてたので、状況全く分からな
かったんだけど、その流れで行ったんです。当時はそんな雰囲気だったんですよ。
何かしなくちゃなんねえんだって。

今、避難所ではどういうお気持ちですか？
避難所生活で、貰うことに慣れてしまうのは良くないことです。自分らで何かをしようっ
ていう動きを作り出すために、警戒区域から避難した人にしか分からない思いを、
行政とか議員さんとか抜きに、底辺の意見の文集というか、そんなものを作れない
かなって。今は思っていたりします。

2011年12月

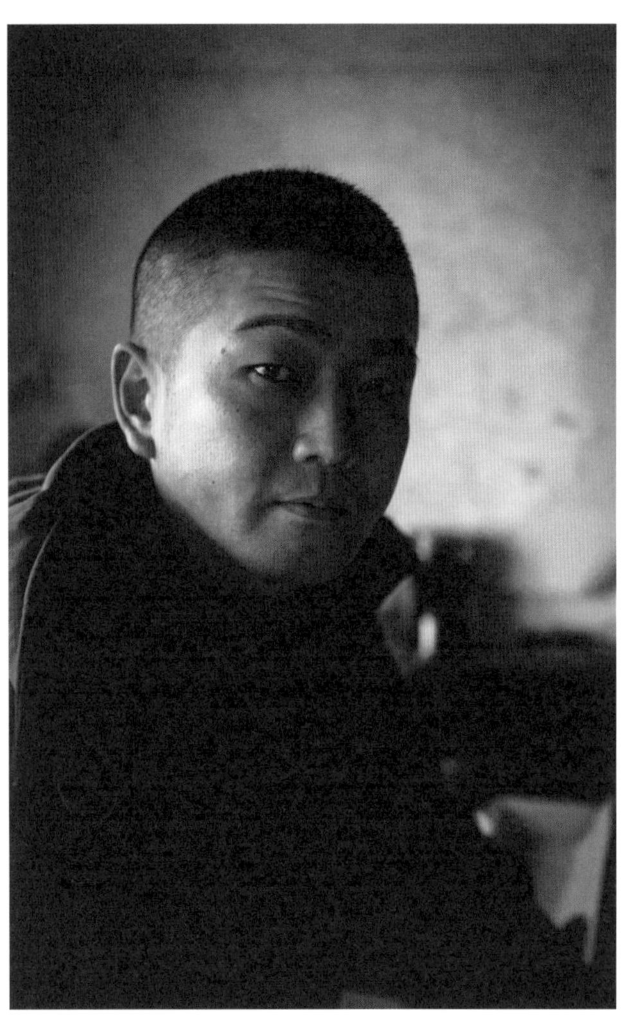

Satoshi Kurita
栗田 覚士
35

"I'm slowly but surely getting contaminated"

私自身も内部被曝が当然少しずつ
進行してます。

Why are you working at the Daiichi reactor?
In my younger years, I was in the Self-Defense Forces and
I served as an official in the reserves until I started working at the
reactor. But I resigned because I wasn't able to fulfill my training
duties anymore. Before, I was working as a "salary man" in property
maintenance but ever since the earthquake disaster I've been
doing volunteer work in Iwate and Miyagi. During all my time with
the Self Defense Forces I was trained to protect the country and the
people. This deeply rooted work ethic of mine was the main reason
for me to come and work at the reactor. I thought I would have
an identity problem if I didn't. You can't make a living off volunteering,
so now I work as an employee for a subcontractor.

What is the current situation like?
I'm slowly but surely getting contaminated myself, but in early
July there were many young people in their twenties who
prided themselves in the amount of radiation they've been over-
exposed to.

December 2011

なぜ原発で働いているのですか？
私は若い時に自衛隊にいて、原発で働くまでは即応自衛官として二足のわらじで
生活していました。でも、現在は訓練出頭義務に応じられないため、退役しました。
以前はビル管理会社のサラリーマンでしたが、震災後は岩手や宮城で
ボランティアの活動をしていました。原発での仕事を決めた一番の理由は、自衛官の
職業意識というか、国と人を守るという訓練をずっとしてきたので、ここで行かなかっ
たら自分自身のアイデンティティがおかしくなってしまうと思ったからです。
でもボランティアでは食べていけないので、下請け業者の社員として働いています。

現状はどうですか？
私自身も内部被曝が当然少しずつ進行してますが、7月初期はもう20代の
人がいっぱいいるような状況で。中では線量浴び過ぎを自慢してしまうような雰囲
気もありましたね。

2011年12月

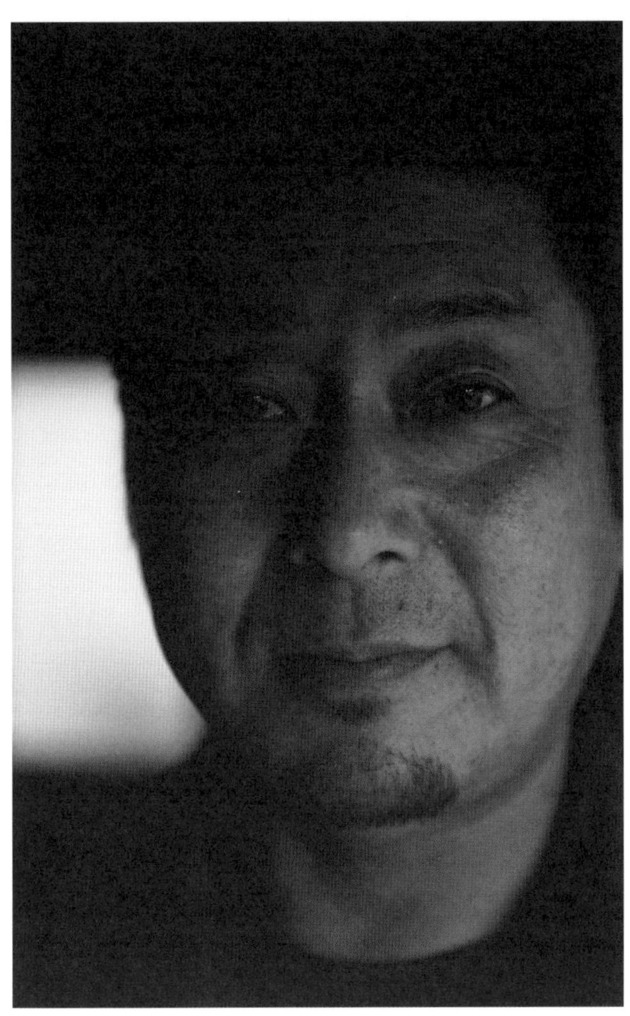

Hiroaki Kikuchi
菊池 広明
46

"I need to feed my family and right now I think working at the reactor is the only long-term employment opportunity."

家族を養っていかなくちゃいけない
ですよね。現状では雇用は原発しかないと
思うんです。

What was your situation like after the accident?
Before the earthquake disaster I worked at a golf course located within the 20-kilometer exclusion zone. After having evacuated to Kanagawa Prefecture I came back to Daiichi in October and am taking advantage of my previous experience in construction.

What about your work at the reactor and the current situation?
I wasn't afraid before going but my father worked at the nuclear power plant since he was young and always told me to never to go to the reactor, ever. He must have known what he was talking about. But now I'm terribly afraid. I think about how I would die if there were another big earthquake or something. As much as it may be cooling down, what if it stops again, what if there's another explosion? I'm working right in front of it now, so I would die for sure. But to be honest, I need to feed my family as well, and right now I think working at the reactor is the only long-term employment opportunity there is. My village is within the emergency evacuation zone and there's no one living in the houses around there. My family has evacuated so I always return alone to the house. I feel lonely going home alone after work when it's pitch-black outside. If I didn't have a house here, I think I would leave and get out of Fukushima Prefecture. But the land I inherited from my parents is here and I can't just abandon the place.

January 2012

震災後どうされていましたか？
震災前は20キロ圏内のゴルフ場に勤務してました。神奈川で避難生活を送った後、以前就いていた土木の経験を活かし、10月から福島第一原発での仕事を始めました。

原発での仕事と現在の状況は？
行く前には恐怖心はありませんでしたが、うちの親父は若いうちから原発で働いていたので、よく言われてたんですよ。原発にだけは絶対行くなって。長かったんで分かってたんでしょうね。でも今はすごく怖いですよ。もしあそこで今度大きい地震とか何かあったら、俺死ぬだろうなって。今あんな半端な状態じゃないですか。冷却してるって言っても、また冷却止まっちゃったり、爆発したりしたら、すぐ目の前で仕事してるから完璧に死ぬなぁって。でも正直なところ、家族を養っていかなくちゃいけないですよね。現状では雇用は原発しかないと思うんです。今、私の集落は緊急避難地域にあるので、周りの家は誰も住んでいないんですよ。家族が避難しているので一人で家に居るんですけど。寂しいですよ、仕事が終わって真っ暗な集落に帰るっていうのは。もしここに家がなければ県外に行くと思います。でも自分の親から頂いた土地がここにあるんで、捨てて行きたくないですね。

2012年1月

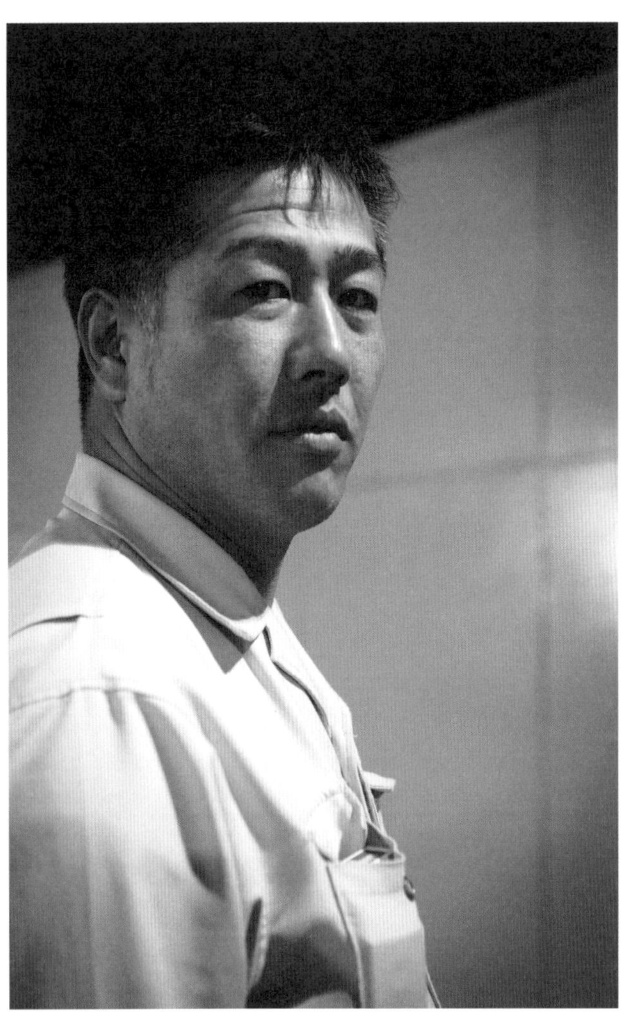

Kazuki Sato
佐藤 一喜
37

"What I saw was worlds apart from what I had seen and heard through the media."

映像で見る情報と全く違いましたよ。

What was it like entering the Daiichi reactor for the first time?
To be honest, I did not want to go. But despite my unease and unwillingness I did, because, after all, it's work. So I went and what I saw was worlds apart from what I had seen and heard through the media. To see it with your own eyes was so intense, I didn't want to get too close. Now you've come, you can't but go whole hog. Well, I've gotten used to it. I guess everyone does. You go in several times and you get used to it. On duty there's not much you can do other than to wear exposure suits. I could have either idled at the evacuation center or worked just because I have to work. My family didn't want me to go. What should I say? I didn't either.

What are your plans for the future?
If there is a possibility of returning to our house and if I can get a job, I think we could stay near Iwaki. The government claims we will be able to go back, that's why I have some hope. Before the disaster I wouldn't even have considered this, but now I think about how I don't want to mark the end of an era by abandoning the land I've inherited from my parents and grandparents. However, thinking of the children, Iwaki's radiation levels aren't low. They say it's 0.15 microsieverts, but they take their measurements above pre-washed concrete where levels are lower.

December 2011

震災当時の状況は？
俺は正直行きたくなかったですね。嫌だな、気持ち悪いな、と思いながらも行ったんです。仕事だから。行ったら行ったで、映像で見る情報と全く違いましたよね。目の前で見れば、うおーすごいことになってるなって。正直、近づくのも嫌でしたけれどもね。でもね、変な話ひっこみつかないですよね。来た以上はやるしかないっていうか。誰でもそうだと思うんですけど、何回も入っていると慣れちゃいますよね。作業には重装備ぐらいしかできないんですけど。家族にはできるなら行ってほしくないって言われましたけど。このまま避難所にいてもっていう気持ちと、仕事をしなくちゃいけないなっていうのがあったんですよね。

今後はどうされますか？
仕事があって、家に戻れる可能性があるんだったら、避難しているいわき市あたりに居てもいいと思うんです。政府が絶対帰れるなんて言うから、期待も持っちゃってます。親と、じいちゃんばあちゃんから貰った土地を手放したくないと言うか、俺の代で終わらせてしまうのが嫌と言うか、そんなこと考えちゃうんですよね。事故が起きて離れる前まではそんなこと考えなかったんですけど。でも、子供のことを考えると、いわき市も線量低いわけじゃない。計っている時は0.15マイクロシーベルトだなんて言ってますけど。そんなのはね、コンクリートの上の洗い流されて線量低くなったとか、そう言う所なんで。

2011年12月

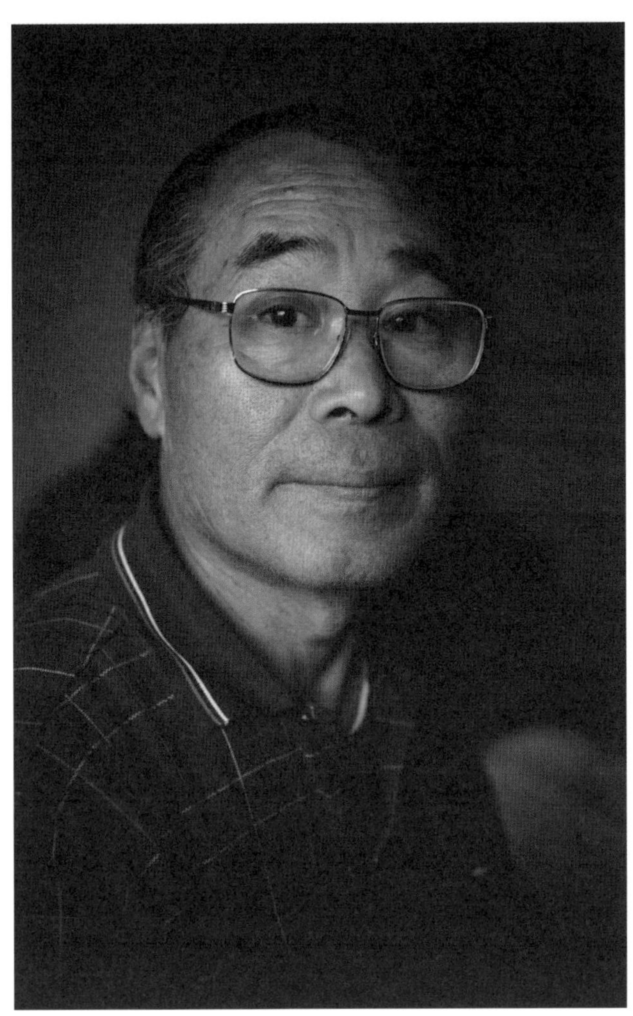

Katsuro Tadano
但野 勝朗
68

"There are people like me who
can't return to their houses anymore.
I don't have anything. Nothing but
the clothes I was wearing."

俺みたいに、うちに帰れなくて途中で止め
られたのもいるんだしさ。本当に何にもねぇ。
本当に着の身着のままで...

What was your job at the Daiichi plant?
Before the accident I had been working as the person in charge
of disaster prevention at the Daiichi and Daini, making sure
the workers would not get injured. I had been in that position
for over 40 years. However, my company got dissolved as a result
of evacuation and so now I'm laid off. At the moment my arm
is immobilized, but I'll go when I get called in. Not because I want
to, but because I'm needed. That's because there are only very
few experienced people available. Accidents have become pretty
common at Daiichi recently.

What has the situation been like since the accident?
Such an accident never ought to happen again. It really is exhausting.
To be honest, I want to beat them to death, those bastards
at TEPCO. But there's no point in getting angry. It's happened and
there's no way back. I do still have a house, one that was rebuilt
anew in its entirety. I just invested money in it. But now you
can't enter the exclusion zone without permission. When it blew up
on March 12, everyone got evacuated, but it was only on the April 22
that they formally restricted traffic into the area. Up until then
it was pretty lawless. What a joke! "You won't be able to re-enter
either starting tomorrow." I told myself and entered the day before.
There were no restrictions whatsoever. So the month before
I hadn't really done anything about it. I've thought of blaming the
government for all the losses, instead of TEPCO. First the government
has everyone evacuated, then they won't assume proper responsibility. There are people like me who can't return to their houses
anymore because they get stopped halfway in. I don't have anything.
Nothing but the clothes I was wearing.

原発では何をされてましたか？
震災前は、作業員が怪我をしないように管理をしている災害防止担当者っていう
立場で、1F、2Fで働いていました。40年以上やってます。避難っていうことで会社
自体が解散して、だから今は無職です。今腕が回んねえから行けねえけど、
要請があったら行きます。行きたいじゃなくて、行きます。なぜかっていうと、長く経験
している人が少ないんですよ。ここまで見逃してもいいっていうのと、こうしたら
危ないっていうのが分かるんですね。これは経験と勘からくるものだと思うん
ですけど。結構今第一原発で事故が多いんです。この前も解体工事中に作業員が
大怪我しました。今は若い人がたくさん入っているんだから最後のご奉公だな。

事故後の状況は？
二度とこういう事故が起きてはいけないし、本当つらいですよ。東京電力、こん畜生、
ぶっ殺すぞって言いたいよ本当は。言いたいけど、怒ってもしょうがないんだ。
もう実際起きちゃったんだから、元に戻るわけじゃないでしょ。家はちゃんとありますよ。
床から壁から全部新しくした。金かけたばかりです。でも実際ねぇ、今は警戒
区域に許可無しに入って行けないでしょう。12日に爆発して、みんな強制避難
させられて、それで4月22日から警察は規制を完全にしたんですけどね。その間、
誰でも入れたんですよ。ふざけたことに。俺も明日から出入りできないよって
言うので、その前の日入ったんですけど。そしたら検問所では全然止められなくて、
あれじゃいくら空き巣に入られたって分からない。警察はそれまでの1ヵ月
弱、野放しにしてたってことだよね。だから、東京電力じゃなくて、政府に
被害請求すっかなぁって言ったんだけどさ。本当いいかげんだからね、そこらへん。
政府が避難させといてさぁ、決めたら政府が責任持たなくちゃまずいでしょう。
俺みたいに、うちに帰れなくて途中で止められたのもいるんだしさ。
本当に何にもねぇ。本当に着の身着のままで...

Tsutomu Tsuji
辻 勉
48

"I don't want my family to worry, so I say I'm okay."

家族には大丈夫だからって言ってますけど。

What was the situation at the time of the disaster?
We were all here on assignment from Yokohama and there was no need to return after we had been evacuated, but the subcontractor had heard of the circumstances at the Fukushima Daiichi Reactor and was seeking people who would go sort out the various emergency goods that had been delivered. Eight days after the disaster I was asked if I couldn't work at the Daiichi reactor itself. I felt torn, but then my boss went ahead in full gear to assess the situation and came back to explain. He wasn't pushing us, nor did I have an overeager feeling that it was my responsibility to go, but I had come this far already. On top of that, my boss with whom I had been working for over 20 years went to verify personally. I wanted to acknowledge that. Also, the local staff had come, which added to my curiosity. When we got there, hundreds of people had been there already. I found that there were many familiar faces, which reassured me to some extent. If it had been just the three of us—Also, TEPCO was really cooperating as much as they could. The following two months were pretty much non-stop work.

What are your present thoughts?
We, the workers, have the mindset, "We just have to do it."
But it goes without saying that those close to us are concerned.
I don't want my family to worry, so I say I'm okay.

November 2011

震災当時の状況は？
僕たちみんな、横浜の方から赴任してたんですよ。だから、避難後に戻っ
てくる必要はなかったんです。ただ、元請けの上司から福島第一原発の状態を聞いて。
色々な緊急物資が福島に届いているから、それをさばいてくれないかと。
それで、震災から8日目に、第一原発で作業してくれないかって言われたんですよ。
ん〜、どうしようかなって。その時、上司が先にフル装備で見に行って、どんな状態
なのか説明してくれました。決して無理にとは言わないと。大それた、
俺がやらなければいけないなんて気持ちはなかったですけど、ここまで来てね。
上司が自ら確認してくると言われて。かれこれ20年以上、一緒にこの仕事やって
きてるので、それにも応えてあげたかった。それに地元の作業員とか社員とか
来てて、その人たちの協力もあったから、一回どんなことやっているのか興味もあってね。
行ったらもうその頃は、何百人単位で人が来てて、見れば同じ業者の顔馴染みも
いっぱいいたし、それで少し安心しましたね。行って俺ら3人だけだよっていう状況
だったらねえ。あと、東電もすごい協力してできる限りやってくれたんで。
その後2ヵ月はほとんど休みなしでした。

現在思われていることは？
僕たち働いている人間は、やるしかねえなっていう気持ちはあるけど、周りの人は
もちろん心配しますよね。家族には大丈夫だからって言ってますけど。

2011年11月

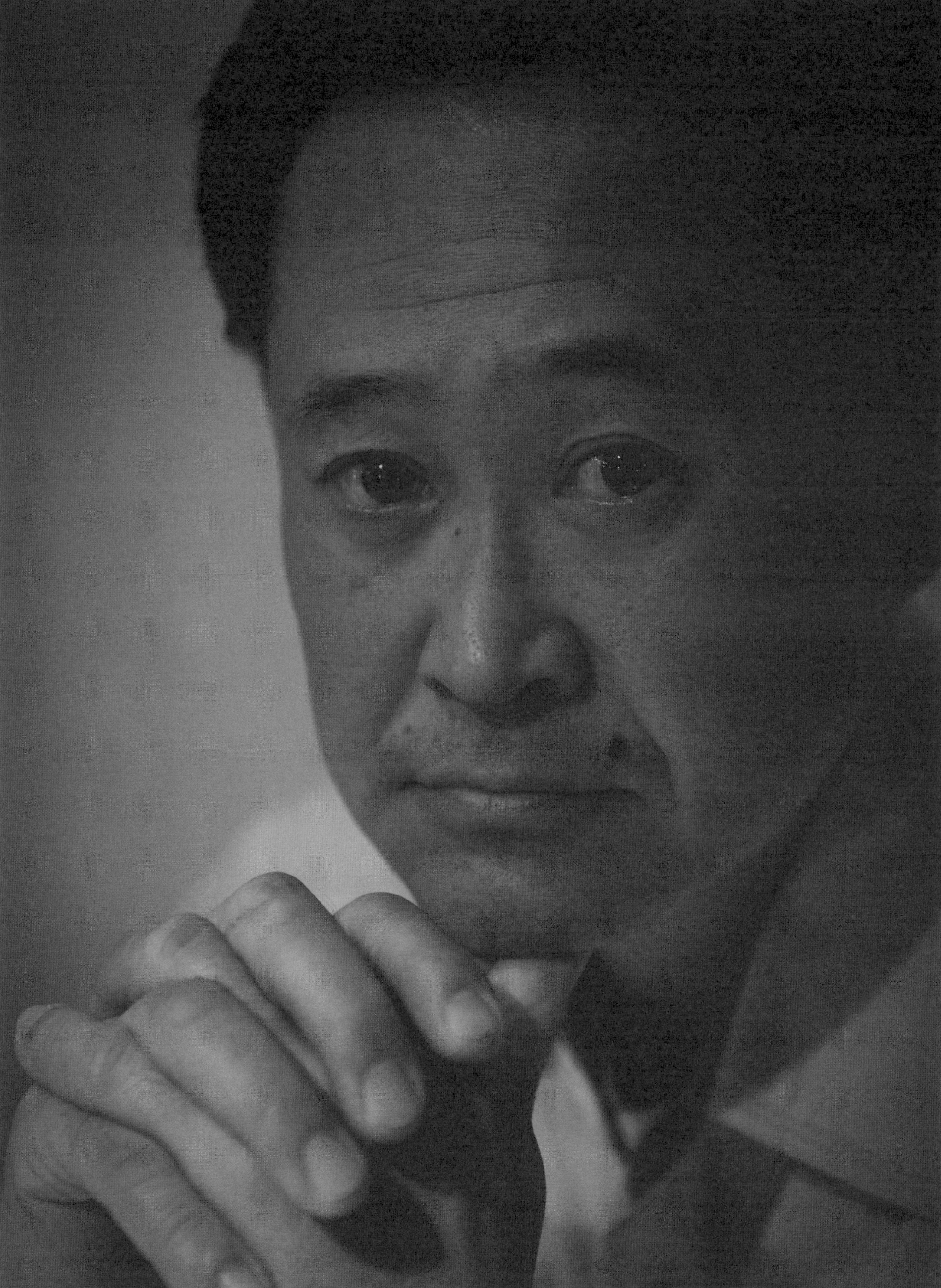

A
Hall

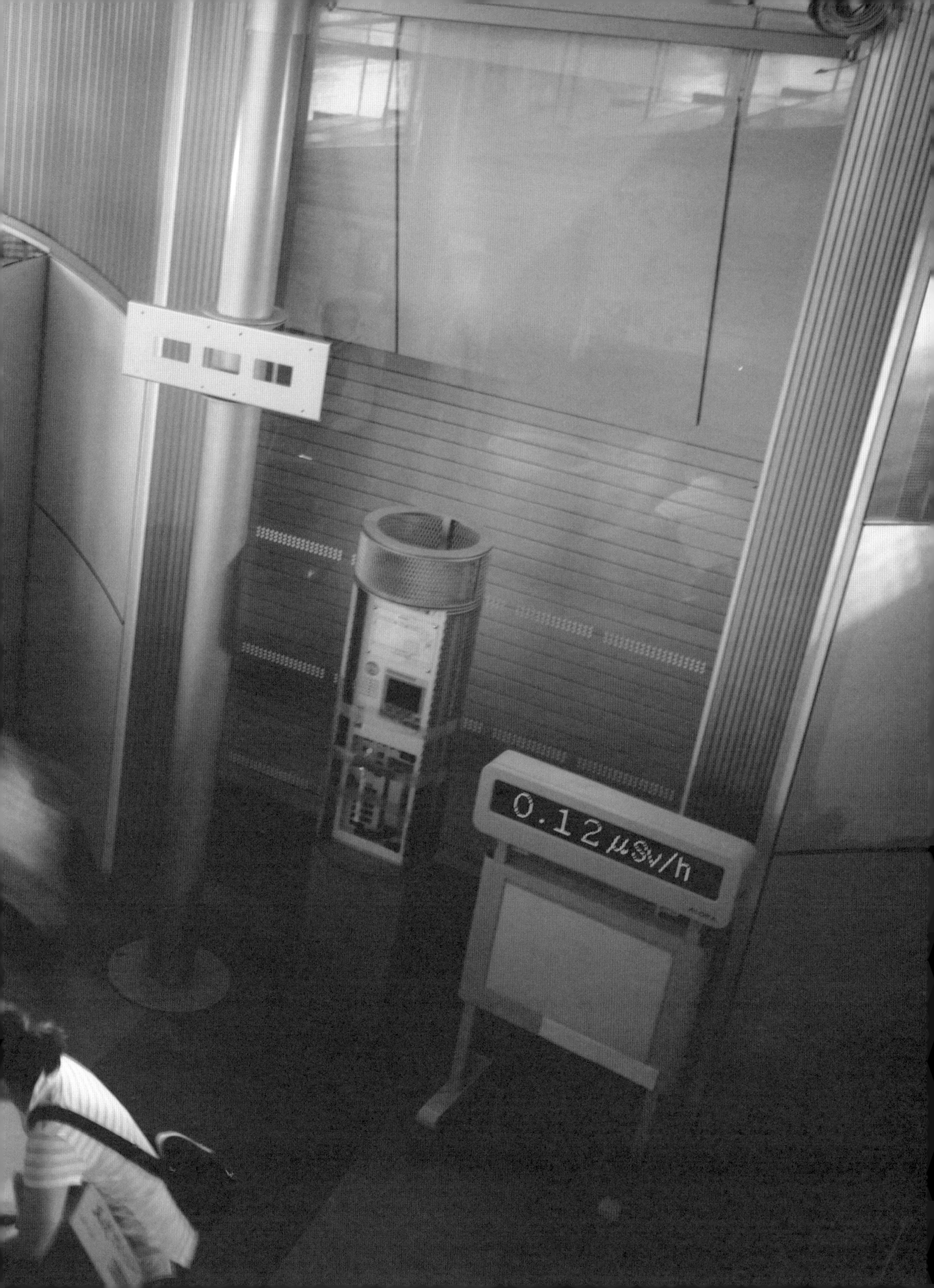
0.12μSv/h

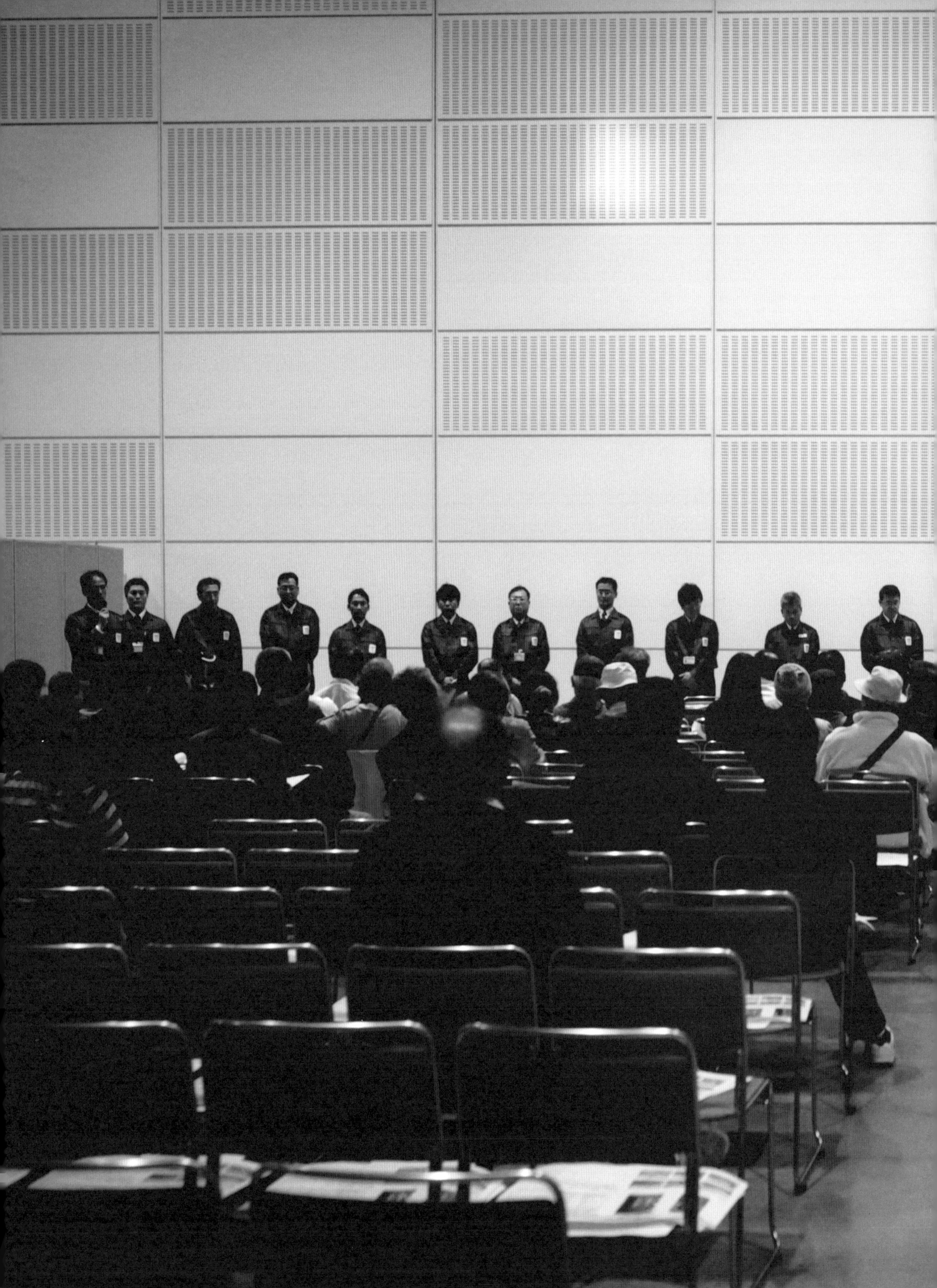

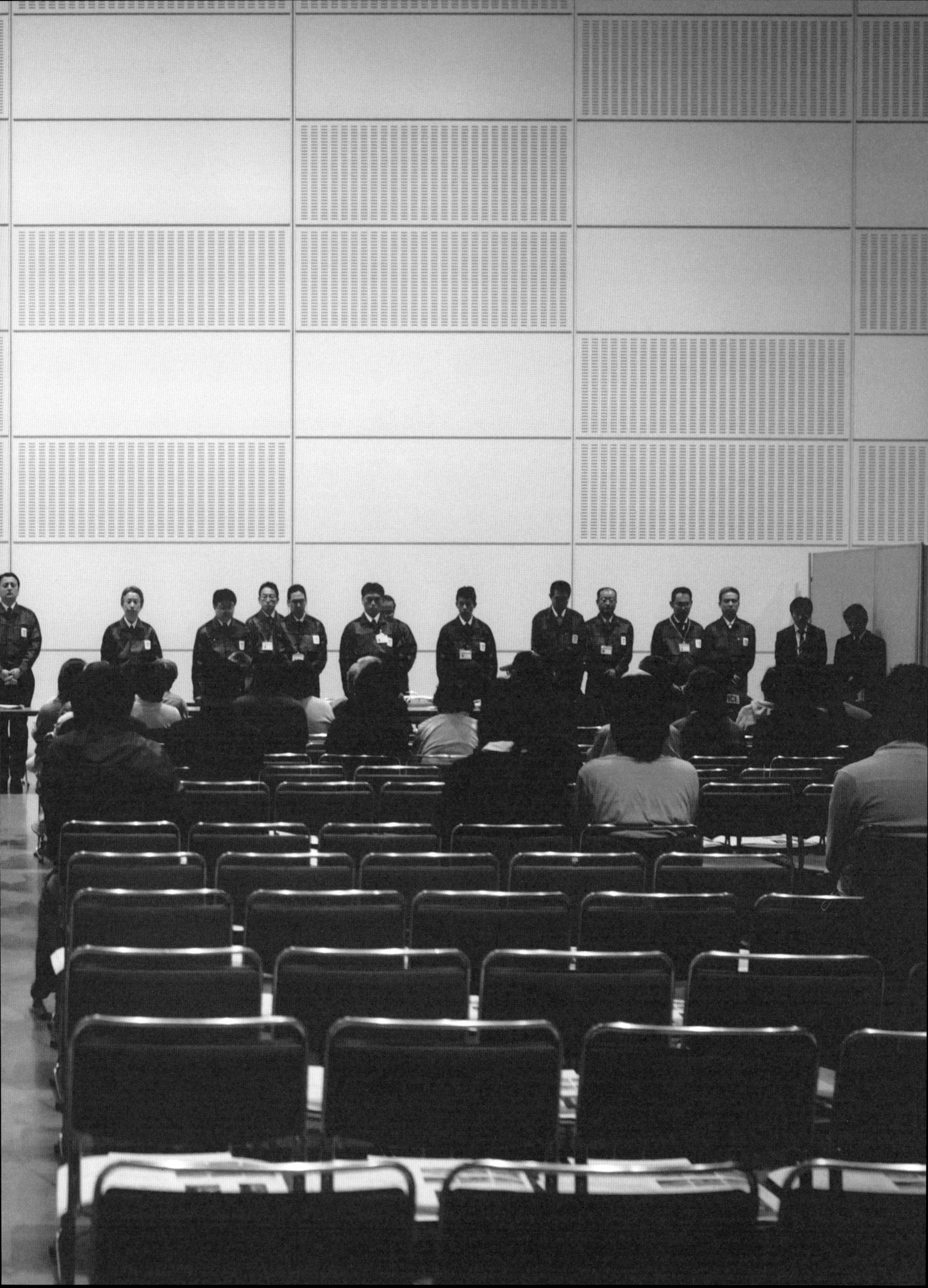

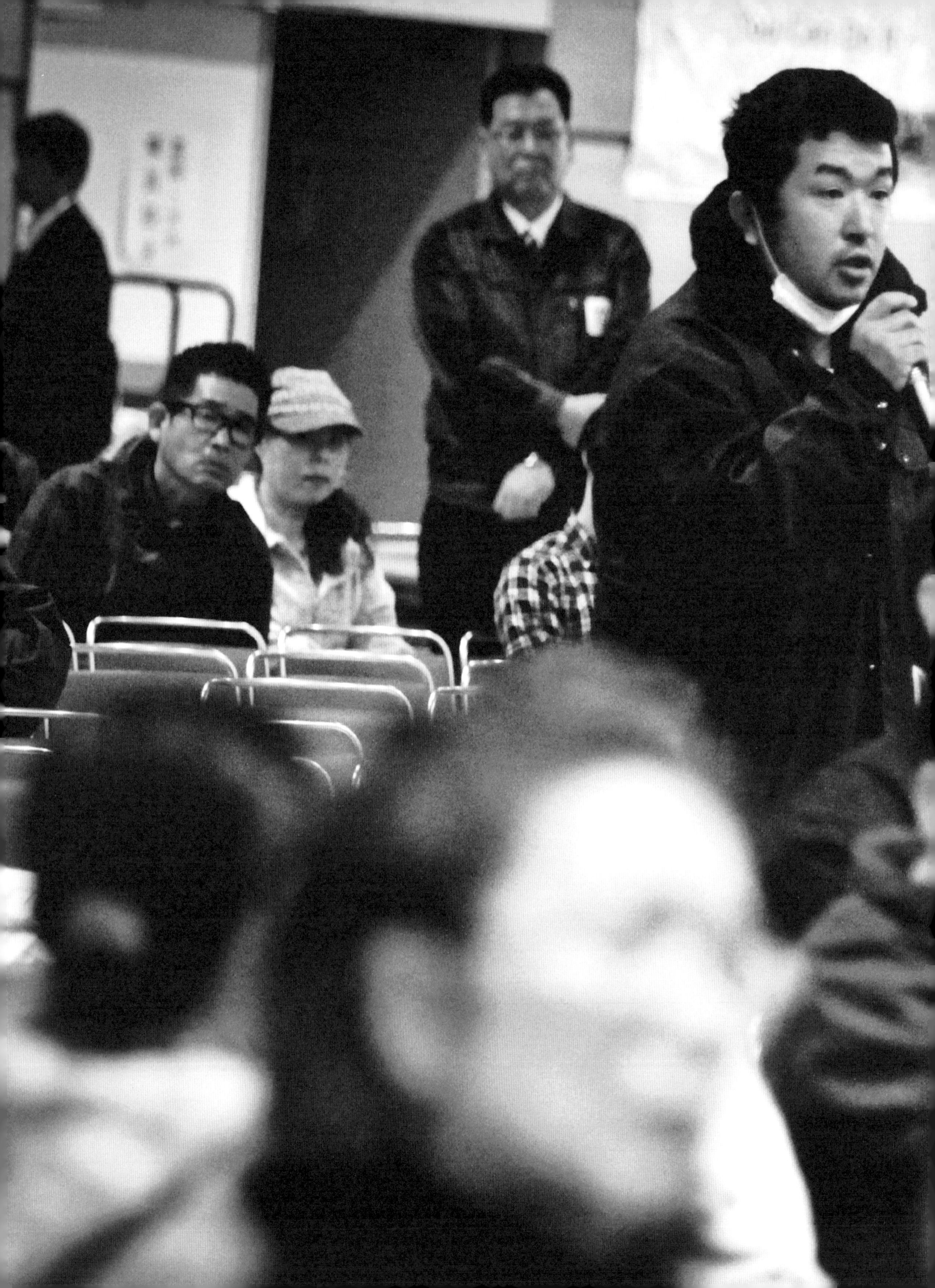

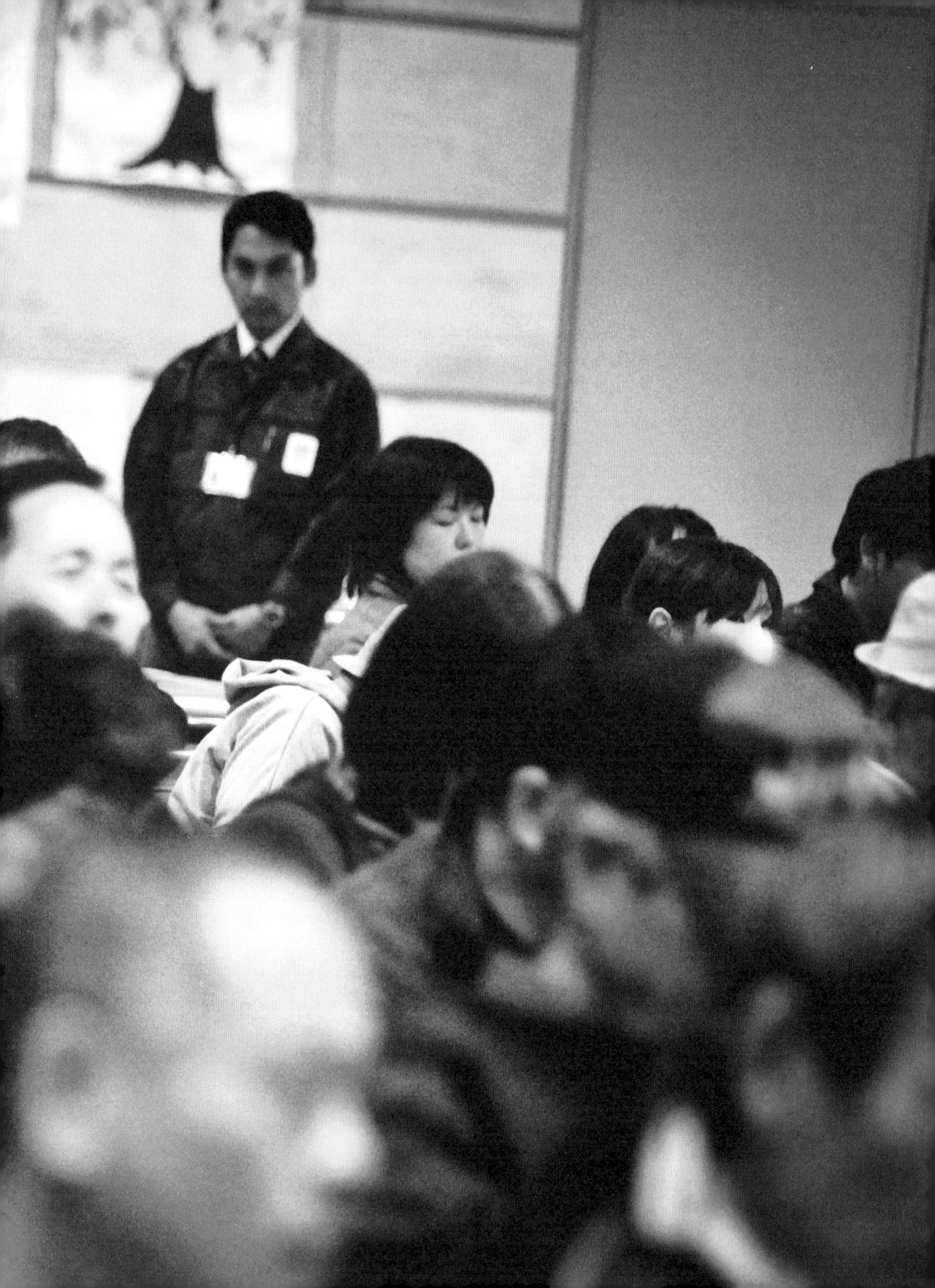

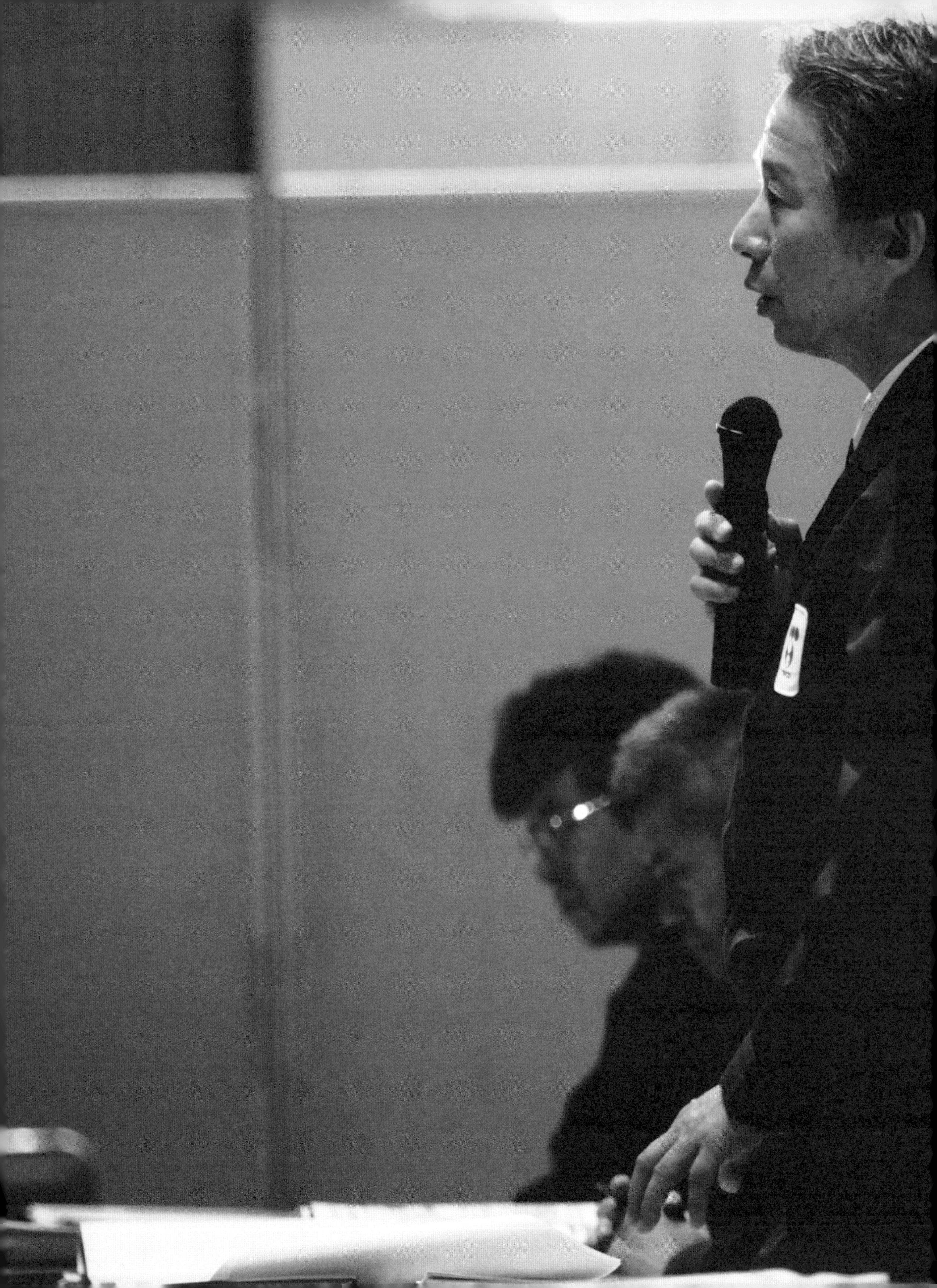

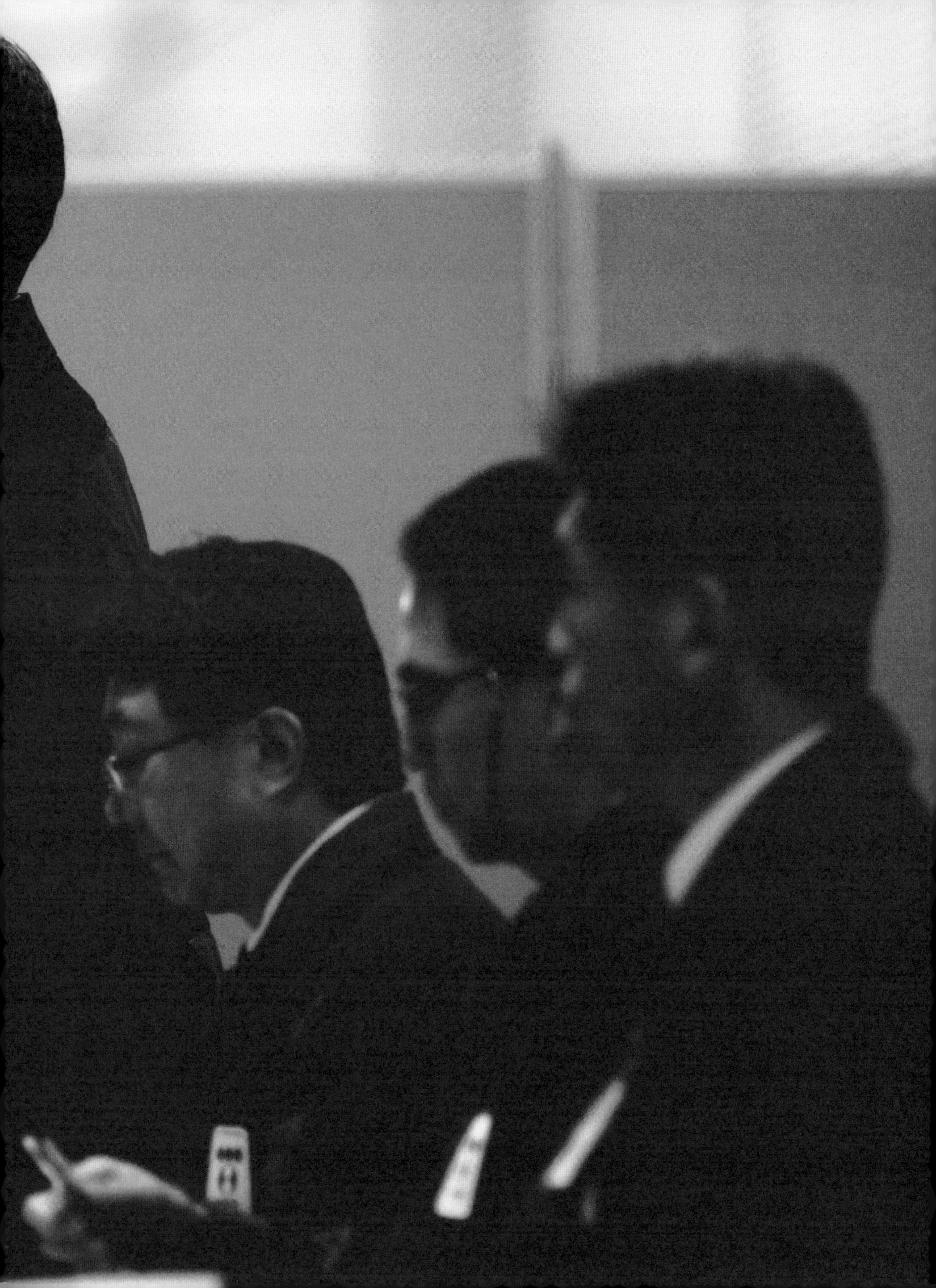

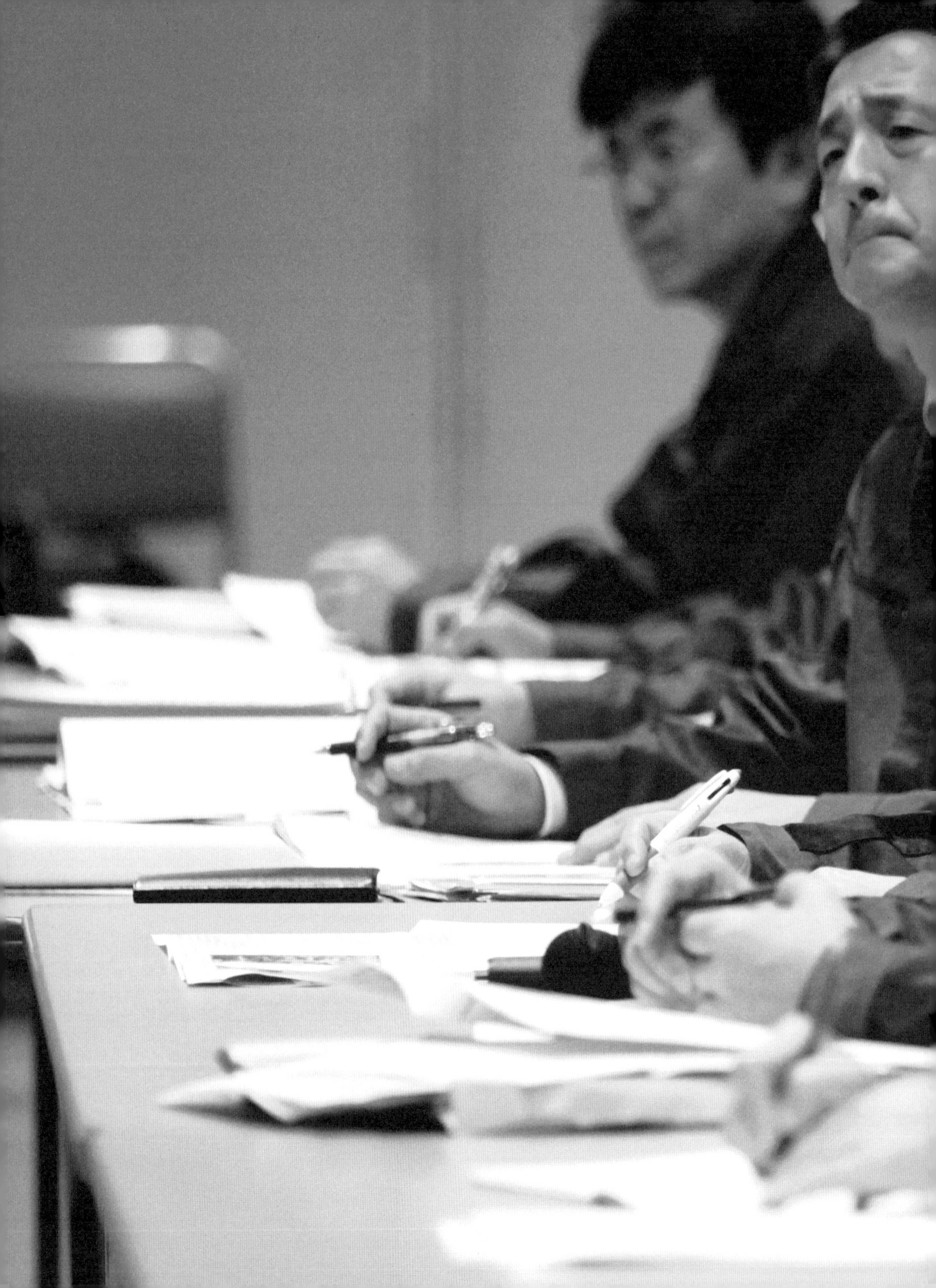

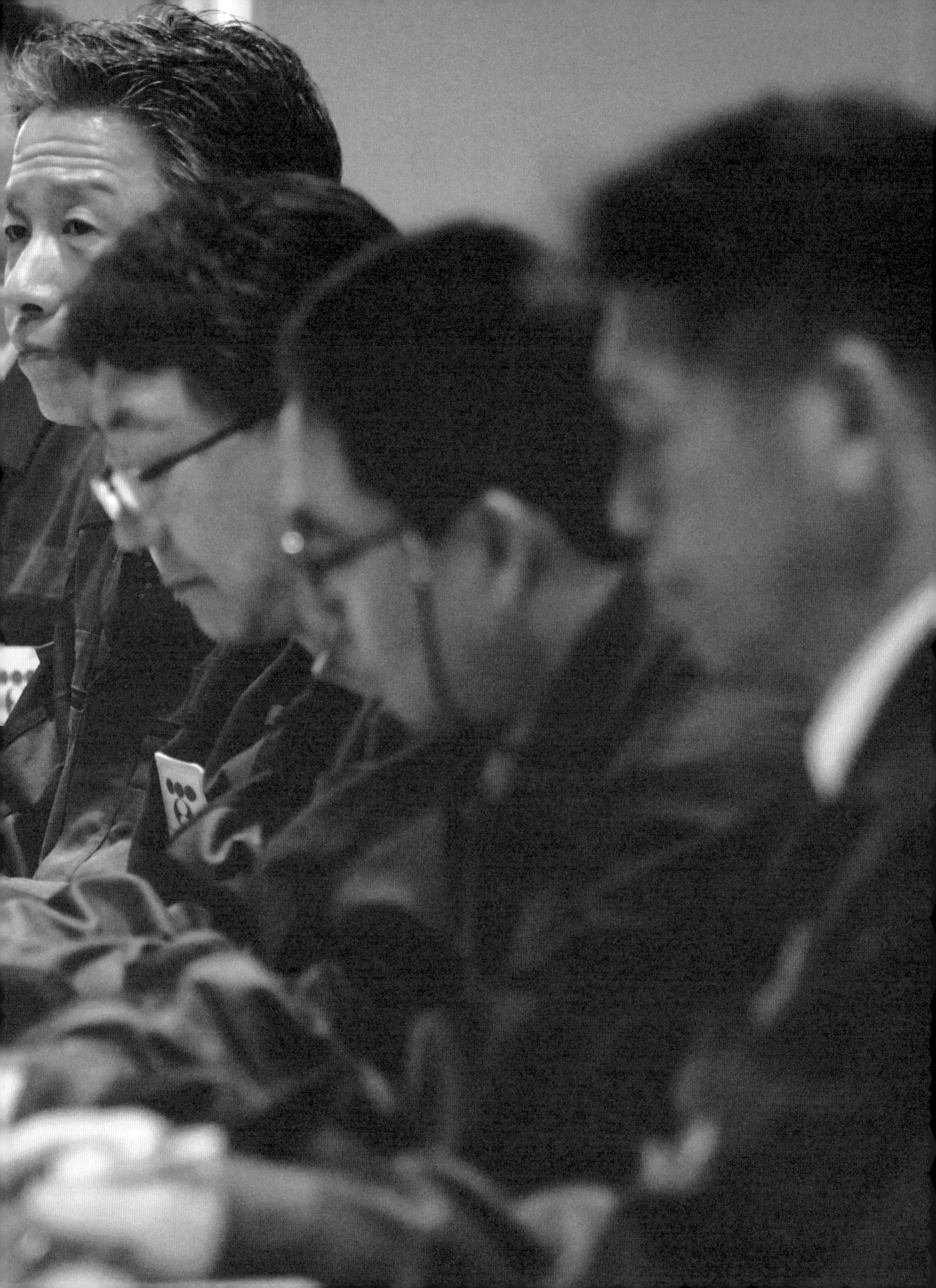

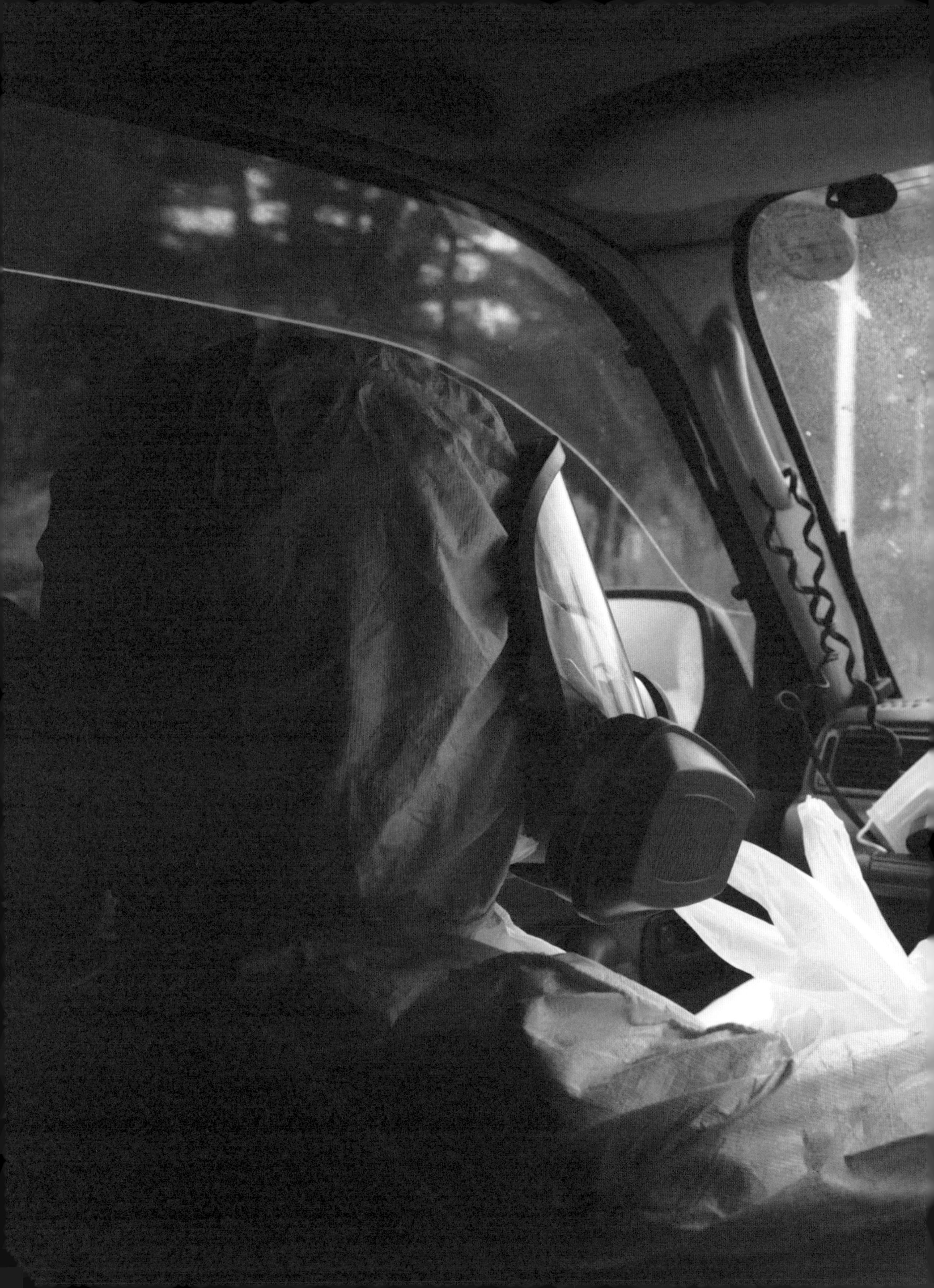

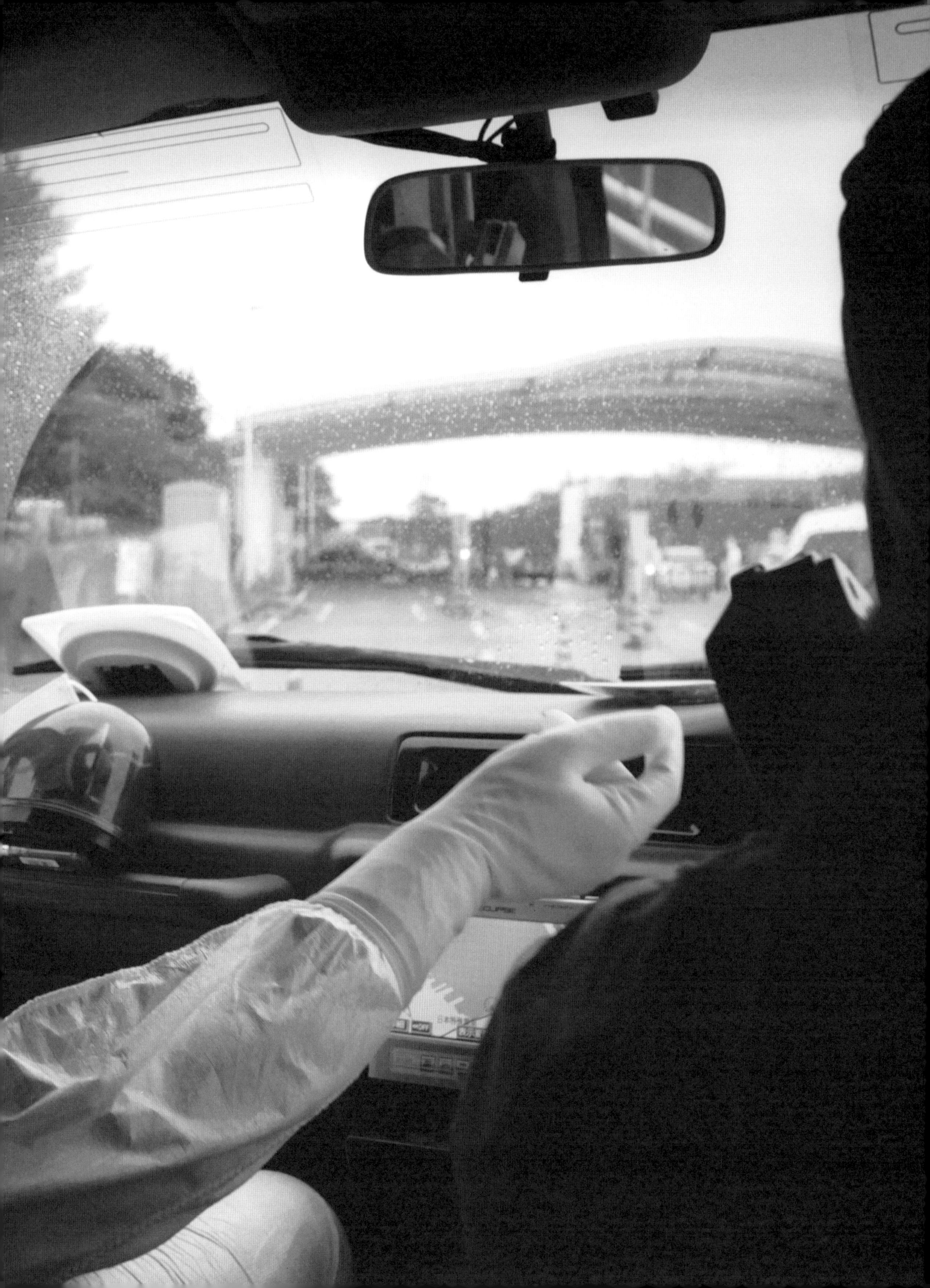

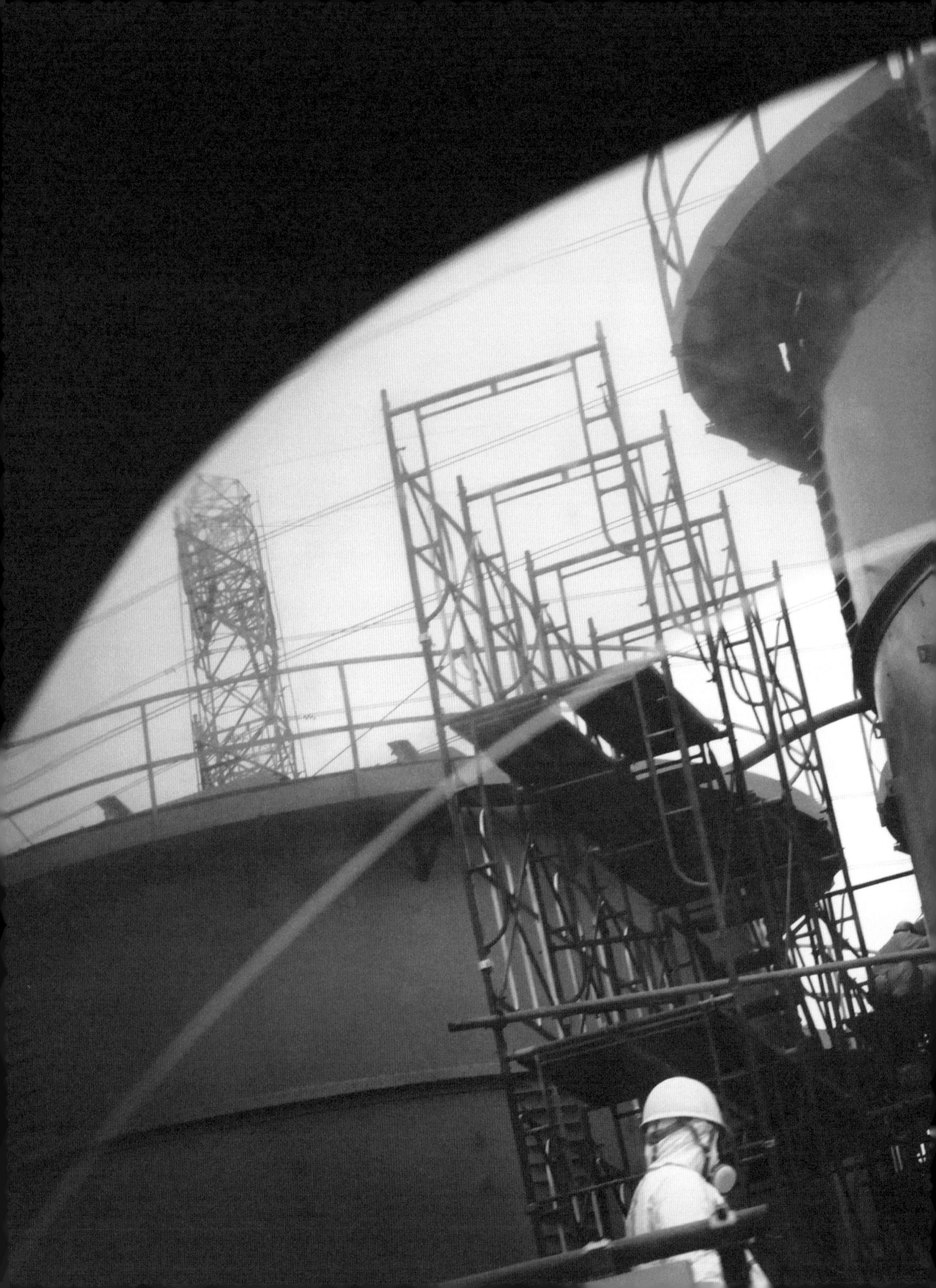

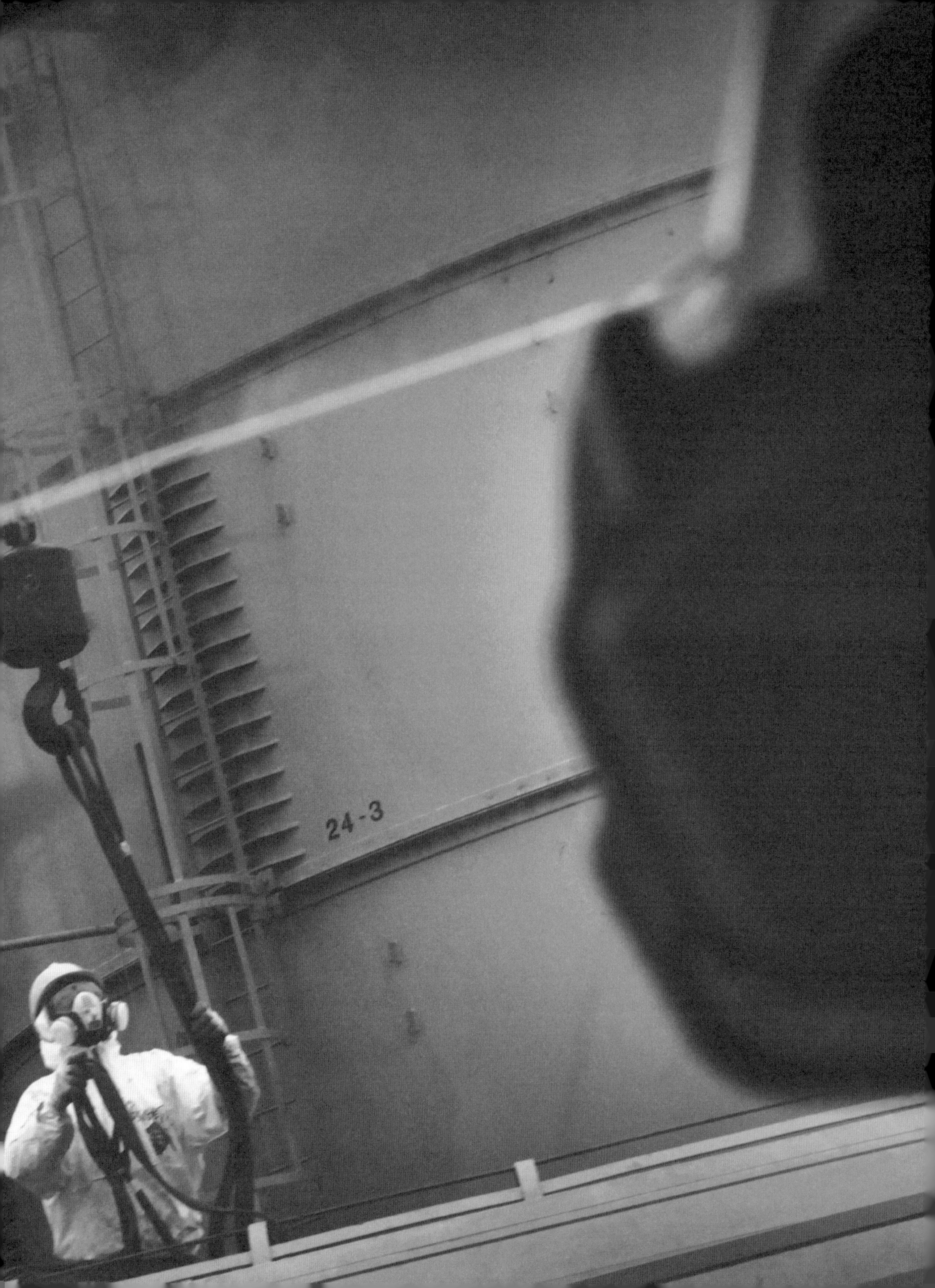
24-3

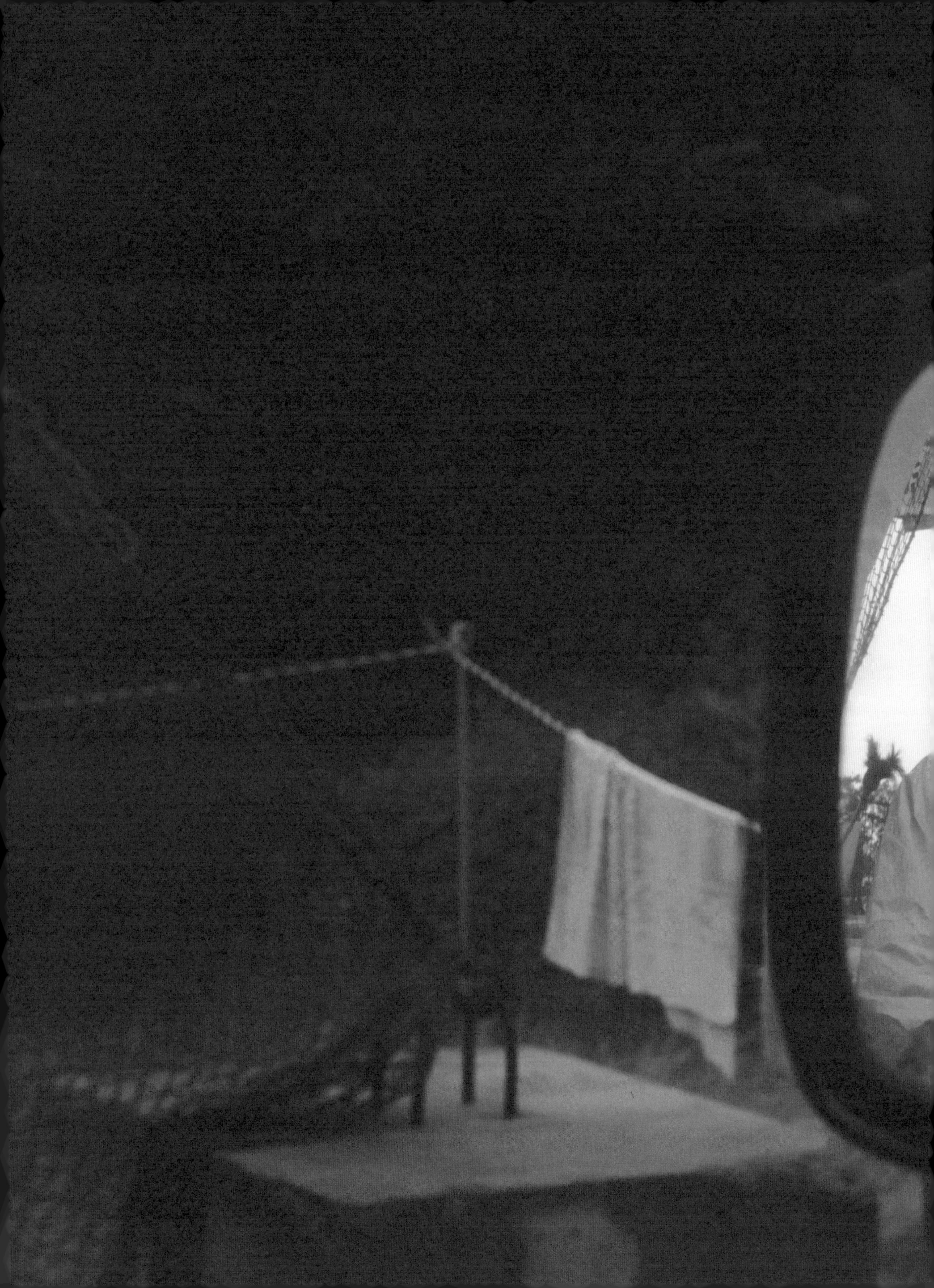

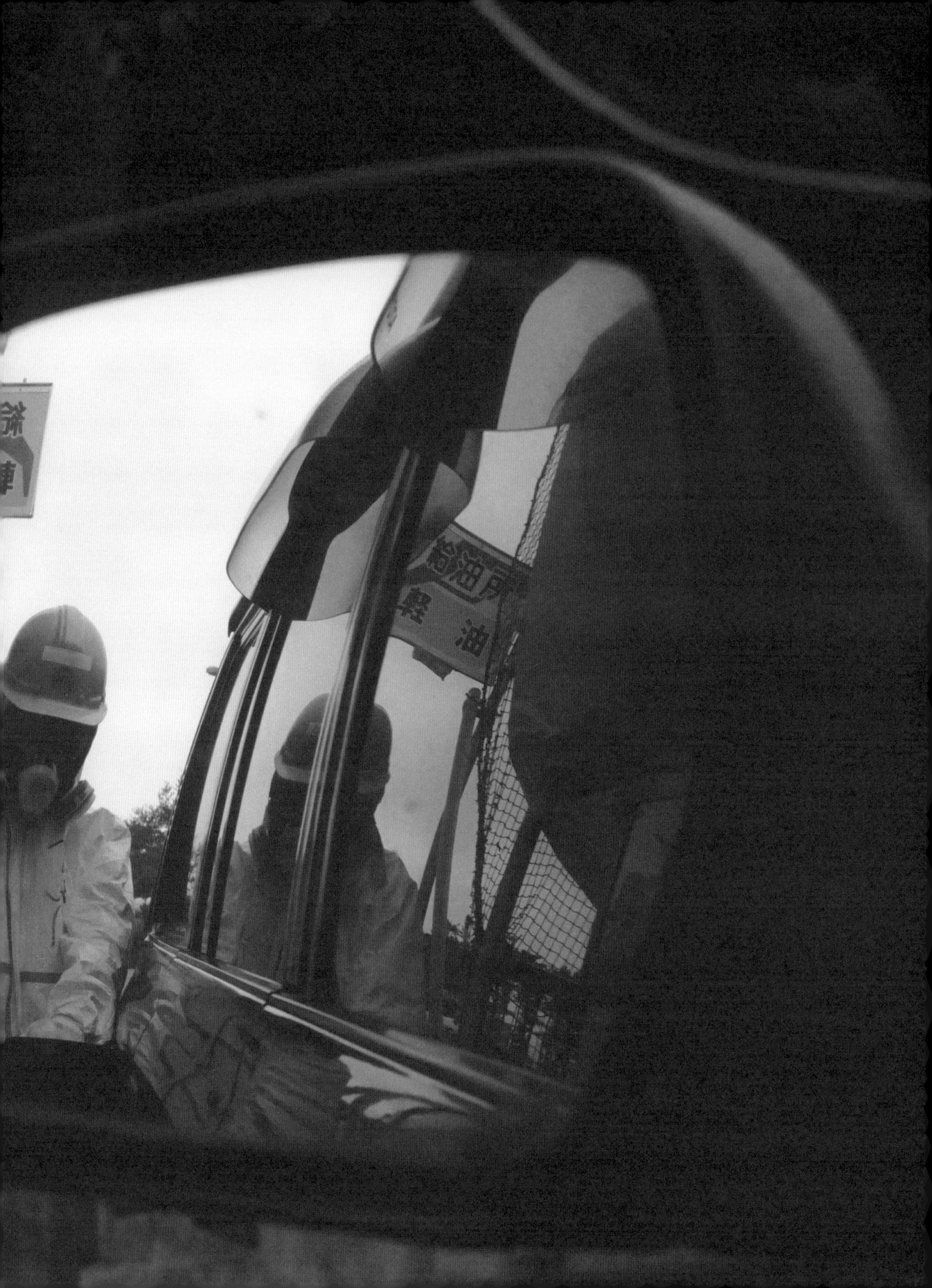
油所
軽油

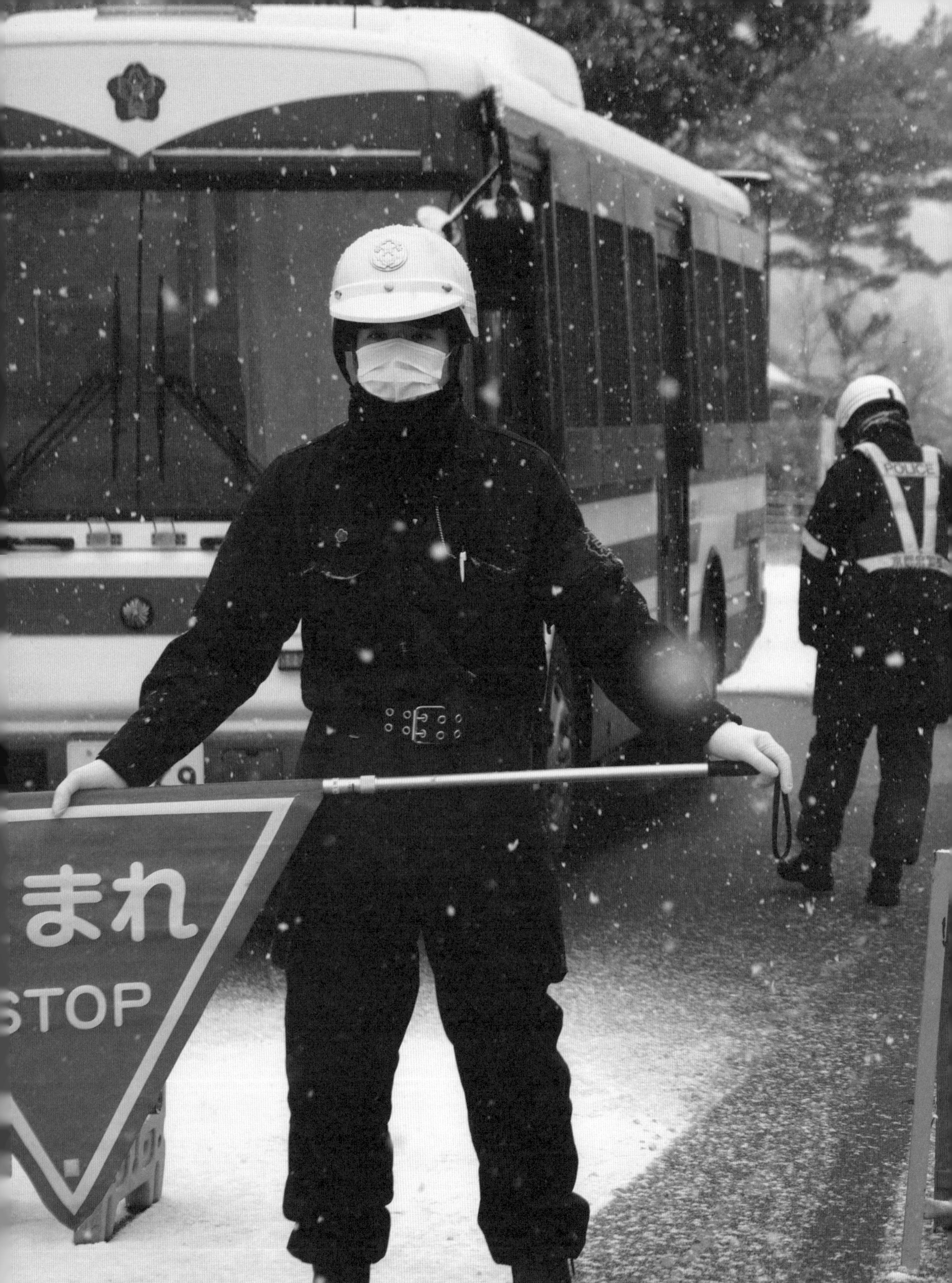
まれ
STOP

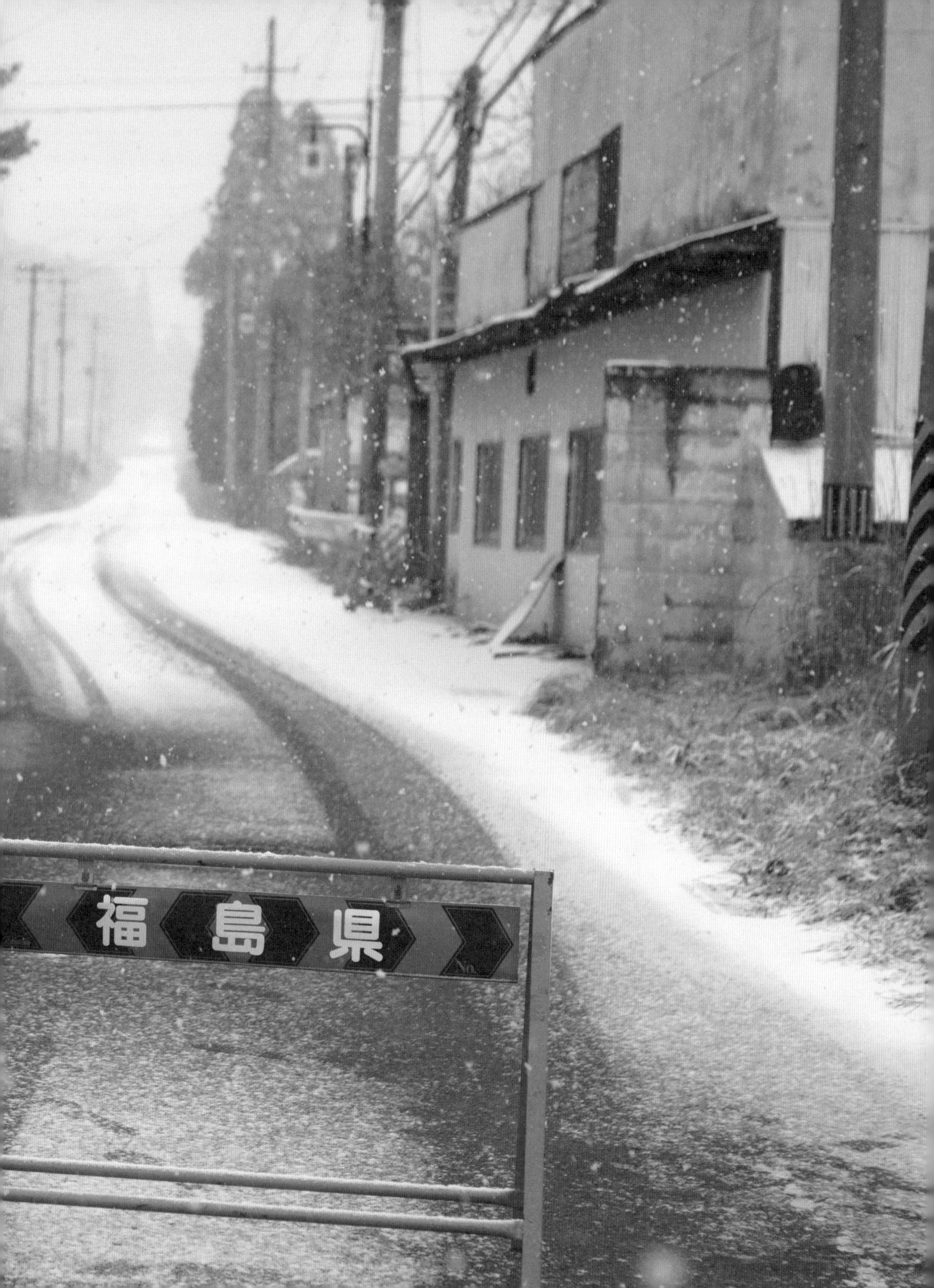
福 島 県

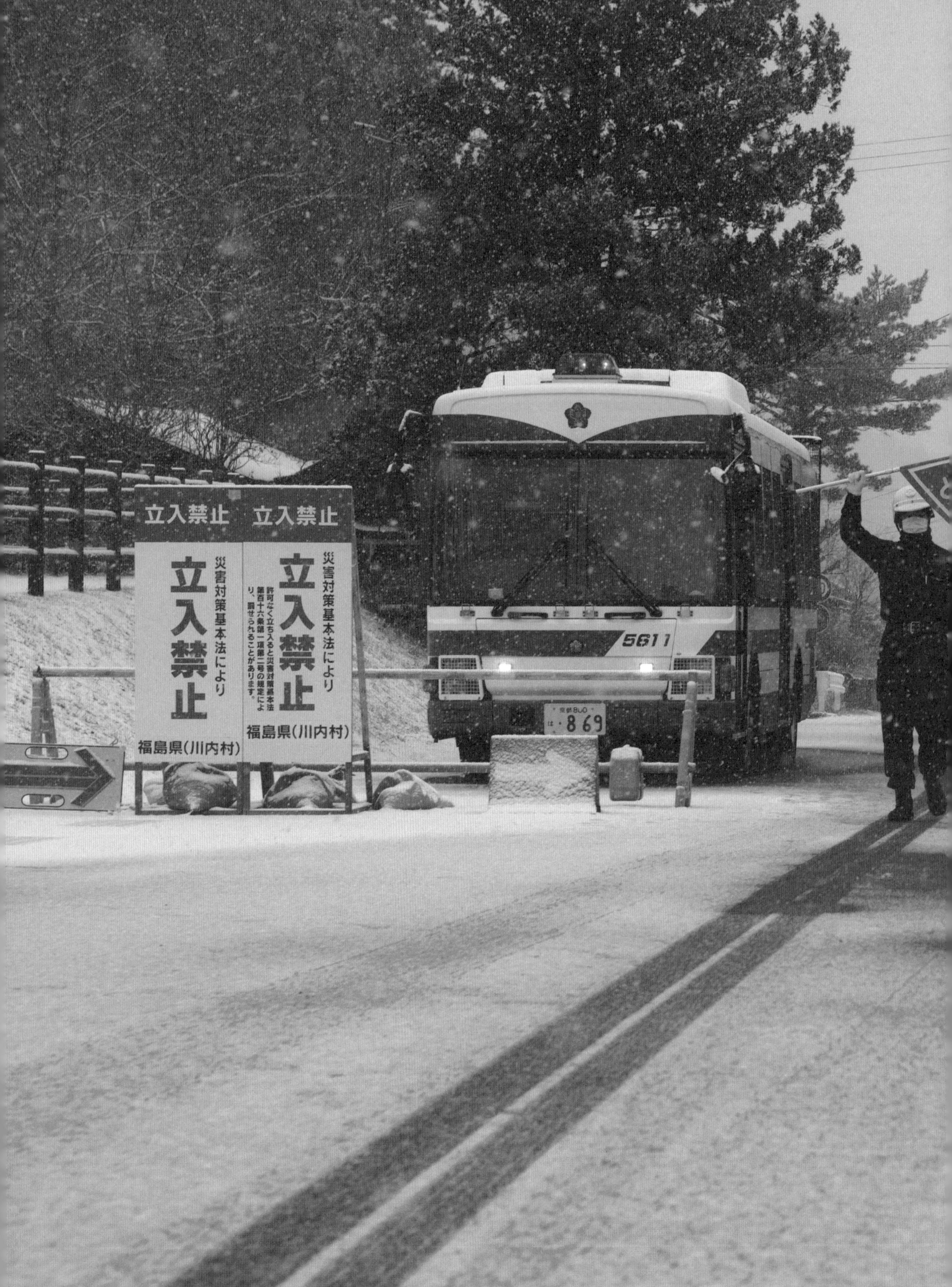

立入禁止　立入禁止
立入禁止
災害対策基本法により
福島県(川内村)
災害対策基本法により
立入禁止
許可なく立ち入ると災害対策基本法
第百十六条第一項第二号の規定によ
り、罰せられることがあります。
福島県(川内村)
5611
京都800
は・869

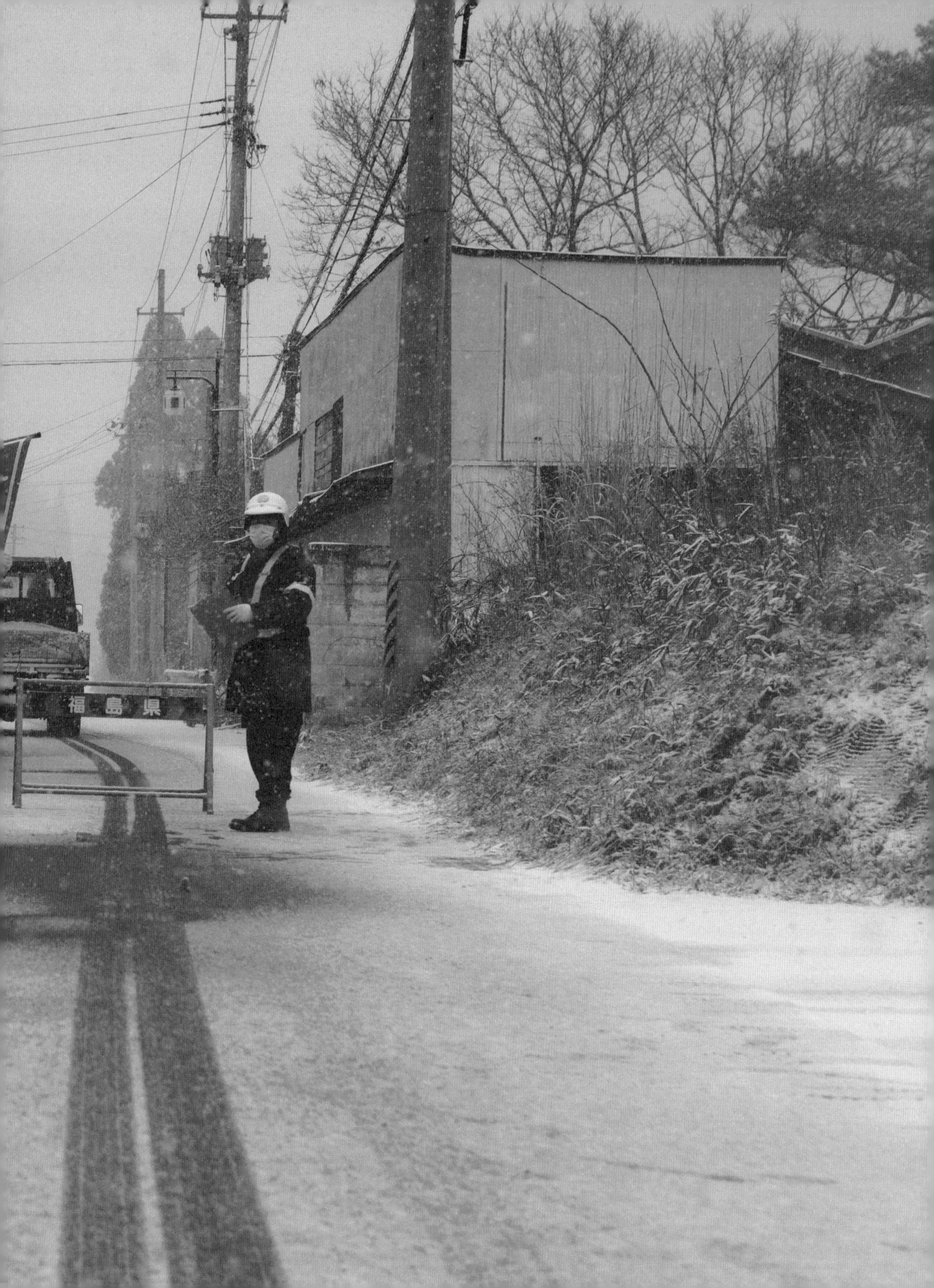

福　島　県

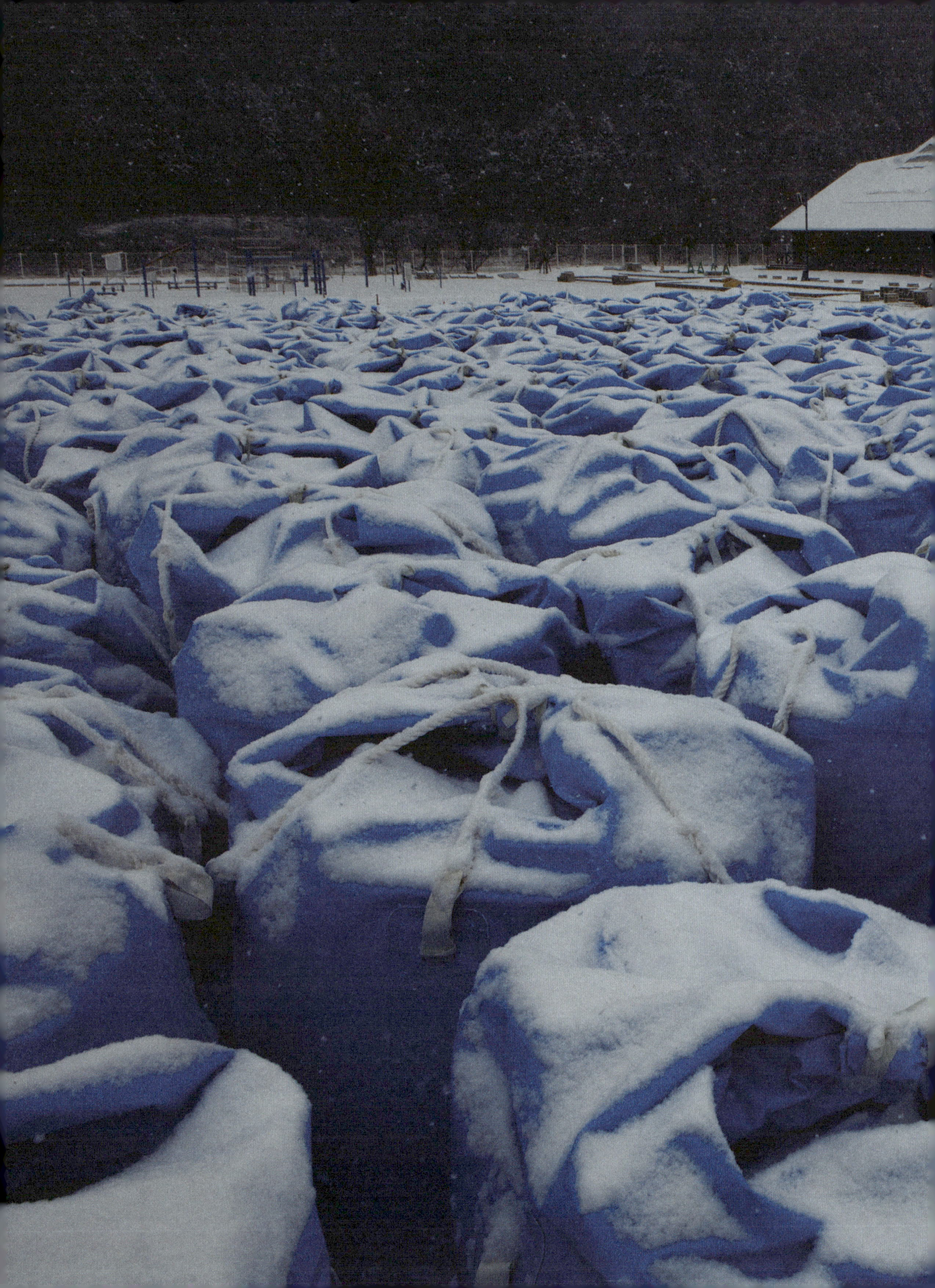

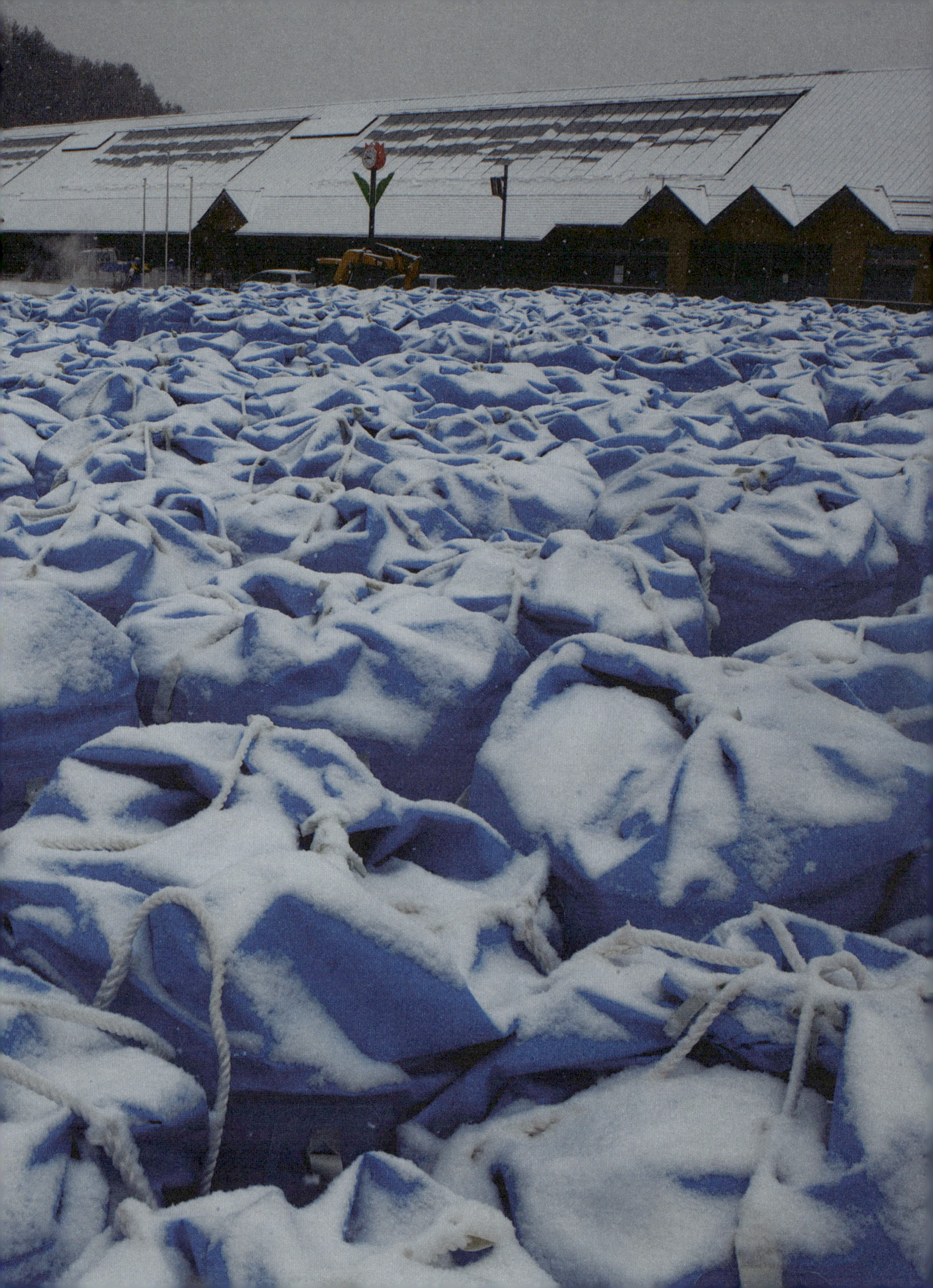

Epilogue

At the time I was far, far away. In the West, the possibility of a meltdown
was immediately reported. While I was feeling overwhelmed by the
sheer mass of video sprawling on the web, I could not stop asking myself
what I could do. As a composer, I felt tormented by this powerlessness.
Horror and shock soon turned into sorrow and prayer, until events
surrounding the nuclear power plant changed the latter into anxiety and
anger. I feel ashamed for not having been aware and critical of the revolting
conspiracy among the government, TEPCO, and the media about the
entire issue of nuclear power until this horrific event happened.

Fukushima not only exposes Japan, but the whole planet to an immense
threat. A certain Greek poet interpreted this calamity as Nemesis.
Due to the countless judgmental errors Japan has been committing,
the world feels a righteous indignation and contempt. Japan now
has to face the question of how to make up for all they've done wrong.

I want to express my sincere respect for the men risking their lives and
fighting to keep the results of the disaster under control. As an individual,
I plead with my fellow men and women to reset, reset their awareness,
their ideals, their reality.

The days of conformity are now over. I want each and every single person
to stand up as a unique individual, with the belief that with our concerted
efforts we can change the face of politics and society in this country.

Jun Miyake, composer

エピローグ

その時僕は遥か遠くに居た。
欧米では即座にメルトダウンの可能性が報じられていた。
ネットから溢れてくる映像に震撼しつつ、
今自分に何ができるのだろうかと問い続けた。
音楽家としての無力感にも苛まれていた。

戦慄と驚愕は、やがて悲しみと祈りに変わり、
原発をめぐる事象が解き明かされるにつれ、
それは焦燥と怒りに変わっていった。

こんなことになるまで、
政府、東電、メディアの醜悪な癒着、
そして原発そのものに問題意識を持てなかった自分を恥ずかしく思う。

今や福島は日本のみならず、地球にとって脅威になろうとしている。
あるギリシャの詩人はこの惨事をネメシスに例えた。
日本の犯した数々の判断ミスに、世界は義憤と侮蔑を覚え始めているのだ。
この負の遺産に我々がどう向き合うかが問われている。

現地で懸命に立ち向かう人々の姿に心から敬意を表しつつ、
一個人として同胞に訴えたい。
リセット・・・意識と理想と現実のリセット。
もう横並びはいい、ひとりひとりが突出した個であってほしい。
個の放つ波動が、政治と社会構造のリセットに繋がっていくことを信じて。

三宅 純（作曲家）

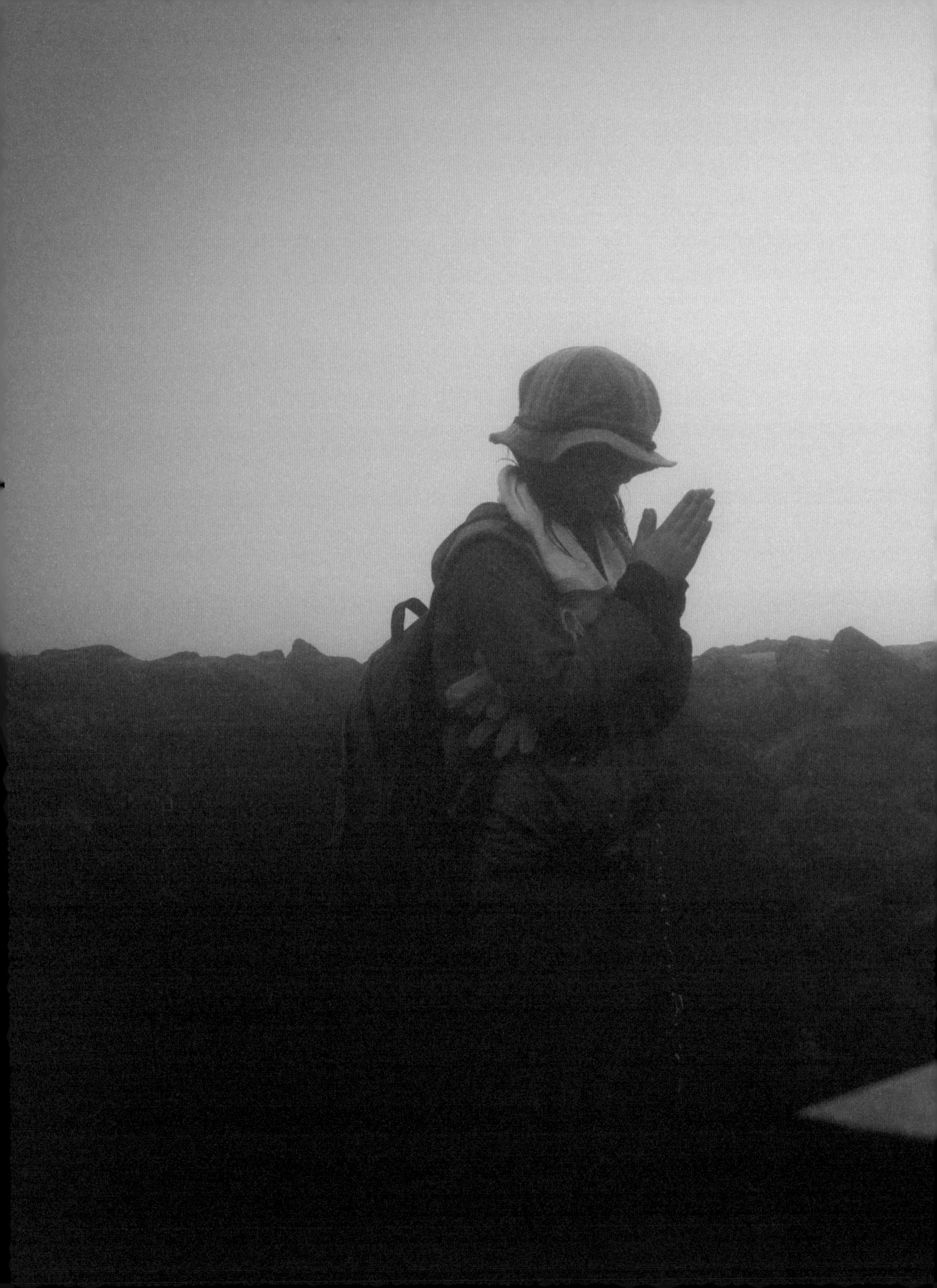

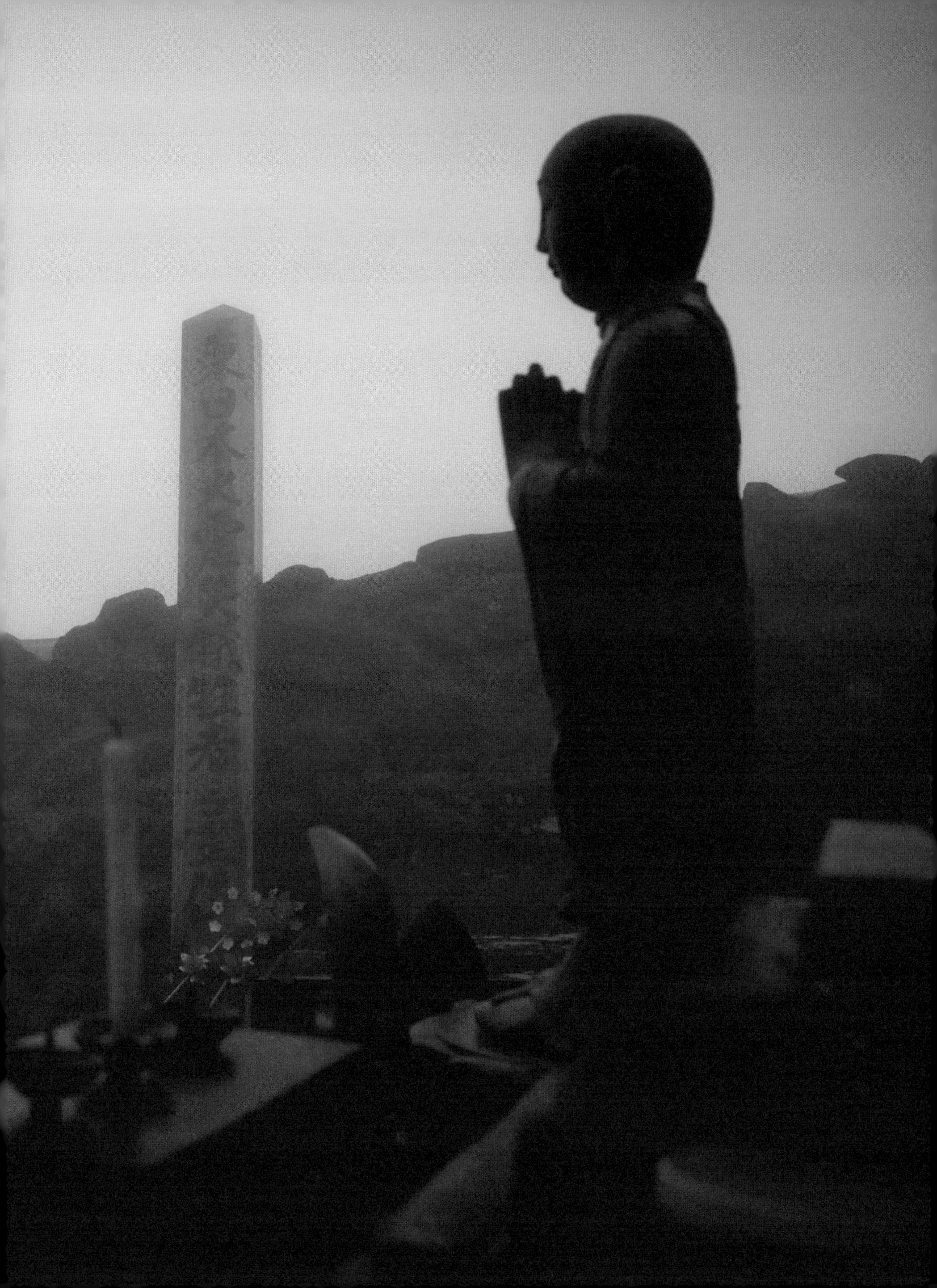

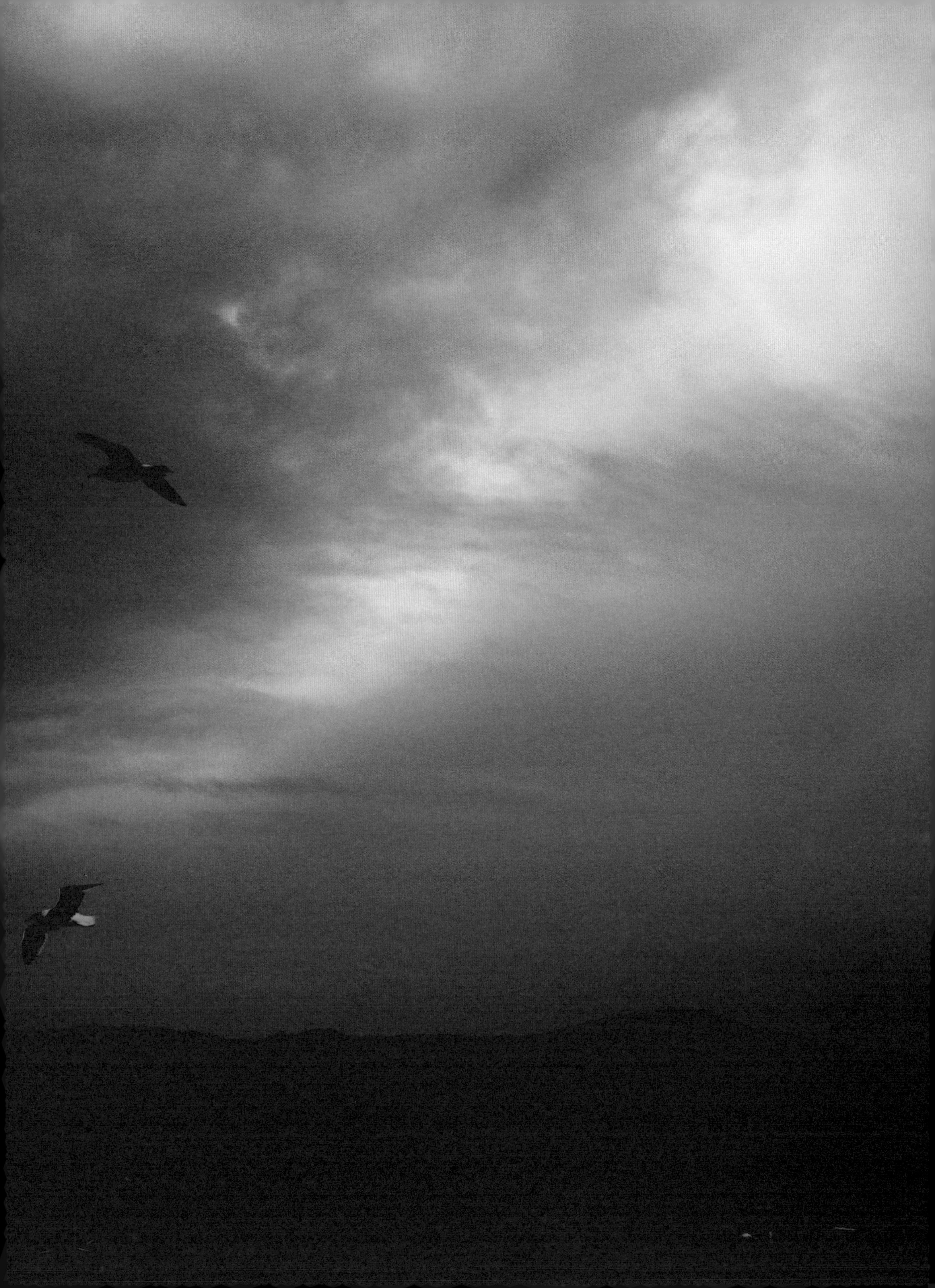

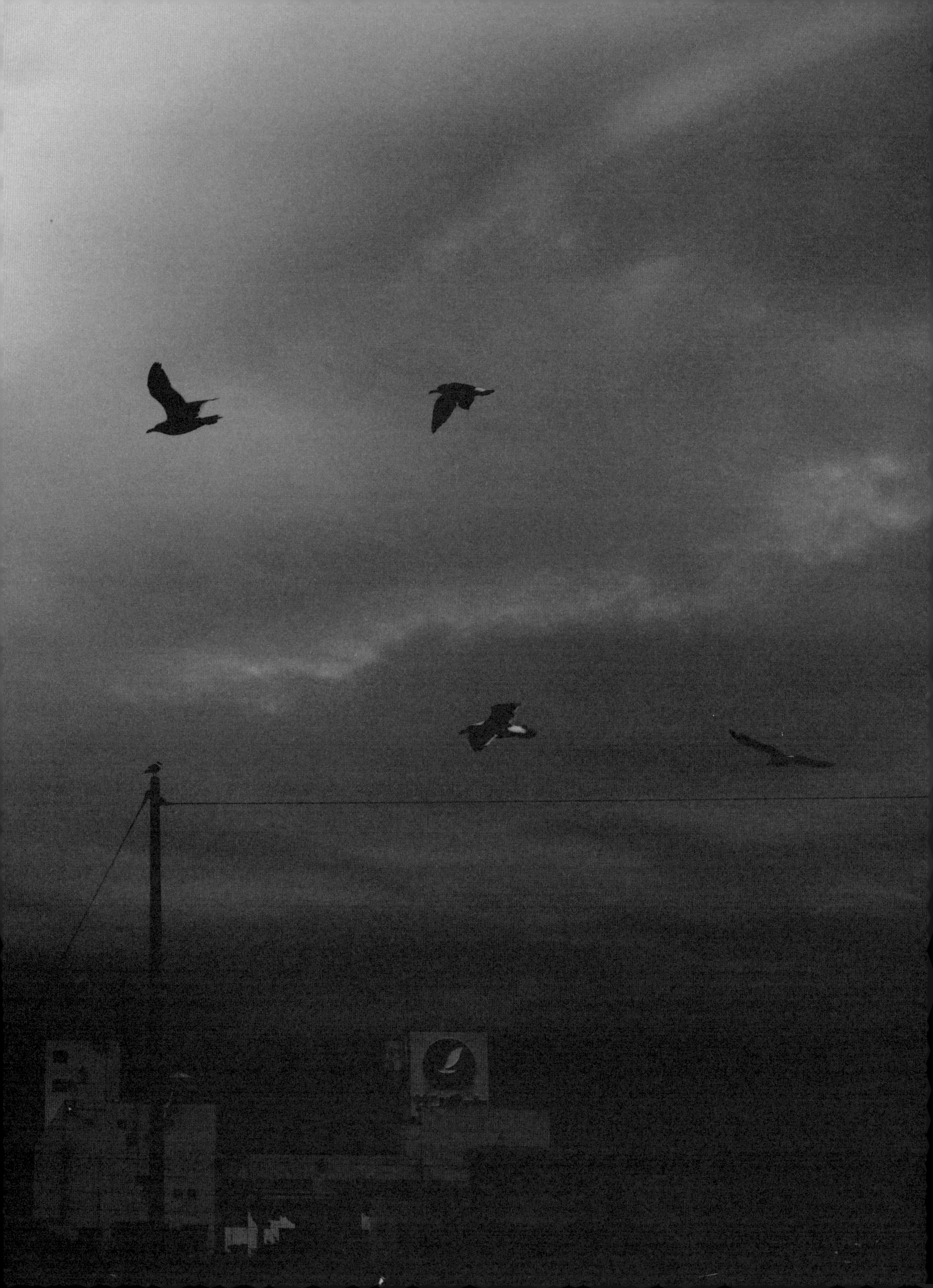

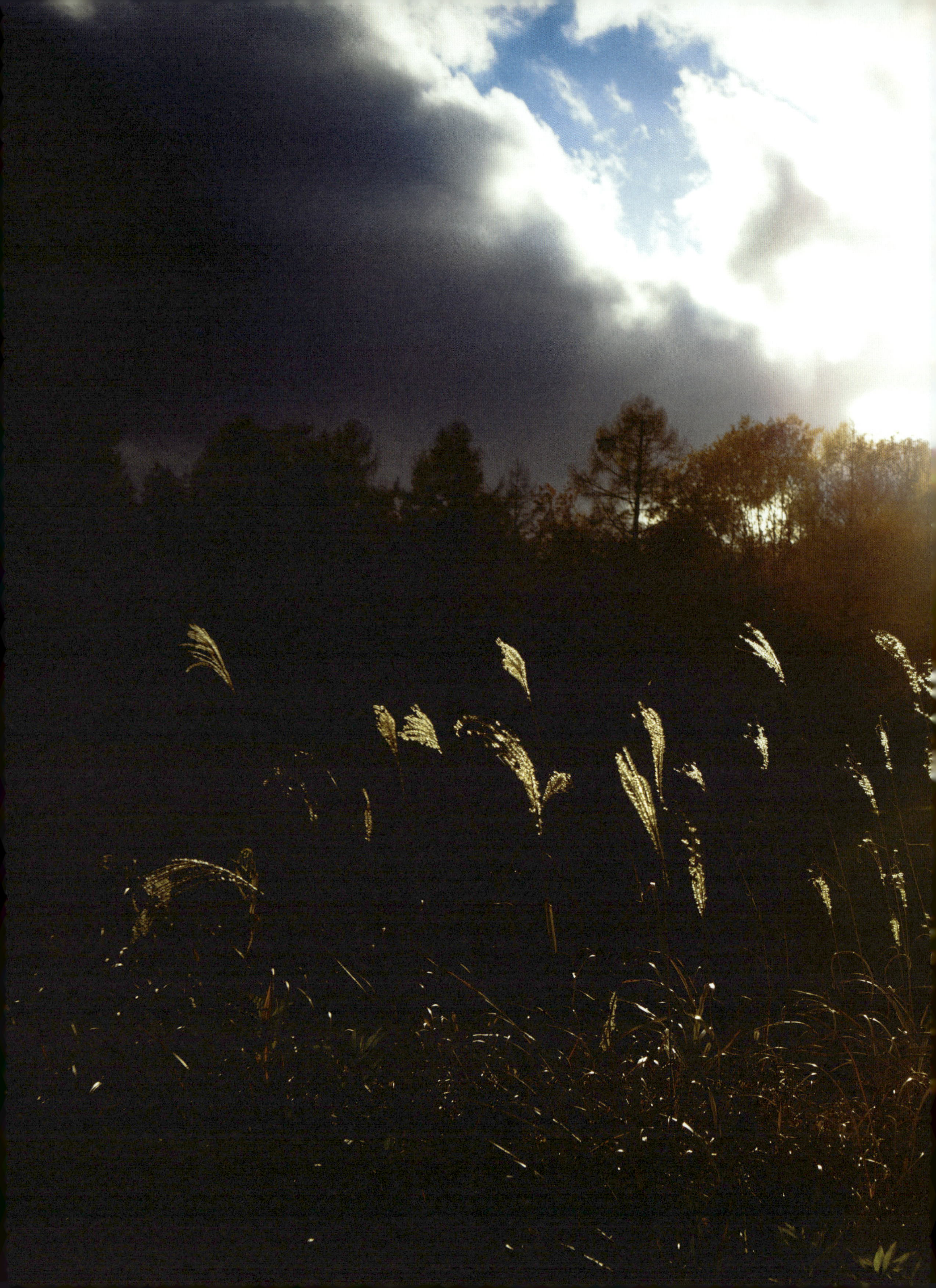

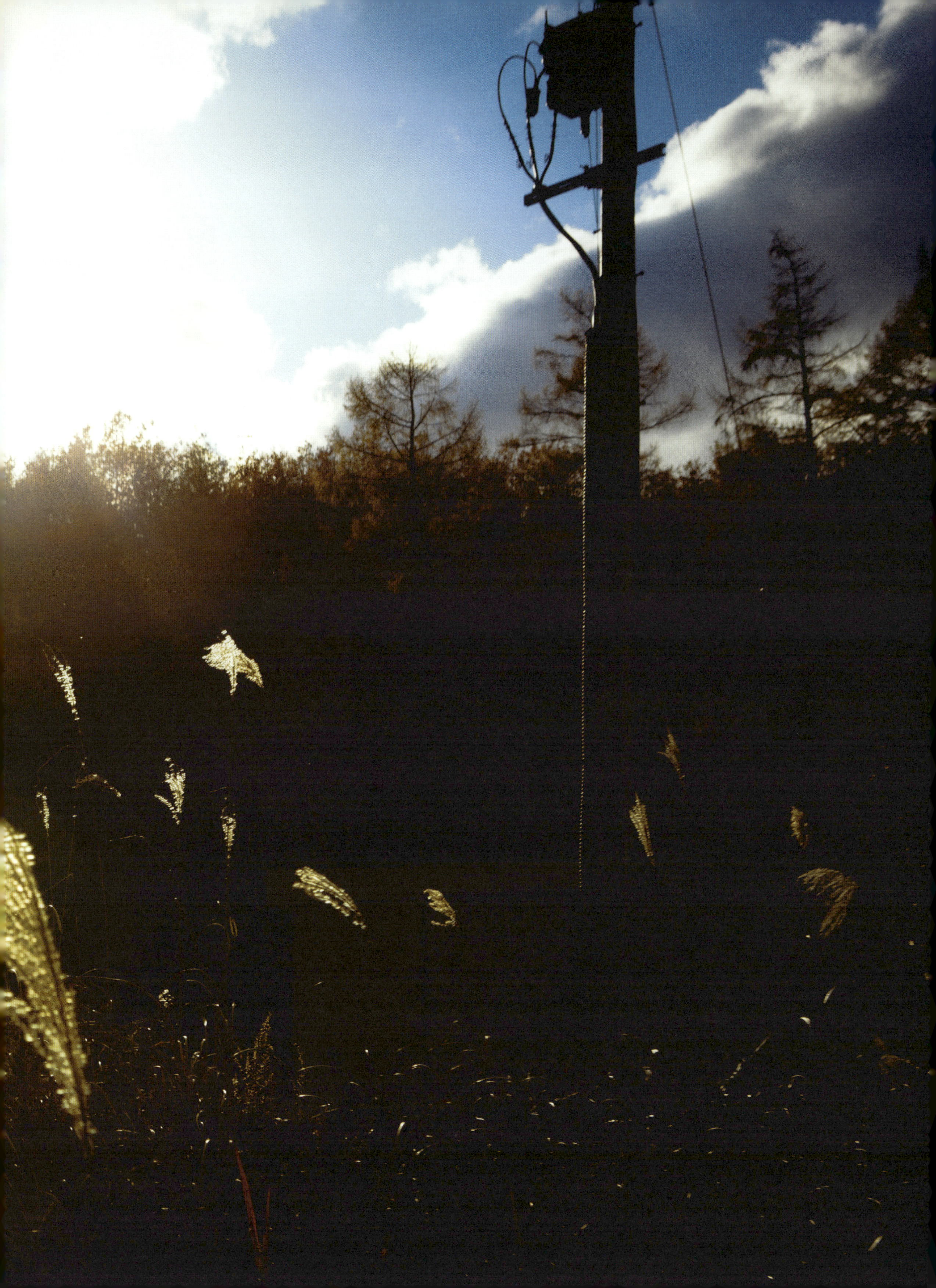

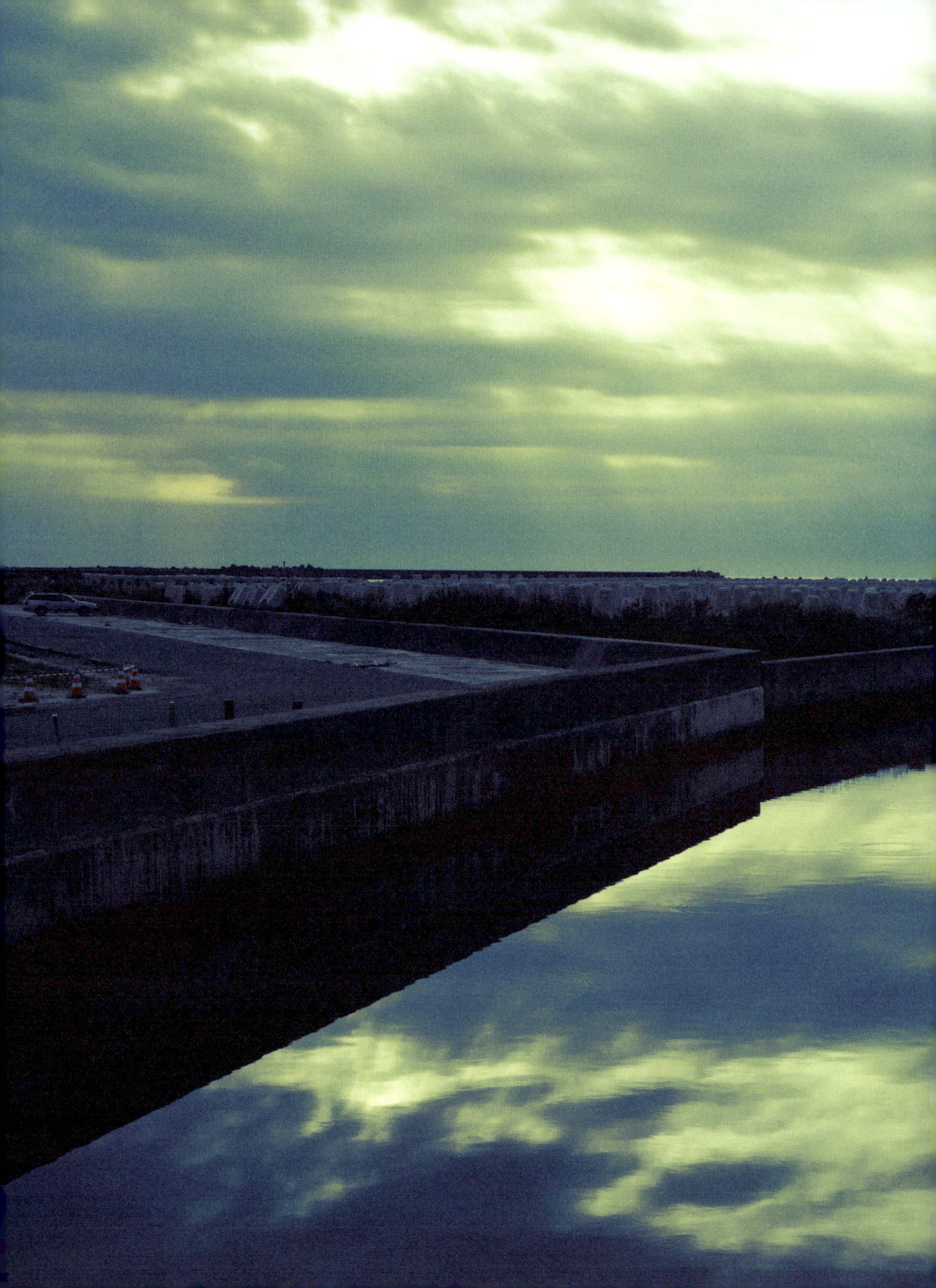

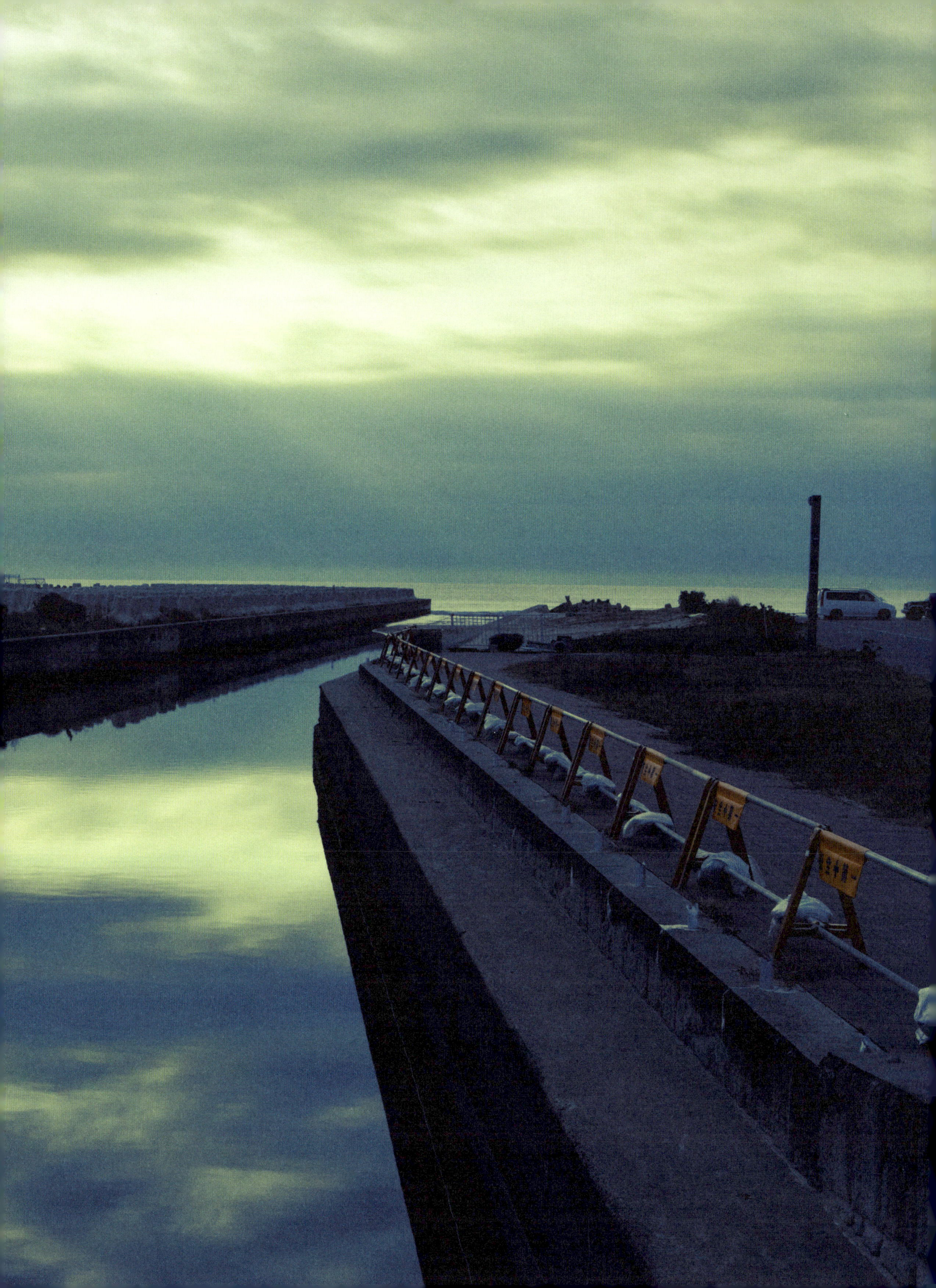

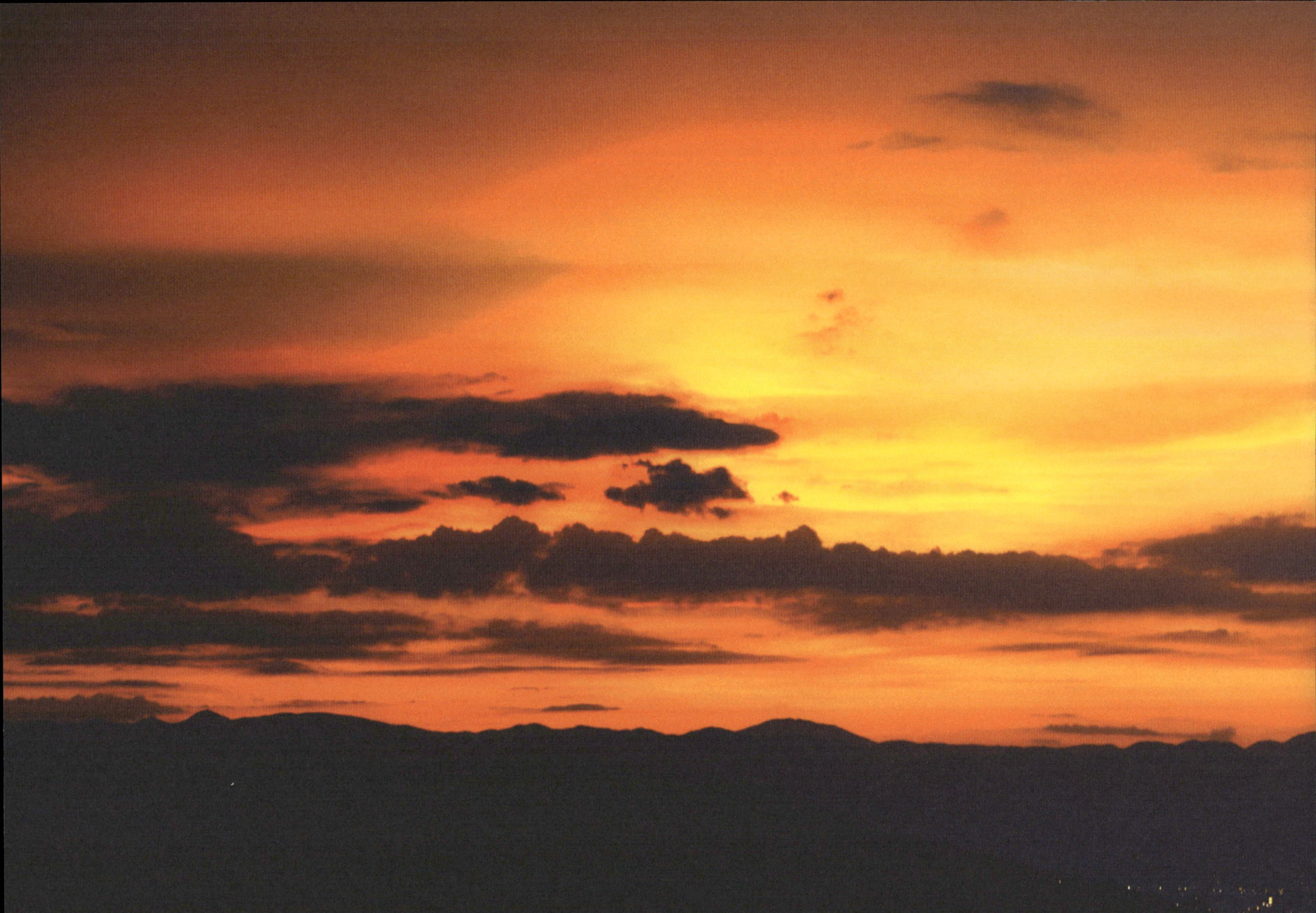

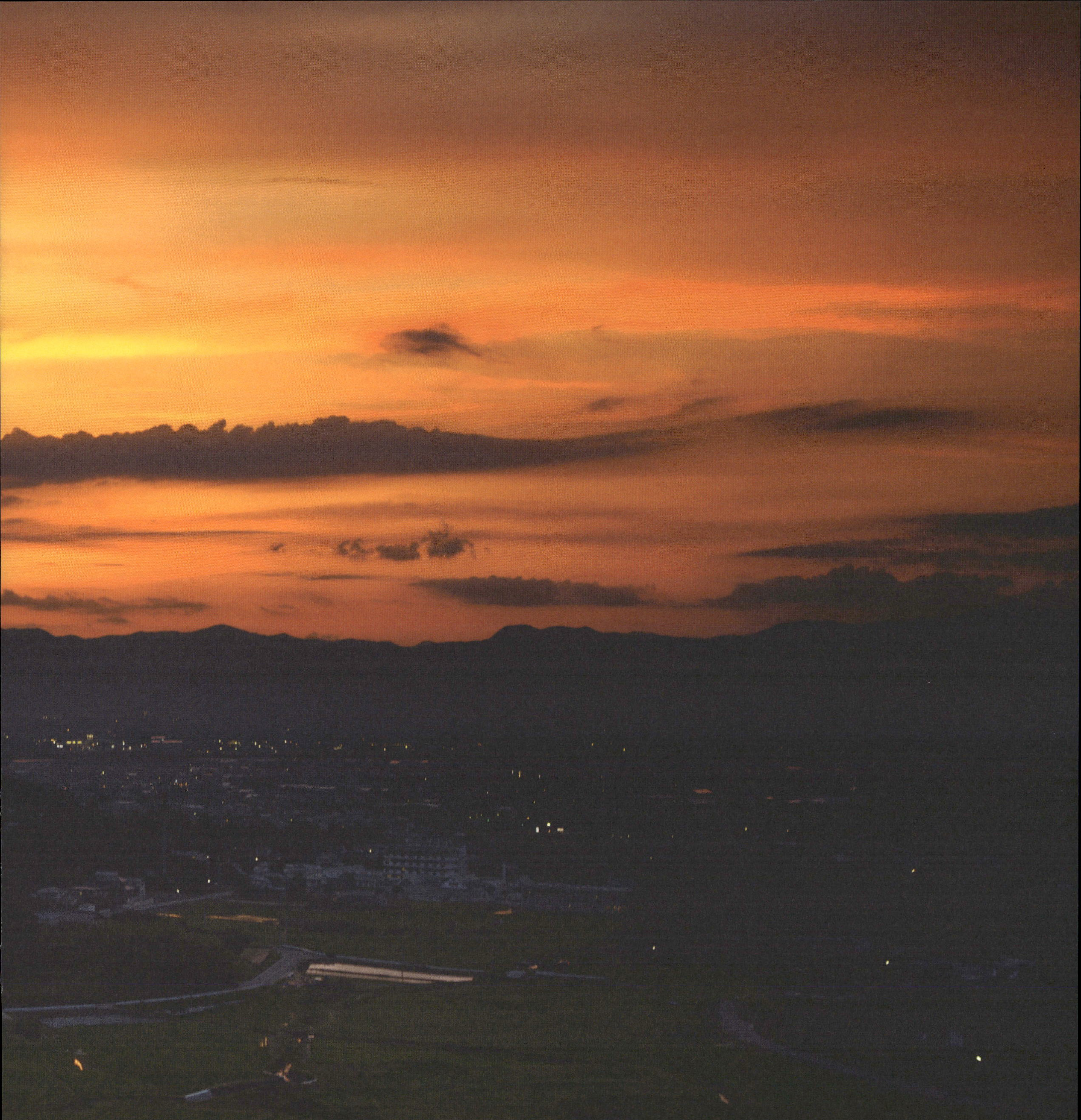

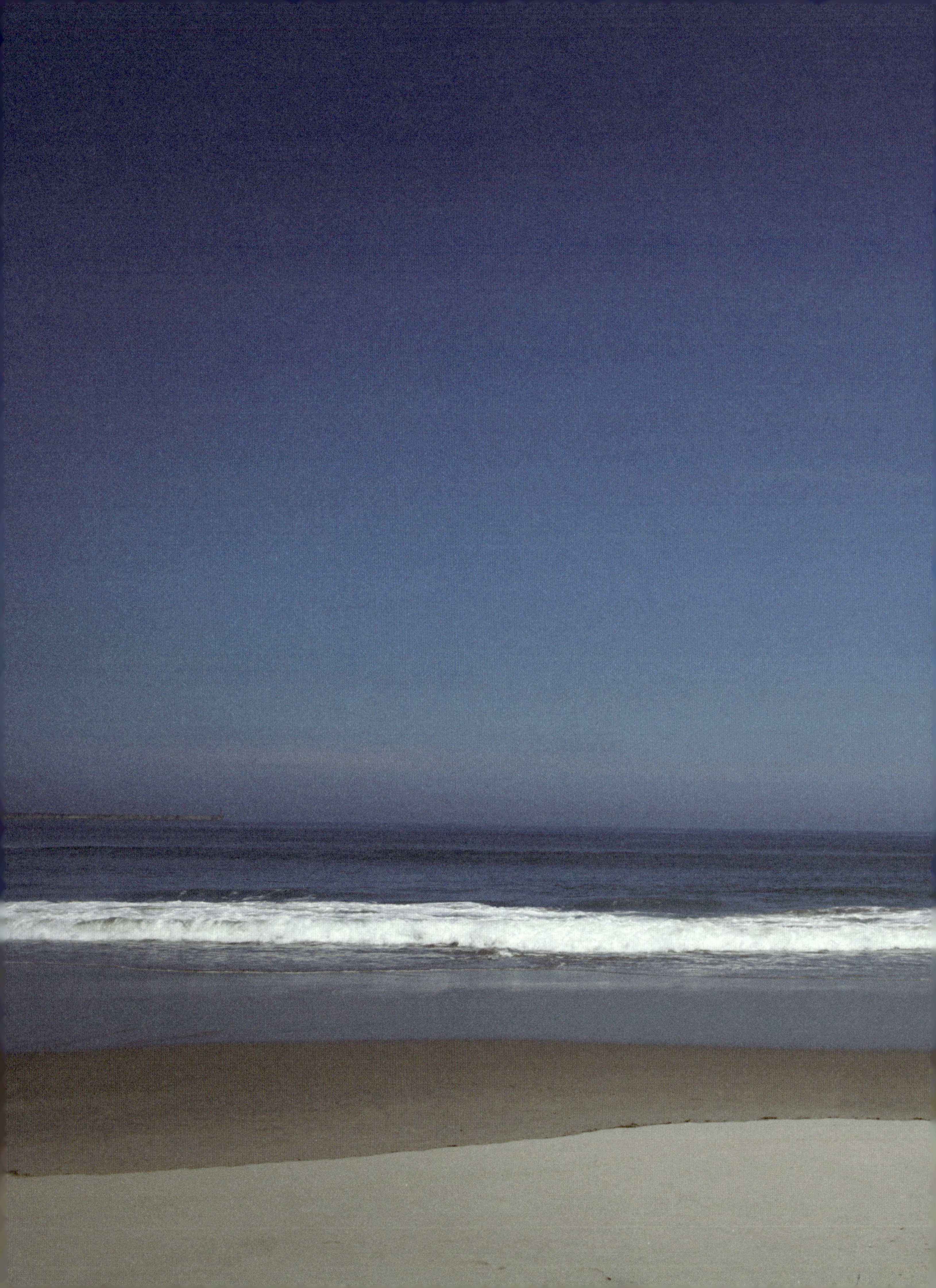

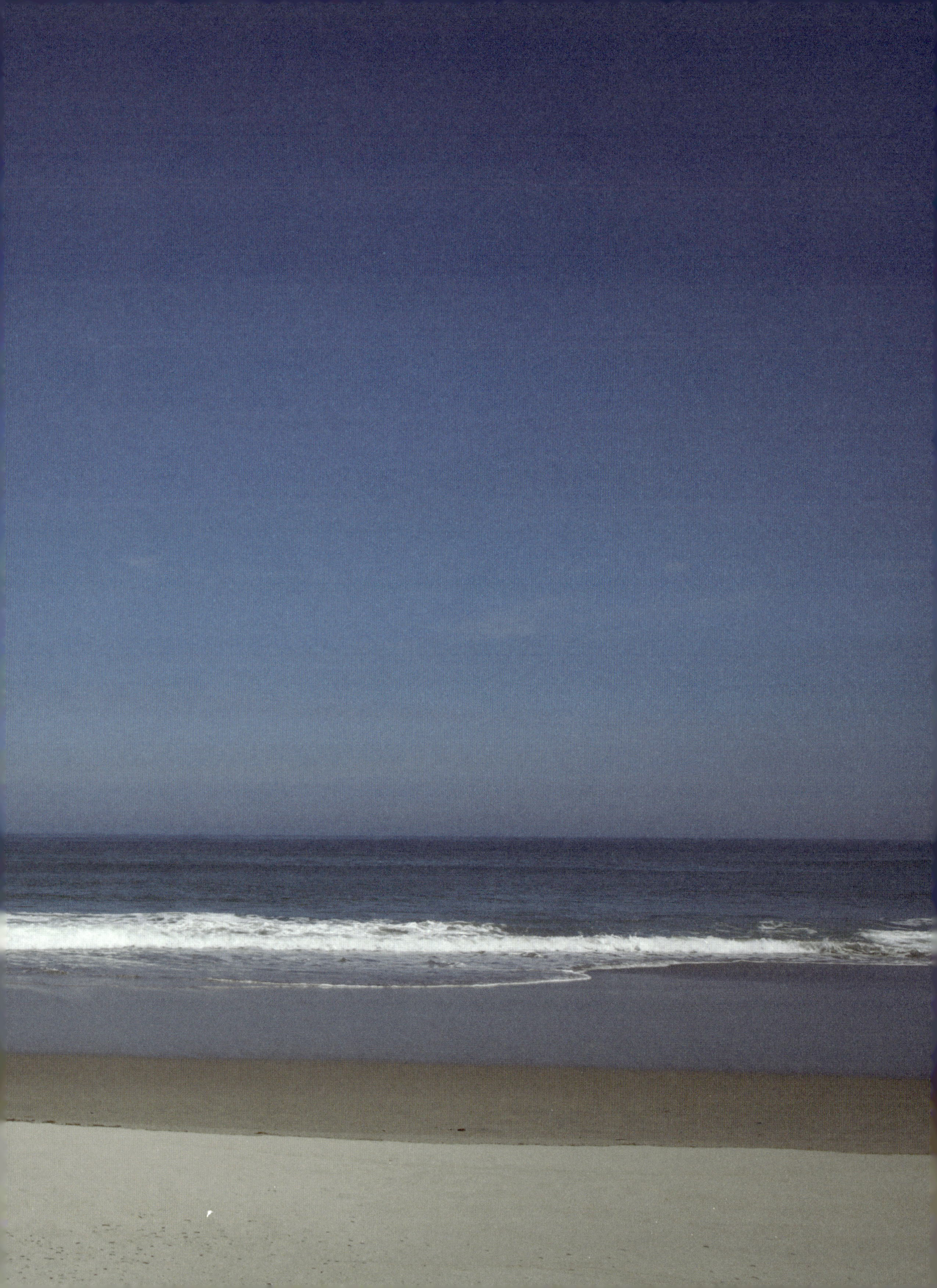

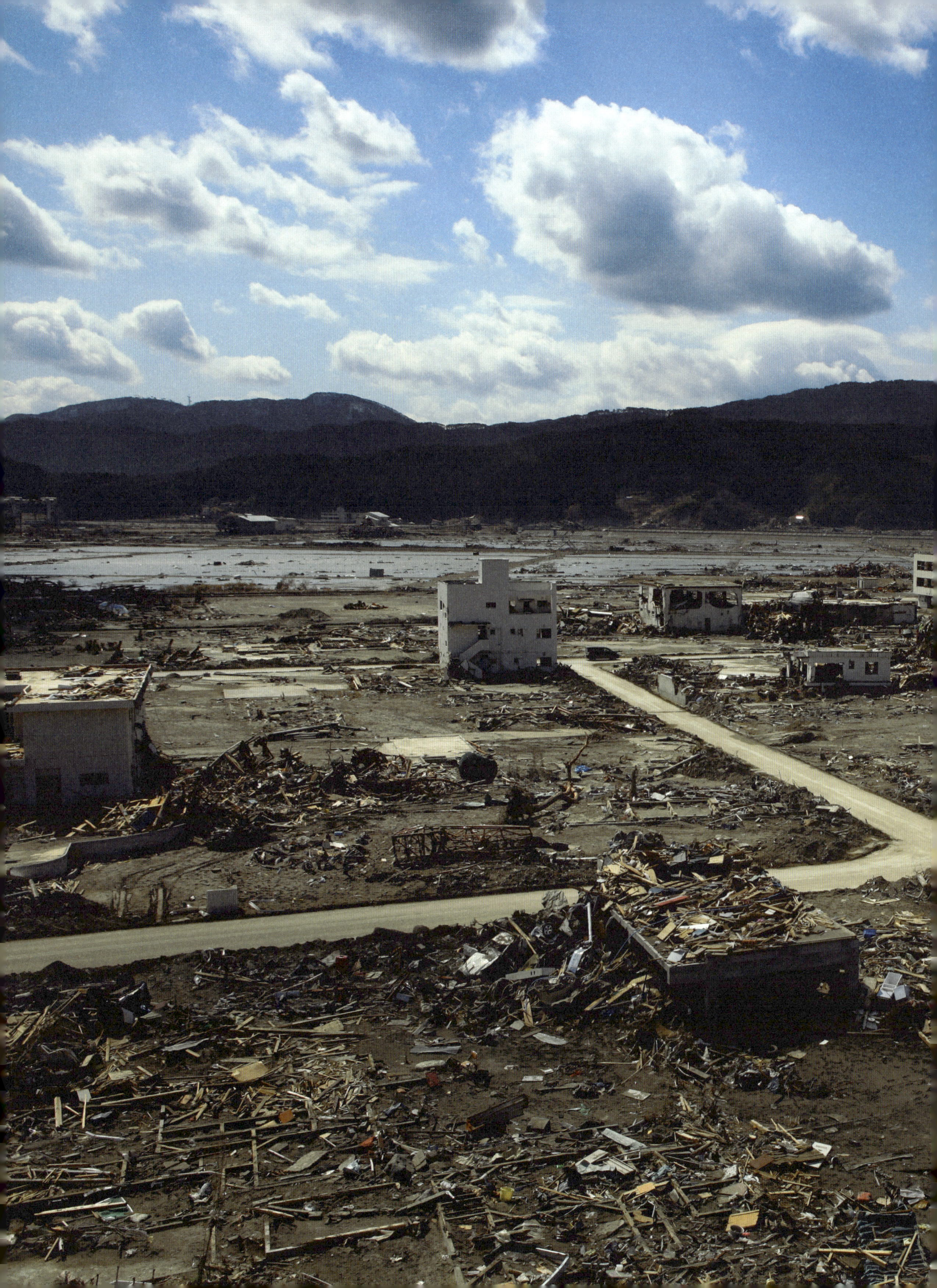

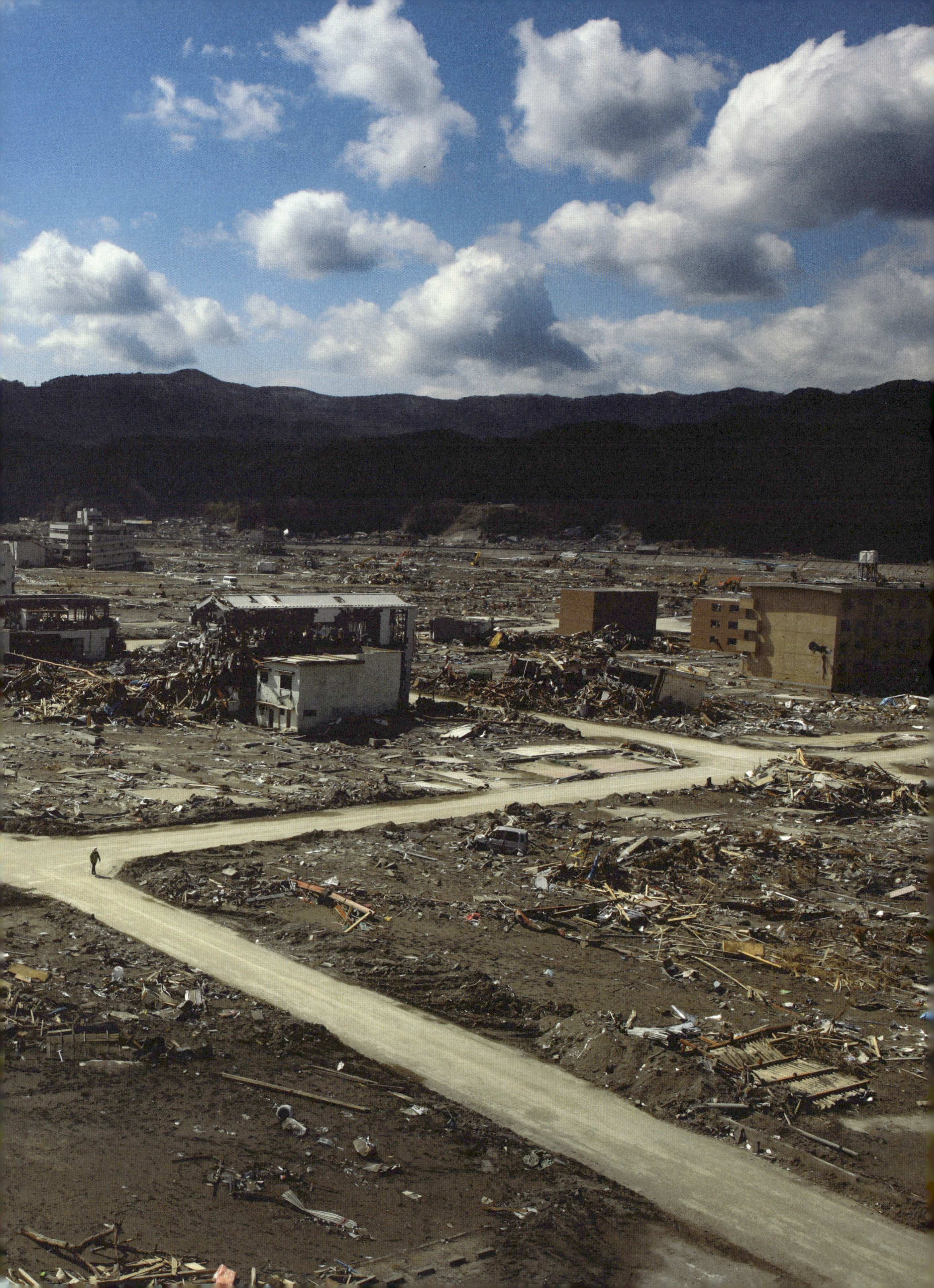

"Prime Minister Declares Nuclear Crisis Under Control"

Asahi Shimbun, December 16, 2011

After temperatures in the affected reactors have been stabilized to below 100 degrees, Japanese Prime Minister Yoshihiko Noda declares that the accident is under control—a statement immediately contested by experts.

野田総理、原発事故収束を宣言

2011年12月16日　朝日新聞

原子炉内の温度が安定基準である100℃以下に保たれたとして、
野田佳彦総理大臣は事故炉が制御下にあることを宣言した。
これについて、専門家から疑問視する声が上がった。

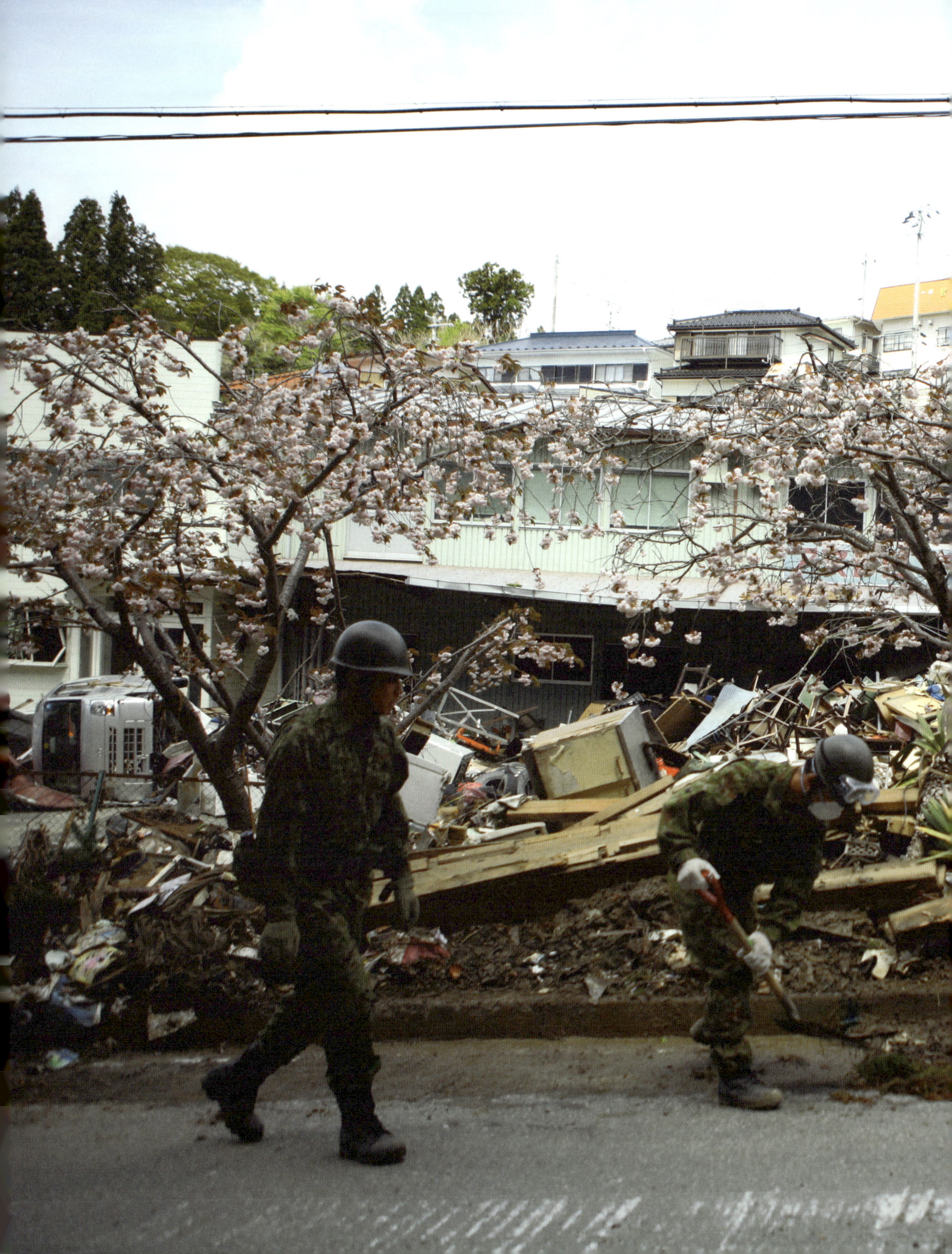

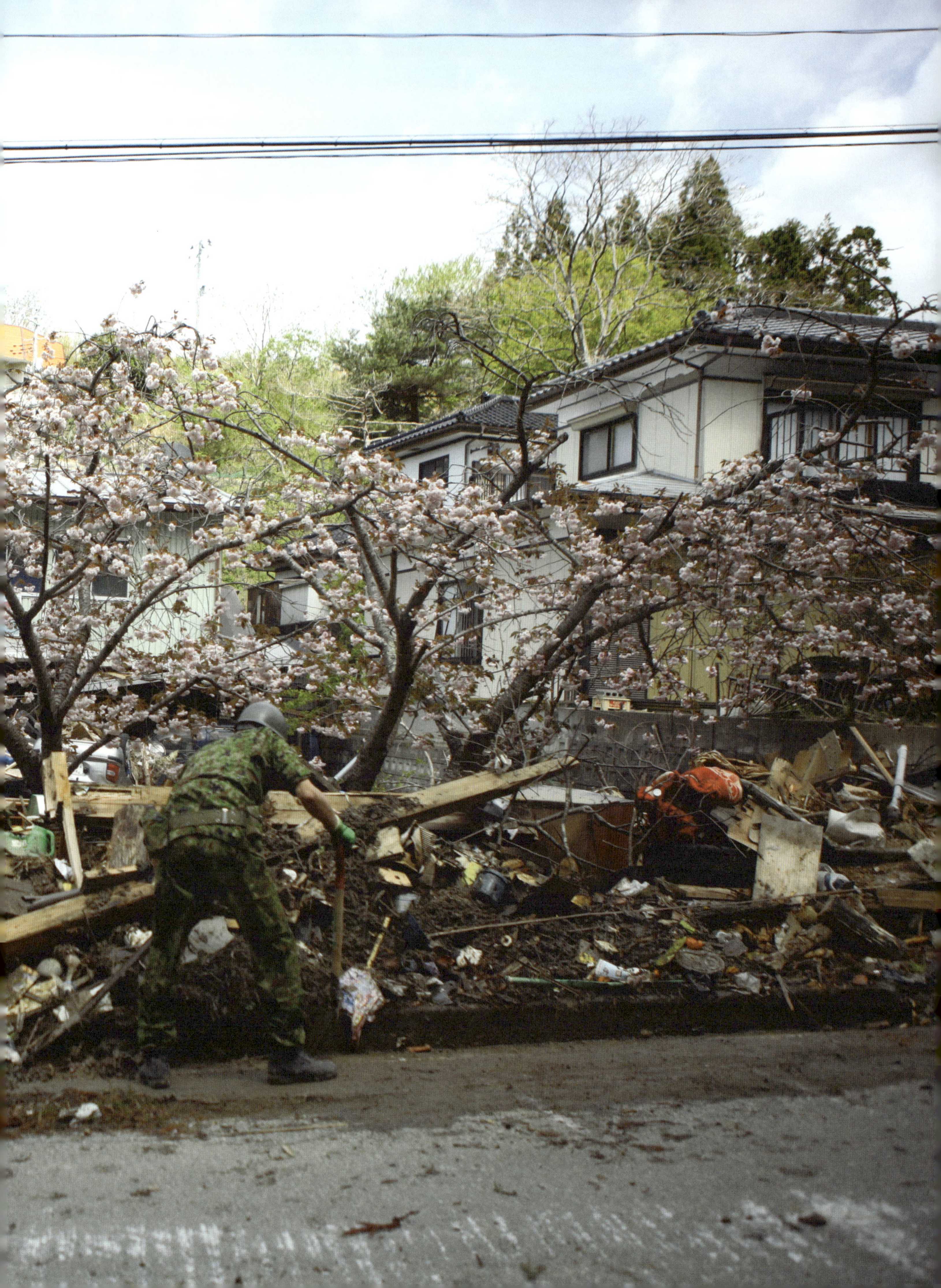

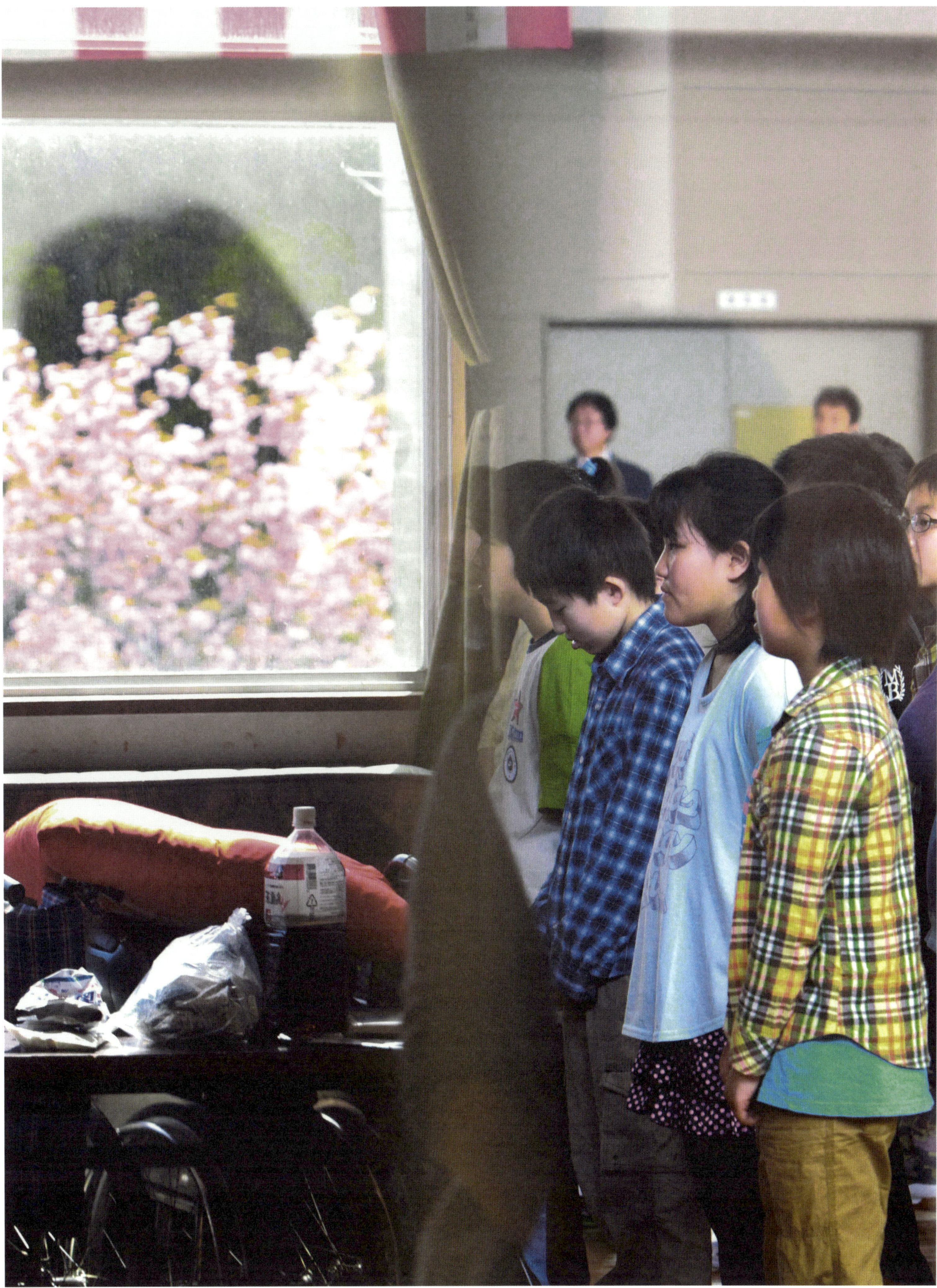

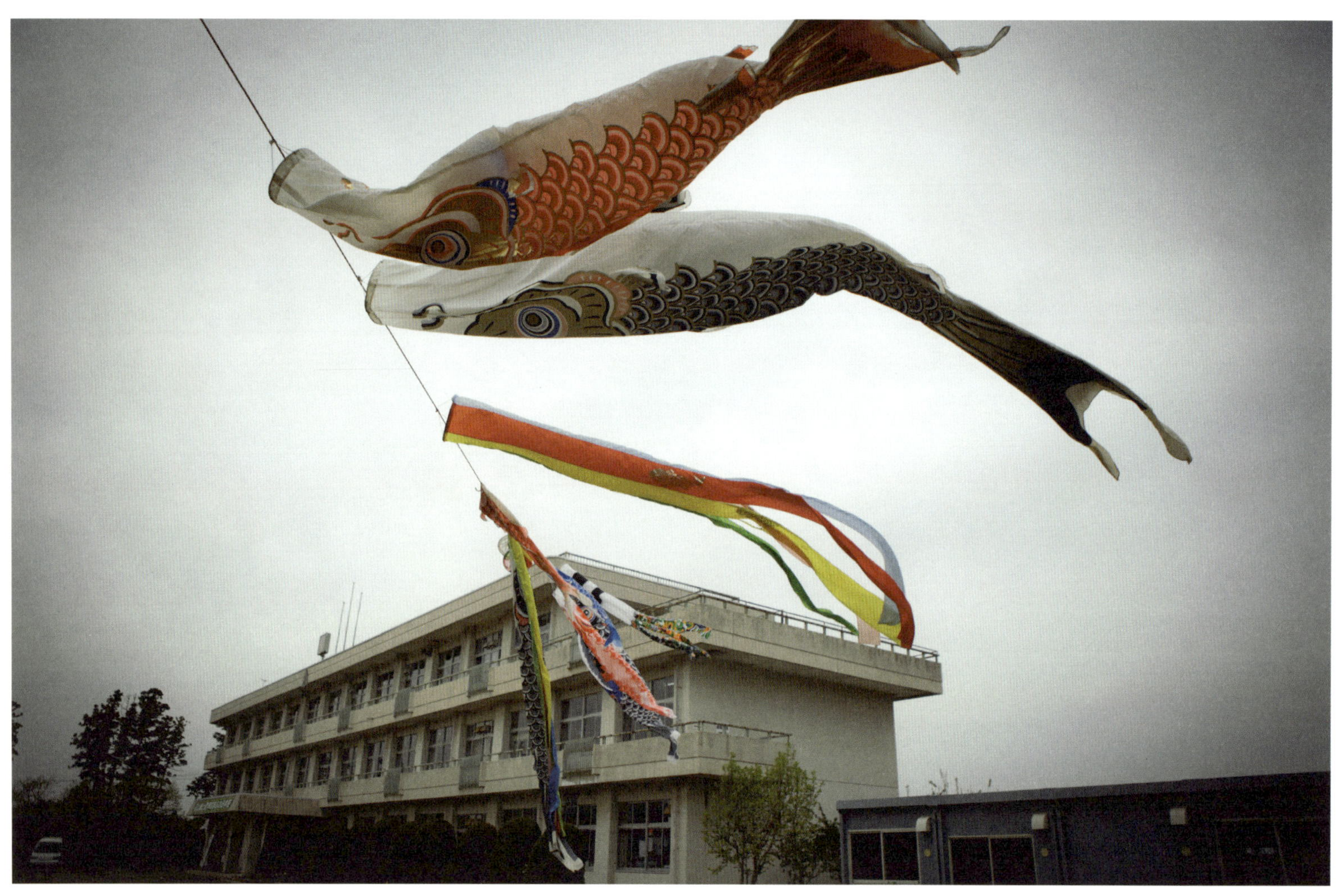

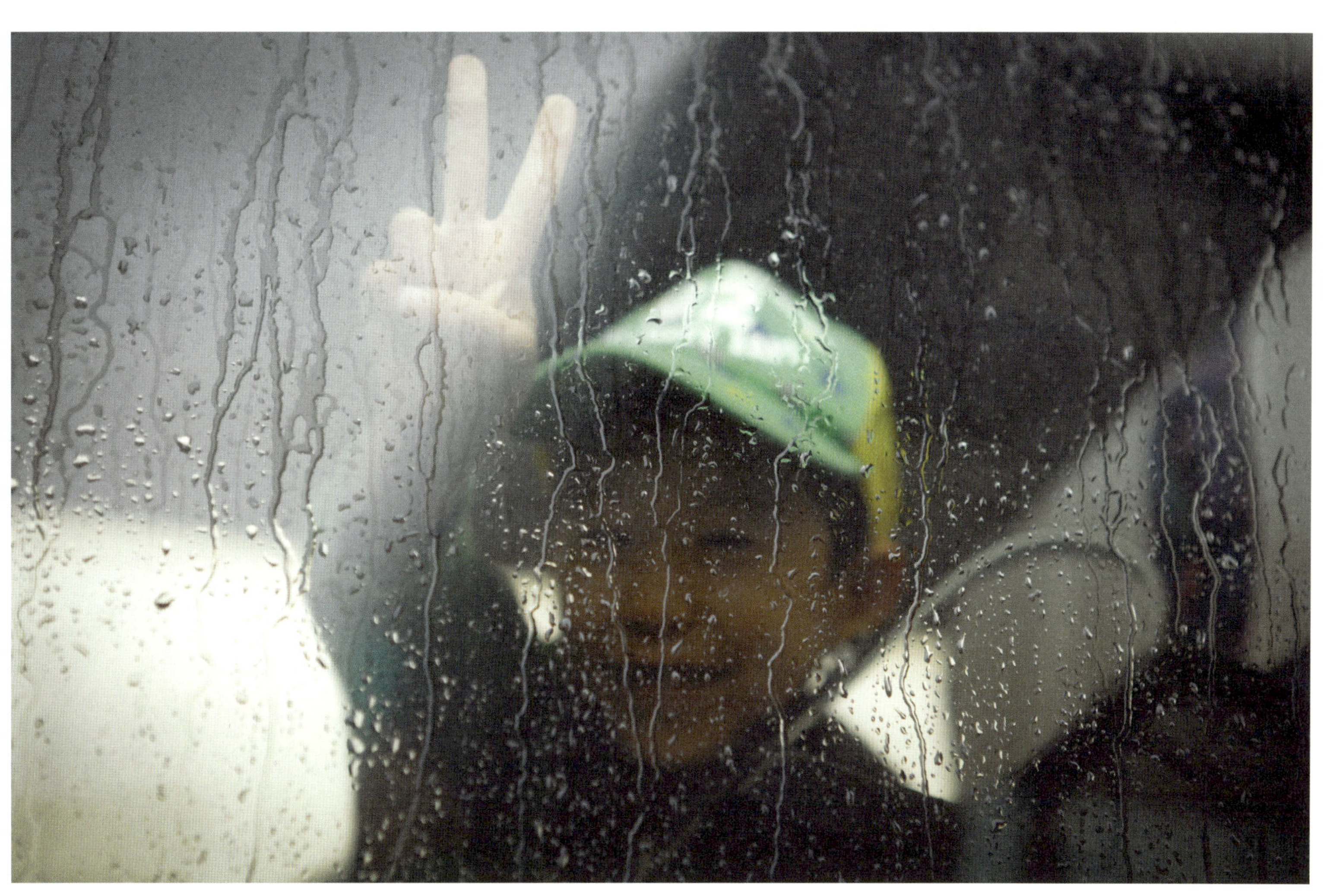

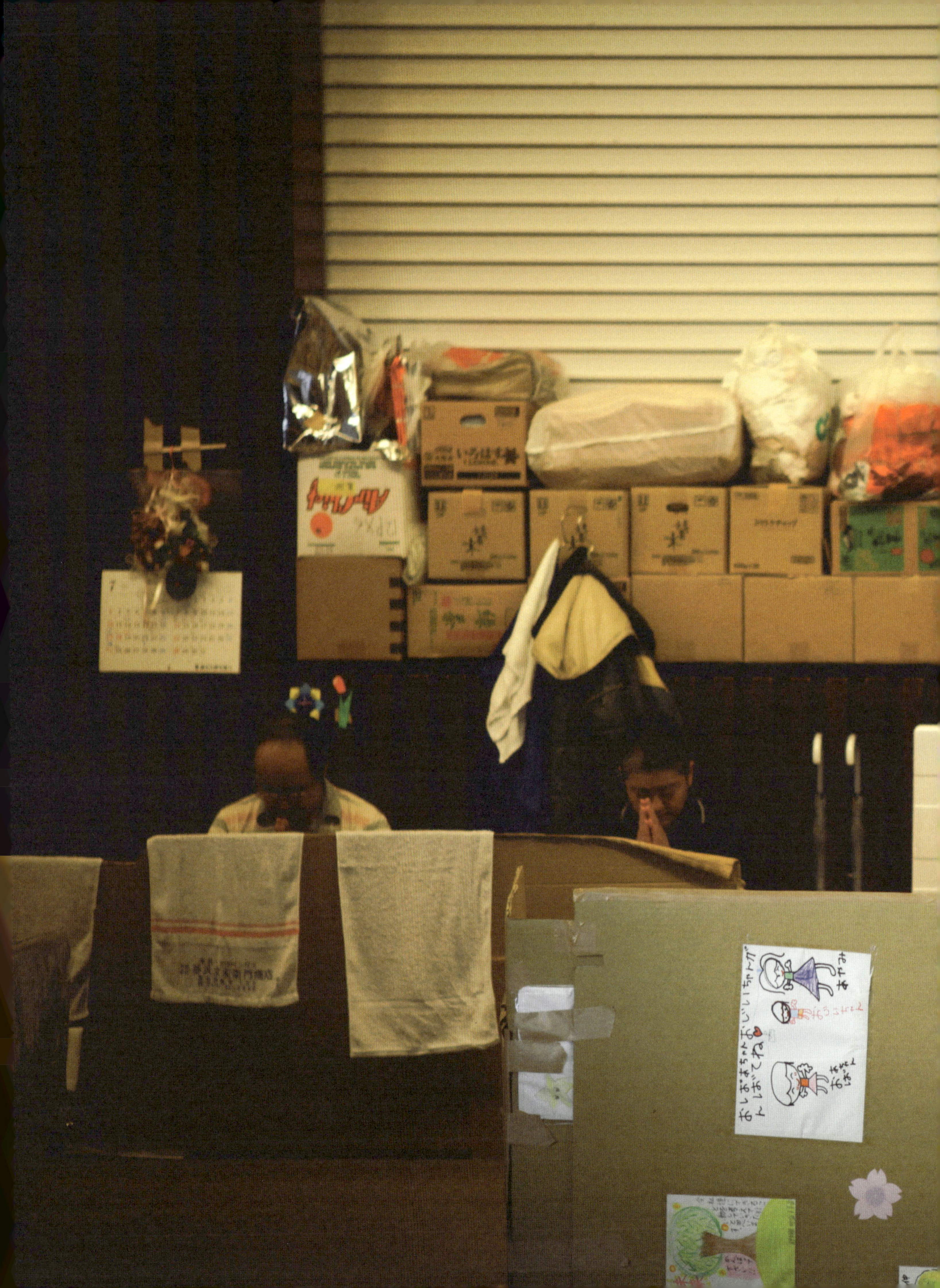

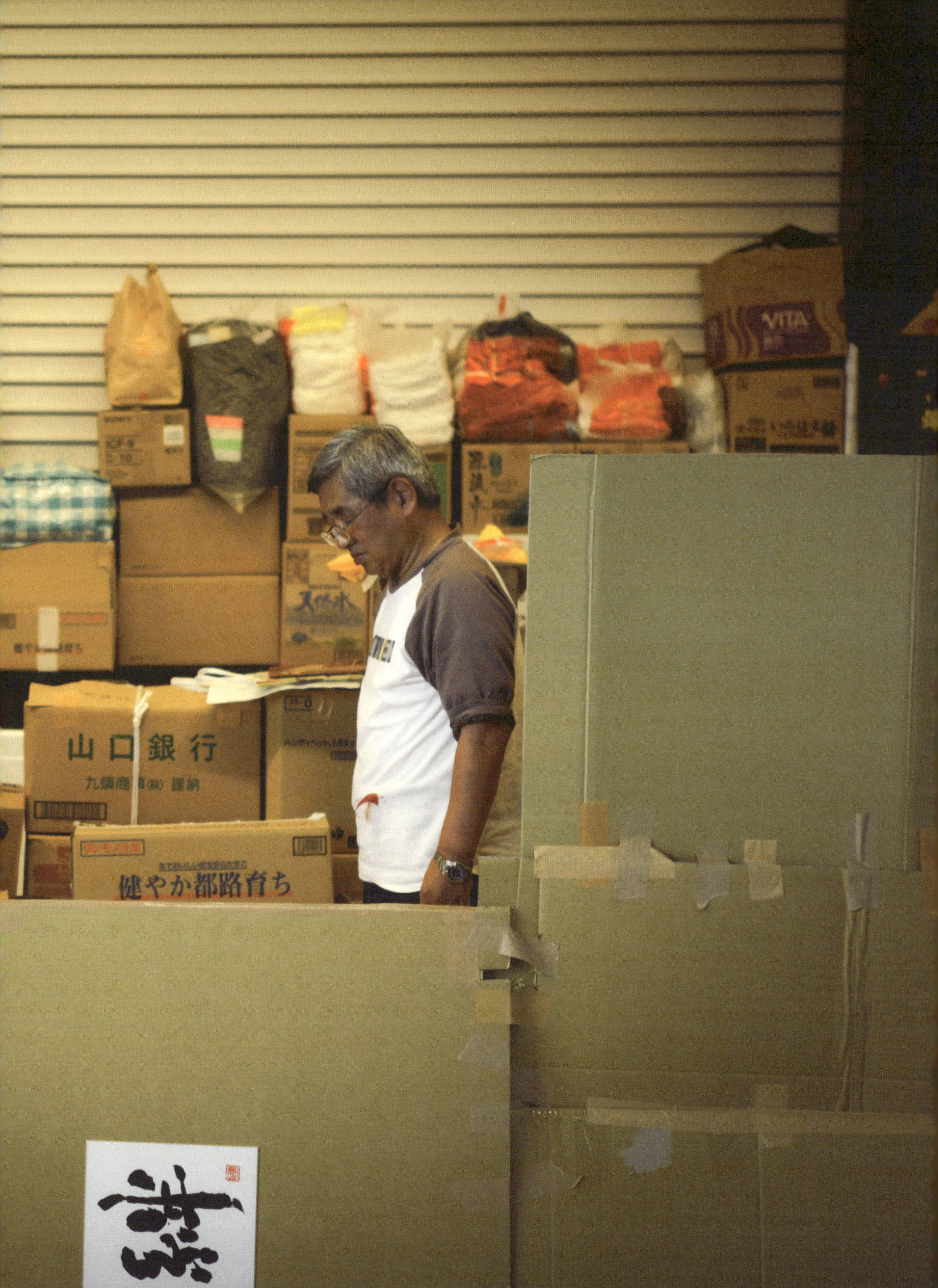

VITA
山口銀行
九州商事㈱ 匯納
健やか都路育ち
SONY
天然水

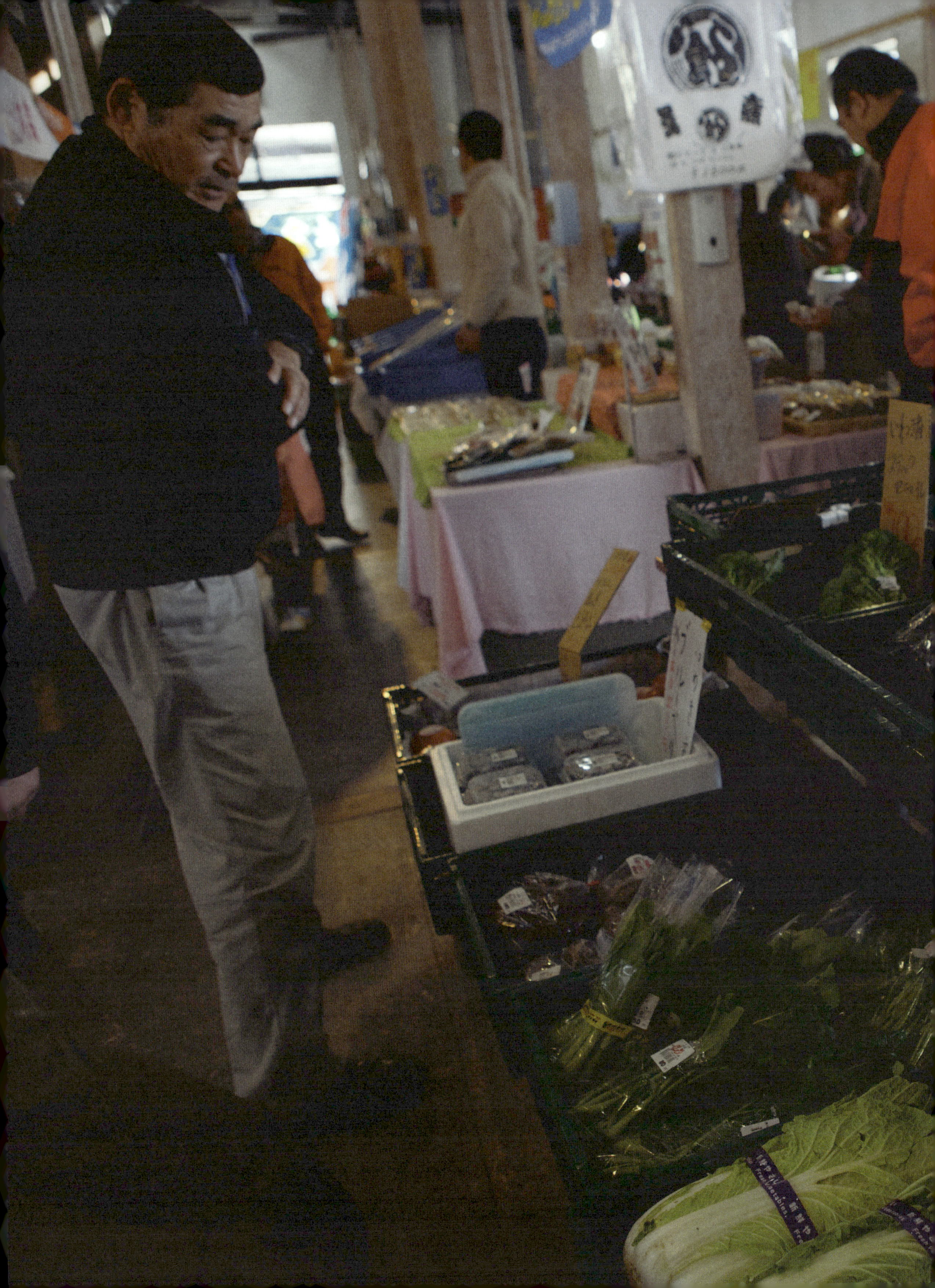

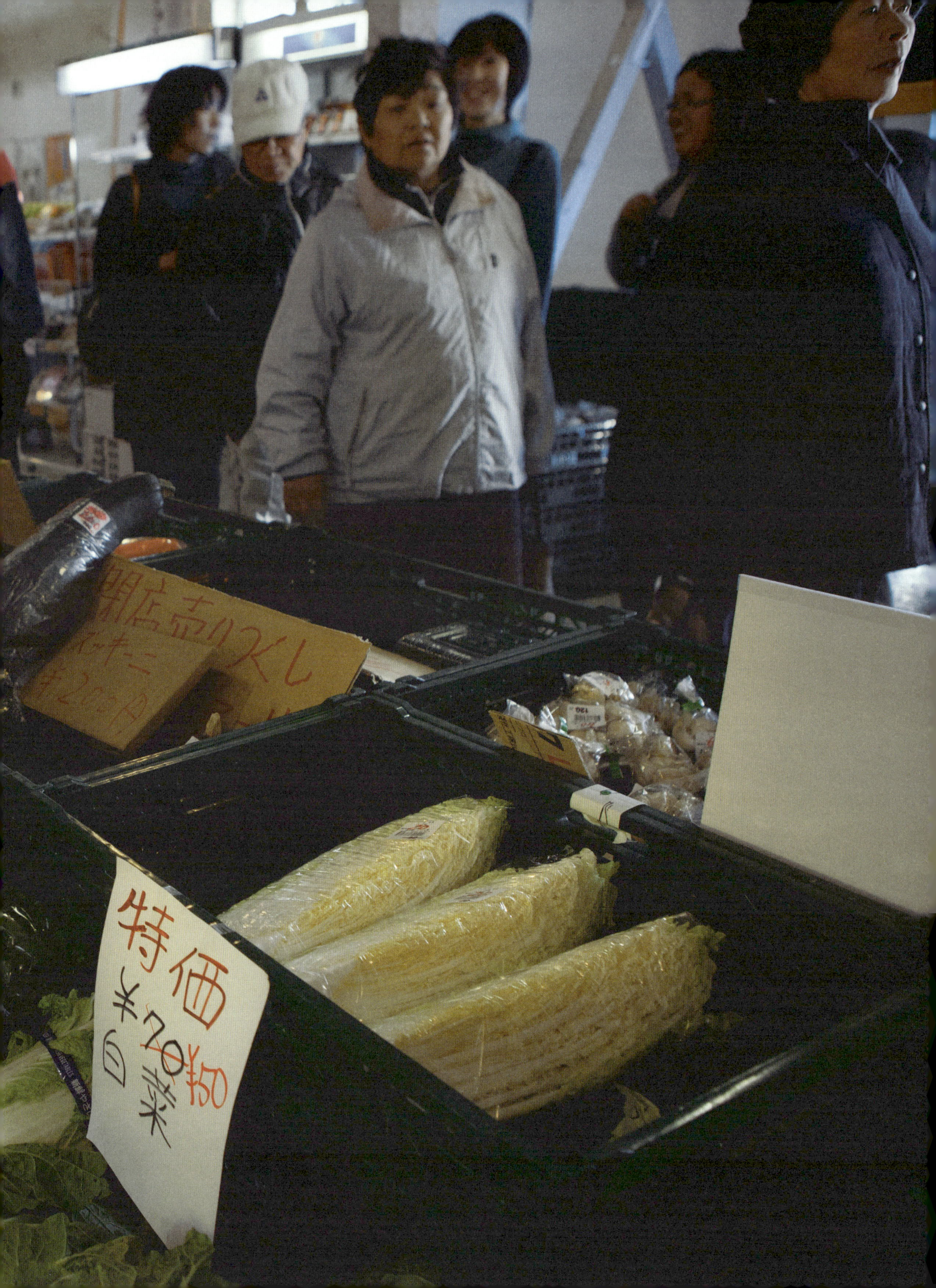
閉店売りつくし
白菜
￥20円
特価
白菜
￥20円

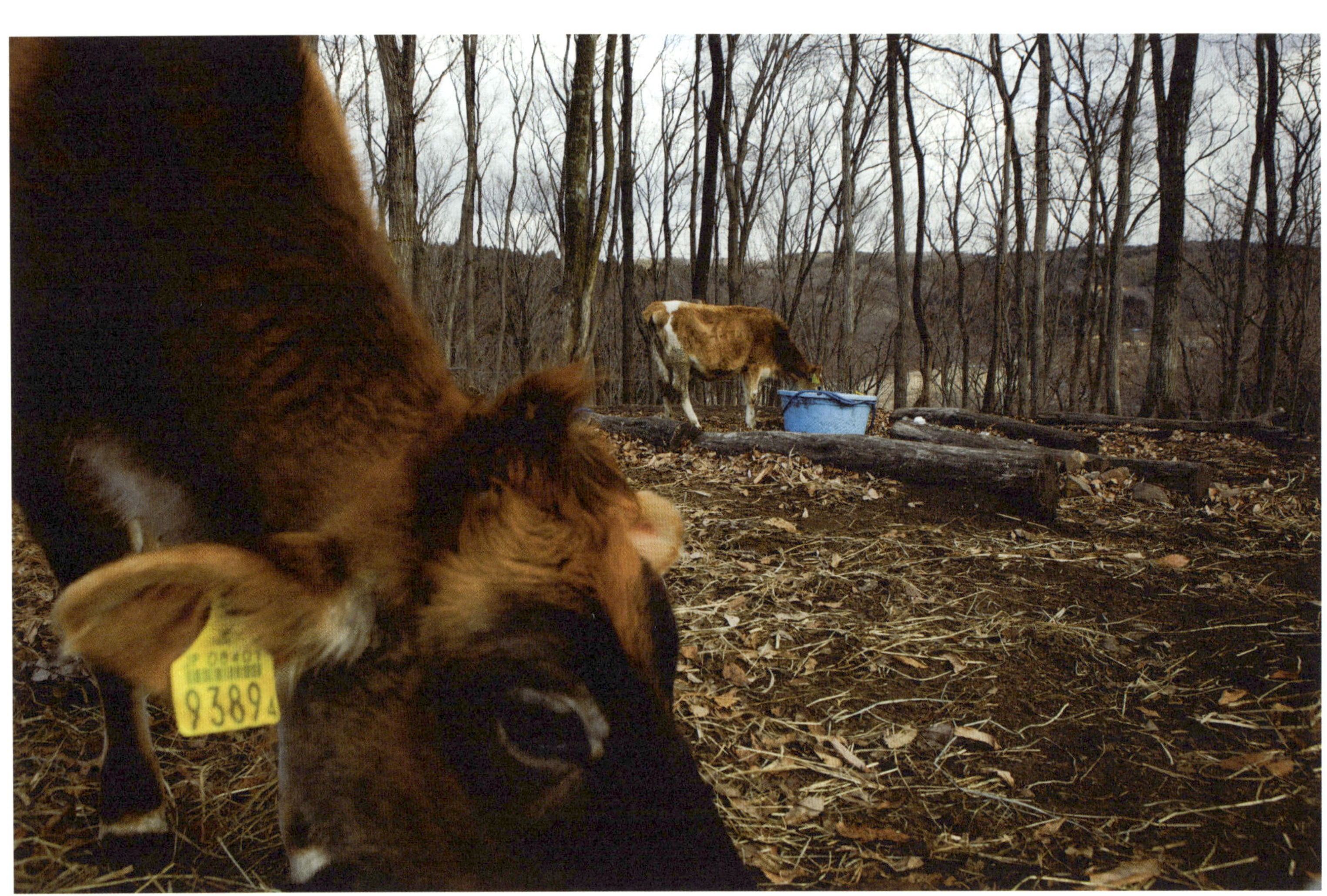

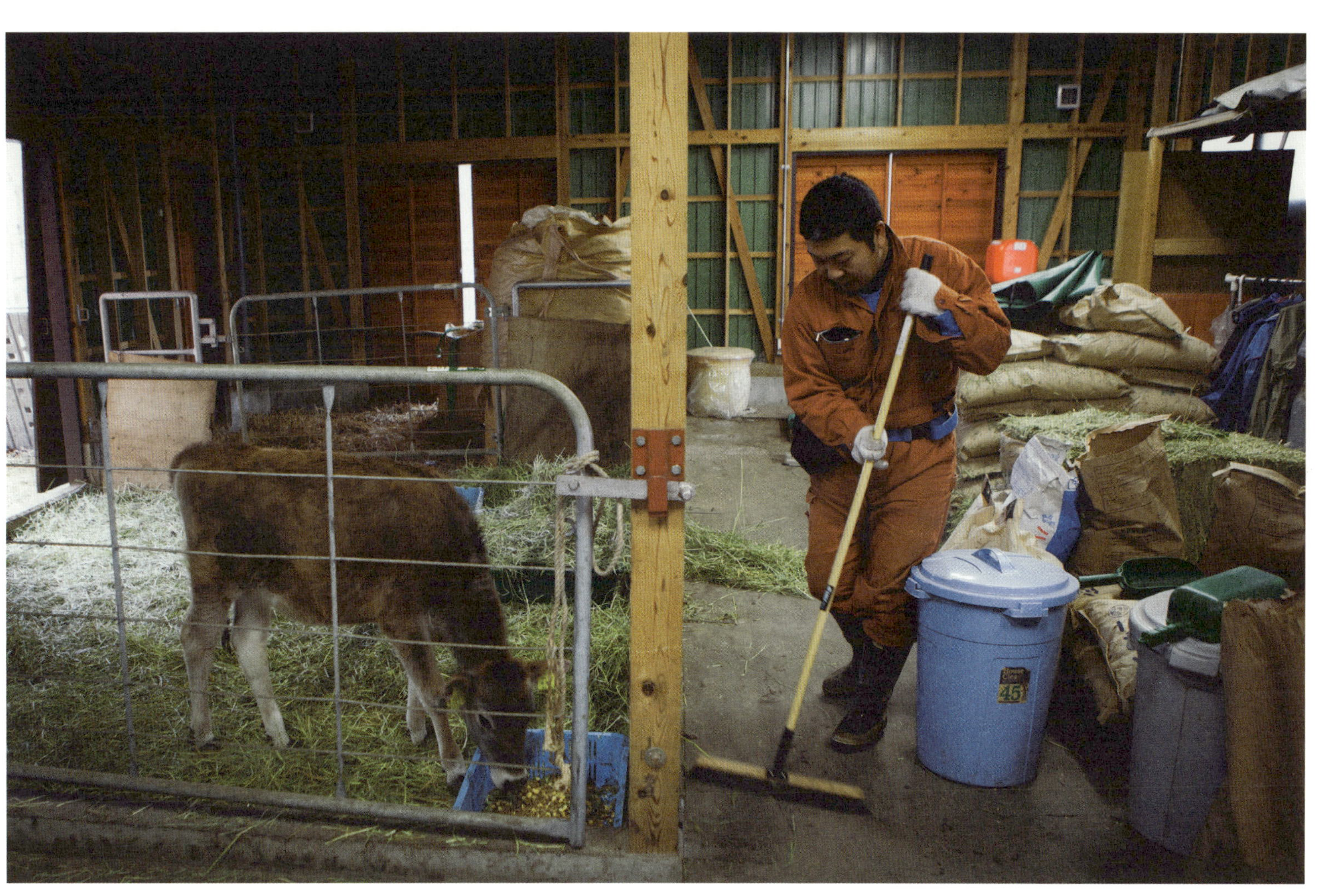

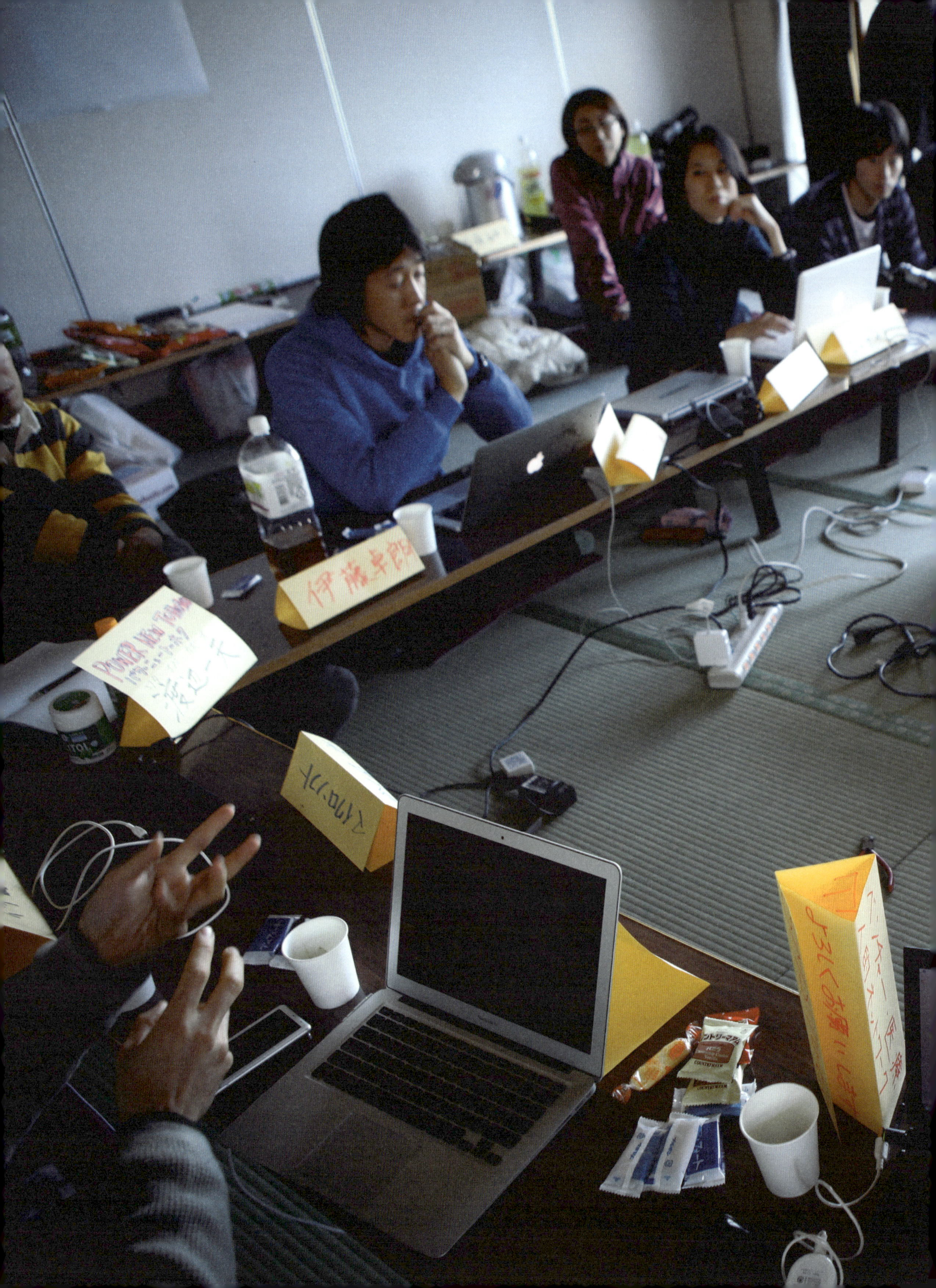

POWER NEW TOKYO
伊藤幸路
スカウター

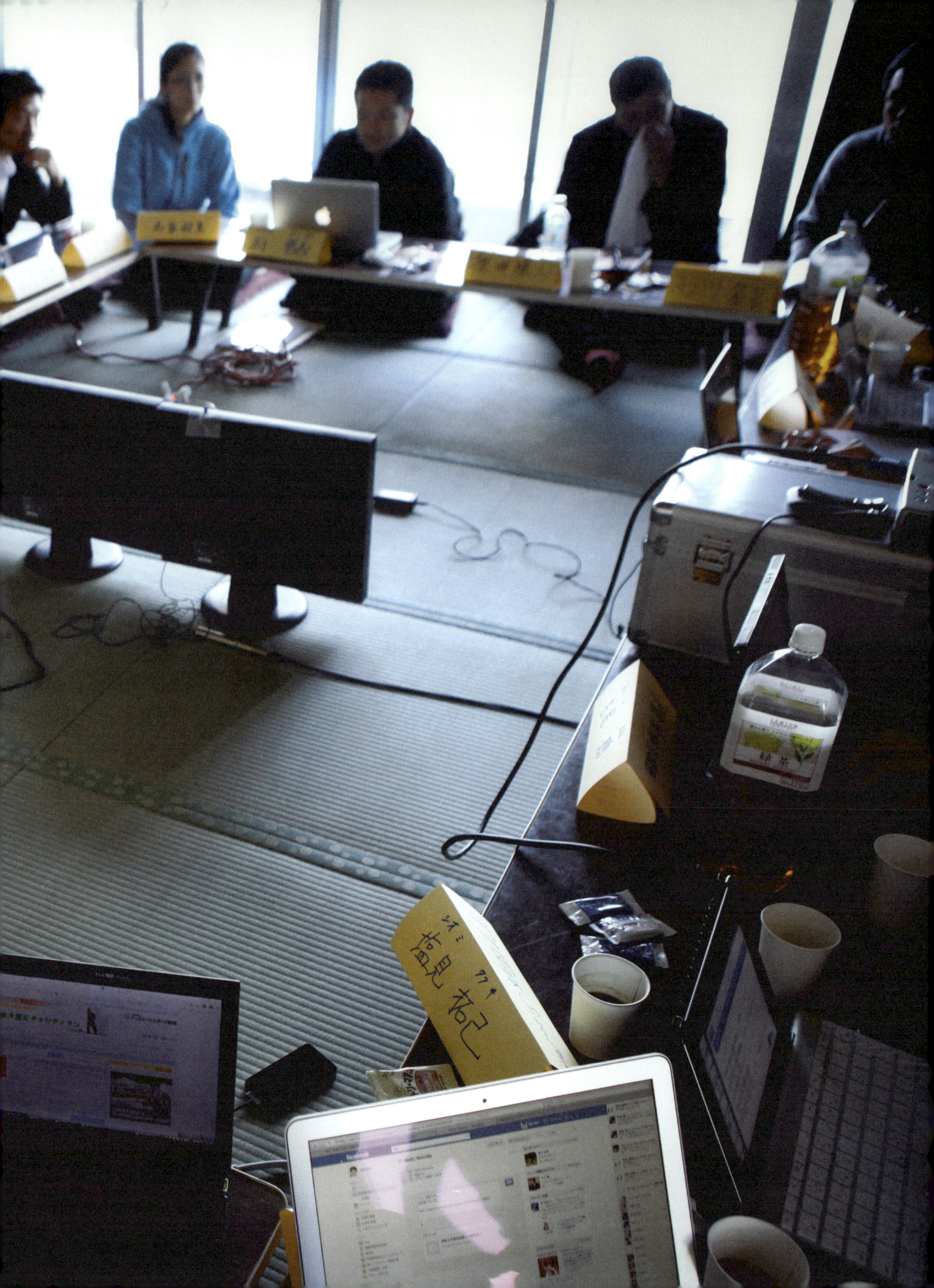

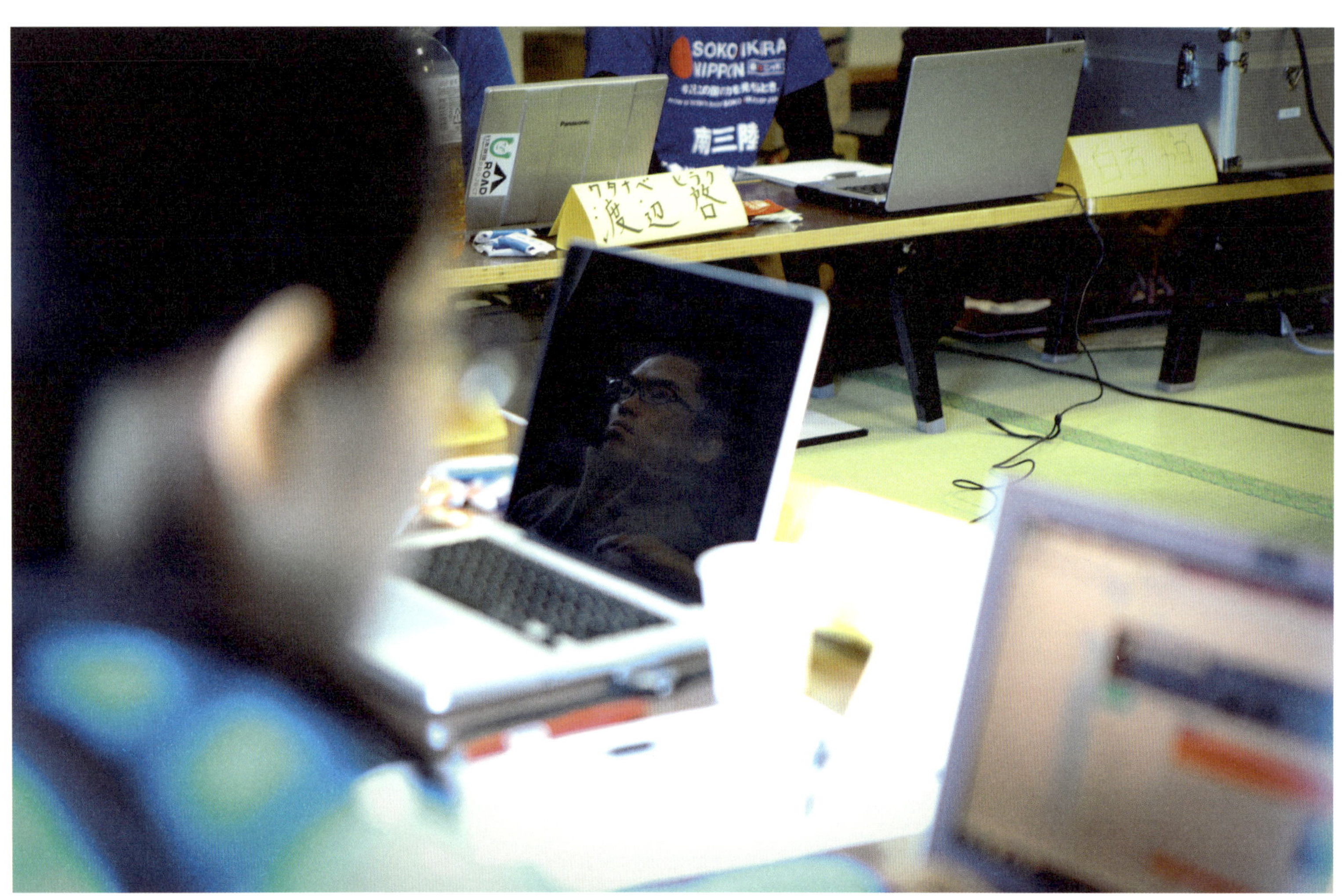

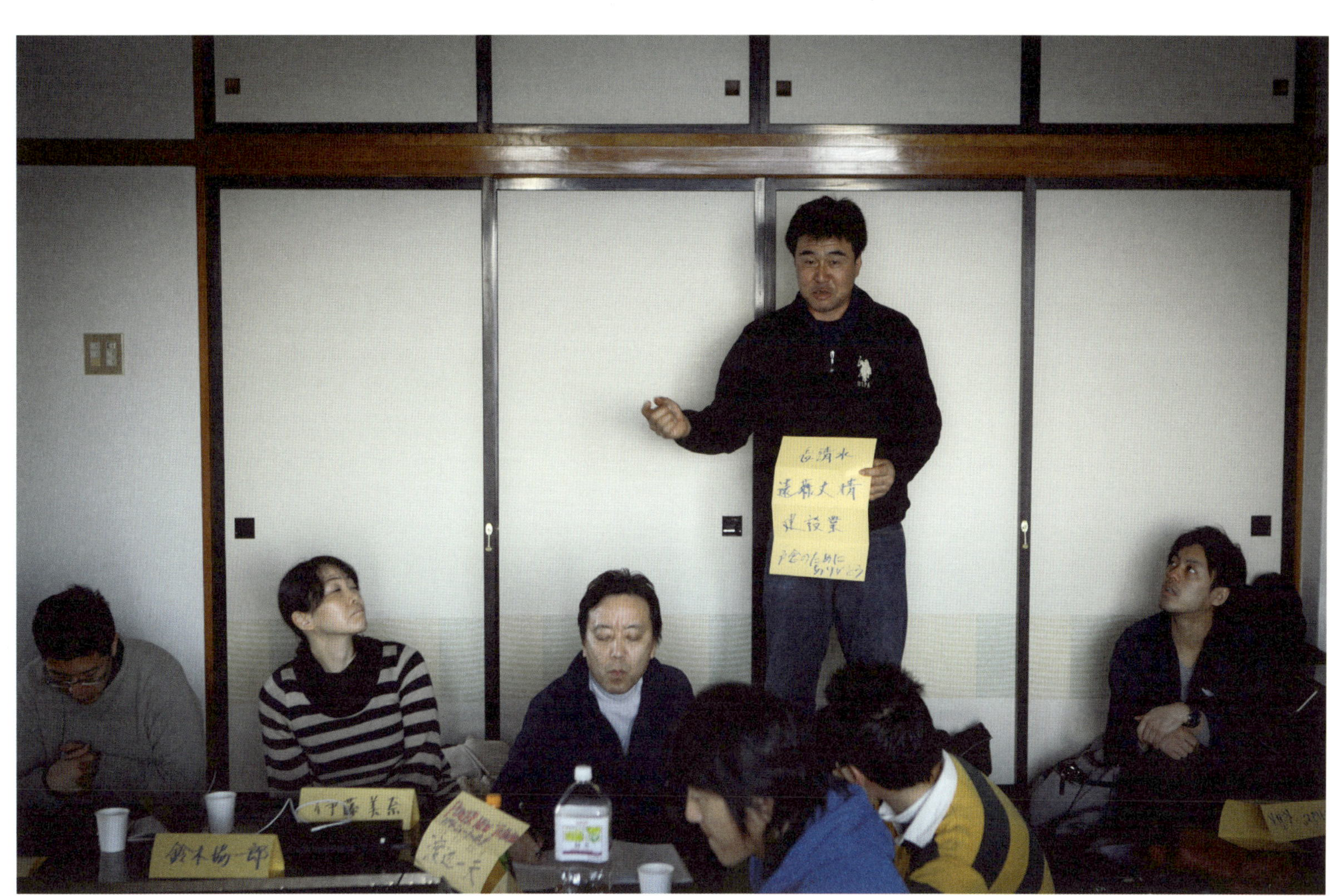
名 清水
遠藤大晴
建設業
子供のために
ありがとう
鈴木陽一郎
伊藤美奈
渡辺一夫

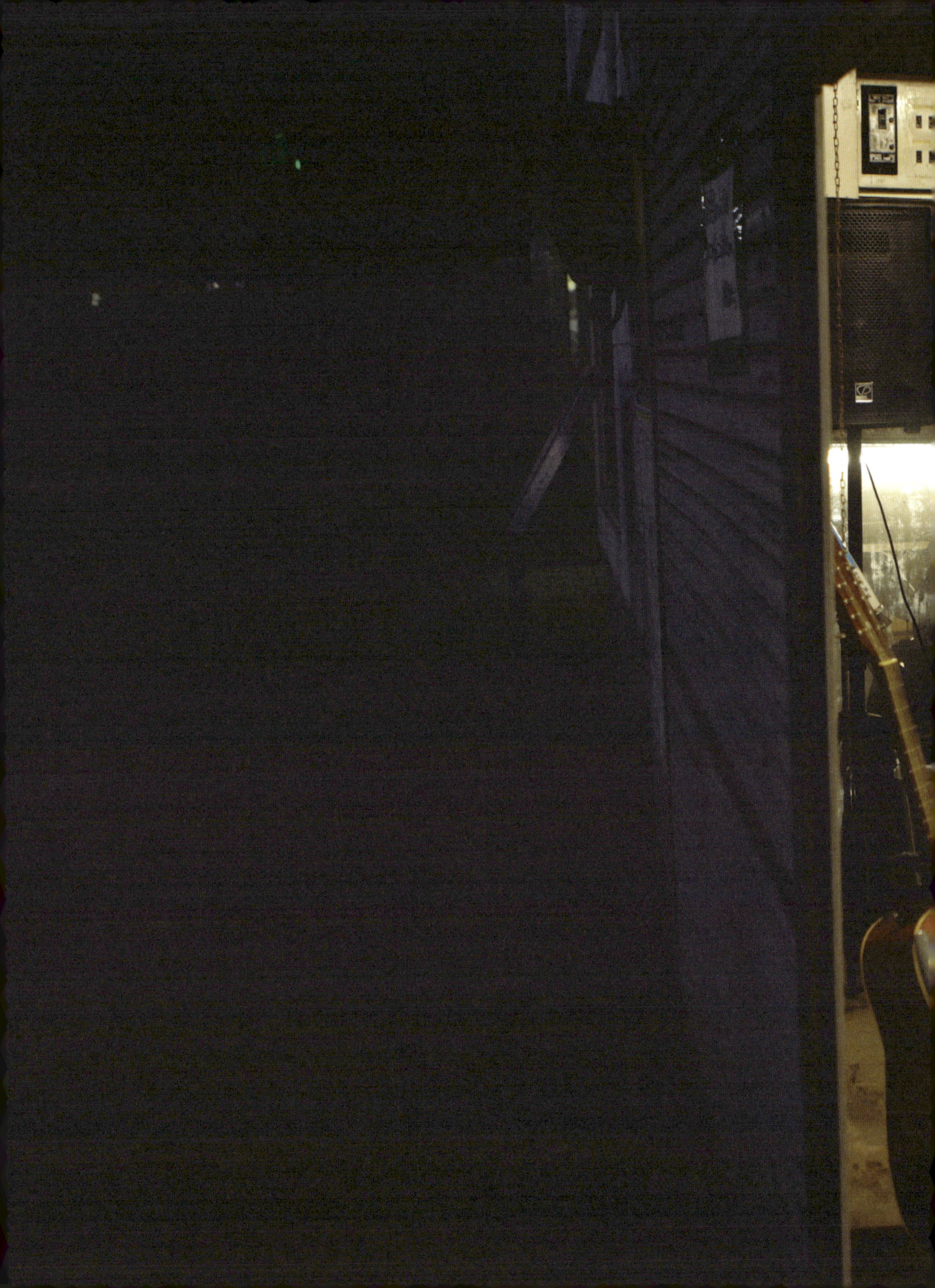

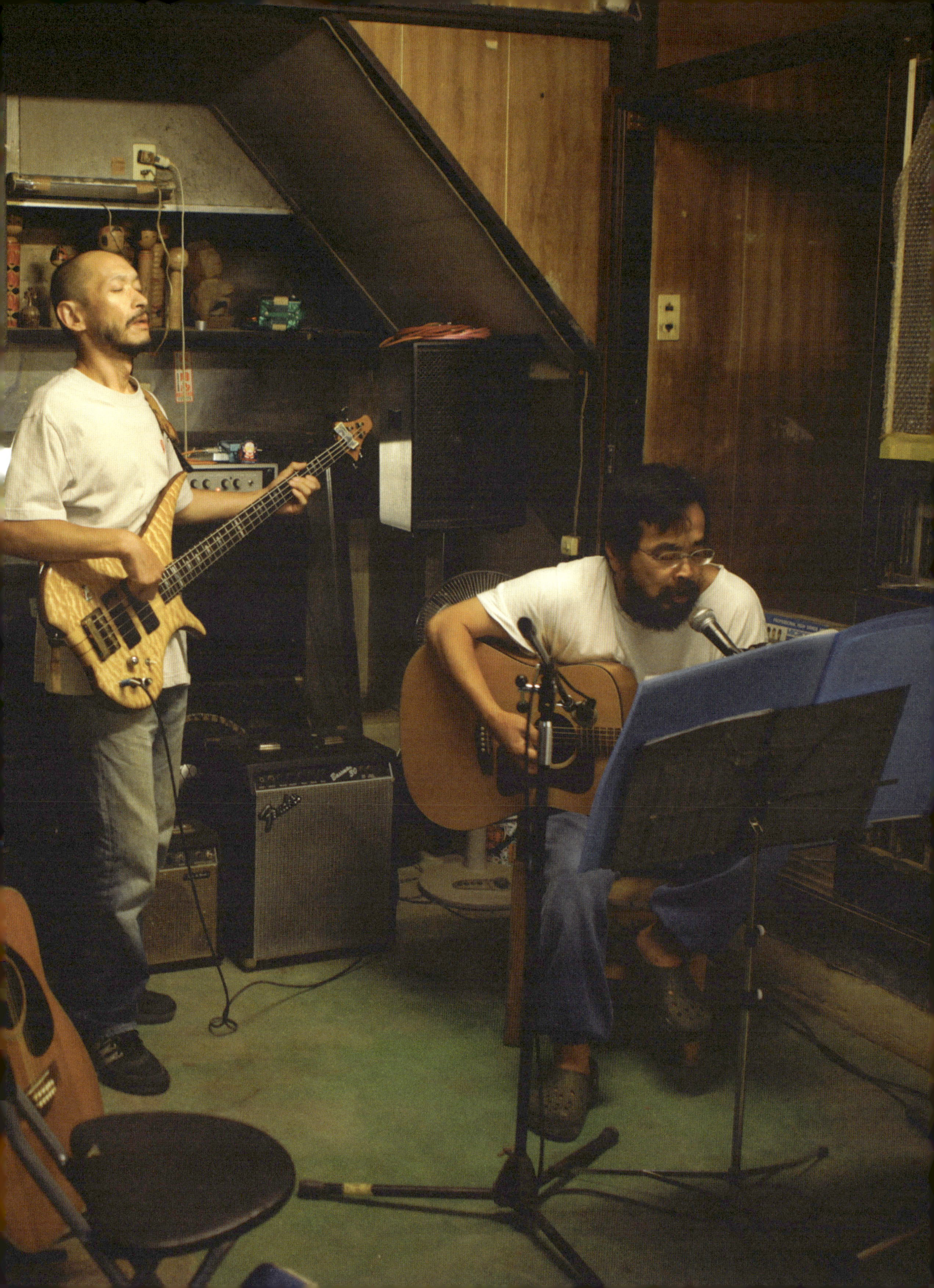

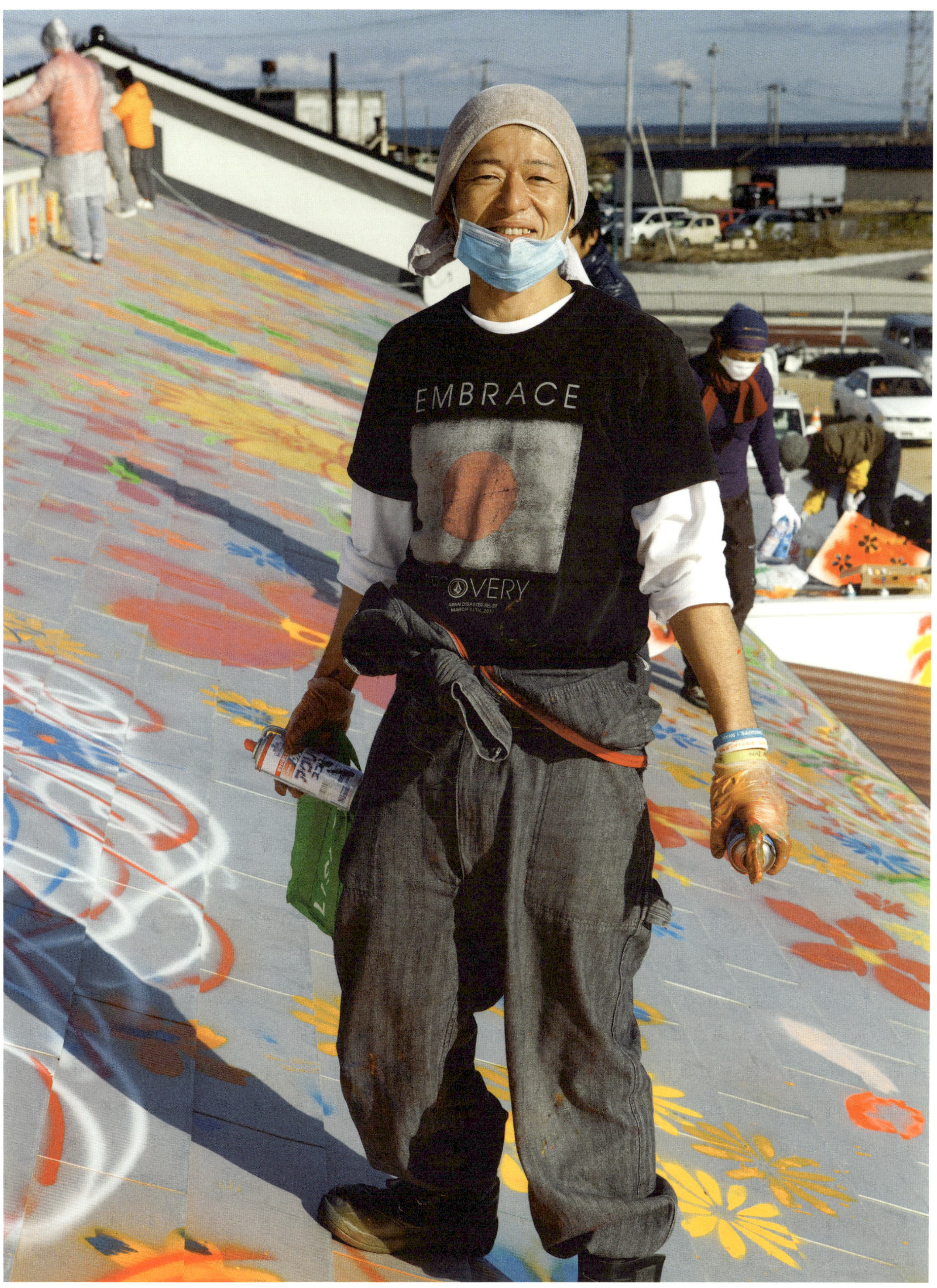
EMBRACE
VERY
JAPAN DISASTER RELIEF
MARCH 11TH, 2011

"United States Approves First Nuclear Reactors since 1978"

Fox News, February 9, 2012

Only eleven months after the beginning of the nuclear disaster in Fukushima Daiichi, the U.S. regulatory commission gives approval for the building of the first nuclear power plant in more than three decades.

米国、原発新設の承認は1978年以来、34年ぶり

2012年2月9日　FOXニュース

福島の原発事故からわずか11ヵ月後、米原子力規制委員会は30年以上建設されていなかった原子力発電所の建設を承認した。

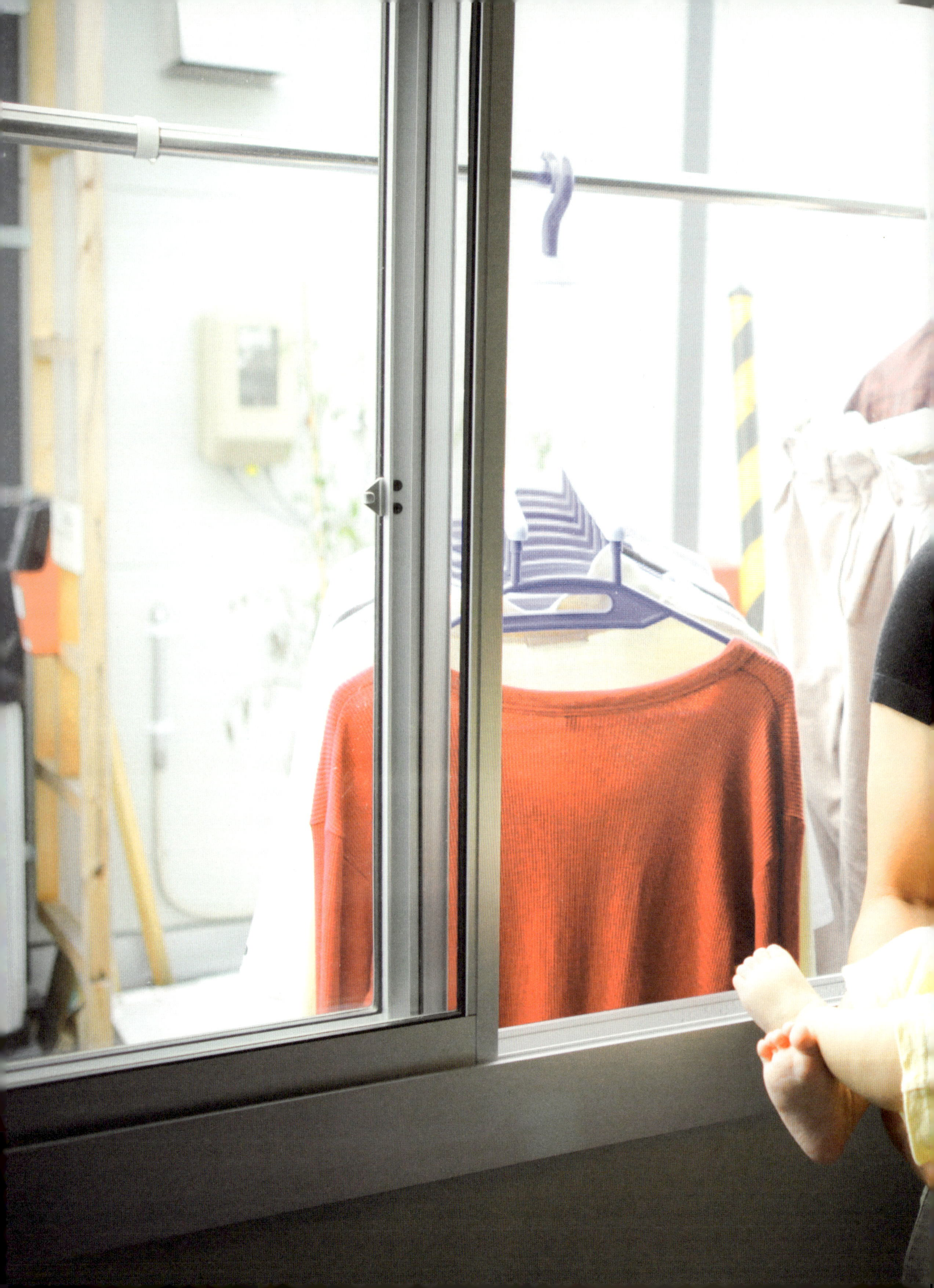

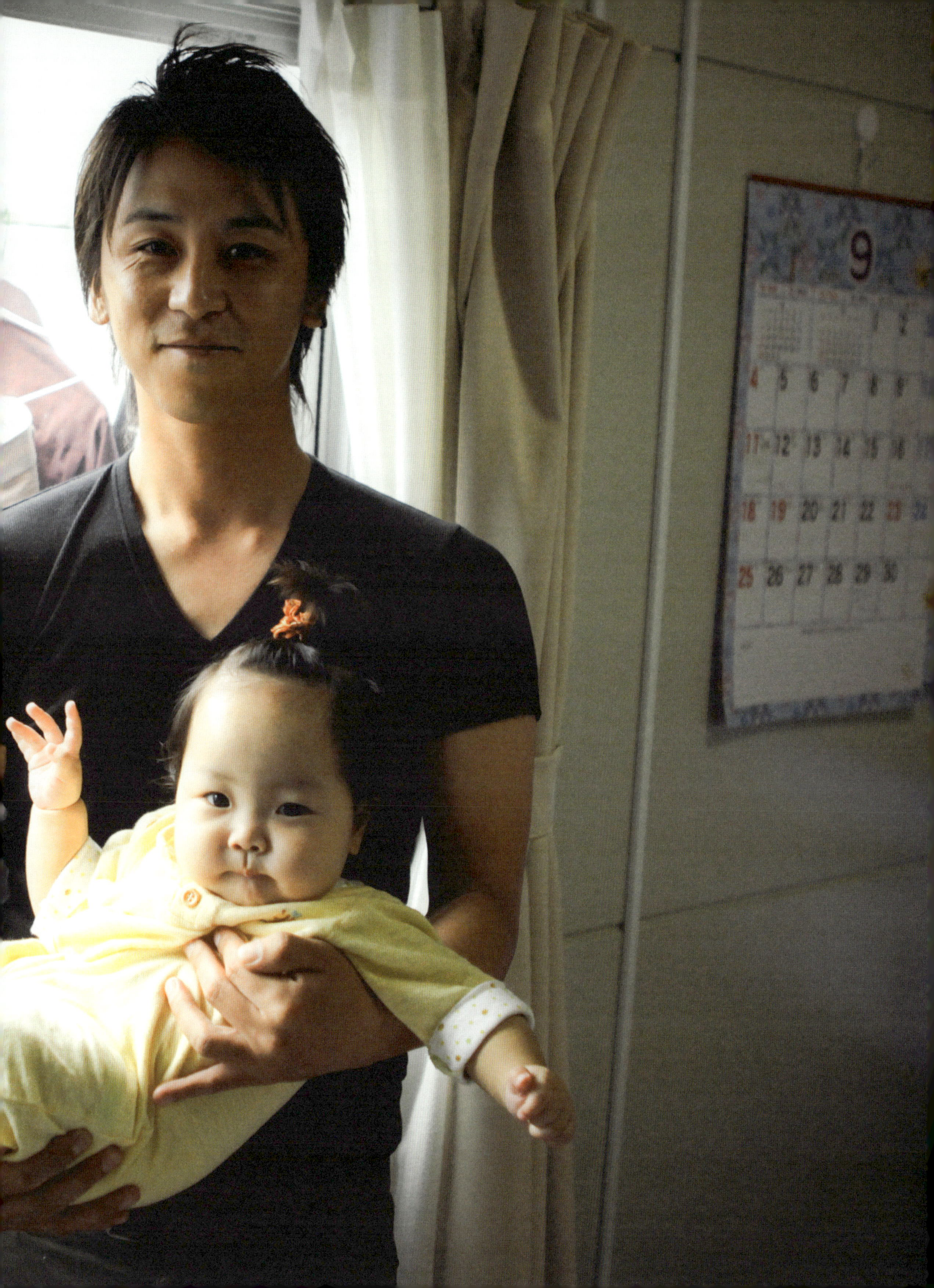

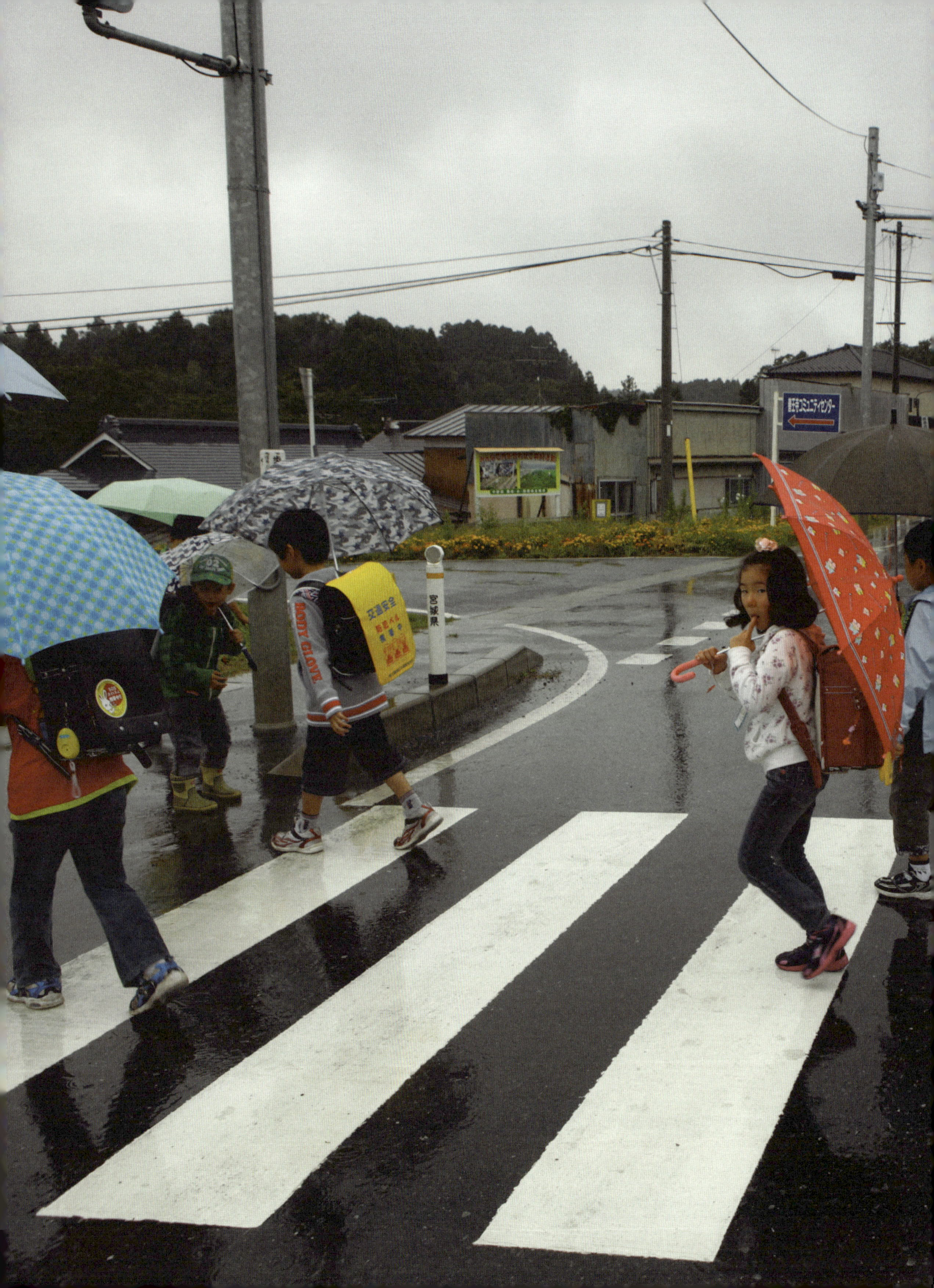

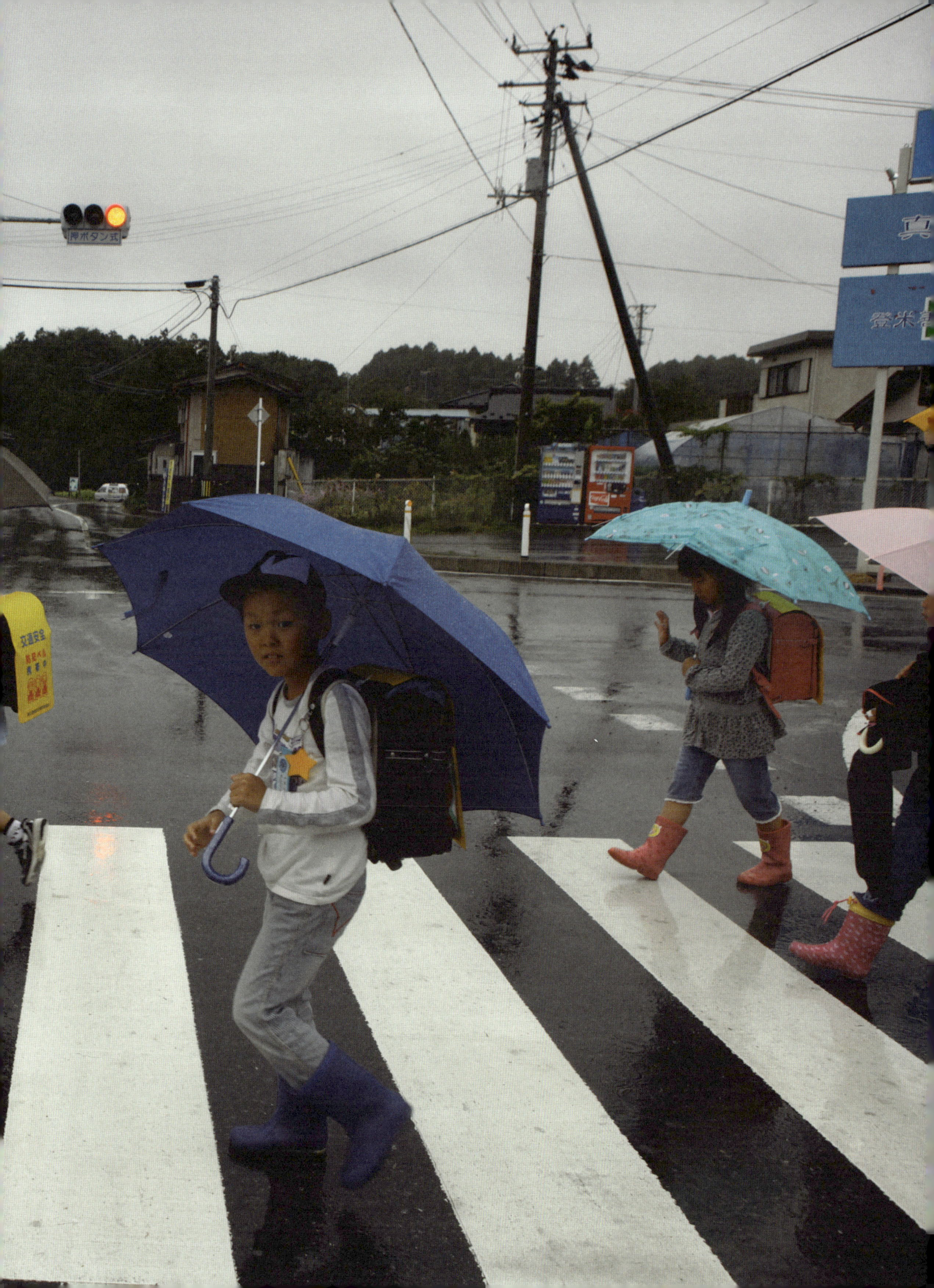

押ボタン式
交通安全

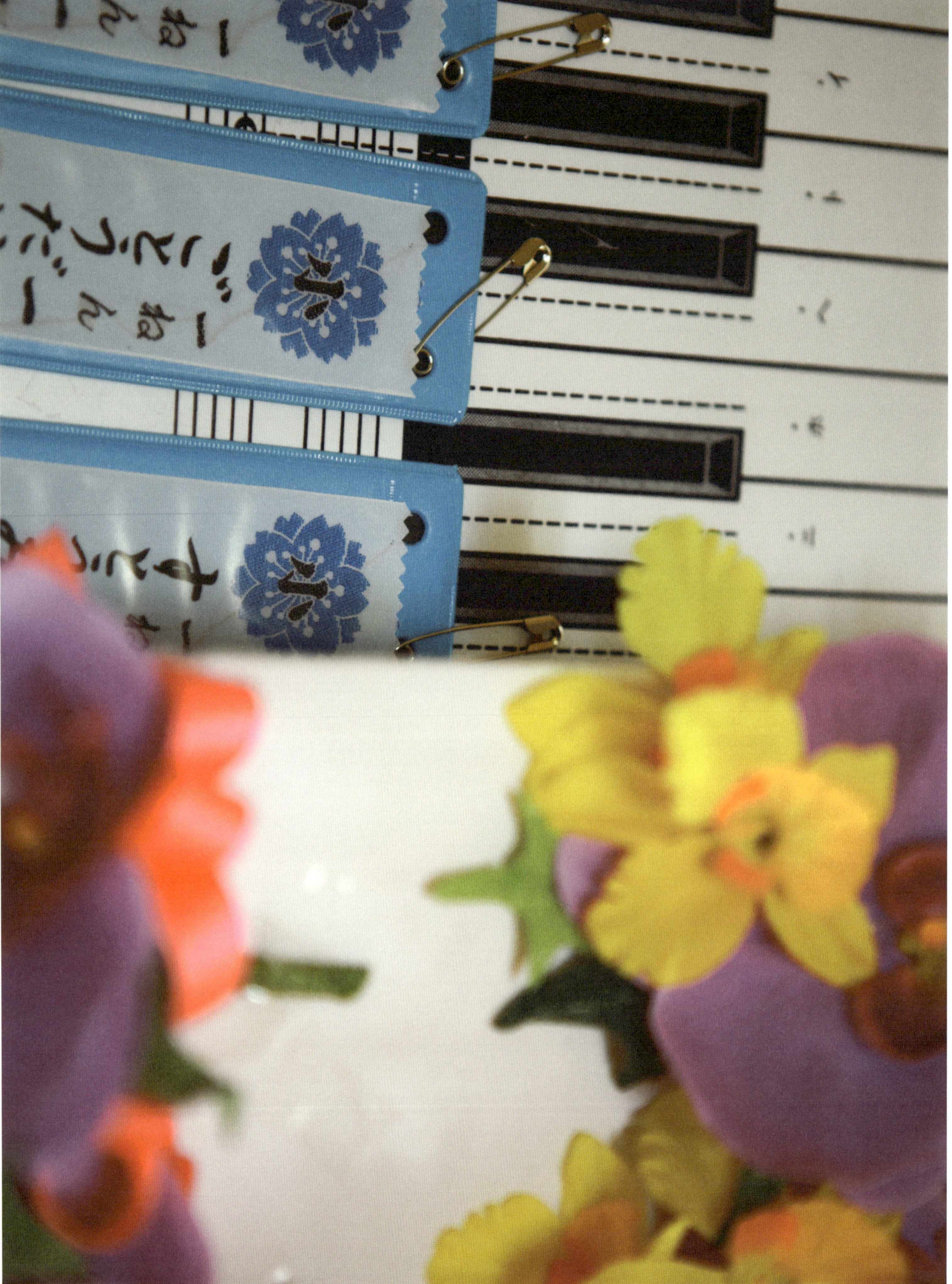

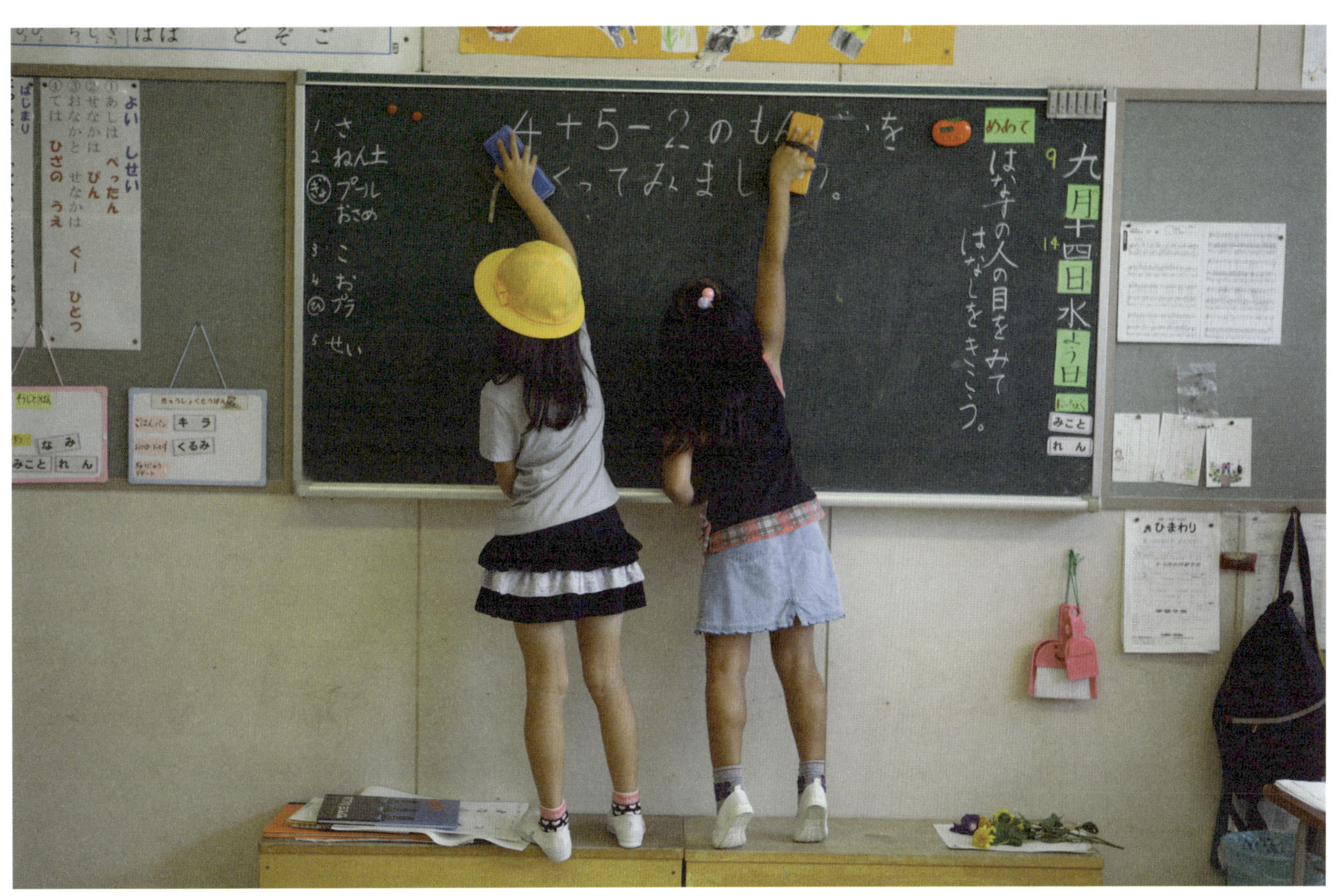
4＋5－2のもんだいを
つくってみましょう。
めあて
はなしの人の目をみて
はなしをきこう。
九月十四日 水よう日
みこと
れん

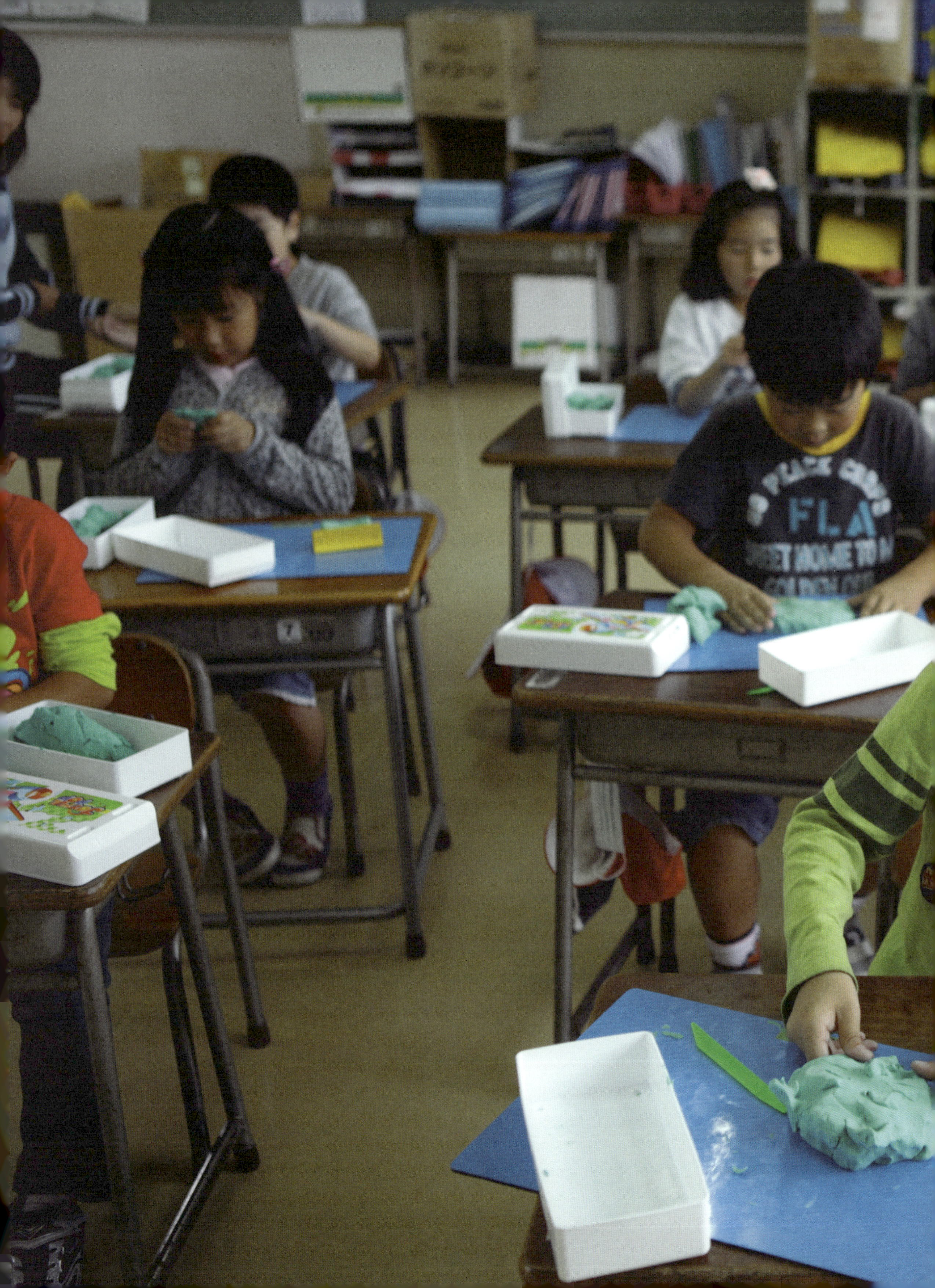

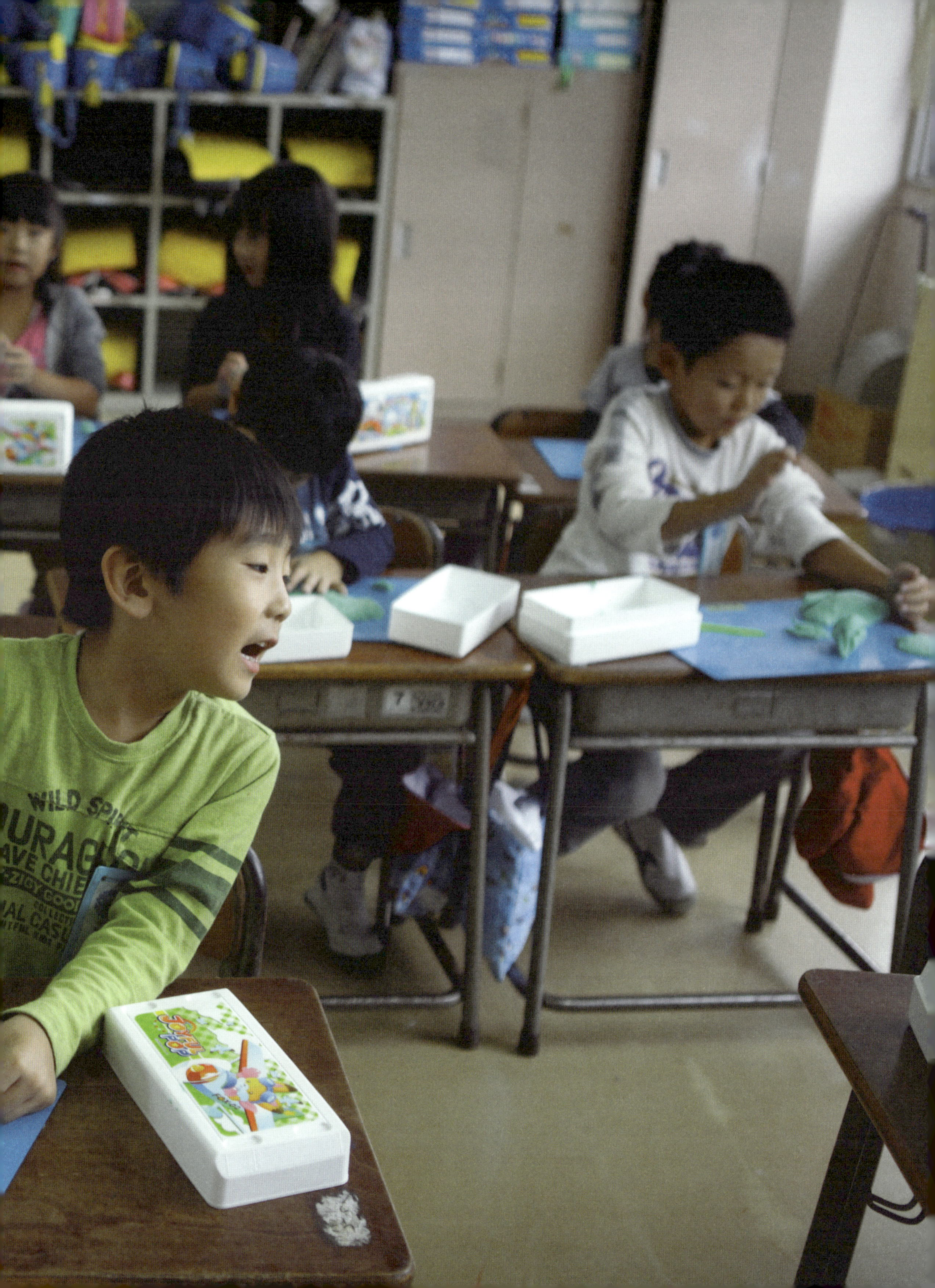

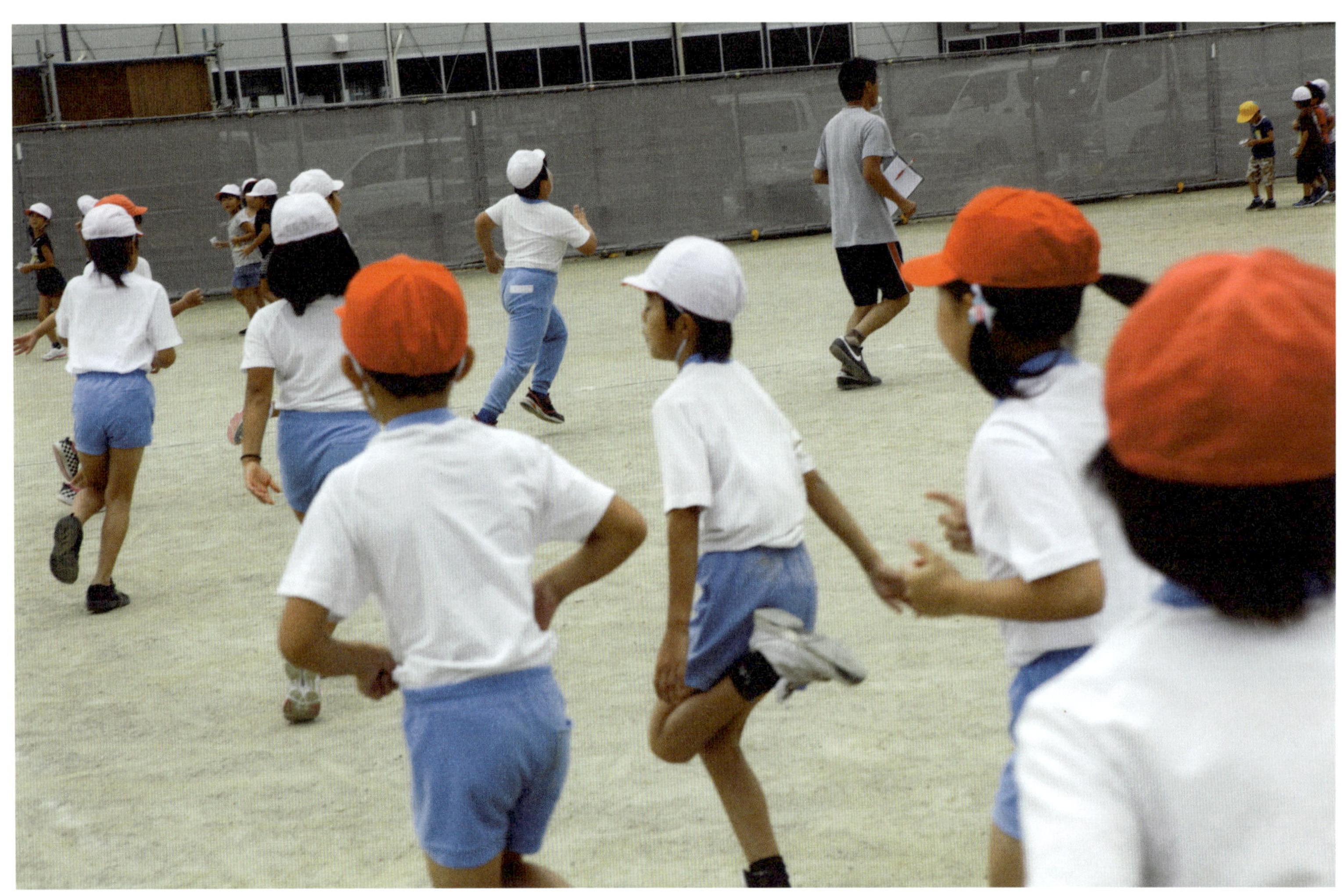

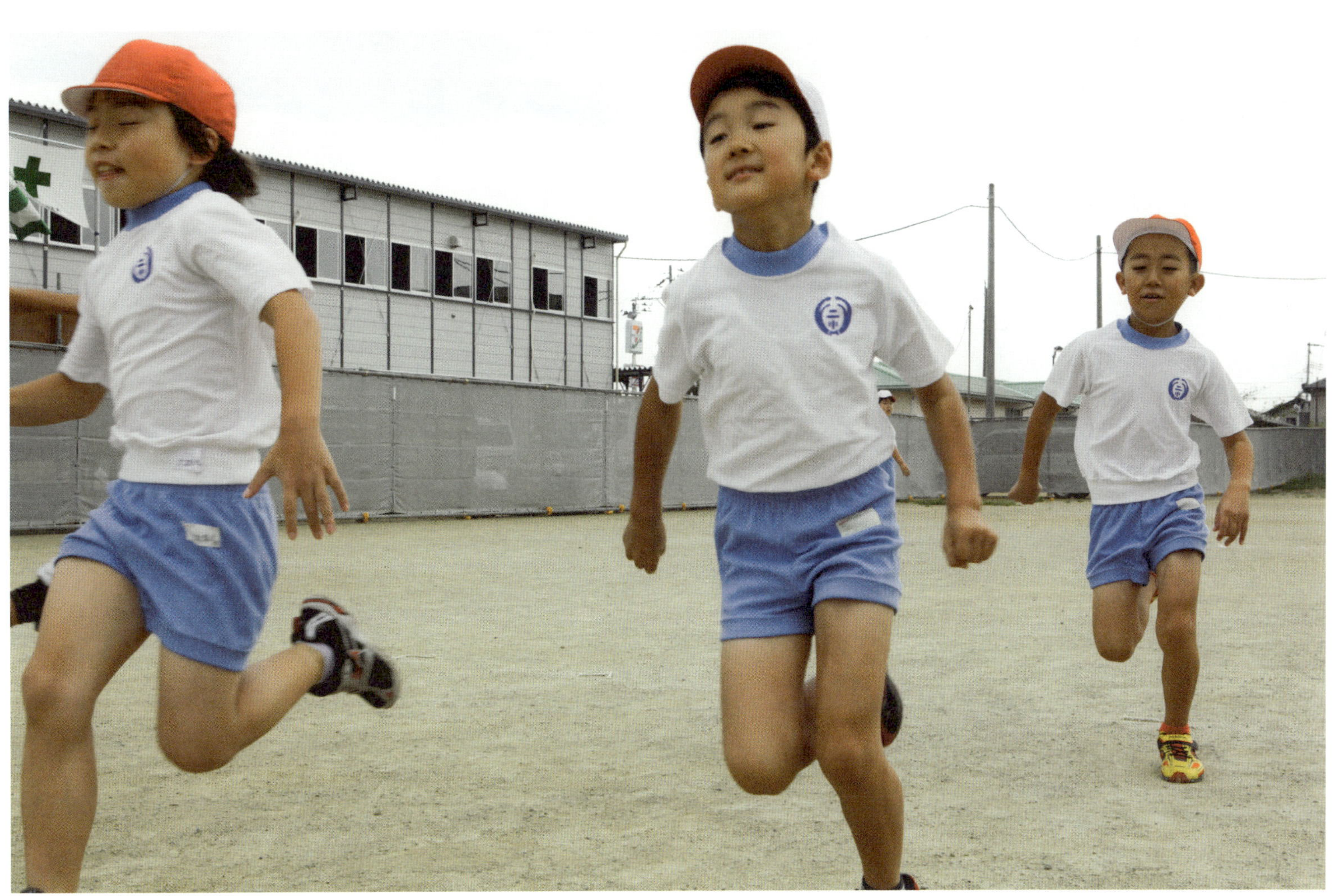

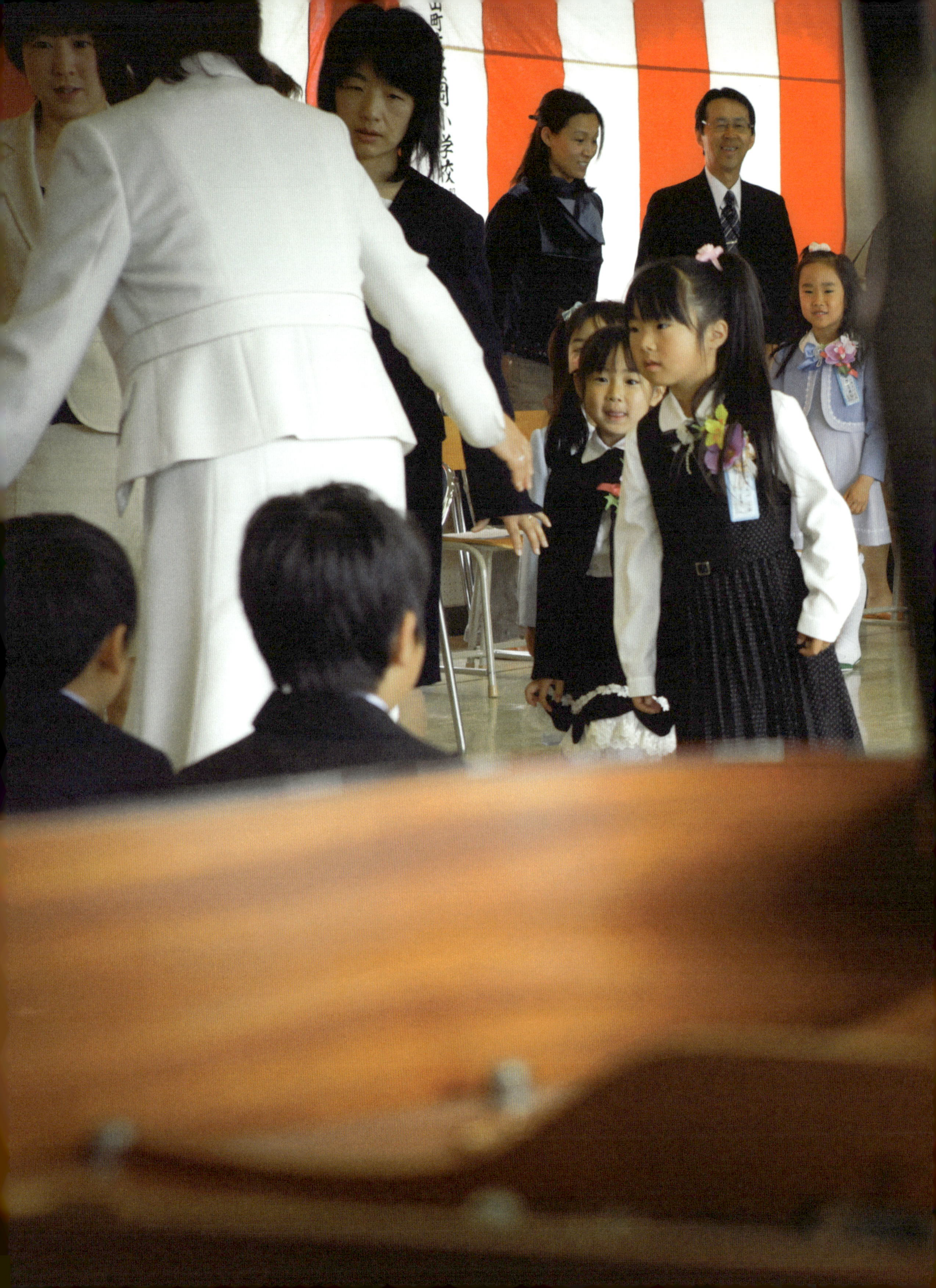

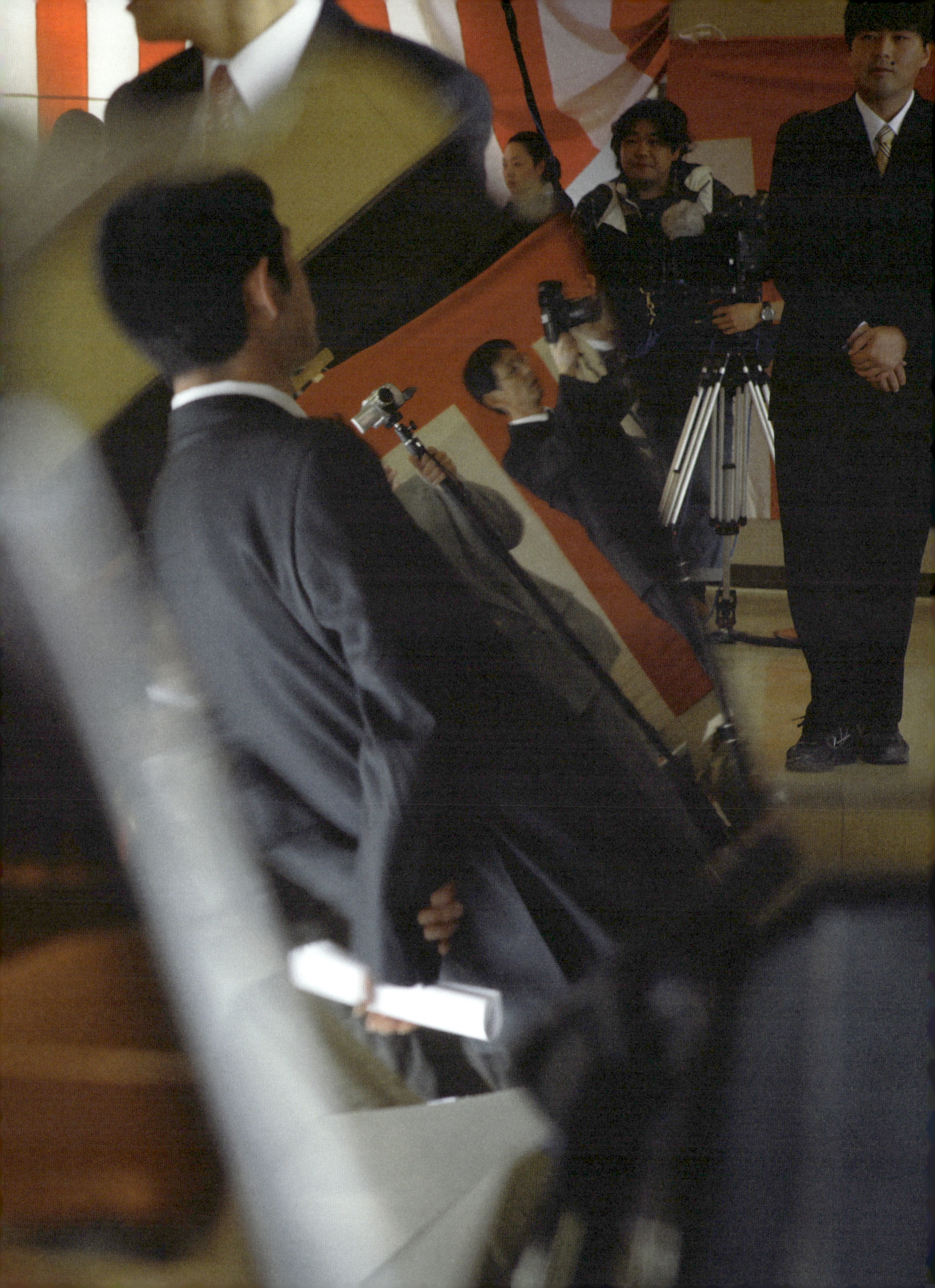

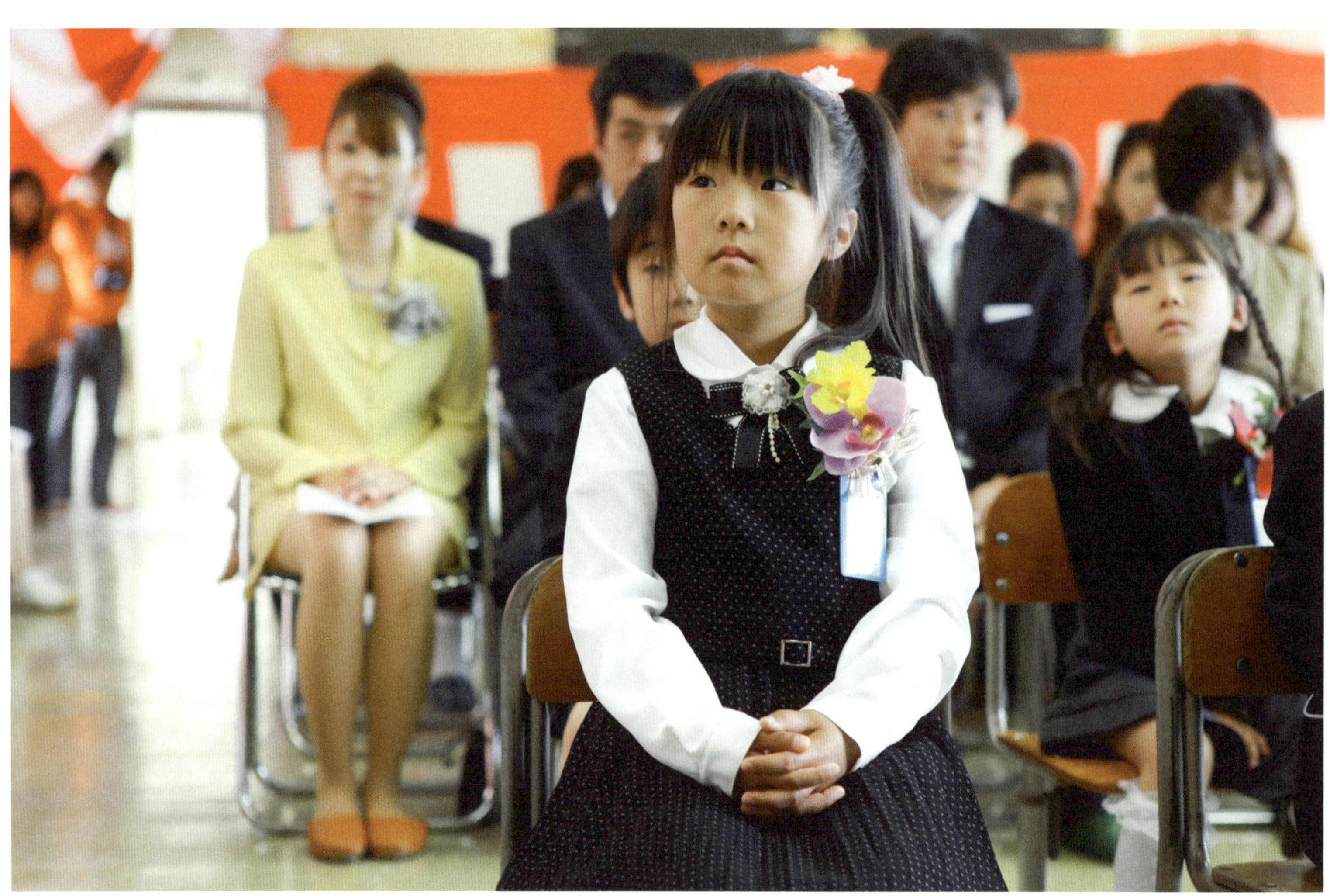

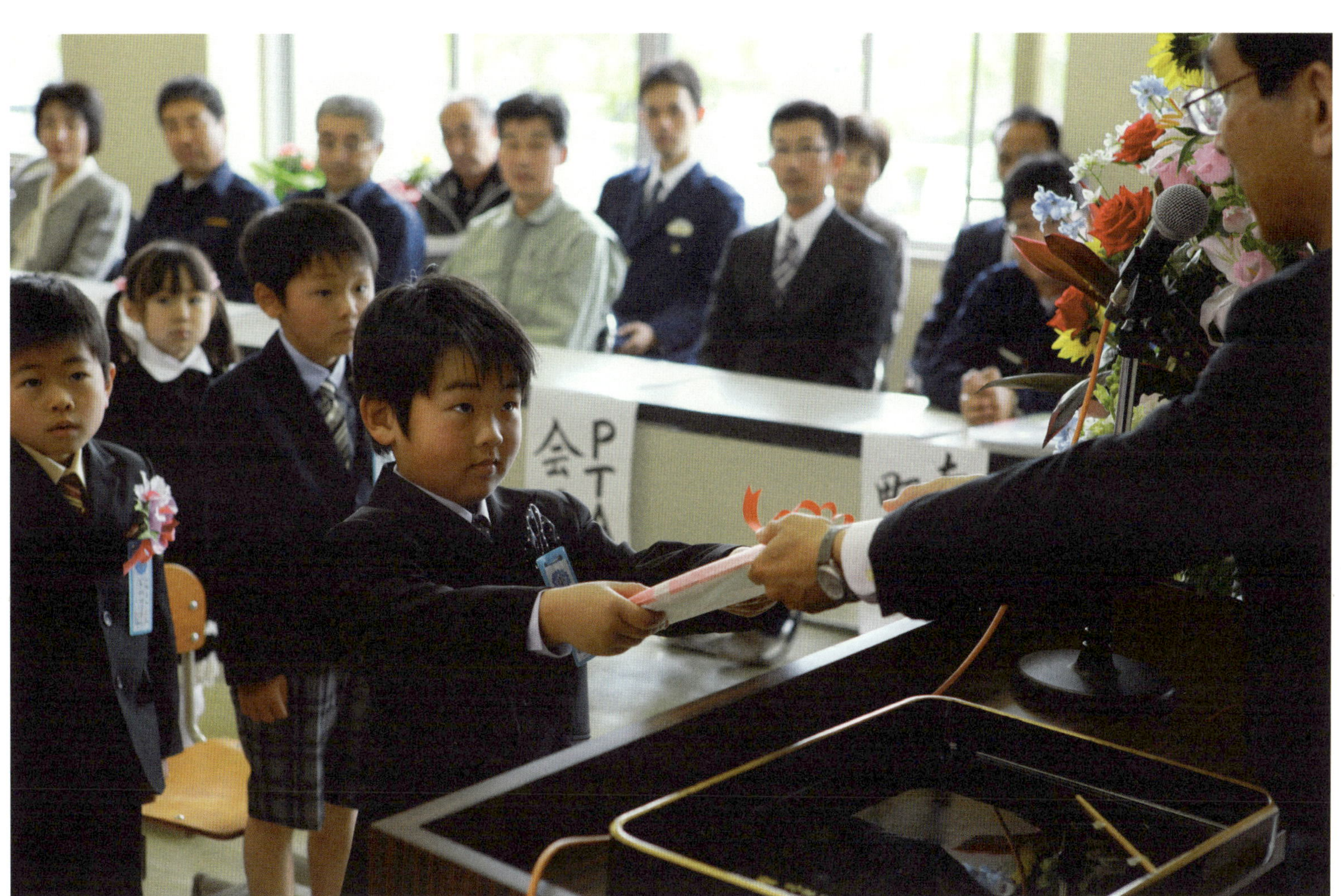

“The days of conformity
are now over.”

Jun Miyake

もう横並びはいい。

三宅 純

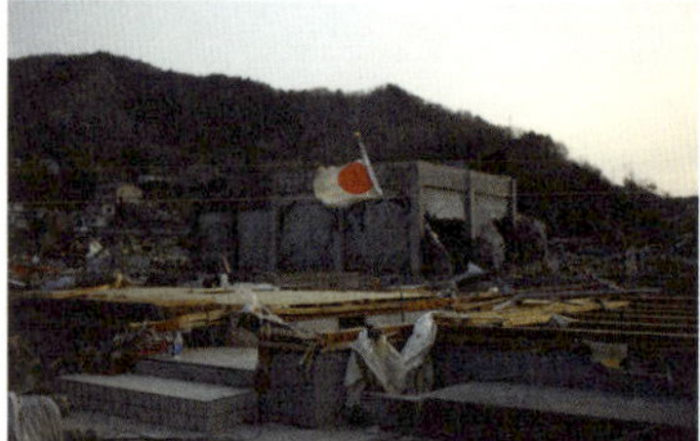

Onagawa, Miyagi, April 2, 2011
2011年4月2日　宮城県女川町

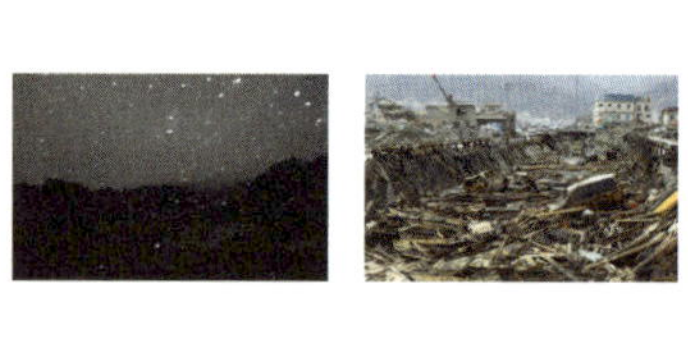

Minamisanriku, Miyagi, March 17, 2011
Ofunato, Iwate, April 7, 2011
2011年3月17日　宮城県南三陸町
2011年4月7日　岩手県大船渡市

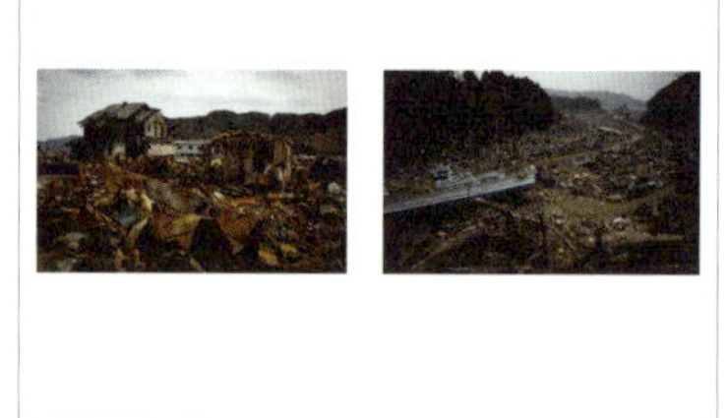

Yamada, Iwate, April 8, 2011. Onagawa, Miyagi, April 2, 2011. The tsunami wave pushed up to 5 km inland.
2011年4月8日　岩手県山田町
2011年4月2日　宮城県女川町
内陸部に向かって最大で5km以上津波が押し寄せた。

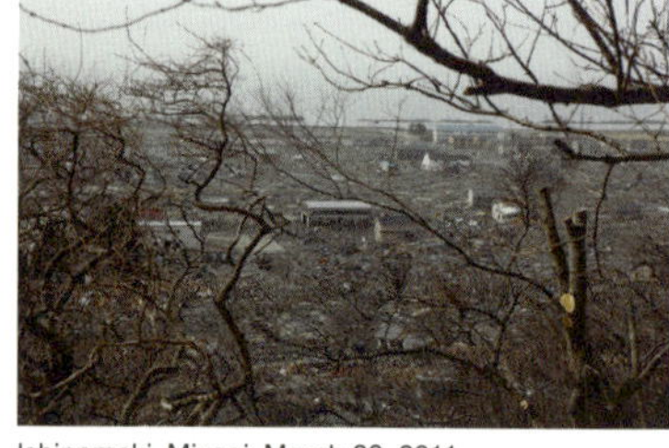

Ishinomaki, Miyagi, March 20, 2011
220,000 houses were damaged, 120,000 of which were completely destroyed.
2011年3月20日　宮城県石巻市
22万棟もの建物が被害を受け、そのうちの約12万棟が全壊。

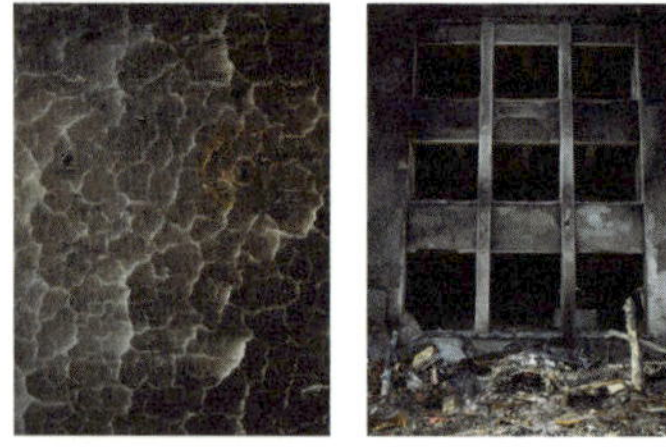

Otsuchi, Iwate, April 8, 2011
Ishinomaki, Miyagi, April 1, 2011
2011年4月8日　岩手県大槌町
2011年4月1日　宮城県石巻市

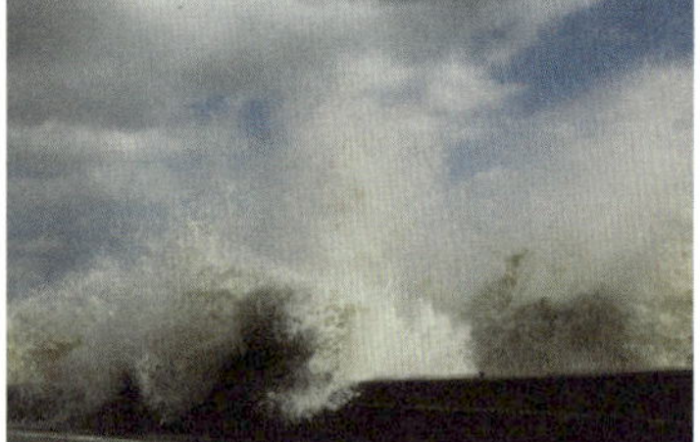

Minamisanriku, Miyagi, March 18, 2011
2011年3月18日　宮城県南三陸町

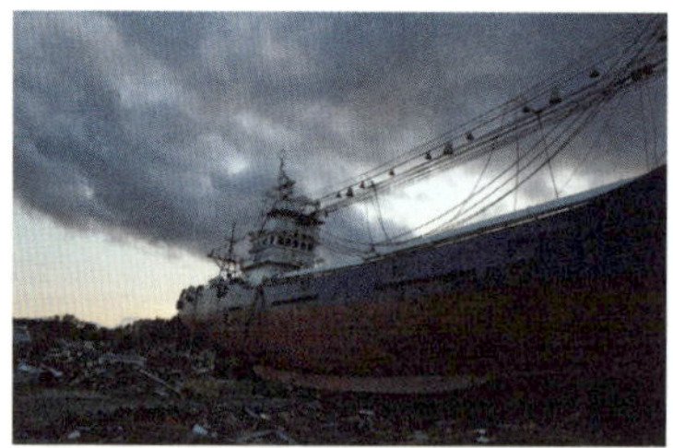

Kesennuma, Miyagi, March 27, 2011
2011年3月27日　宮城県気仙沼市

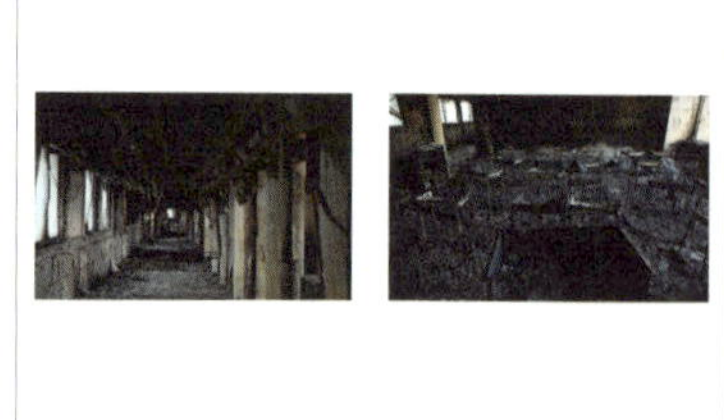

Ishinomaki, Miyagi, March 26, 2011
2011年3月26日　宮城県石巻市

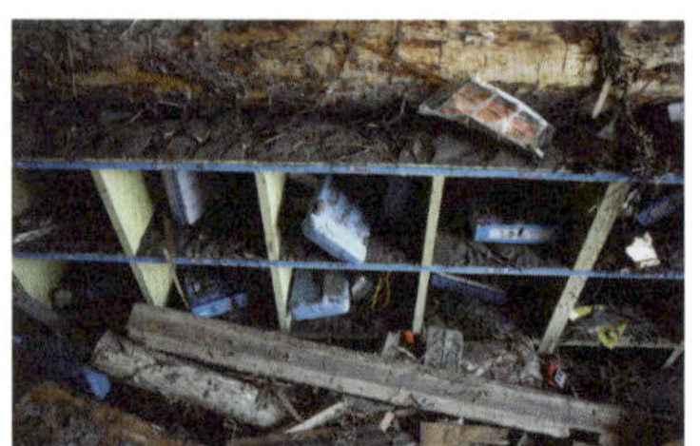

Ishinomaki, Miyagi, April 1, 2011
2011年4月1日　宮城県石巻市

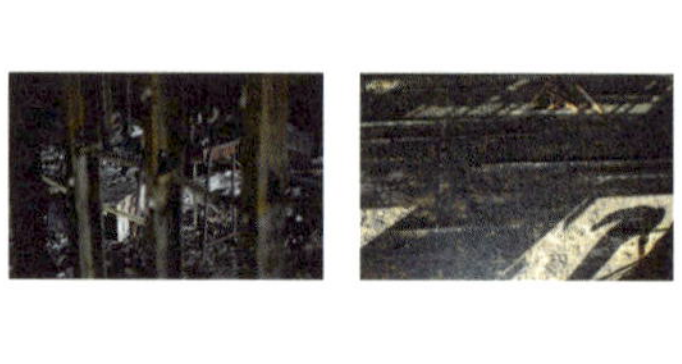

Otsuchi, Iwate, April 8, 2011
Kesennuma, Miyagi, March 29, 2011
2011年4月8日　岩手県大槌町
2011年3月29日　宮城県気仙沼市

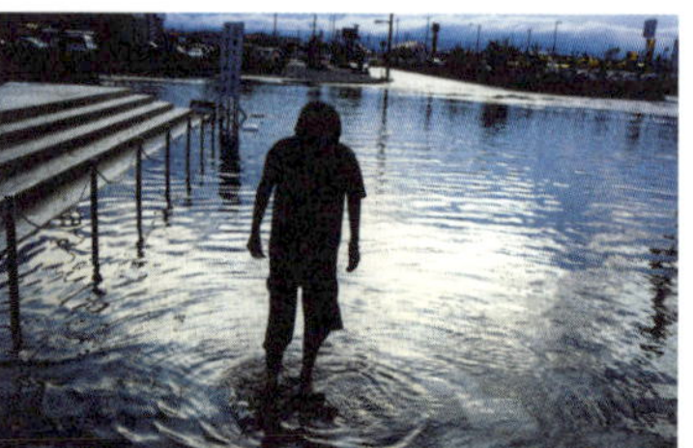

Koriyama, Fukushima, July 11, 2011
2011年7月11日　福島県郡山市

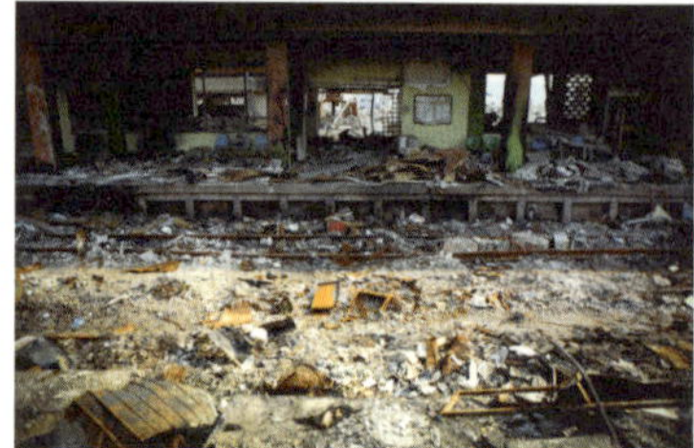

Yamada, Iwate, April 7, 2011
2011年4月7日　岩手県山田町

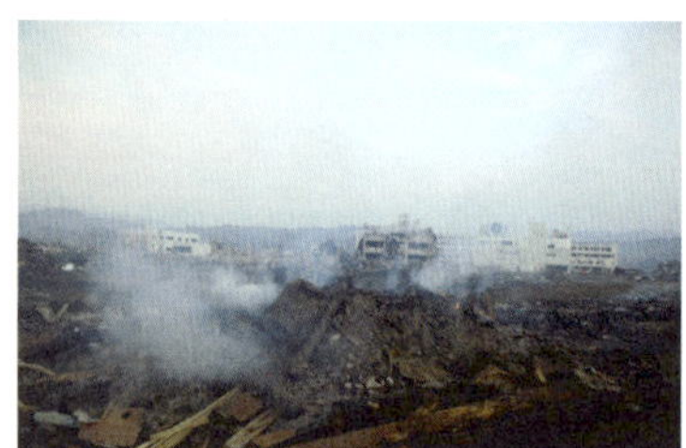

Minamisanriku, Miyagi, March 31, 2011
2011年3月31日　宮城県南三陸町

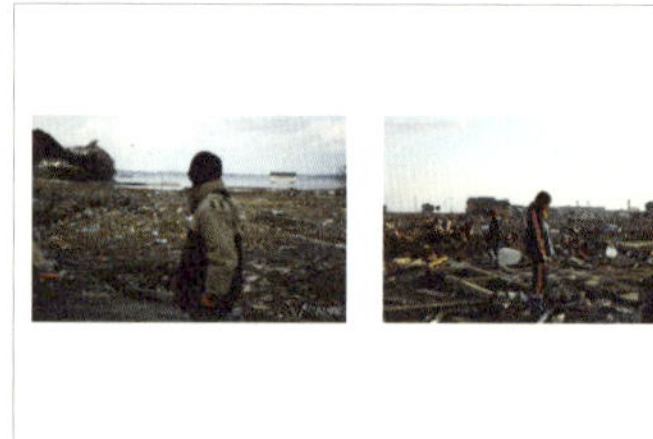

Minamisanriku, Miyagi, March 17, 2011
Ishinomaki, Miyagi, March 26, 2011
2011年3月17日　宮城県南三陸町
2011年3月26日　宮城県石巻市

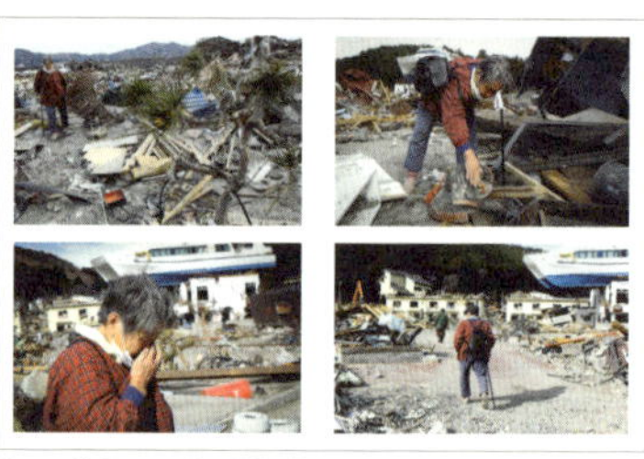

Otsuchi, Iwate, April 8, 2011
2011年4月8日　岩手県大槌町

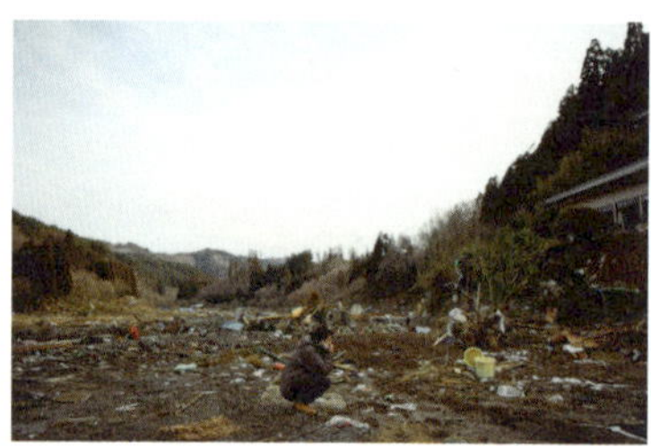

Minamisanriku, Miyagi, March 17, 2011
2011年3月17日　宮城県南三陸町

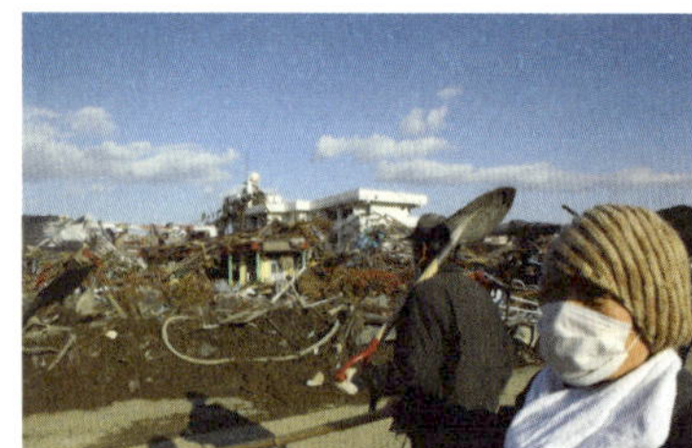

Minamisanriku, Miyagi, March 18, 2011
2011年3月18日　宮城県南三陸町

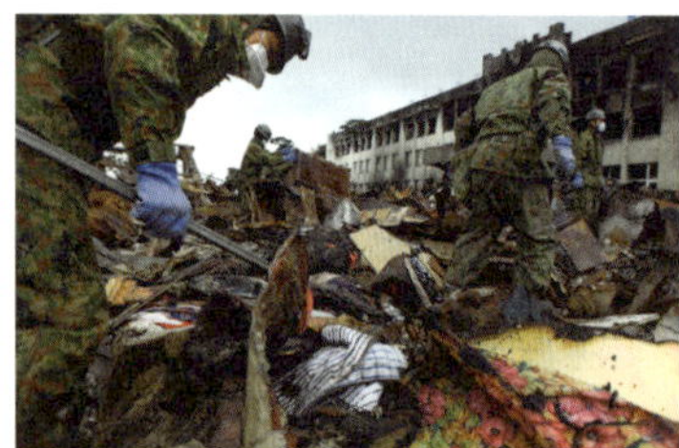

Ishinomaki, Miyagi, March 26, 2011
A total of 180,000 officials of the Self Defense Force were dispatched to save lives and recover bodies.
2011年3月26日　宮城県石巻市。延べ18万人の自衛隊員が派遣され、人命救助や遺体収容を行った。

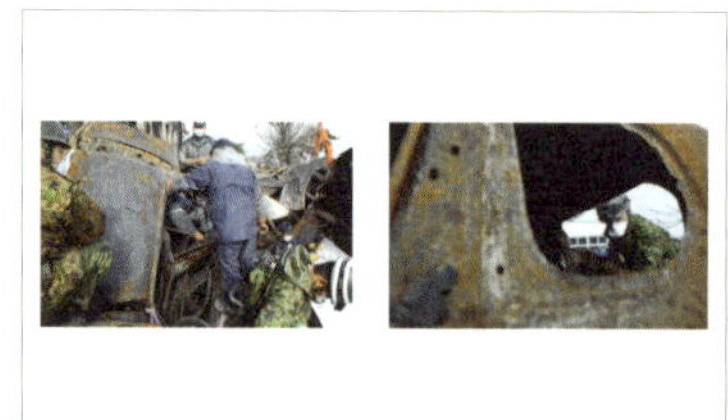

Ishinomaki, Miyagi, March 26, 2011
2011年3月26日　宮城県石巻市

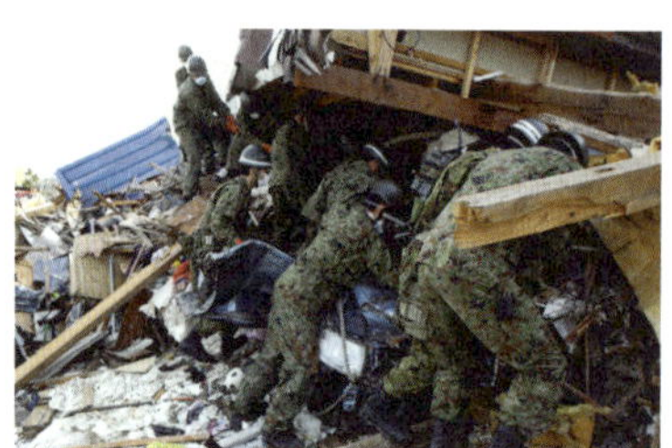

Ishinomaki, Miyagi, April 1, 2011
2011年4月1日　宮城県石巻市

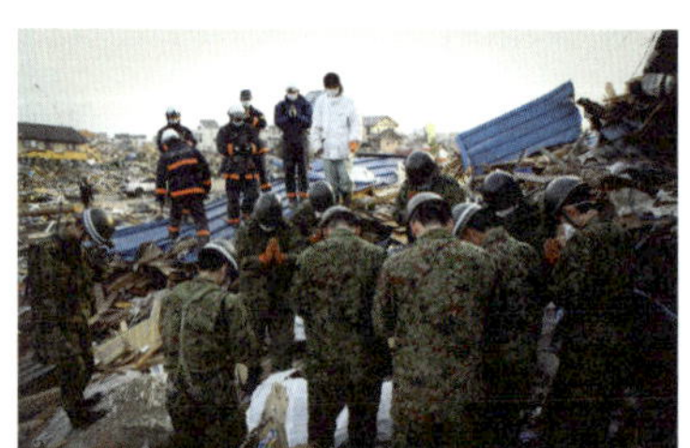

Ishinomaki, Miyagi, April 1, 2011
2011年4月1日　宮城県石巻市

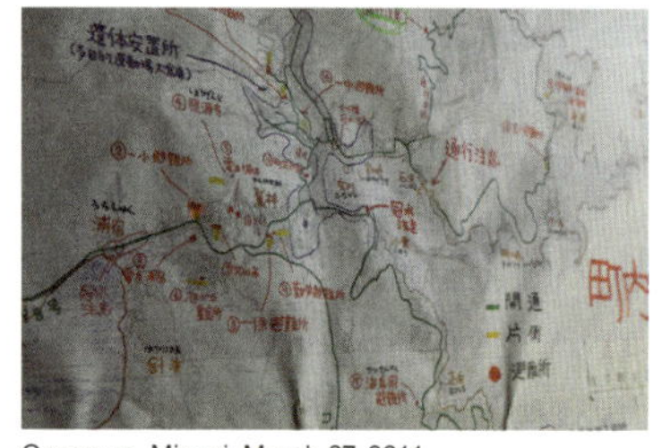

Onagawa, Miyagi, March 27, 2011
At evacuation centers and morgues, maps indicated the road conditions.
2011年3月27日　宮城県女川町
避難所や遺体安置所、道路状況が示された地図。

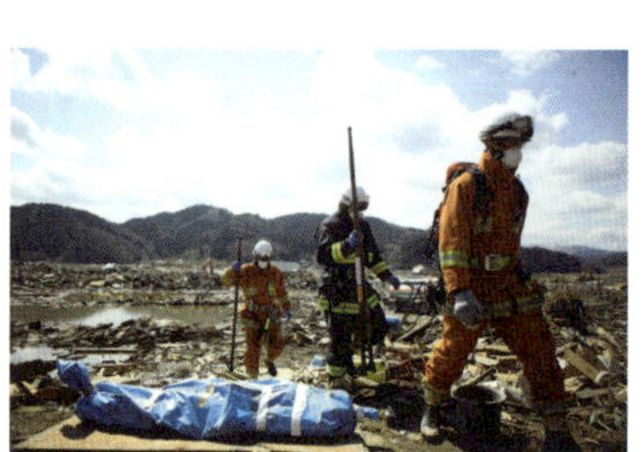

Rikuzentakada, Iwate, March 28, 2011
2011年3月28日　岩手県陸前高田市

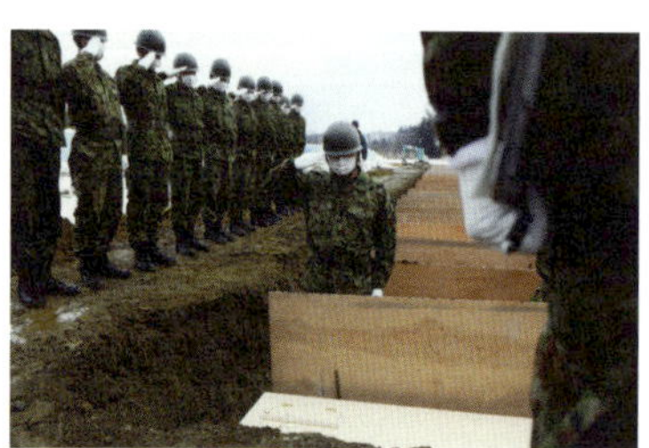

Higashimatsushima, Miyagi, March 26, 2011
Lacking time for proper cremation, temporary burials take place in every district.
2011年3月26日　宮城県東松島市
火葬が間に合わず、各地で仮土葬が行われた。

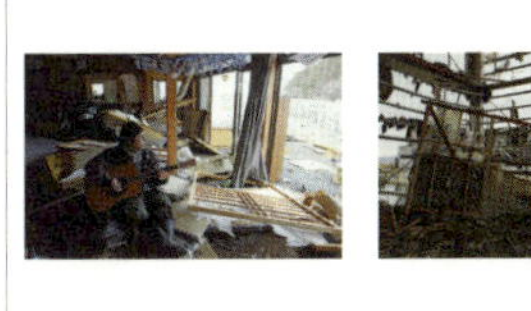 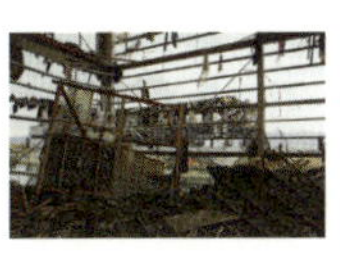

Minamisanriku, Miyagi, March 31, 2011
Ishinomaki, Miyagi, March 31, 2011
2011年3月31日　宮城県南三陸町
2011年3月31日　宮城県石巻市

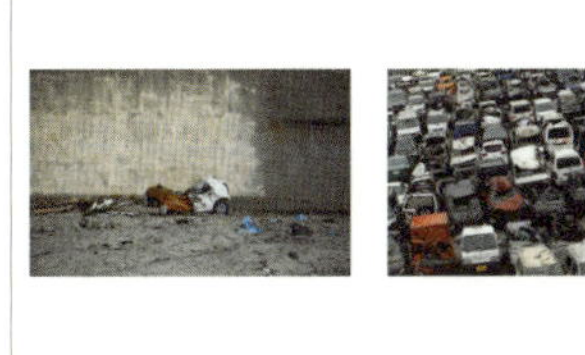

Ishinomaki, Miyagi, March 20, 2011
Kamaishi, Iwate, April 7, 2011
2011年3月20日　宮城県石巻市
2011年4月7日　岩手県釜石市

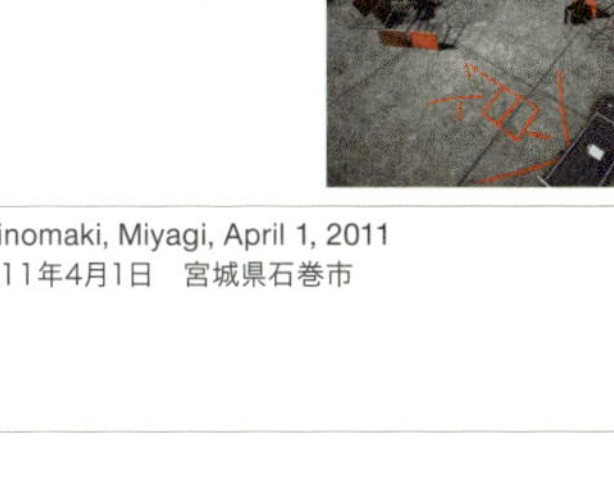

Ishinomaki, Miyagi, April 1, 2011
2011年4月1日　宮城県石巻市

Ishinomaki, Miyagi, April 1, 2011
The teachers' lounge at a primary school.
2011年4月1日　宮城県石巻市
小学校の職員室。

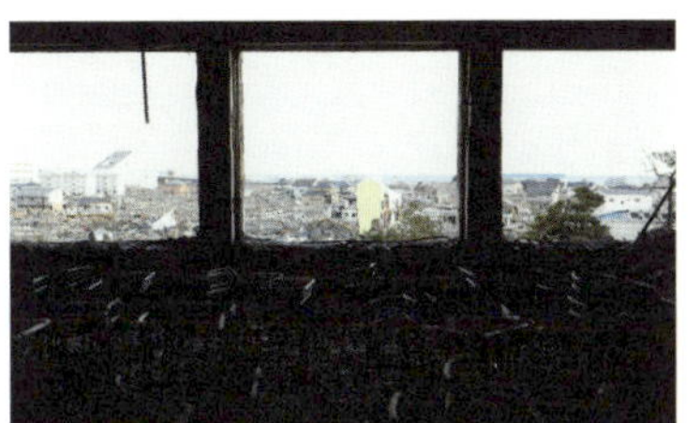

Ishinomaki, Miyagi, March 26, 2011
16,000 people lost their lives; 3,000 remain missing.
2011年3月26日　宮城県石巻市
約1万6000人が死亡、未だ3000人以上が行方不明。

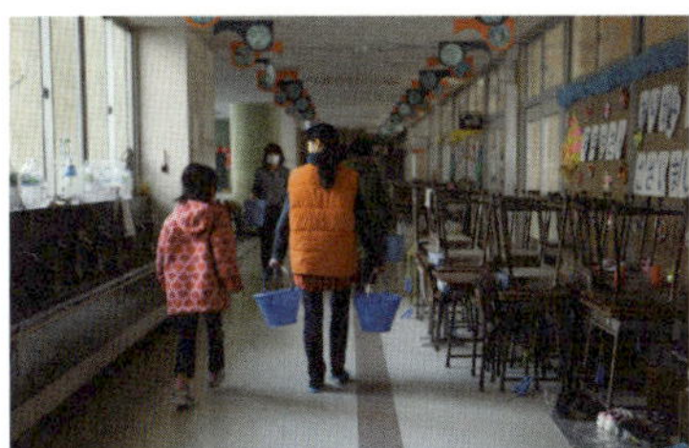

Minamisanriku, Miyagi, March 30, 2011
2011年3月30日　宮城県南三陸町

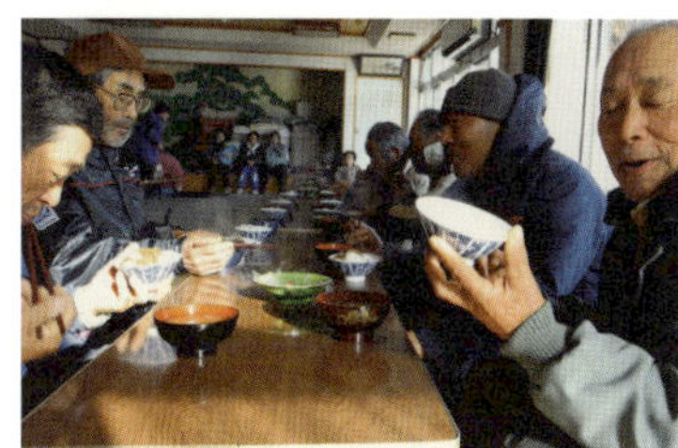

Minamisanriku, Miyagi, April 6, 2011
Minamisanriku, Miyagi, March 30, 2011
2011年4月6日　宮城県南三陸町
2011年3月30日　宮城県南三陸町

Minamisanriku, Miyagi, March 18, 2011
Due to the tsunami and the nuclear accident,
330,000 people were evacuated.
2011年3月18日　宮城県南三陸町。津波、原発事故により33万以上の人が避難生活を送っている。

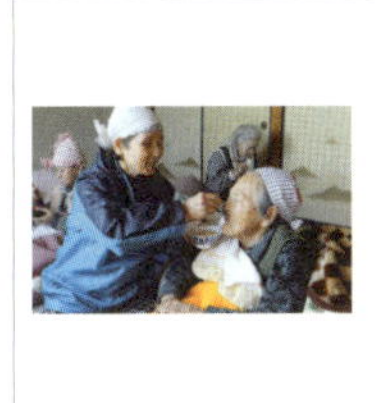 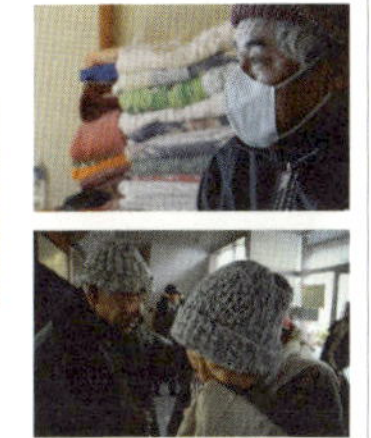

Minamisanriku, Miyagi, March 18, 2011
2011年3月18日　宮城県南三陸町

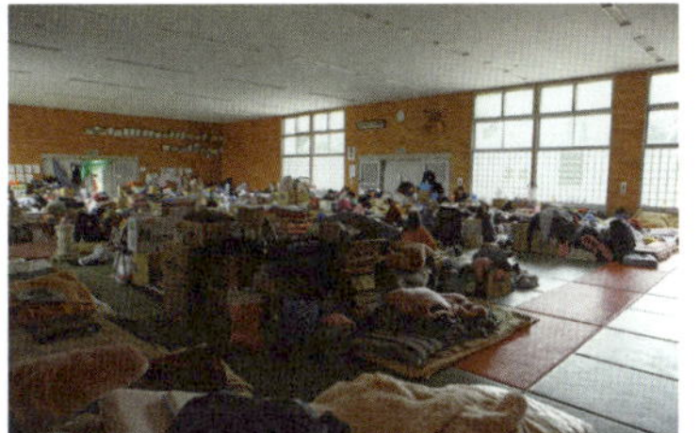

Minamisanriku, Miyagi, March 30, 2011
2011年3月30日　宮城県南三陸町

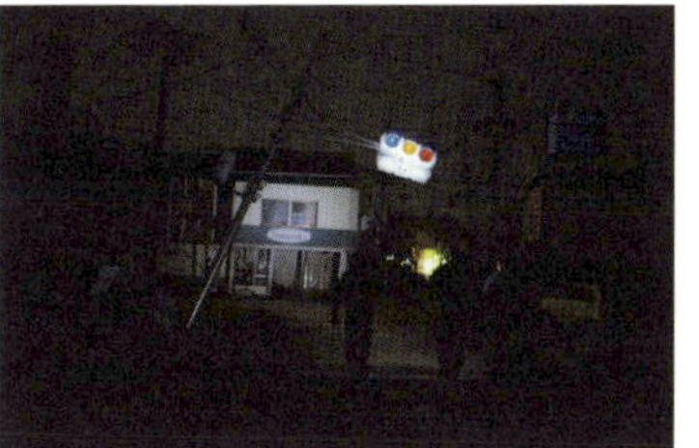

Ishinomaki, Miyagi, March 19, 2011
2011年3月19日　宮城県石巻市

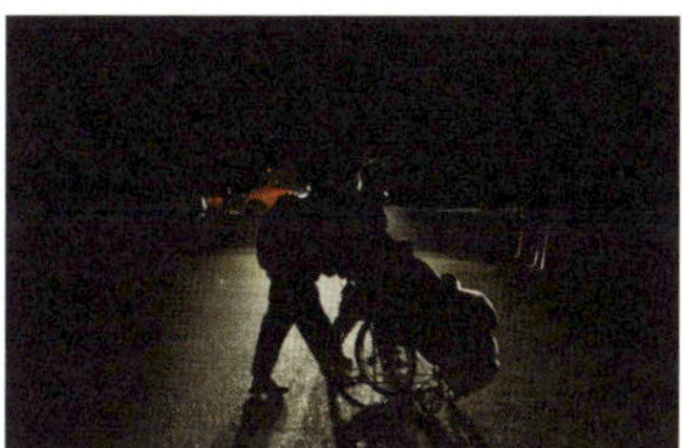

Kamaishi, Iwate, April 7, 2011
2011年4月7日　岩手県釜石市

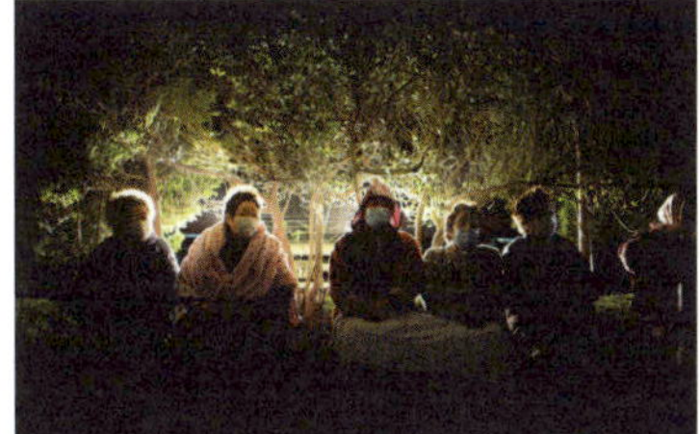

Kamaishi, Iwate, April 7, 2011
2011年4月7日　岩手県釜石市

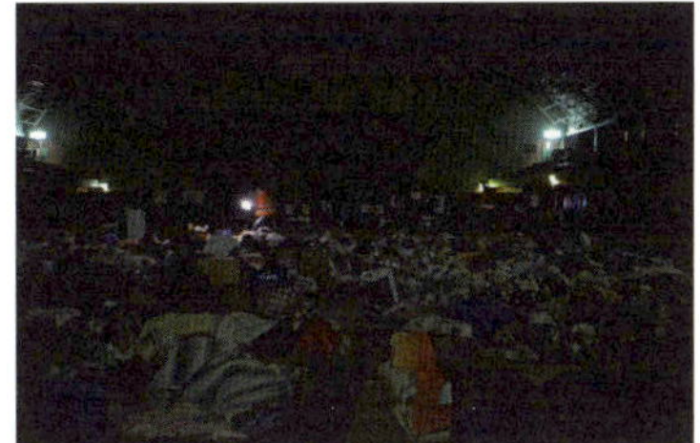

Kamaishi, Iwate, April 7, 2011
2011年4月7日　岩手県釜石市

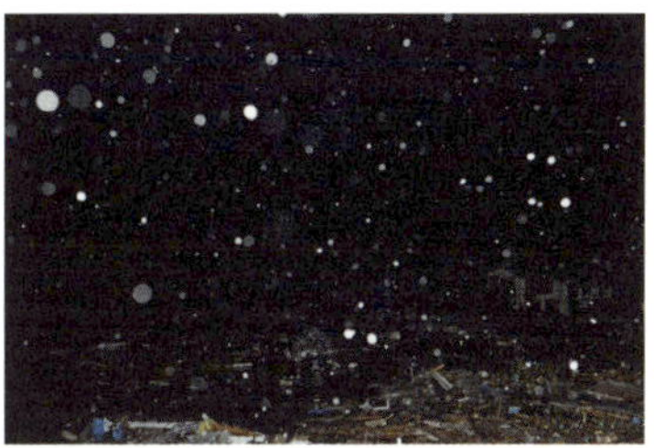

Minamisanriku, Miyagi, March 17, 2011
2011年3月17日　宮城県南三陸町

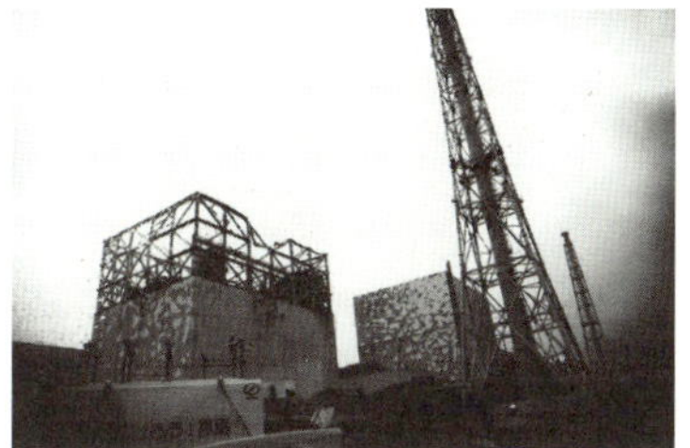

Fukushima Daiichi Nuclear Power Plant,
August 2011
2011年8月　福島第一原子力発電所

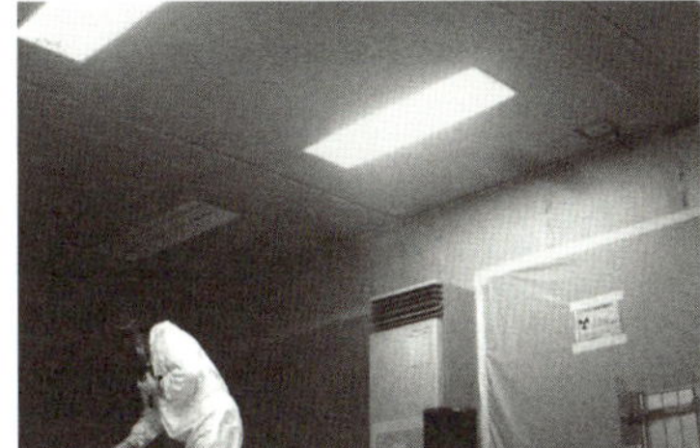

Fukushima Daiichi Nuclear Power Plant, August 2011
Workers rest at the seismically isolated building
located 200 meters from Reactor No. 1.
2011年8月　福島第一原子力発電所。1号炉から200mほどに位置する免震重要棟。作業員の休憩所にも使われる。

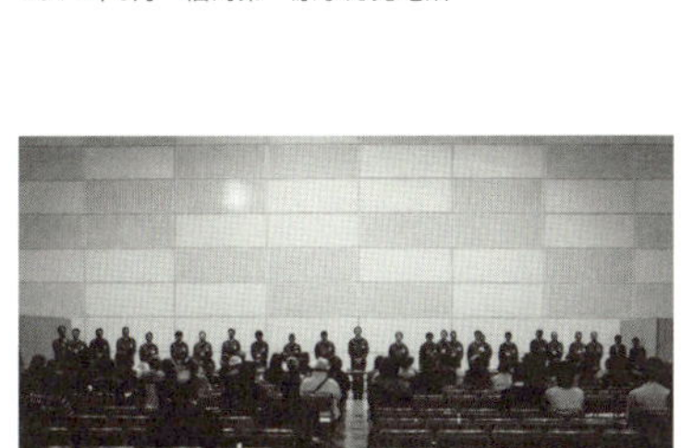

Fukushima Daiichi Nuclear Power Plant, August 2011
2011年8月　福島第一原子力発電所

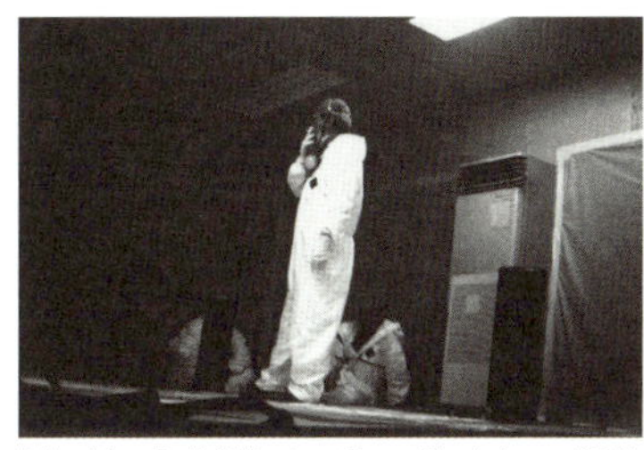

Fukushima Daiichi Nuclear Power Plant, August 2011
2011年8月　福島第一原子力発電所

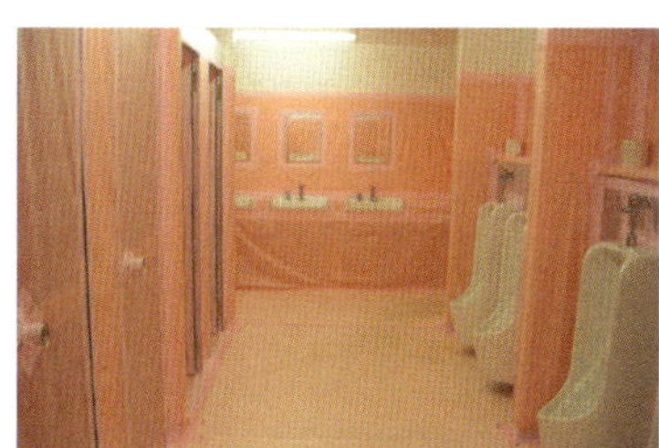

Fukushima Daiichi Nuclear Power Plant, August 2011
The bathroom in the seismically isolated building.
The walls are covered in pink foil.
2011年8月　福島第一原子力発電所。免震重要棟内のトイレ。棟内の壁はピンク色のシートで覆われている。

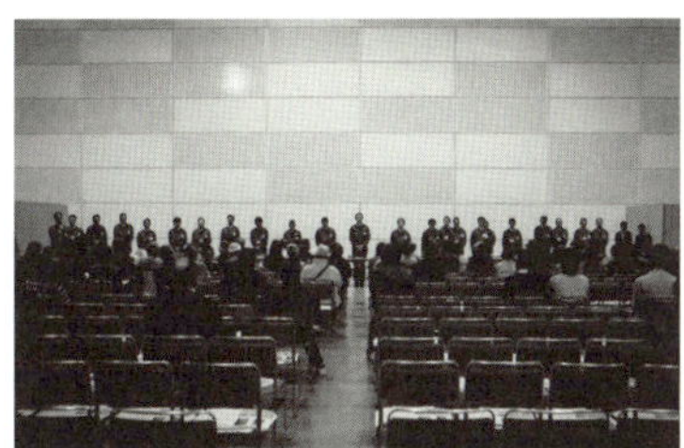

Koriyama, Fukushima, July 11, 2011
2011年7月11日　福島県郡山市

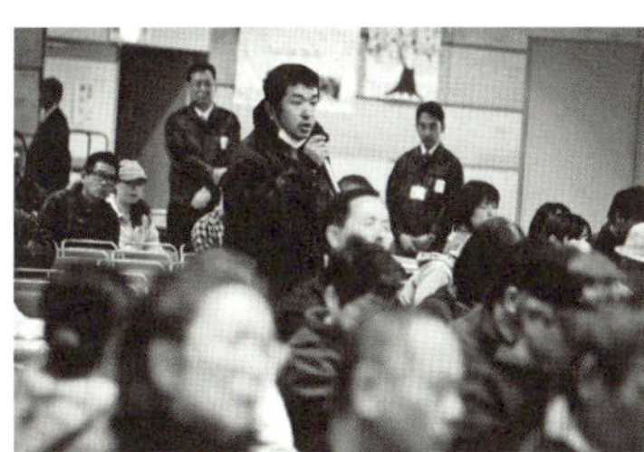

Koriyama, Fukushima, November 8, 2011
TEPCO giving an explanation regarding compensation to an entirely evacuated village population.
2011年11月8日　福島県郡山市
全村避難した住民へ東京電力が補償の説明を行う。

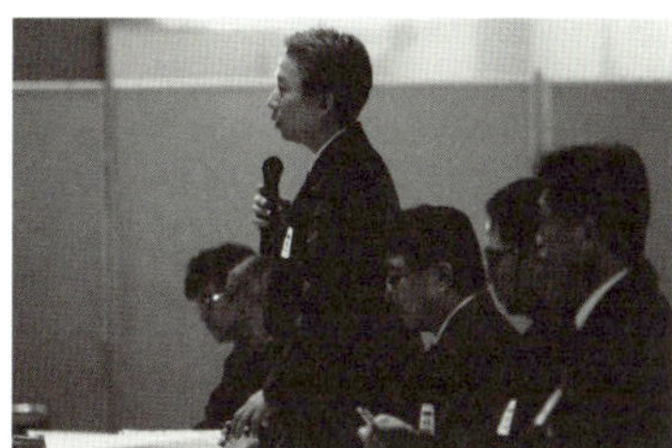

Koriyama, Fukushima, November 8, 2011
Citizens standing up against TEPCO in anger.
2011年11月8日　福島県郡山市
東京電力の対応に怒りをぶつける住民。

Koriyama, Fukushima, November 8, 2011
TEPCO is not providing a sincere answer towards a solution.
2011年11月8日　福島県郡山市
東京電力から誠意ある回答はない。

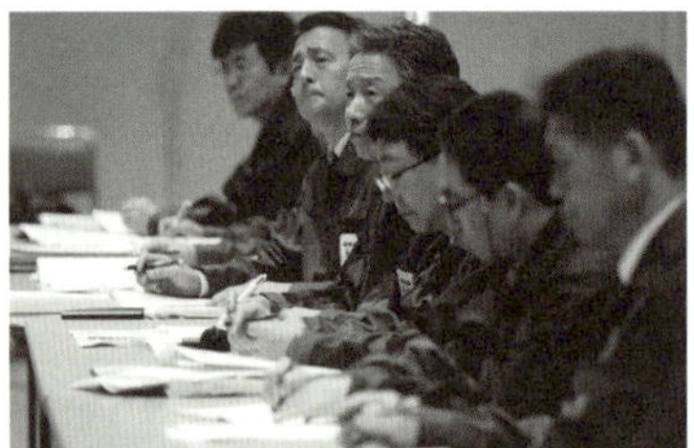

Koriyama, Fukushima, November 8, 2011
2011年11月8日　福島県郡山市

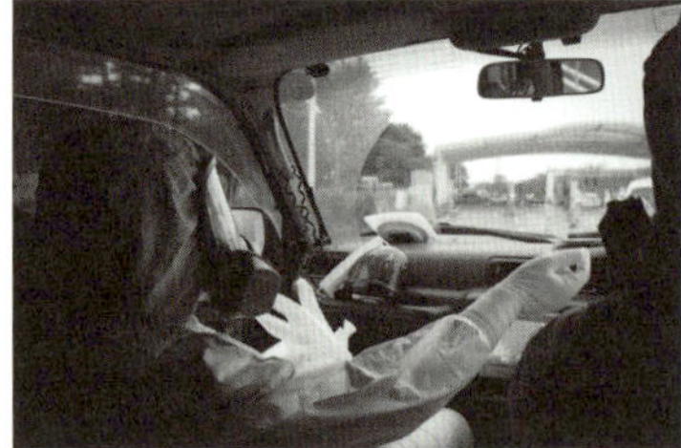

Fukushima Daiichi Nuclear Power Plant, August 2011
2011年8月　福島第一原子力発電所

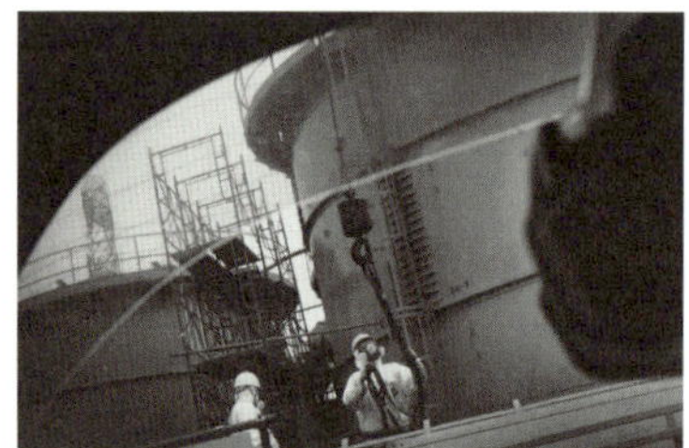

Fukushima Daiichi Nuclear Power Plant, August 2011
2011年8月　福島第一原子力発電所

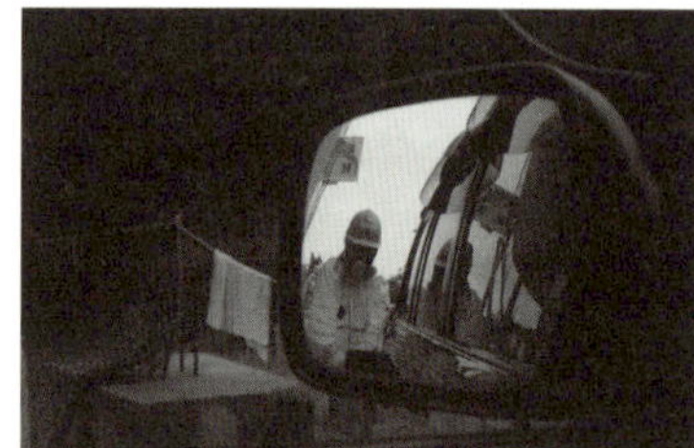

Fukushima Daiichi Nuclear Power Plant, August 2011
2011年8月　福島第一原子力発電所

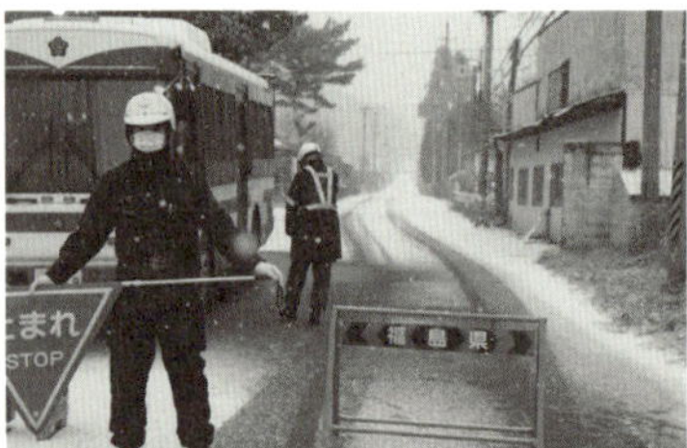

Kawauchi, Fukushima, January 11, 2011
The checkpoint to the exclusion zone.
Police officers regulate traffic on a 24-hour basis.
2011年1月11日　福島県川内村。警戒区域への検問所。
警官が24時間態勢で出入りを規制している。

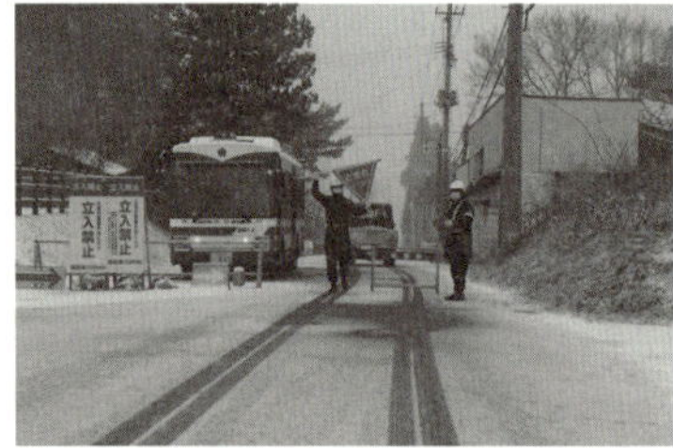

Kawauchi, Fukushima, January 11, 2011
2011年1月11日　福島県川内村

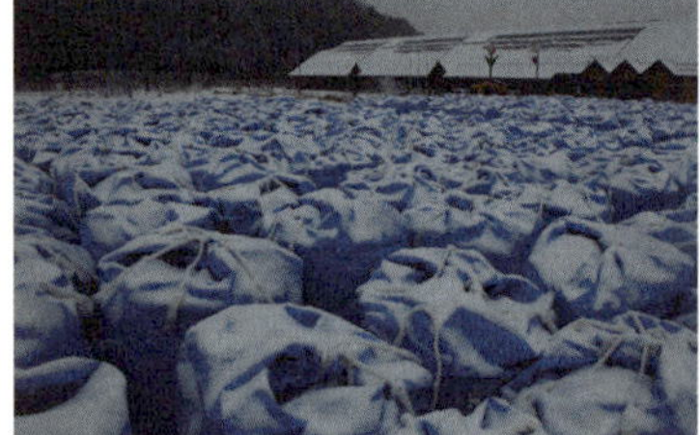

Kawauchi, Fukushima, January 11, 2011
Polluted soil removed for decontamination.
It remains unclear where or how it will be disposed of.
2011年1月11日　福島県川内村
除染による汚染土。未だ貯蔵場所は決まっていない。

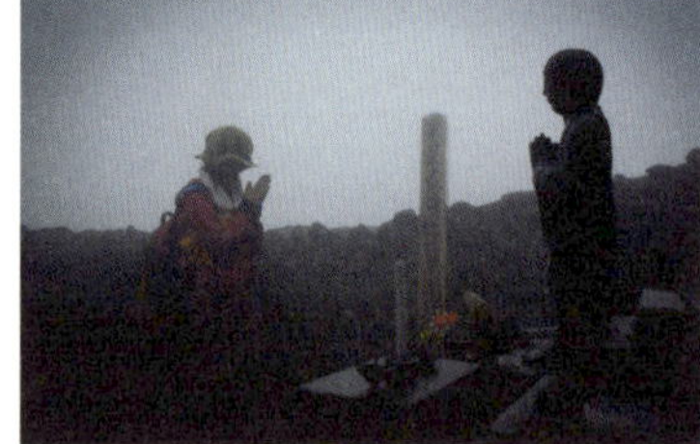

Gassan, Yamagata, September 11, 2011
2011年9月11日　山形県月山

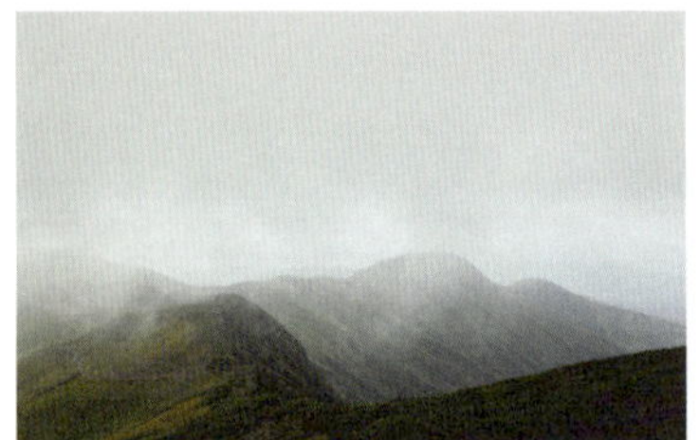

Gassan, Yamagata, September 11, 2011
2011年9月11日　山形県月山

Gassan, Yamagata, September 11, 2011
2011年9月11日　山形県月山

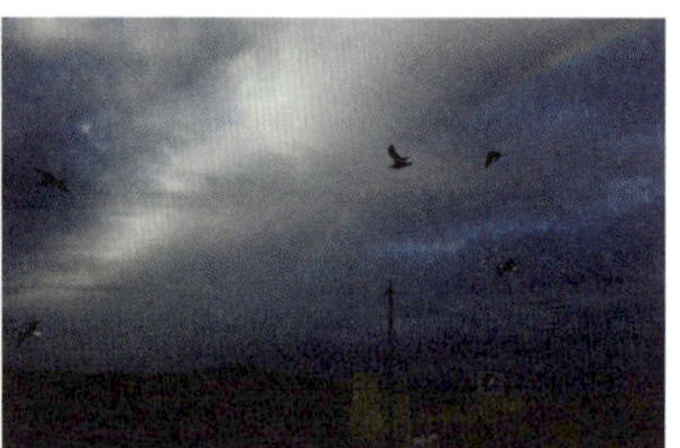

Minamisanriku, Miyagi, September 22, 2011
2011年9月22日　宮城県南三陸町

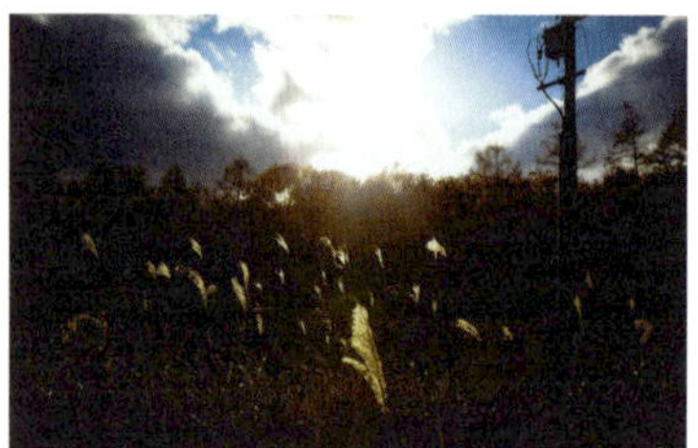

Tamura, Fukushima, November 15, 2011
2011年11月15日　福島県田村市

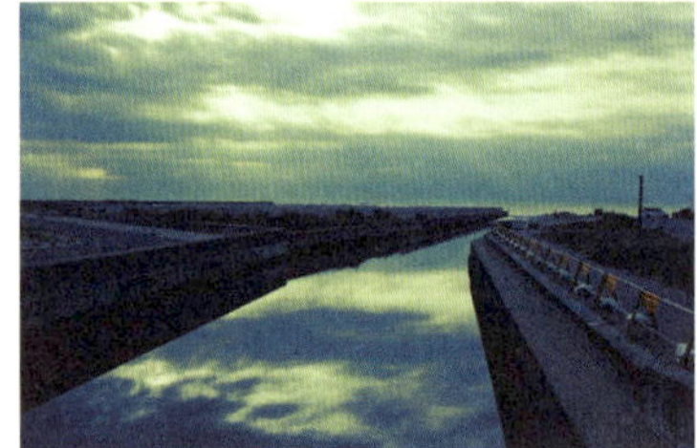

Iwaki, Fukushima, December 1, 2011
2011年12月1日　福島県いわき市

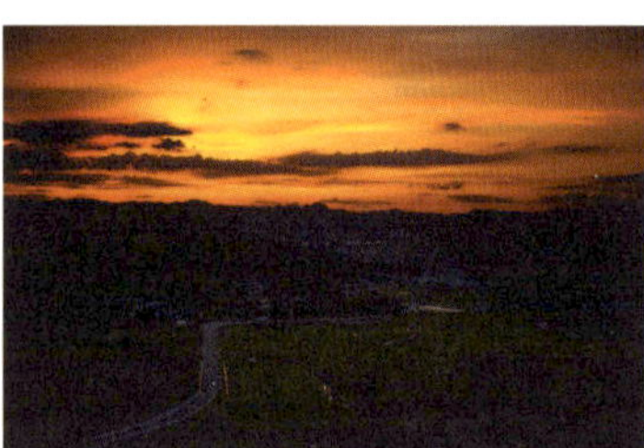

Fukushima, Fukushima, July 11, 2011
2011年7月11日　福島県福島市

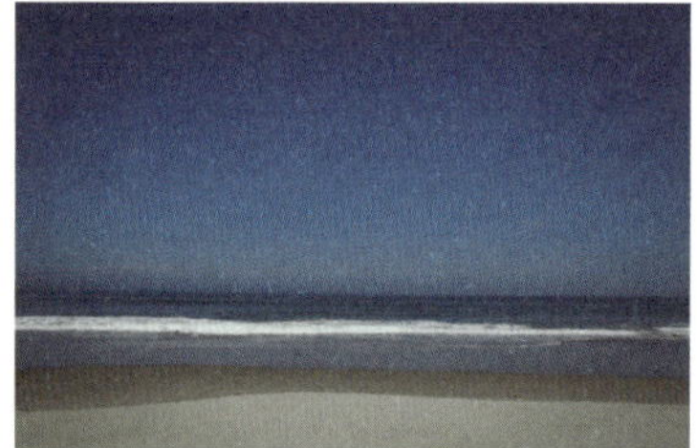

Minamisouma, Fukushima, July 12, 2011
2011年7月12日　福島県南相馬市

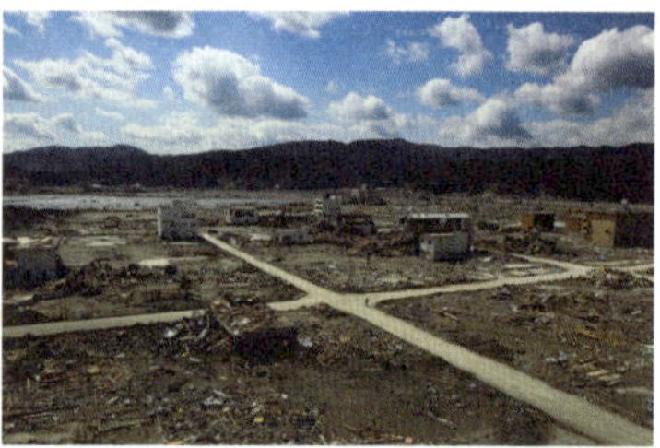

Rikuzentakada, Iwate, March 28, 2011
2011年3月28日　岩手県陸前高田市

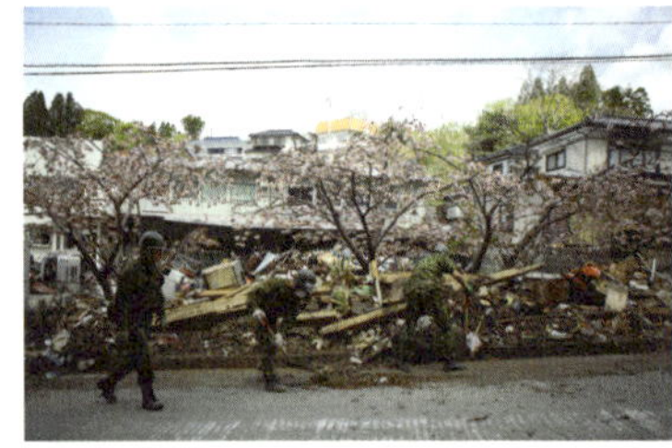

Minamisanriku, Miyagi, May 10, 2011
2011年5月10日　宮城県南三陸町

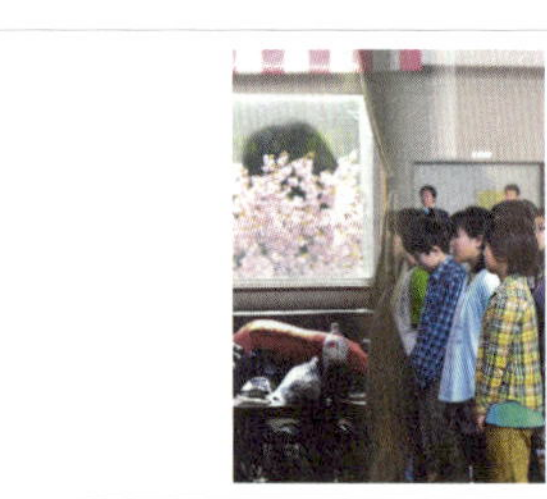

Minamisanriku, Miyagi, May 10, 2011
2011年5月10日　宮城県南三陸町

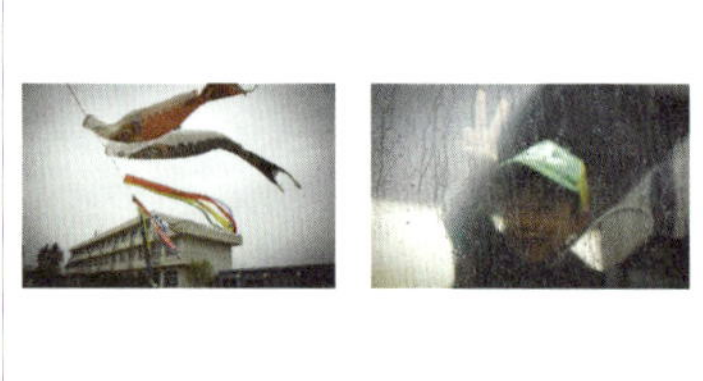

Tome, Miyagi, May 11, 2011
Tome, Miyagi, September 20, 2011
2011年5月11日　宮城県登米市
2011年9月20日　宮城県登米市

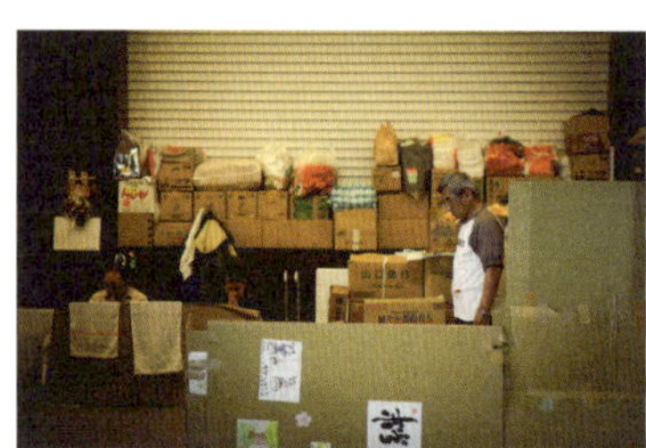

Koriyama, Fukushima, July 11, 2011
2011年7月11日　福島県郡山市

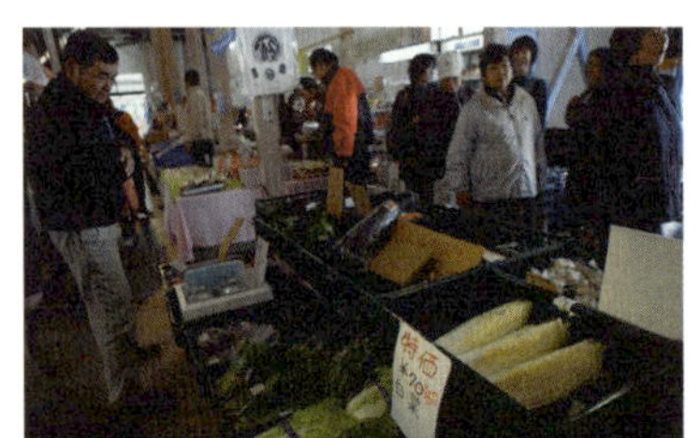

Iwaki, Fukushima, December 11, 2011
2011年12月11日　福島県いわき市

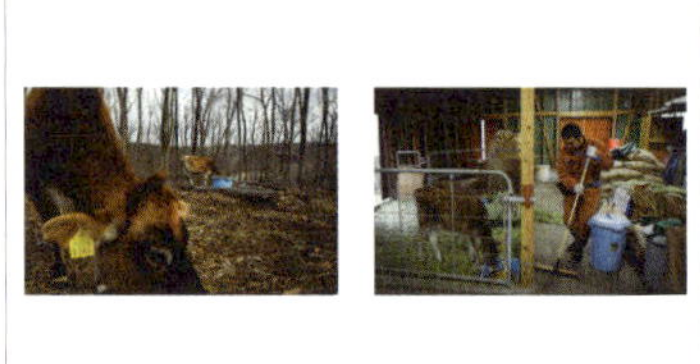

Nasu, Tochigi, January 13, 2012
Farmers within and outside Fukushima prefecture
were advised not to let their cattle graze freely.
2012年1月13日　栃木県那須町。広範囲にわたる放射
能汚染で福島県外の牛も放牧の自粛を迫られた。

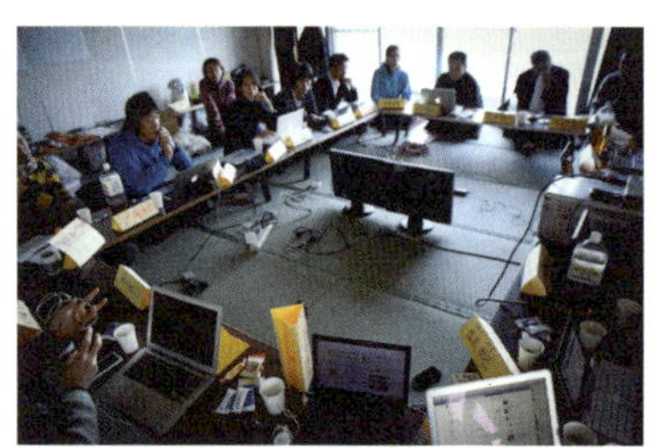

Minamisanriku, Miyagi, January 8, 2012
2012年1月8日　宮城県南三陸町

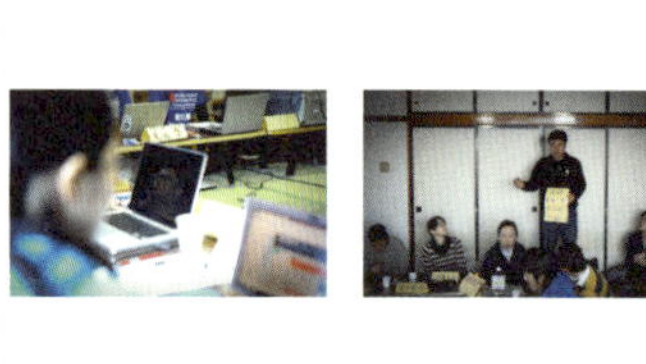

Minamisanriku, Miyagi, January 8, 2012
People from outside the areas affected gather to
collect ideas for the reconstruction.
2012年1月8日　宮城県南三陸町。被災地内外から集ま
った人々が復興に向けてアイディアを出し合う。

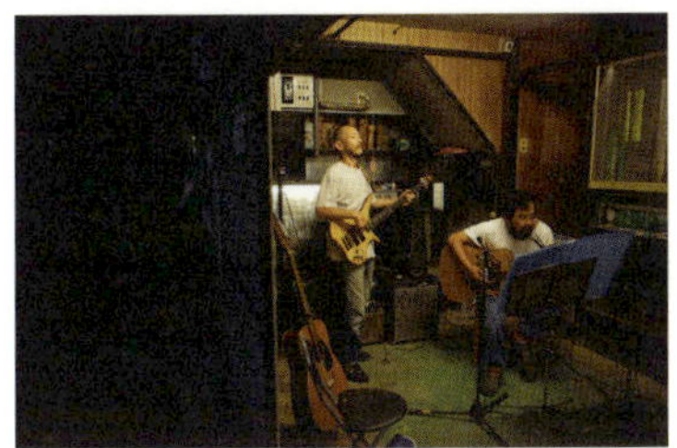

Ishinomaki, Miyagi, September 14, 2011
2011年9月14日　宮城県石巻市

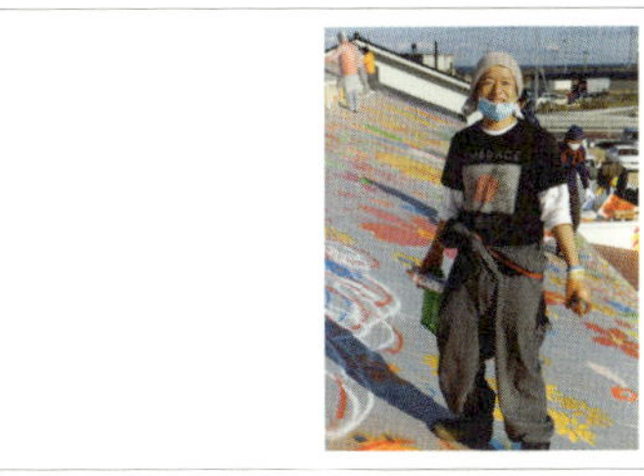

Iwaki, Fukushima, December 11, 2011
Citizens and painting a building before its demolition.
2011年12月11日　福島県いわき市
取り壊し前の建物に飾り付けをする住民たち。

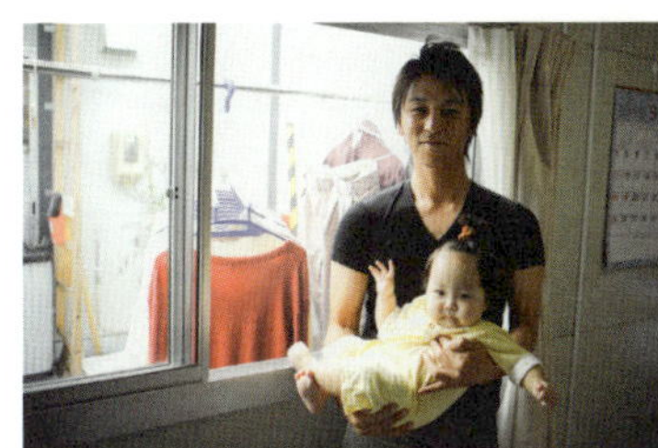

Minamisanriku, Miyagi, September 22, 2011
2011年9月22日　宮城県南三陸町

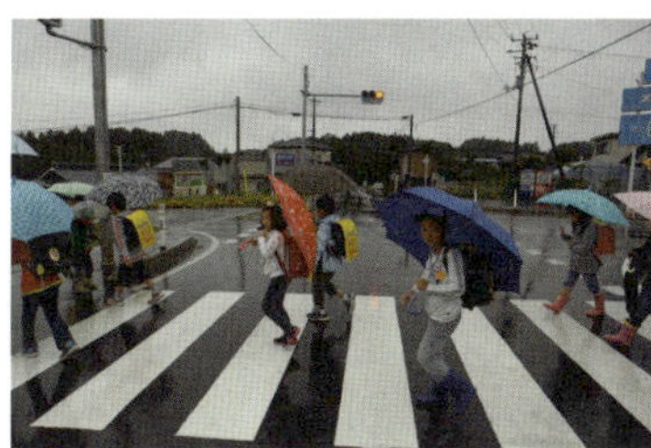

Tome, Miyagi, September 20, 2011
2011年9月20日　宮城県登米市

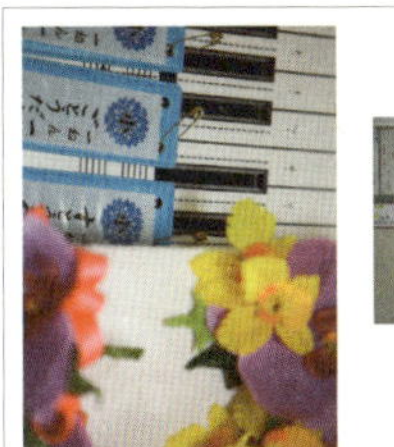

Tome, Miyagi, May 11, 2011
Ishinomaki, Miyagi, September 14, 2011
2011年5月11日　宮城県登米市
2011年9月14日　宮城県石巻市

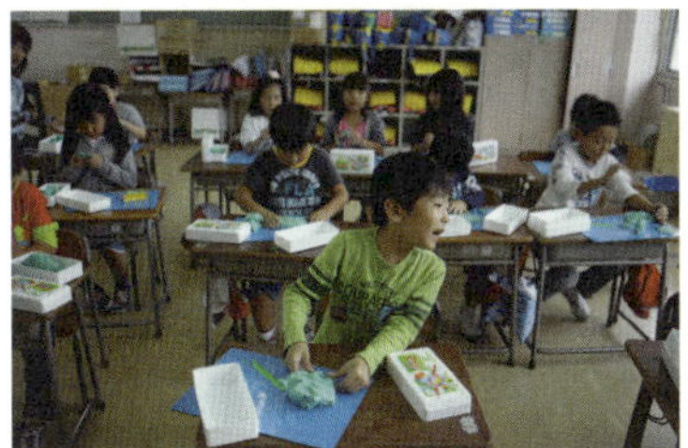

Tome, Miyagi, September 20, 2011
2011年9月20日　宮城県登米市

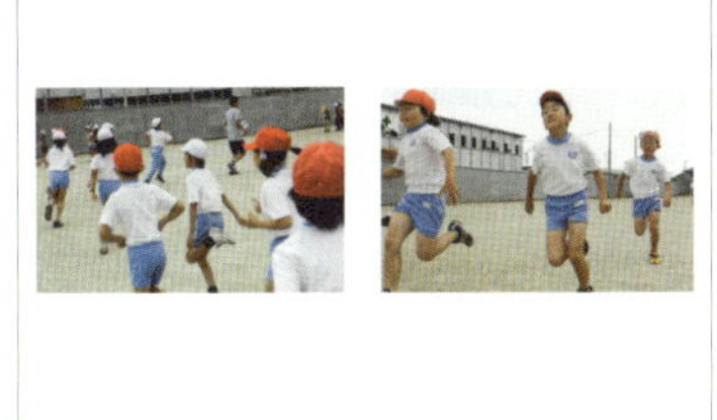

Ishinomaki, Miyagi, September 14, 2011
2011年9月14日　宮城県石巻市

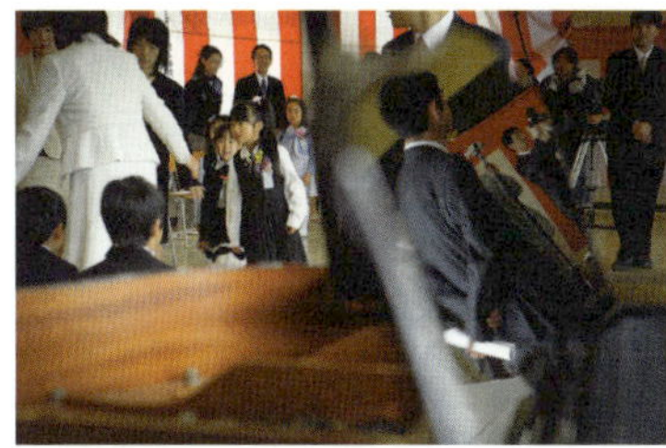

Tome, Miyagi, May 11, 2011
2011年5月11日　宮城県登米市

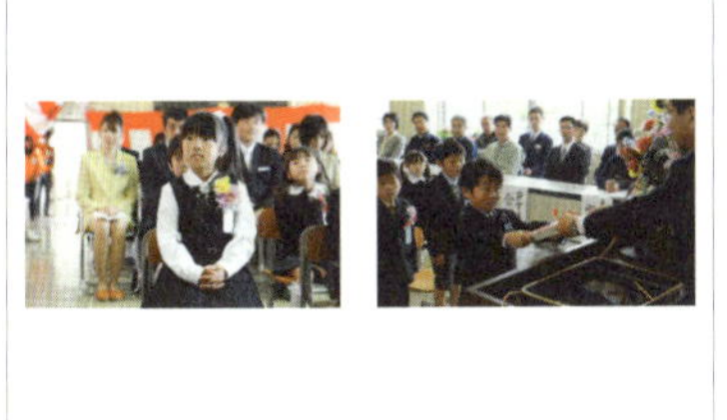

Tome, Miyagi, May 11, 2011
2011年5月11日　宮城県登米市

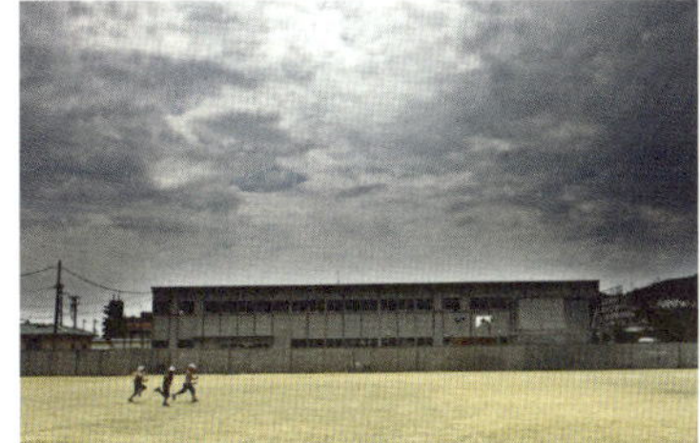

Ishinomaki, Miyagi, September 14, 2011
2011年9月14日　宮城県石巻市

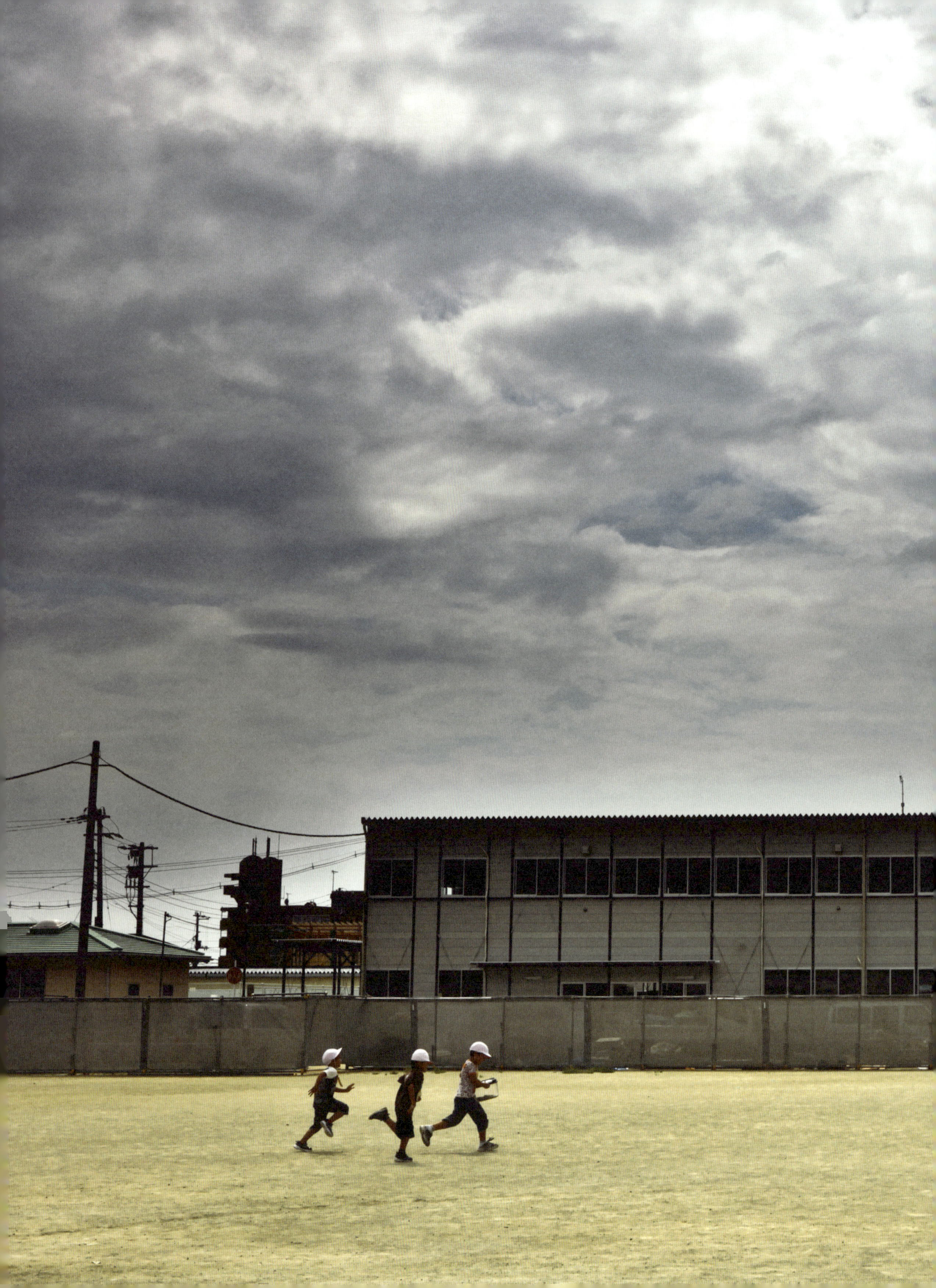

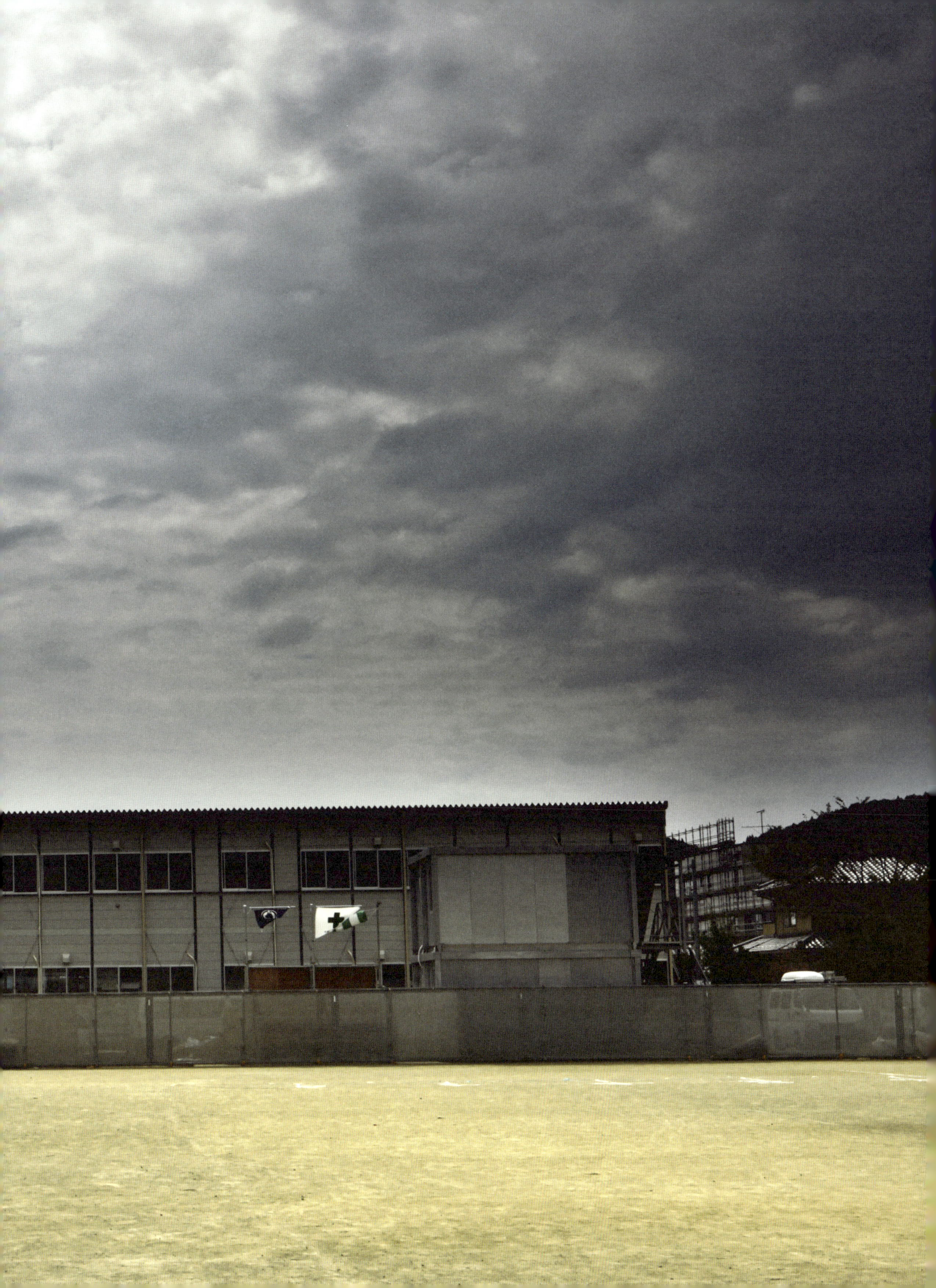

Adriano A. Biondo, born in Basel in 1961, is a photographer and creative director. He works in the worlds of advertising, publishing, and art. A recipient of the New York Art Directors Club Award, he is a frequent guest lecturer in visual communication and architecture at several universities. Due to his work in Japan beginning in the mid-1980s, he has also become known as a mediator between the world of Japan and the West.

Akira A. Biondo, born in Basel in 1991, is a translator and environmentalist. She is currently studying social anthropology and environmental sciences at Universität Zürich and working as a project coordinator for the ocean conservation organization PangeaSeed. After having experienced the earthquake disaster first-hand, she worked as a volunteer in the towns of Ishinomaki and Kesennuma, Miyagi Prefecture.

Jun Miyake, born in Kyoto in 1958, is a composer, focusing his work on the blind spot of time. He has worked with Pina Bausch, Wim Wenders, Robert Wilson, Oliver Stone, Jean Paul Goude, Philippe Decouflé, and Katsuhiro Otomo, and his music has been praised around the world for its unique crossbred sound. He has lived in Paris since 2005. His latest album *Stolen from Strangers* was awarded the Preis der Deutschen Schallplattenkritik (German Record Critics Award) in 2008.

Lars Müller, born in Oslo in 1955, is a designer and publisher, and has run a studio for visual communication since 1982. Since 1983 has been working as a publisher in the fields of art, design, architecture, photography, and society. He teaches visual design at several universities.

Kazuma Obara, born in Iwate in 1985, Japan, is a photojournalist. He studied social sciences at Utsunomiya University and continued his studies at Days Japan Photo Journalism School while working in the financial industry. Three days after the earthquake disaster, voices from his hometown called to him; he resigned from his job to begin documenting what was happening on the frontline. His photographs from the Fukushima Daiichi Nuclear Power Plant have been published all over Europe.

アドリアーノ・A・ビオンド　1961年、スイス、バーゼル生まれ。写真家、クリエイティブディレクター。広告、エディトリアル、アートプロジェクトにて活躍する。様々な機関の審査員務め、大学で客員講師としてビジュアルコミュニケーションと建築の教鞭を執る。80年代半ばより、日本での仕事を通して欧米と日本を結ぶアドバイザーとしても知られる。

ビオンド 晶　1991年、スイス、バーゼル生まれ。翻訳家、環境保護活動家。チューリヒ大学にて社会人類学と環境科学を専攻する傍ら、海洋保護団体パンジアシードのコーディネーターとして活動。3月11日の震災を体験し、宮城県石巻と気仙沼にてボラティア活動をする。

三宅 純　1958年、京都府生まれ。作曲家。時代の盲点をついたアーティスト活動の傍ら、作曲家としてピナ・バウシュ、ヴィム・ヴェンダース、ロバート・ウィルソン、オリバー・ストーン、ジャン・ポール・グード、フィリップ・ドゥクフレ、大友克洋らの作品に参加。異種交配を多用した個性的なサウンドは国際的賞賛を受けている。05年秋よりパリに拠点を設け、最新アルバム"Stolen from strangers"は欧米音楽誌で「年間ベストアルバム」「音楽批評家大賞」などを受賞。

ラース・ミュラー　1955年、ノルウェイ、オスロ生まれ。グラフィックデザイナー、出版者。82年、ビジュアルコミュニケーションのスタジオを設立。83年より世界のアート、デザイン、建築、写真、社会のフィールドにて多くの書籍を出版する。大学にて客員講師を務める。

小原 一真　1985年、岩手県生まれ。フォトジャーナリスト。宇都宮大学にて社会学を専攻。金融機関で働く傍ら、Days Japanフォトジャーナリスト学校にて学ぶ。3.11の3日後、故郷から届く被災地の声に引き寄せられ、会社を退職、取材を開始する。福島第一原発での取材はヨーロッパ各国で報道される。

RESET
BEYOND FUKUSHIMA
Will the Nuclear Catastrophe Bring Humanity to Its Senses?

Edited by Adriano A. Biondo and Lars Müller
in collaboration with Kazuko Shimada
Photography: Kazuma Obara
Design: Integral Lars Müller/Lars Müller and Sarah Pia
Copyediting: Brian Currid (English), Yoko Suzuki (Japanese)
Translations: Akira Biondo
Lithography: Ast & Fischer, Wabern, Switzerland
Printing and binding: Kösel, Altusried-Krugzell, Germany
Paper: Munken Lynx 150 g/m²

Lars Müller Publishers
Zurich, Switzerland
www.lars-mueller-publishers.com

ISBN 978-3-03778-292-7

Printed in Germany

Published with the generous support of

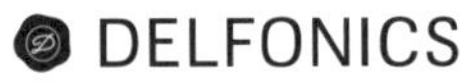

www.delfonics.com

Salomee and Edwin Faeh
of CARHARTT, Work In Progress

RESET
福島の彼方に
原発の巨大事故は私たちを目覚めさせるだろうか？

編集：　アドリアーノ・A・ビオンド ＆ ラース・ミュラー
企画：　島田 和子
写真：　小原 一真
デザイン：　インテグラール・ラース・ミュラー／ラース・ミュラー ＆ サラ・ピア
英文校正：　ブライアン・カリッド
日本語校正：　鈴木 陽子
翻訳：　ビオンド 晶
リトグラフ：　アスト＆フィッシャー、スイス、ワーベルン
印刷・製本：　ケーゼル、ドイツ、アルトゥスリート＝クルークツェル
紙：　Munken Lynx 150 g/m2

© 2012　ラース・ミュラー・パブリッシャーズ、チューリヒ ＆ 小原 一真

本書の無断複写、引用、複製はいかなる方法でも、書評を除き禁じます。

ラース・ミュラー・パブリッシャーズ
スイス、チューリヒ
www.lars-mueller-publishers.com

ISBN 978-3-03778-292-7

Printed in Germany

本書は以下の各社の寛大なサポートにより出版されました。

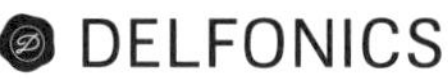

www.delfonics.com

Salomee and Edwin Faeh
of CARHARTT, Work In Progress